Jamaica Ladies

Jamaica Ladies

Female Slaveholders and the Creation of Britain's Atlantic Empire

CHRISTINE WALKER

Published by the
OMOHUNDRO INSTITUTE OF
EARLY AMERICAN HISTORY AND CULTURE,
Williamsburg, Virginia,
and the
UNIVERSITY OF NORTH CAROLINA PRESS,
Chapel Hill

The Omohundro Institute of Early American History and Culture (OI) is sponsored by William & and Mary. On November 15, 1996, the OI adopted the present name in honor of a bequest from Malvern H. Omohundro, Jr., and Elizabeth Omohundro

Manufactured in the United States of America

Cover illustration: *A Mulatto Woman with Her White Daughter Visited by Negro Women in Their House in Martinique.* Le Masurier (b. 1710). 1775 (oil on canvas), Ministere d l'Outre Mer, Paris, France. Bridgeman Images

Library of Congress Cataloging-in-Publication Data
Names: Walker, Christine (Christine Millen), author. | Omohundro Institute of Early American History & Culture, publisher.
Title: Jamaica ladies : female slaveholders and the creation of Britain's Atlantic empire / Christine Walker.
Description: Williamsburg, Virginia : Omohundro Institute of Early American History and Culture ; Chapel Hill : Omohundro Institute of Early American History and Culture and the University of North Carolina Press, [2020] | Includes bibliographical references and index.
Identifiers: LCCN 2019053442 | ISBN 9781469655260 (cloth : alk. paper) | ISBN 9781469658797 (paperback : alk. paper) | ISBN 9781469655277 (ebook)
Subjects: LCSH: Women colonists—Jamaica—History—18th century. | Women colonists—Jamaica—History—17th century. | Slaveholders—Jamaica—History. | Women, Black—Jamaica—History. | Women—Jamaica—Social conditions—History. | Great Britain—Colonies—America—Economic conditions.
Classification: LCC HQ1517 .W35 2020 | DDC 305.40941—dc23
LC record available at https://lccn.loc.gov/2019053442

The University of North Carolina Press has been a member of the Green Press Initiative since 2003.

For Will & Finn

Acknowledgments

This book is, not the work of a solitary writer, but rather the fruition of years of mentorship, intellectual generosity, emotional and financial sustenance, and painstaking labor done by various people living in different parts of the world. A number of organizations opened their purse strings, offering generous funding that made it possible for me to transform the rough sketch of an idea into a legitimate research project. The University of Michigan assisted my initial forays to archives in Jamaica and Britain with a Rackham Graduate Student Research Grant, a Peter and Barbara Benedek Graduate Fellowship, and a Rackham Humanities Candidacy Fellowship. A Fulbright Research Grant enabled me to spend a substantial amount of time in the Jamaican archives and give this work the evidentiary depth that it required. A short-term grant from the Huntington Library further enhanced the scope of my research. The largess of the Mellon / ACLS Dissertation Completion Fellowship afforded me the luxury of a full year to write my dissertation findings, while a Bernard and Irene Schwartz Postdoctoral Fellowship at the New-York Historical Society gave me a year to transform the dissertation into a book manuscript. Finally, the generous maternity and medical leave provided by Yale-NUS College made it possible for me to complete this work while also bringing two children into the world.

The Atlantic scope of this project necessitated research at numerous archives in three different countries, and I am deeply appreciative of the archivists who gave me their patient and skillful assistance during my research journey. Staff at the Island Record Office, the National Library of Jamaica, and the Jamaica Archives allowed me to spend months at their institutions sifting through thousands of rare manuscripts. Employees at the National Archives of Scotland and England and the British Library quickly retrieved a trove of material for me, while the archivists at smaller record offices, including the East Sussex Record Office and the Bristol Record Office, shared crucial knowledge of the holdings at their institutions with me. Altogether, the expertise and the efforts of a cadre of unnamed staff yielded the rich manuscript collections that form the basis of this book.

Jamaica Ladies developed from the kernel of an idea that was nurtured and enhanced by the exceptional guidance that I received at the dissertation stage from my advisors. David Hancock continually challenged me to reexamine my ideas from new angles and spent hours line editing a rough dissertation into a feasible project. I still employ the lessons he taught me about the necessity of explaining, both in writing and in speech, why my work matters to a wide range of audiences. Susan Juster guided the project from its inception to its completion, imparting sharp insights about contradictory or unconvincing elements in the dissertation and inciting me to improve it. Mary Kelley and Dena Goodman invested their tenacious intellects, not only in the dissertation, but in my development as a scholar. Years later, I remain both grateful for and inspired by this remarkable group of faculty members.

Other scholars have made important contributions to this work along the way. The faculty at the University of the West Indies, Mona, including Sir Roy Augier, Johnathan Dalby, David Gosse, and Kathleen Monteith, supplied valuable insights that shaped my plans at a key moment in my research in Jamaica. James Robertson liberally shared his unparalleled knowledge of Jamaican archives and sources. Anthony Bogues has been a steadfast supporter of this project, inviting me to present my research to faculty and graduate students at the Center for the Study of Slavery and Social Justice at Brown University twice. The critical feedback that I received as a participant in the inaugural Lapidus Scholars' Workshop at the Omohundro Institute of Early American History and Culture from Josh Piker, Brett Rushforth, Fredrika Teute, Karin Wulf, and Nadine Zimmerli convinced me that the Institute was the place that I wanted to publish my book.

Many scholars of early America, the Caribbean, the Atlantic world, the British Empire, and women's and gender studies have further enriched my work. I met Trevor Burnard when I was just beginning my dissertation research in Britain; he continues to be one of the most enthusiastic supporters of my work, generously sharing his time and his vast knowledge of Jamaica and the Atlantic world with me. Nina Dayton and Thomas Foster have both made considerable contributions to this project. I am also grateful for the feedback that I have received from Sarah Barringer, Rick Bell, Kathleen Brown, Kit Candlin, Amy Erickson, Amy Froide, Marisa Fuentes, Alison Games, Sheryllynne Haggerty, Catherine Hall, Dirk Hartog, Michelle McDonald, Roderick McDonald, Diana Paton, Christer Petley, David Ryden, and Nuala Zahedieh.

I am greatly indebted to the team at the Omohundro Institute who have supported this project. Together, their unmatched skills have turned an ungainly dissertation into a polished book. The manuscript's two readers, Ellen Hartigan-O'Connor and Simon Newman, delivered scrupulous and shrewd advice that incited me to make substantial enhancements to its structure and argument. My editor Nadine Zimmerli shepherded the project from the proposal to the copyediting stage, conferring her judicious expertise every step of the way. Her support, which has often involved phone calls made from different time zones, has been unwavering, while her ability to develop and clarify arguments and to creatively rearrange chapters is unmatched. Catherine Kelly ensured the smooth and timely completion of the work. I marvel at Kaylan Stevenson's capacity for reshaping ungainly and repetitive text into sparkling prose and am grateful for the assistance of the Institute's apprentices, whose painstaking efforts have ensured the credibility of every line in this book.

A global network of friends and colleagues at various institutions and locations throughout the world have both sustained me and contributed to this project at various points. In graduate school, Emma Amador, Benjamin Cronin, Kara French, Aston Gonzalez, Suzi Linsley, Daniel Livesay, Elspeth Martini, Jennifer Palmer, and Edgardo Pérez-Morales established a stimulating and encouraging cohort. During my tenure at Texas Tech University, my colleagues in the history department, Alan Barenberg, Jacob Baum, Justin Hart, Karlos Hill, Matthew Johnson, Erin-Marie Legacey, Miguel Levario, Emily Skidmore, and Abigail Swingen, welcomed me into their congenial and intellectually vibrant community. Aaron Jakes, T. Cole Jones, Matthew Karp, and Brandon O'Malley provided a year of comradery at the New-York Historical Society and the New School, while Zara Anishanslin, Celine Carayon, Glenda Goodman, Rana Hogarth, and Whitney Martinko shared hours of laughter and hours of insightful commentary at the Omohundro Institute's Lapidus Scholars' Workshop. Yale-NUS College's richly interdisciplinary community, including Nienke Boer, Kevin Goldstein, Jessica Hanser, Gabriele Koch, and Rohan Mukherjee, has prompted me to expand my scholarly boundaries beyond the Atlantic world and beyond history.

I've worked through numerous iterations of this book in multiple countries. Over the years, family members have traveled thousands of miles to offer essential encouragement and moments of respite. My husband has kept me on an even keel throughout this entire voyage, while the arrival of our children infused the final stages of the project with a renewed sense of curiosity and joy.

Contents

Illustrations

PLATES

FIGURES

TABLES

Jamaica Ladies

Introduction

When Elizabeth Keyhorne sat down to write her last will and testament in 1713, she might have been distracted by the din of hammering and sawing and the shouts of dockworkers outside. Located on West Street, Keyhorne's house was on the fringes of the rapidly growing port town of Kingston, just a few blocks from the waterfront that lined one of the deepest harbors in the world (Plate 1). She lived amid a flurry of construction and maritime activity. An ever-increasing number of ships sailed to Jamaica each year. They carried an amalgam of goods acquired from every corner of the globe. Gloves, stockings, and sewing needles arrived alongside packages of pepper, cinnamon, and printed calicoes. Although expanding trade increased the variety of items that were available to locals like Keyhorne, most of the merchandise was earmarked to be sold illegally as contraband to Spanish customers who paid high prices for illicit goods. Keyhorne would have also been familiar with the sights and sounds that emanated from another type of vessel—one that carried human cargo in the form of African captives to Kingston's shores. After spending a few months of "seasoning" in the pens that lined the harbor, most of the enslaved people who had survived the Middle Passage would be forced back onto ships and carried along with the manufactured imports to customers in New Spain.[1]

1. See, for example, Gregory E. O'Malley, *Final Passages: The Intercolonial Slave Trade of British America, 1619–1807* (Williamsburg, Va., and Chapel Hill, N.C., 2014); Vincent Brown, *The Reaper's Garden: Death and Power in the World of Atlantic Slavery* (Cambridge, Mass., 2008); Colin Palmer, *Human Cargoes: The British Slave Trade to Spanish America, 1700–1739* (Urbana, Ill., 1981).

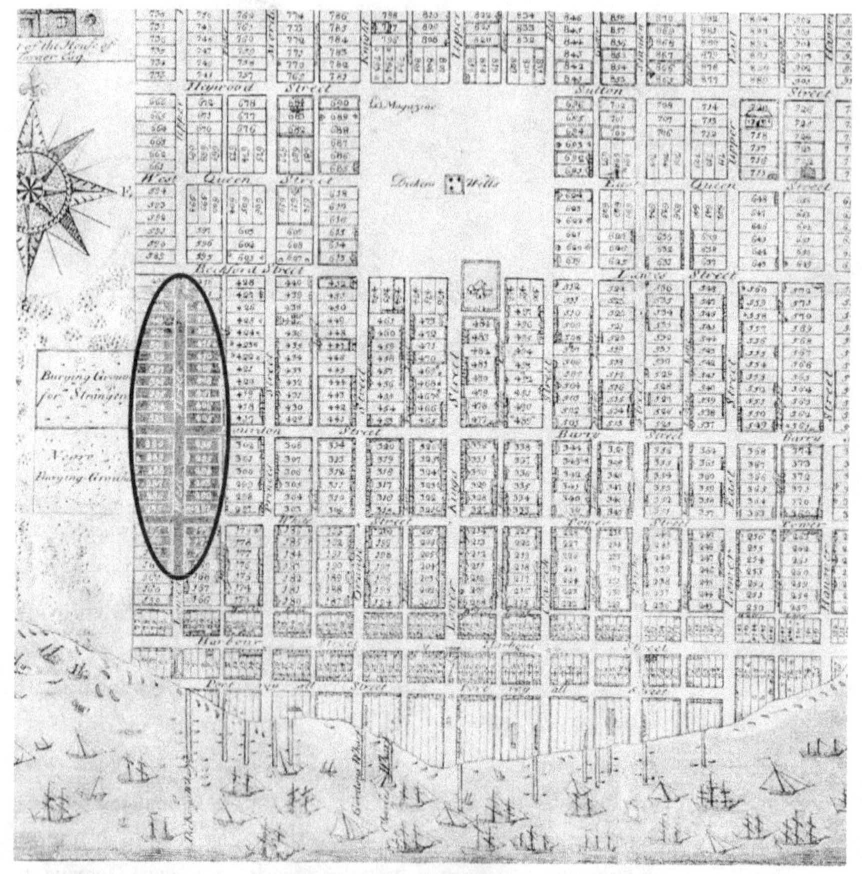

PLATE 1. Location of Elizabeth Keyhorne's property. Detail from [Plan of Kingston], by Michael Hay. [1745?]. Courtesy, Library of Congress, Geography and Maps Division, G4964.K5646 1745 .H3

Elizabeth Keyhorne's property was located on West Street, which still exists in Kingston. The harbor, which is depicted as swarming with ships, was a short walk down the street. When Keyhorne made her will in 1713, the harbor would have been less crowded but still busy. The map was engraved by Michael Hay, a local engraver.

In the early eighteenth century, Kingston was poised to become the largest transshipment depot for enslaved Africans in the Atlantic world. Keyhorne exploited this situation to acquire her own slaves. At the end of her life, Keyhorne possessed two enslaved women, Jenny and Daphne, and their two daughters. The widow bequeathed all of them to her son, Joseph, who was apprenticed to a joiner to learn detailed carpentry skills. Joseph's training ensured him a profitable career as a craftsman in a town that was undergoing a construction boom. When his mother died, Joseph would assume ownership of the captive women and children, who would either act as his domestic servants or be sold to fund his career. As she faced her own demise, Keyhorne might have taken comfort in her ability to contribute these people—who embodied both labor and material wealth—toward Joseph's promising future.[2]

During her lifetime, Keyhorne had married, raised a son, and acquired real estate in Kingston, achieving middling respectability and financial security for her family. Becoming a slaveholder signified one of her most important accomplishments. In the context of eighteenth-century Jamaica, these features of Keyhorne's life marked her as ordinary, rather than unusual. The island, and Kingston in particular, was home to a large number of legally independent female colonists, and slaveholding enabled women like Keyhorne to achieve a level of affluence that few other colonists in British America could hope to attain. A more careful reading of Keyhorne's will, however, suggests that her life—and her relationship to slavery—was far more complicated than it initially appears. Joseph, it turns out, was not Keyhorne's only child. The mother also made bequests "to my four daughters . . . now being slaves." When she left instructions for disbursing her estate in 1713, Keyhorne's other children, Molly, Margaritta, Flora, and Franky, were being held in bondage. Keyhorne gave the girls her linen, woolen, and silk clothing—the kinds of intimate personal items that women commonly offered to their daughters—but her will did not include plans for obtaining their freedom. Perhaps Keyhorne lacked the funds to purchase their manumissions. Or maybe the man who owned her children refused to release them from captivity. It is also possible that Keyhorne and her son agreed that he would sell Jenny, Daphne, and their daughters and use the proceeds to purchase his own siblings. In a colony where people served as currency, such transactions were commonplace.[3]

Whatever the case, Keyhorne's reference to Molly, Margaritta, Flora, and Franky, "now being slaves," dramatically alters our interpretation of the woman's life. Though Keyhorne identified herself by her marital status as a widow, not her race, the presence of her enslaved daughters hints at a very different trajectory from the one that the rest of her will constructs. Her connection to the captive girls and the early date of her will suggest that Key-

2. Will of Elizabeth Keyhorne, 1713, Jamaica Wills, 1661–1771, XIV, Island Record Office (IRO), Spanish Town, Jamaica. Kathleen Wilson refers to Michael Hay, the engraver of the map of Kingston (Plate 1), in *The Island Race: Englishness, Empire, and Gender in the Eighteenth Century* (Milton, U.K., 2003), 160.

3. Will of Elizabeth Keyhorne, 1713, Jamaica Wills, XIV.

horne was born in Africa and then transported along with an ever-growing number of captives to the Caribbean. Once there, Keyhorne gave birth to four daughters, whose father was likely enslaved. The free status and expensive apprenticeship held by her son, Joseph, on the other hand, point toward a free father. His mother's relationship with this man probably initiated her own remarkable transformation from slavery to freedom, marriage, and her adoption of the name Elizabeth Keyhorne. At the end of her life, Keyhorne resided just a few blocks from the shore where she might have disembarked from a slave ship years earlier.

A few brief sentences in Keyhorne's 1713 will unravel long-held assumptions about the interplay of gender, race, marital status, legal status, and kinship ties in the Anglo-Atlantic world. This document illuminates a pivotal moment in the history of the British Empire. It tells the story of a person's traumatic dislocation and relocation across the Atlantic and of her transition from subjectification to subjecthood. As a slave who became an enslaver herself, Keyhorne challenges a historical account that casts the typical slaveholder as a white male. If Keyhorne's actions appear contradictory to us, they made perfect sense in the context of the early modern Atlantic world. Her life describes slavery as an invasive social practice, one that demanded the participation of every free and freed person, including those of African and Euro-African descent, to extract a profit and ensure colonial stability. Keyhorne was not a marginalized outlier who operated on the periphery of the empire. On the contrary, from Brazil to Saint Domingue, free and freed women acquired slaves to protect their own tenuous claims to status and independence. Slaveholding was a vector for social mobility and financial success, and Keyhorne lived in Kingston, Jamaica, at the very moment when it was becoming a crucial node in the thickening web of the Atlantic slave trade. Her life was indelibly stamped by colonialism and slavery, which she both experienced and participated in.[4]

4. Freed people of African descent and even slaves acted as slaveholders throughout the Atlantic world. See, for instance, James H. Sweet, *Domingos Álvares, African Healing, and the Intellectual History of the Atlantic World* (Chapel Hill, N.C., 2013); Dominique Rogers and Stewart King, "Housekeepers, Merchants, Rentières: Free Women of Color in the Port Cities of Colonial Saint-Domingue, 1750–1790," in Douglas Catterall and Jodi Campbell, eds., *Women in Port: Gendering Communities, Economies, and Social Networks in Atlantic Port Cities, 1500–1800* (Leiden, Neth., 2012), 369; Gwyn Campbell, Suzanne Miers, and Joseph C. Miller, eds., *Women and Slavery*, I, *Africa, the Indian Ocean World, and the Medieval North Atlantic* (Athens, Ohio, 2007); Stewart R. King, *Blue Coat or Powdered Wig: Free People of Color in Pre-Revolutionary Saint Domingue* (Athens, Ga., 2001); Yesenia Barragan, "Gendering Mastery: Female Slave-

Focusing on Keyhorne and the other free and freed women who migrated to Jamaica, either by choice or by force, reconfigures our understanding of how the island became the wealthiest colony with the largest enslaved population in the Anglo-Atlantic world. If male merchants and sailors oversaw the purchase and transportation of captive Africans to America, then free and freed women acted as the handmaidens of empire, weaving these captives into the warp and weft of colonial societies. During an era when social, familial, and professional connections were intertwined, their actions were instrumental. Jamaica's notoriously deadly mortality rates, its mercantile focus, and its involvement in imperial warfare made free families even more reliant on female members to secure local estates, to fill crucial niches in urban markets, to manage plantations, and to facilitate overseas trade. Most importantly, the investment made by female colonists in unfree labor ensured the commitment not just of individual men but also of entire families to a slave labor regime that, in turn, drove the growth of Britain's commercial empire during the eighteenth century.

Jamaica Ladies is the first comprehensive and multidimensional account of the contributions made by free and freed women of European, Euro-African, and African descent to these fundamental historical developments in the Atlantic world.[5] The book questions long-standing beliefs about who

holders in the Columbian Pacific Lowlands," *Slavery and Abolition*, XXXIX (2018), 1–26; Wendy Wilson-Fall, "Women Merchants and Slave Depots: Saint-Louis, Senegal, and St. Mary's, Madagascar," in Ana Lucia Araujo, ed., *Paths of the Atlantic Slave Trade: Interactions, Identities, and Images* (Amherst, N.Y., 2011), 273–303.

5. Although work has been done on female slaveholding during the early modern period in the Atlantic world, *Jamaica Ladies* is the first book to systematically scrutinize multiple dimensions of women's involvement in chattel slavery in Jamaica. An edited edition of Lucille Mathurin Mair's 1970s dissertation is the only comparable study of the activities of female colonists on the island (Mathurin Mair, *A Historical Study of Women in Jamaica, 1655–1844*, ed. Hilary McD. Beckles and Verene A. Shepherd [Kingston, 2006]). More recent research by Cecily Jones shows that free women of European descent actively participated in the construction of whiteness as slaveholders in Barbados and South Carolina (Jones, *Engendering Whiteness: White Women and Colonialism in Barbados and North Carolina, 1627–1865* [Manchester, U.K., 2007]). Kit Candlin and Cassandra Pybus, in *Enterprising Women: Gender, Race, and Power in the Revolutionary Atlantic* (Athens, Ga., 2015), offer a study of free women of color in the British Caribbean, but female slaveholding is not the focus of their work. Although Marie Jenkins Schwartz has written about the involvement of the wives of the "founding fathers" in slavery, she studies a small group of elite women (Schwartz, *Ties That Bound: Founding First Ladies and Slaves* [Chicago, 2017]). Marisa J. Fuentes's work includes a section on white women slaveowners; see *Dispos-*

perpetuated chattel slavery and reaped the profits of settler colonialism during the early modern era, arguing that female colonists played crucial roles in constructing a society that depended on enslaved labor. Drawing on thousands of largely unstudied manuscript records, including wills, parish registers, court cases, probated inventories, and personal letters, *Jamaica Ladies* reshapes a historical narrative that either emphasizes women's absence or

---

sessed Lives: Enslaved Women, Violence, and the Archive (Philadelphia, 2016), chap. 3. See also Hilary McD. Beckles, *Centering Woman: Gender Discourses in Caribbean Slave Society* (Kingston, 1999), part 2.

The following articles reference female slaveholding in British America: Sarah E. Yeh, "'A Sink of All Filthiness': Gender, Family, and Identity in the British Atlantic, 1688–1763," *Historian,* LXVIII (2006), 79–82; Inge Dornan, "Masterful Woman: Colonial Women Slaveholders in the Urban Low Country," *Journal of American Studies,* XXXIX (2005), 383–402; Linda L. Sturtz, "The 'Dimduke' and the Duchess of Chandos: Gender and Power in Jamaican Plantation Management—A Case Study; or, A Different Story of 'A Man [and His Wife] from a Place Called Hope,'" *Revista/Review Interamericana,* XXIX (1999), [1–15]; Cara Anzilotti, "Autonomy and the Female Planter in Colonial South Carolina," *Journal of Southern History,* LXIII (1997), 239–268; Barbara Bush, "White 'Ladies,' Coloured 'Favourites,' and Black 'Wenches': Some Considerations on Sex, Race, and Class Factors in Social Relations in White Creole Society in the British Caribbean," *Slavery and Abolition,* II, no. 3 (December 1981), 245–262. For comparative work on women slaveholders living in non-British regions of the Atlantic world, see Jennifer L. Palmer, *Intimate Bonds: Family and Slavery in the French Atlantic* (Philadelphia, 2016); Pernille Ipsen, *Daughters of the Trade: Atlantic Slavers and Interracial Marriage on the Gold Coast* (Philadelphia, 2015); Barragan, "Gendering Mastery," *Slavery and Abolition,* XXXIX (2018), 1–26; Danielle Terrazas Williams, "'My Conscience Is Free and Clear': African-Descended Women, Status, and Slave Owning in Mid-Colonial Mexico," *Americas,* LXXV (2018), 525–554.

Although focusing on the seventeenth and eighteenth century reveals much earlier precedents for women's actions a century later, more work has been done on female slaveholders in antebellum America. See, for example, Thavolia Glymph, *Out of the House of Bondage: The Transformation of the Plantation Household* (Cambridge, 2008); Stephanie E. Jones-Rogers, *They Were Her Property: White Women as Slave Owners in the American South* (New Haven, Conn., 2019); Kirsten E. Wood, *Masterful Women: Slaveholding Widows from the American Revolution through the Civil War* (Chapel Hill, N.C., 2004); Marli F. Weiner, *Mistresses and Slaves: Plantation Women in South Carolina, 1830–80* (Chicago, 1998); Drew Gilpin Faust, "'Trying to Do a Man's Business': Slavery, Violence, and Gender in the American Civil War," *Gender and History,* IV (1992), 197–214; Catherine Clinton, *The Plantation Mistress: Woman's World in the Old South* (New York, 1982); Elizabeth Fox-Genovese, *Within the Plantation Household: Black and White Women of the Old South* (Chapel Hill, N.C., 1988); Suzanne Lebsock, *The Free Women of Petersburg: Status and Culture in a Southern Town, 1784–1860* (New York, 1984).

characterizes their disempowerment in Atlantic slave societies.[6] The British Caribbean, in particular, has been portrayed as a hypermasculine space—one that was dominated by male pirates, merchants, and planters.[7] Femi-

6. This book draws on records culled from archives in Jamaica, Britain, and the United States, including all of the last wills and testaments authored by Jamaican women and a substantial sample of Jamaican men's wills. Although wealthier women have left behind faint traces in the archives, few collections of private letters, diaries, or journals have survived from the early colonial period. It is even more difficult to figure out how impoverished free and freed women survived. To depict the widest socioeconomic spectrum, I use a variety of source material to highlight broader trends.

7. The literature on slavery in British America is vast. However, the majority of the scholarship does not treat free and freed women as important agents of colonialism and slavery. In the Anglo-Atlantic context, historians have argued that the emergence of the racial categories that justified chattel slavery relied on divorcing white women from labor. Hilary McD. Beckles, for instance, writes that white women were "considered unfit for manual labour on account of [their] endemic fragility," "faint heart and delicate skin." See Beckles, "Sex and Gender in the Historiography of Caribbean Slavery," in Verene Shepherd, Bridget Brereton, and Barbara Bailey, eds., *Engendering History: Caribbean Women in Historical Perspective* (New York, 1995), 133. See also Kathleen M. Brown, *Good Wives, Nasty Wenches, and Anxious Patriarchs: Gender, Race, and Power in Colonial Virginia* (Williamsburg, Va., and Chapel Hill, N.C., 1996); Rhys Isaac, *Landon Carter's Uneasy Kingdom: Revolution and Rebellion on a Virginia Plantation* (New York, 2004); Edmund S. Morgan, *American Slavery, American Freedom: The Ordeal of Colonial Virginia* (New York, 1975); Richard S. Dunn, *Sugar and Slaves: The Rise of the Planter Class in the English West Indies, 1624–1713* (Williamsburg, Va., and Chapel Hill, N.C., 1972); Philip D. Morgan, *Slave Counterpoint: Black Culture in the Eighteenth-Century Chesapeake and Lowcountry* (Williamsburg, Va., and Chapel Hill, N.C., 1998). The Caribbean, and Jamaica in particular, is normally characterized as an aggressively masculine space. Trevor Burnard, who has produced a substantial corpus of work on Jamaica, generally attributes the brutality and violence of colonial society to white men. Likewise, Vincent Brown concludes that Jamaica was intensively patriarchal, with white men controlling the island's female inhabitants. See Burnard, *Mastery, Tyranny, and Desire: Thomas Thistlewood and His Slaves in the Anglo-Jamaican World* (Chapel Hill, N.C., 2004); Burnard, "'Rioting in Goatish Embraces': Marriage and Improvement in Early British Jamaica," *History of the Family*, XI (2006), 185–197; Burnard, "A Failed Settler Society: Marriage and Demographic Failure in Early Jamaica," *Journal of Social History*, XXVIII (1994), 63–82; and Brown, *Reaper's Garden*. Natalie A. Zacek critiques these portrayals, writing that British colonies in the Caribbean were more than "armed camps of aggressive men, or machines for the making of fortunes quickly dissipated by the lavish lifestyles of absentee planters." See Zacek, "Between Lady and Slave: White Working Women in the Eighteenth-Century Leeward Islands," in Catterall and Campbell, eds., *Women in Port*, 150. She also offers a more-nuanced portrait of

nist scholars who study the region have focused on enslaved women, revealing how slaveholders co-opted the productive and reproductive capacities of female captives and subjected them to sexual exploitation. However, their research still configures the normative slaveholder as a white male. Consequently, women's activities in the region as colonizers and as slaveholders—and the gendered implications of their pursuits—remain largely unexamined and undertheorized.[8] Scholarship on the intersection of race, gender, and sexuality in British North America offers a more robust point of departure for *Jamaica Ladies.* Collectively, this literature identifies the emergence of punitive laws that targeted white women's sexuality and banned interracial relationships and marriage. Kathleen Brown, Clare Lyons, and Kirsten Fischer, for instance, contend that white women were subjected to stricter legal and social regimes during the eighteenth century. My book also explores the degree to which early modern beliefs about gender and, gradually, racial differences were naturalized, embedded in legal, political, economic, and religious systems, and mapped onto bodies, but it draws different conclusions about how these dynamics played out in the colonial context.[9]

---

white manhood in the region; see Zacek, "'Banes of Society' and 'Gentlemen of Strong Natural Parts': Attacking and Defending West Indian Creole Masculinity," in Thomas A. Foster, ed., *New Men: Manliness in Early America* (New York, 2011), 116–133.

8. The work on enslaved women in the Caribbean has significantly enhanced our understanding of the gendered and sexualized dimensions of slavery. This substantial body of scholarship includes edited volumes such as Judith A. Byfield, LaRay Denzer, and Anthea Morrison, eds., *Gendering the African Diaspora: Women, Culture, and Historical Change in the Caribbean and Nigerian Hinterland* (Bloomington, Ind., 2010); and Gwyn Campbell, Suzanne Miers, and Joseph C. Miller, eds., *Women and Slavery*, II, *The Modern Atlantic* (Athens, Ohio, 2007). Scholarly monographs include Shawna Sweeney, "A Free Enterprise: Market Women, Insurgent Economies, and the Making of Caribbean Freedom" (unpublished manuscript); Sasha Turner, *Contested Bodies: Pregnancy, Childrearing, and Slavery in Jamaica* (Philadelphia, 2017); Sowande' M. Mustakeem, *Slavery at Sea: Terror, Sex, and Sickness in the Middle Passage* (Urbana, Ill., 2016); Fuentes, *Dispossessed Lives;* Jennifer L. Morgan, *Laboring Women: Reproduction and Gender in New World Slavery* (Philadelphia, 2004); Diana Paton, *No Bond But the Law: Punishment, Race, and Gender in Jamaican State Formation, 1780–1870* (Durham, N.C., 2004); Hilary McD. Beckles, *Natural Rebels: A Social History of Enslaved Black Women in Barbados* (New Brunswick, N.J., 1989); Marietta Morrissey, *Slave Women in the New World: Gender Stratification in the Caribbean* (Lawrence, Kans., 1989); Barbara Bush, *Slave Women in Caribbean Society, 1650–1838* (Kingston, 1990); and Bernard Moitt, *Women and Slavery in the French Antilles, 1635–1848* (Bloomington, Ind., 2001).

9. A spate of scholarship over the past two decades has changed our understanding of how

This study is not a chronicle of free women's disempowerment and oppression. Nor does it celebrate female agency. Instead, it offers a far more ambivalent account of the gendered dimensions of power. Recognizing women as powerful agents of slavery and colonialism calls into question the extent to which normative European gender ideologies were imported and adopted across the Atlantic. Female slaveholders wielded novel and significant legal, social, economic, and cultural authority, which they enacted inside and outside the household. The title *Jamaica Ladies* draws attention to this divergence between metropolitan ideals and colonial practice. In Britain, *lady* conveyed multiple meanings. It was an honorific title that signified a woman's membership in the aristocracy, a term that recognized her refined and genteel qualities, and a label for the female head of a household who commanded servants. In sum, *lady* signified feminine respectability and rank.[10]

---

bodies were racialized and gendered in early America. See Brown, *Good Wives, Nasty Wenches;* Kirsten Fischer, *Suspect Relations: Sex, Race, and Resistance in Colonial North Carolina* (Ithaca, N.Y., 2002); Jennifer M. Spear, *Race, Sex, and Social Order in Early New Orleans* (Baltimore, 2009); Sharon Block, *Rape and Sexual Power in Early America* (Williamsburg, Va., and Chapel Hill, N.C., 2006); Clare A. Lyons, *Sex among the Rabble: An Intimate History of Gender and Power in the Age of Revolution, Philadelphia, 1730–1830* (Williamsburg, Va., and Chapel Hill, N.C., 2006); and Morgan, *Laboring Women.* Kirsten Fischer and Jennifer Morgan have argued, however, that most of the scholarship on sexuality in early America focuses on white men, reducing both free and enslaved women to objects of male desire. See Fischer and Morgan, "Sex, Race, and the Colonial Project," *WMQ*, 3d Ser., LX (2003), 197–198.

10. See Joan Wallach Scott, "Gender: A Useful Category of Historical Analysis," in Scott, *Gender and the Politics of History* (New York, 1988), 45–46. Michel Foucault's multipart definition of power is useful for theorizing the dynamics that existed between women enslavers and the people whom they held in captivity. I do not treat power as an "institution" or a "structure." Instead, I study the ways women exercised their authority from "innumerable points" that show "the interplay of nonegalitarian and mobile relations." The "major domination" of free over enslaved people on the island was the "hegemonic" effect of these countless confrontations (Foucault, *The History of Sexuality*, I, *An Introduction*, trans. Robert Hurley [New York, 1990], 92–94 [quotations, 94]). See *Oxford English Dictionary*, s.v. "lady," http://www.oed.com. As Alexandra Shepard notes, the household functioned as "the primary structural locus of male supremacy . . . and the marital relations at its core were the justification for men's subordination of women" in early modern England; see Shepard, *Meanings of Manhood in Early Modern England* (Oxford, 2003), 70. For more on women, gender, and the early modern household in Britain, see Amy Froide, *Never Married: Singlewomen in Early Modern England* (New York, 2005); and Margaret R. Hunt, *The Middling Sort: Commerce, Gender, and the Family in England, 1680–1780* (Berkeley, Calif., 1996). For more on these topics in Early America, see Karin Wulf, *Not All Wives: Women of Colonial Philadelphia* (Ithaca, N.Y., 2000); Lorri Glover, *All Our Relations: Blood Ties*

The attributes that defined femininity, of course, were not static. At the end of the seventeenth century, women were conceived of as inherently lustful and prone to sin. Marriage was viewed as a necessary means of containing female sexuality and ensuring a woman's sexual virtue, which underwrote her honor. Although the woman was believed to be an inferior version of the ideal male type, the sexes were not defined as binary opposites; rather, male and female existed on a continuum. During the eighteenth century, however, a two-sex model gained popularity, whereby men and women were viewed as inherently distinctive, and femininity was correlated with passivity, delicacy, and domesticity.[11]

From the British perspective, Jamaica's female colonists did not manifest the attributes that were correlated with newer gender ideologies. Portrayed as lustful, sexually capacious, passionate, and ungovernable, they were certainly not "ladies" according to metropolitan standards. Rather, they seemed to invoke the older notions of passionate and unruly womanhood. When the English minister James White traveled to the island in the 1720s, for instance, he accused a local judge of living "as a married person w[i]th his Brothers wife." Instead of ostracizing the woman for adultery, White claimed, "all society seemed to happily socialize" with the "incestuous wife" as if she "was a virtuous woman." According to White, a woman could maintain her status as a "lady" in spite of her transgressive sexual behavior on the island. In their role as slaveholders, female colonists further upset British gender ideals. By commanding absolute authority over enslaved dependents, they claimed masculine prerogatives for themselves and rejected their position as submissive dependents.[12]

---

and Emotional Bonds among the Early South Carolina Gentry (Baltimore, 2000); and Linda L. Sturtz, *Within Her Power: Propertied Women in Colonial Virginia* (New York, 2002).

11. In Britain, women accrued social status and respect on marrying and playing an important—albeit unequal—role in the "male-headed household family," which was the "fundamental institution of society" (Amanda Vickery, *Behind Closed Doors: At Home in Georgian England* [New Haven, Conn., 2009], 193). See also Brown, *Good Wives, Nasty Wenches,* 30–31; Fischer, *Suspect Relations,* 3–4; Tim Hitchcock, *English Sexualities, 1700–1800* (New York, 1997), 100–101; and Thomas Laqueur, *Making Sex: Body and Gender from the Greeks to Freud* (Cambridge, Mass., 1990).

12. James White to [Bishop Gibson], Mar. 5, 1723/4, fols. 173–174, Apr. 23, 1724, fols. 185–188, Fulham Papers, Colonial, 1626–1822, General Correspondence, West Indies, XVII, Lambeth Palace Library (LPL), London. As Kathleen Wilson observes, "white Creole women" became associated with promiscuity, excess, and savageness, which British writers attributed to their intimacies with people of African descent; see Wilson, *Island Race,* 144–145. See also Yeh, " 'A

Early in the eighteenth century, observers like White associated the Caribbean—and the women who lived there—with sexual and social disorder. Although the texts authored by British men tell us little about colonists' lived experiences, they do point toward a society that adopted a notably lenient approach toward female sexuality. A combination of local conditions, especially the omnipresence of slavery, persistently high mortality rates, and an intensively commercial environment, altered gender norms in Jamaica. The colonial government, which was focused on surveilling and controlling a skyrocketing enslaved population, ignored the sexual activities of free people. In turn, a large number of colonists started families outside wedlock, and illegitimacy rates were strikingly high. By the 1750s, Jamaica was a place where a woman like Teresia Constantia Phillips, who was viewed as a notorious profligate in Britain after publishing memoirs of her sexual escapades, received a warm welcome. Indeed, Phillips was made the Mistress of Revels, the first official political post ever offered to a woman in the colony. As the example of Phillips shows, islanders did not necessarily equate femininity or being a "lady" with sexual virtue. A free woman's social status, instead, emanated from the complex interplay of a variety of characteristics, including her legal status as a free person, her ability to enslave others, her marital status, her kinship ties, her wealth, her education, and her religion, all of which aided in the construction of her position.[13]

Sink of All Filthiness,'" *Historian,* LXVIII (2006), 79–82; Melissa K. Downes, "Ladies of Ill-Repute: The South Sea Bubble, the Caribbean, and *The Jamaica Lady,*" *Studies in Eighteenth-Century Culture,* XXXIII (2004), 23–48; Erin Mackie, "Jamaican Ladies and Tropical Charms," *ARIEL,* XXXVII (2006), 189–192; Vickery, *Behind Closed Doors;* Amanda Vickery, *The Gentleman's Daughter: Women's Lives in Georgian England* (New Haven, Conn., 1998); Dror Wahrman, *The Making of the Modern Self: Identity and Culture in Eighteenth-Century England* (New Haven, Conn., 2004); Richard Godbeer, *Sexual Revolution in Early America* (Baltimore, 2002); Anthony Fletcher, *Gender, Sex, and Subordination in England, 1500–1800* (New Haven, Conn., 1995); and Hitchcock, *English Sexualities.* If male authority over women was rooted in men's control of property, as Kathleen Brown observes of early modern England, then the influx of enslaved people as a form of human property that women commanded in Jamaica had the potential to unsettle male power (Brown, *Good Wives, Nasty Wenches,* 30–31). Amanda Vickery notes that "ungoverned girls" who were not under the care of parents or husbands were "an anathema to patriarchy" (Vickery, *Behind Closed Doors,* 202). Sarah Yeh describes women's participation in the violence of slave societies as a "disturbing aberration" from British gender norms (Yeh, "'A Sink of All Filthiness,'" *Historian,* LXVIII [2006], 79–82).

13. See Wilson, *Island Race,* 160–161. My sources have led me to reach different conclusions about the relationship between gender, race, and sexuality from those of Marisa Fuentes and

In a labor regime where enslaved status was only mapped onto nonwhite bodies, race also influenced the lives of female colonists in significant ways. When Keyhorne wrote her will in 1713, colonial assemblies throughout the Anglo-Atlantic world were developing racialized legal distinctions between servants and slaves. Jamaica followed this trend. Borrowing, in part, from Barbadian laws, Jamaica's legislature, for example, required masters and mistresses to obtain legal permission to physically punish servants, but not slaves. Similarly, men were supposed to compensate employers for impregnating female servants, but the assembly passed no acts to regulate enslaved women's reproductive capacities. Such laws confirmed the correlation of whiteness with legal, economic, cultural, and sexual privilege in relation to nonwhite people and equated enslaved status with African descent.[14]

Barbara Bush, who study Barbados. Whereas they argue that the privileged positions of white women rested on their sexual virtue and honor in comparison with enslaved women, my findings, which are detailed in Chapter 5, indicate that the sexual virtue of free women, irrespective of race, was not treated as a culturally important value in eighteenth-century Jamaica, nor did the concept of the "domestic sphere"—the site of gender production in the nineteenth century—exist on the island during this era. It is possible that Barbados and Jamaica developed different sexual cultures in relation to women. See Fuentes, *Dispossessed Lives,* 75, 79–80; and Bush, *Slave Women in Caribbean Society,* 112. Daniel Livesay also makes this point in relation to Jamaica in *Children of Uncertain Fortune: Mixed-Race Jamaicans in Britain and the Atlantic Family, 1733–1833* (Williamsburg, Va., and Chapel Hill, N.C., 2018), especially the introduction and chapter 1. Jessica Marie Johnson describes similarly complicated means of signifying status in colonial New Orleans; see Johnson, "Death Rites as Birthrights in Atlantic New Orleans: Kinship and Race in the Case of María Teresa v. Perine Dauphine," *Slavery and Abolition,* XXXVI (2015), 233–256. See also Yvonne Fabella, "Redeeming the 'Character of the Creoles': Whiteness, Gender, and Creolization in Pre-Revolutionary Saint Domingue," *Journal of Historical Sociology,* XXIII (2010), 40–72.

14. Masters and mistresses wanted to squeeze as much work as possible out of servants who were indentured for specific periods of time. They controlled the labor of enslaved people in perpetuity. For more on the distinction between servants and slaves in the British Caribbean, see Jenny Shaw, *Everyday Life in the Early English Caribbean: Irish, Africans, and the Construction of Difference* (Athens, Ga., 2013); Hilary McD. Beckles, "A 'Riotous and Unruly Lot': Irish Indentured Servants and Freemen in the English West Indies, 1644–1713," *WMQ,* 3d Ser., XLVII (1990), 503–522; and Edward B. Rugemer, "The Development of Mastery and Race in the Comprehensive Slave Codes of the Greater Caribbean during the Seventeenth Century," *WMQ,* 3d Ser., LXX (2013), 429–458. Though the law requiring compensation to employers was designed to protect the employer from the loss of labor that would result from a pregnancy, it also acted as a potential deterrent to sexual abuse, but it did not extend to enslaved women. See *The Laws of Jamaica, Passed by the Assembly and Confirmed by His Majesty in Council, Feb. 23, 1683* . . .

In this context, women like Keyhorne who were not far removed from slavery themselves needed to be especially vigilant about cultivating and performing free status in ways that white women did not. However, Keyhorne's life also reflects a certain plasticity in local perceptions of race. She lived in an era when Europeans believed that environmental and cultural conditions determined skin color and therefore considered race to be a mutable characteristic, rather than an inherent facet of a person's identity. Though local administrators used terms like "white," "negro," and "mulatto" to describe Jamaica's free populace, efforts to establish a legible racial hierarchy and racially segregate people were haphazard. Indeed, in the face of devastating mortality rates, the colonial government occasionally recognized and, to an extent, legitimized the proliferation of interracial relationships in hopes of bolstering the free population.[15]

(London, 1683); and *The Laws of Jamaica, Passed by the Assembly and Confirmed by His Majesty in Council, April 17, 1684*... (London, 1684).

15. As James H. Sweet argues, Europeans treated skin color as an important marker of cultural superiority well before the development of the Atlantic slave trade. See Sweet, "The Iberian Roots of American Racist Thought," *WMQ*, 3d Ser., LIV (1997), 143–166. This point is also made by Jennifer L. Morgan in "'Some Could Suckle over Their Shoulder': Male Travelers, Female Bodies, and the Gendering of Racial Ideology, 1500–1770," ibid., 167–192. Yet Europeans did not necessarily view race as permanent or heritable until the end of the eighteenth century. The belief in monogenesis led European naturalists to explain racial differences in terms of cultural degeneration. See Fischer, *Suspect Relations*, 86–87. Writing about French Louisiana, Jennifer Spear describes French observers adopting a similarly "malleable" view of skin color in the early eighteenth century (Spear, *Sex, Race, and Social Order*, 35–36). See also Roxann Wheeler, *The Complexion of Race: Categories of Difference in Eighteenth-Century British Culture* (Philadelphia, 2000), 46. Craig Steven Wilder and Rana A. Hogarth chart the emergence of scientific and medicalized racism at the end of the eighteenth century, when the belief in race as climatically and culturally produced was replaced with biologized notions of heritable difference. See Wilder, *Ebony and Ivy: Race, Slavery, and the Troubled History of America's Universities* (New York, 2013), esp. chapter 6; and Hogarth, *Medicalizing Blackness: Making Racial Difference in the Atlantic World, 1780–1840* (Chapel Hill, N.C., 2017). Natalie Zacek's observation from her study of poor and middling white women in the Leeward Islands that we should "reconceptualize these societies in terms beyond the oversimplified binary oppositions of white and black, enslaved and free" is useful in asking us to construct a more-nuanced portrait of colonial Caribbean societies (Zacek, "Between Lady and Slave," in Catterall and Campbell, eds., *Women in Port*, 139). As Wheeler points out, our assumptions about interracial sex as a source of contamination or a cause of degeneration did not emerge until the end of the eighteenth century (Wheeler, *Complexion of Race*, 143). Daniel Livesay charts this development. He observes that the Jamaica Assembly chose to imitate the Spanish legal precedent of considering people to be white who were four generations

The actions of Keyhorne and other free and freed people who maintained ambiguous racial identities challenged institutional attempts to demarcate boundaries along racial lines. In practice, the intimate connections forged between colonists of European, African, and Euro-African descent fortified the island. Together they transformed a sparsely populated Spanish outpost into a profit-generating engine for the empire. Islanders accomplished this metamorphosis by establishing more expansive, flexible, and inclusive families. In the early modern era, the family included blood relatives, kin through marriage, servants, and, in the colonial context, slaves, who shared the same household. Free and freed people in Jamaica enlarged their kin groups to include illegitimate, freed, and sometimes enslaved relatives. In doing so, colonists who were positioned in the crosshairs of a world characterized by demographic and economic volatility managed to survive and prosper. Epidemiological crises, natural disasters, and imperial warfare did not result in a "failed settler society," as we might expect. Instead, islanders developed remarkably durable kinship networks that became the lynchpin for Britain's ongoing control of Jamaica, and women played fundamental roles in this process.[16]

---

removed from an African ancestor. The colony also allowed wealthy people of Euro-African descent to petition for "white" status. See Livesay, *Children of Uncertain Fortune*, 38–41.

16. *Jamaica Ladies* contributes to a body of scholarship that stresses the centrality of the family to the formation of early modern empires. See, for instance, Sarah M. S. Pearsall, *Atlantic Families: Lives and Letters in the Later Eighteenth Century* (New York, 2008); Emma Rothschild, *The Inner Life of Empires: An Eighteenth-Century History* (Princeton, N.J., 2011); Palmer, *Intimate Bonds;* and Livesay, *Children of Uncertain Fortune.* On the extended definition of "family" in the early modern era, see Robert Shell, *Children of Bondage: A Social History of the Slave Society at the Cape of Good Hope, 1652–1838* (Hanover, N.H., 1994), 214–215. As Sarah Pearsall points out, imperial expansion meant that people who considered one another to be kin might live thousands of miles apart (*Atlantic Lives*, 28–29). Trevor Burnard's important article popularized this conception of Jamaica; see Burnard, "A Failed Settler Society," *Journal of Social History*, XXVIII (1994), 63–82. Daniel Livesay also describes the more "fluid" nature of the free family in Jamaica, as well as the centrality of kinship to the empire, writing that the family functioned as a "true" and "normalized" family unit on the island just as it did in Britain; see Livesay, *Children of Uncertain Fortune*, 4–5, 12. I offer a detailed discussion about the relationship between marriage and Atlantic trade in Chapter 2, below. See also Richard Grassby, *Kinship and Capitalism: Marriage, Family, and Business in the English-Speaking World, 1580–1740* (Cambridge, 2001); Peter Mathias, "Risk, Credit, and Kinship in Early Modern Enterprise," in John J. McCusker and Kenneth Morgan, eds., *The Early Modern Atlantic Economy* (Cambridge, 2000), 15–35; and Pearsall, *Atlantic Families.* Work has been done that traces the involvement of

Jamaica Ladies crafts a granular portrait of colonial society that shows how the first few generations of families, rather than individual men acting in isolation, secured the island for the empire. Starting in the 1670s and ending in the 1760s, it focuses on a critical yet poorly understood period of colonial expansion that saw Atlantic trade, contrabanding, privateering, planting, and especially slavery transform Jamaica. Typically, scholars either investigate seventeenth-century Port Royal or they focus on the late eighteenth century, when the sugar plantation economy was already well established. Yet, in the years between these two bookends, the island gained its ascendency. By the 1730s, no other colony could rival Jamaica's economic and strategic importance or compete with the financial and political power wielded by its constituents in London. All of these factors make Jamaica more "representative" of early America, as Vincent Brown has argued, than other regions such as New England and the Chesapeake, which have received the majority of the attention from historians of British America.[17]

---

families in the slave trade. These books generally focus on individual families, however, rather than investigating how alterations to the gendered family structure itself propagated and benefited from slavery. For more on family involvement in Atlantic slavery, see S. D. Smith, *Slavery, Family, and Gentry Capitalism in the British Atlantic: The World of the Lascelles, 1648–1834* (New York, 2006); Andrea Stuart, *Sugar in the Blood: A Family's Story of Slavery and Empire* (New York, 2013); and Thomas Norman DeWolf, *Inheriting the Trade: A Northern Family Confronts Its Legacy as the Largest Slave-Trading Dynasty in U.S. History* (New York, 2008). Jennifer Palmer's work, which studies slaveholding families who moved between Saint Domingue and La Rochelle, is a notable exception; see Palmer, *Intimate Bonds.*

17. Brown, *Reaper's Garden,* 258–259. The few works that do include aspects of Jamaica's role in colonial expansion in the early eighteenth century include Jack P. Greene, *Settler Jamaica in the 1750s: A Social Portrait* (Charlottesville, Va., 2016); Adrian Finucane, *The Temptations of Trade: Britain, Spain, and the Struggle for Empire* (Philadelphia, 2016); and O'Malley, *Final Passages.* For works focusing on seventeenth-century Port Royal or late eighteenth-century Jamaica, see, for example, Mark G. Hanna, *Pirate Nests and the Rise of the British Empire, 1570–1740* (Williamsburg, Va., and Chapel Hill, N.C., 2015); Nuala Zahedieh, "The Merchants of Port Royal, Jamaica, and the Spanish Contraband Trade, 1655–1692," *WMQ,* 3d Ser., XLIII (1986), 570–593; Carla Gardina Pestana, *The English Conquest of Jamaica: Oliver Cromwell's Bid for Empire* (Cambridge, Mass., 2017); Trevor Burnard and John Garrigus, *The Plantation Machine: Atlantic Capitalism in French Saint-Domingue and British Jamaica* (Philadelphia, 2016); Richard S. Dunn, *A Tale of Two Plantations: Slave Life and Labor in Jamaica and Virginia* (Cambridge, Mass., 2014); Paton, *No Bond But the Law;* B. W. Higman, *Plantation Jamaica, 1750–1850: Capital and Control in a Colonial Economy* (Kingston, 2005); Brown, *Reaper's Garden;* Christer Petley, *Slaveholders in Jamaica: Colonial Society and Culture during the Era of Abolition* (New York, 2009); Andrew Jackson O'Shaughnessy, *An Empire Divided: The American Revolution and the*

England's initial foray in Jamaica, however, did not lead to high expectations about the island's potential. After a disastrous attempt to seize Hispaniola from Spain as part of Oliver Cromwell's "Western Design," a motley crew of half-starved English soldiers and colonial recruits made a last-minute decision to take the sparsely populated island of Jamaica. Though their numbers were small, English women were involved in efforts to colonize Jamaica from the start. Some, like the wife of General Robert Venables, likely joined their husbands on the military expedition to the Caribbean. When they landed on the island in 1655, this group encountered a small contingent of Spanish and Afro-Spanish colonists, who, together with their slaves, had subsisted as ranchers, rearing and selling cattle to the treasure-laden flotillas traveling through the Caribbean on their way to Spain, for more than 150 years. During the 1660s, the English fought a guerilla war with these resilient Spanish inhabitants while struggling to survive on the island.[18]

A few decades later, English settlers had established themselves on the south coast, where they built a military outpost and port. Initially called Cagway and then renamed Port Royal after the Restoration of Charles II, the town was flourishing by the 1670s. Port Royal became one of the wealthiest and busiest towns in the Anglo-Atlantic world, supporting a thriving trade in licit and illicit goods—one that women actively participated in. After a devastating earthquake destroyed much of Port Royal in 1692, male and female colonists began relocating to the new port town of Kingston, where they continued to prosper from a range of legal and illegal maritime activities. When Britain acquired the valuable asiento from Spain in 1713, making it the chief contractor of enslaved Africans in the Atlantic world, Kingston's role in the empire grew exponentially. Ideally located near Spanish territories in America, Kingston became the primary transshipment entrepôt for the British slave trade, ushering in a torrent of human captives, money, ships, goods, and visitors to the island.[19]

British Caribbean (Philadelphia, 2000); and Trevor Burnard, *Planters, Merchants, and Slaves: Plantation Societies in British America, 1650–1820* (Chicago, 2015), 221.

18. Carla Pestana claims that Spanish colonists were unable to import a large number of African slaves to the island because it was a "backwater" in the Spanish Empire that few slave ships wanted to visit; see Pestana, *English Conquest of Jamaica*, 47–48. David Wheat has found evidence of French and Portuguese slavers bringing a few hundred Africans to Jamaica in the late sixteenth and early seventeenth centuries; see Wheat, *Atlantic Africa and the Spanish Caribbean, 1570–1640* (Williamsburg, Va., and Chapel Hill, N.C., 2016), 77, 98–99.

19. Zahedieh, "Merchants of Port Royal, Jamaica, and the Spanish Contraband Trade," *WMQ*, 3d Ser., XLIII (1986), 570–593; Palmer, *Human Cargoes*.

The investment made by Keyhorne and other early settlers in slaveholding made Jamaica a prison for the most substantial unfree African population in British America. The island's enslaved population swelled from 9,504 in 1673 to 74,525 in 1730. (In comparison, 50,000 enslaved people inhabited Virginia, and 21,000 captives lived in South Carolina in the 1730s.) The Royal African Company transported 18,801 enslaved Africans to Jamaica between 1680 and 1693; the island received another 44,376 from the company and private traders between 1698 and 1707. By 1752, 110,000 enslaved people inhabited Jamaica—the majority of whom were born in Africa, coming from the Bight of Biafra, the Gold Coast, West Central Africa, Sierra Leone, the Bight of Benin, and Senegambia. To maintain control of this African slave majority, Jamaica established a brutal labor regime and harsh slave codes that provoked frequent insurgencies. Enslaved people who fled from their owners joined the Maroons—free descendants of slaves who had been transported by the Spanish—aiding them in a war of attrition against settlers. After decades of failed attempts to defeat the Maroons, the British army acknowledged defeat and signed a treaty with them in 1739.[20]

These violent conditions did not rend the social fabric of free society. Instead, local men and women adapted to—and even flourished in—the precarious world they were forming. Free families were able to survive and succeed by enhancing the roles played by female kin in relation to inheritance,

20. See Edward Long, *The History of Jamaica; or, General Survey of the Antient and Modern State of That Island with Reflections on Its Situation, Settlements, Inhabitants, Climate, Products, Commerce, Laws, and Government,* I (London, 1774), 376; Dunn, *Sugar and Slaves,* 155; Burnard, *Planters, Merchants, and Slaves,* 68–70; and Fischer, *Suspect Relations,* 27. See also Table III in David Eltis, "The Volume and Structure of the Transatlantic Slave Trade: A Reassessment," *WMQ,* 3d Ser., LVIII (2001), 17–46. A large portion of the captives were destined for regions in the Spanish Empire. Colin Palmer estimates that 18,180 of the captives were exported from the island to Spanish territories between 1702 and 1714. After the signing of the asiento between Britain and Spain, a total of 19,662 slaves were legally shipped to Spanish colonies between 1715 and 1738—most of them would pass through Jamaica. See Palmer, *Human Cargoes,* 97, 99, 103. Using *Voyages: Transatlantic Slave Trade Database,* http://www.slavevoyages.org, several scholars conclude in a co-authored article that 1,205,000 Africans arrived alive in Jamaica between 1661 and 1807. Between 1650 and 1750, 154,126 people disembarked from the Gold Coast, 105,291 from the Bight of Benin, and 99,930 from the Bight of Biafra. See Simon P. Newman et al., "The West African Ethnicity of the Enslaved in Jamaica," *Slavery and Abolition,* XXXIV (2013), 378–379. Vincent Brown provides a map detailing the origins of enslaved immigrants to Jamaica. He also determines that people from the Bight of Biafra and the Gold Coast composed the majority of the captives who were transported to Jamaica. See Brown, *Reaper's Garden,* 25–27.

commerce, marriage, and slaveholding. For instance, they established inheritance strategies that divided estates more equitably and took measures to protect married women's property, a large portion of which was composed of slaves. By strengthening the property rights of individuals irrespective of gender, the colonial government supported and encouraged local adaptations. Altogether, colonists devised flexible and practical customs that were designed to navigate both Caribbean and Atlantic conditions. In doing so, they developed a form of colonialism that was secular, legalistic, and aggressively profit-oriented, yet also intensively family-focused and deeply reliant on female members.[21]

Free and freed women, in turn, benefited from their elevated positions within colonial society. Working as merchants, shopkeepers, seamstresses, and tavernkeepers, female islanders of European, African, and Euro-African descent helped to suture together local, Atlantic, and global markets.[22] Al-

21. These changes occurred at a time when the "Bloody code" was established in England, which harshly protected the rights of property owners by treating any form of minor theft as a capital offense, suggesting that the trend toward the privileging of private property was Atlantic in nature. See Amanda Vickery, "An Englishman's Home Is His Castle? Thresholds, Boundaries, and Privacies in the Eighteenth-Century London House," *Past and Present,* no. 199 (May 2008), 159. In response to Trevor Burnard's article, "A Failed Settler Society," *Journal of Social History,* XXVIII (1994), 63–82, Vincent Brown describes Jamaica as "more than a failed settler society." He also observes that colonists "struggled to establish intelligible patterns for group cohesion, and the reproduction of family, hierarchy, and prosperity—however they defined these." See Brown, *Reaper's Garden,* 59. My findings indicate that colonial families relied heavily on female members to secure family estates and thereby maintain social order on the island.

22. Adhering to the assertion that the particular and the individual are the best sites for studying the Atlantic economy, *Jamaica Ladies* places free and freed women's commercial activities at the center, rather than at the margins, of an increasingly global marketplace. See David Hancock, *Citizens of the World: London Merchants and the Integration of the British Atlantic Community, 1735–1785* (Cambridge, 1995). Although *Jamaica Ladies* is not a microhistory, Chapters 2 and 3, in particular, draw on work that uses individual lives to tell larger stories about the British Empire. For exemplary histories that inspired my own approach, see Miles Ogborn, *Global Lives: Britain and the World, 1550–1800* (New York, 2008); Linda Colley, *The Ordeal of Elizabeth Marsh: A Woman in World History* (New York, 2007); and Rothschild, *Inner Life of Empires.* Kit Candlin and Cassandra Pybus emphasize the entrepreneurial activities of free Euro-African and African women in *Enterprising Women.* Ellen Hartigan-O'Connor examines the economic activities of free women and shows how they profited from the practice of hiring out enslaved people in Charleston, South Carolina, and Newport, Rhode Island; see Hartigan-O'Connor, *The Ties That Buy: Women and Commerce in Revolutionary America* (Philadelphia,

though sugar planting became ever more important to the Jamaican economy, the island never became a sugar monoculture like Britain's other Caribbean colonies, thus creating opportunities for women to engage in a variety of agricultural and ranching ventures. Of course, the holdings of female colonists paled in comparison with the gargantuan fortunes amassed by elite male planters and merchants.[23] Still, free and freed women in Jamaica were significantly richer than most Britons. The average female colonist owned a median estate valued at £285 and a mean estate worth £803 (between £41,500 to £116,900, respectively, today).[24] Her wealth far surpassed the modest £42 estate possessed by an ordinary person living in Britain or in mainland North America. Female property holders on the higher end of the scale also equaled their male peers in the West Indies, whose fortunes, amounting to £1,042, made them the wealthiest people in the British Empire.[25] For most Britons, this level of wealth was unattainable; for lower-status women like London's

---

2009). Linda Sturtz, in *Within Her Power,* has uncovered similar evidence of free women's legal and economic autonomy in colonial Virginia.

23. Trevor Burnard calculates that between 1700 and 1724 the average planter's estate was valued at £860 and the average merchant's at £1,985. He finds that in Kingston between 1700 and 1784 an average male merchant's estate was valued at £3,604, whereas an estate held by the average woman was worth £671 (Burnard, *Planters, Merchants, and Slaves,* 179, 207).

24. I calculated both the median and the mean values of women's estates from all 915 of the probated inventories of women's estates made between 1674 and 1770. See Jamaica Inventories, 1674–1784, Jamaica Archives (JA), Spanish Town, Jamaica. My figures are derived from the database of probated inventories compiled by Trevor Burnard. I have also converted Jamaican currency to British pounds sterling throughout the book for consistency's sake. To illustrate the scale of colonists' wealth, I use the calculator on *Measuring Worth.com*—a tool that was developed by professors of economics from several universities; see "Purchasing Power of British Pounds from 1270 to Present," https://www.measuringworth.com/calculators/ppoweruk/. It calculates what the "simple" purchasing power of a given amount would be in the present. I use the "real price" estimate, which is the most conservative of four options (real price, labor value, income value, and economic share).

25. Of the estates that were probated in Jamaica between 1674 and 1765, 13 percent—a little more than one in ten—belonged to women (Jamaica Inventories). A probate account offers a snapshot of an estate after all the debts have been settled. Probates were normally filed one year after a person died. See Amy Louise Erickson, *Women and Property in Early Modern England* (1993; rpt. London, 1995), 34. The list of the wealthiest men in Jamaica includes men like William Beckford, Simon Taylor, and Rose Fuller who converted colonial slavery into metropolitan political power. For a complete list, see Burnard, *Planters, Merchants, and Slaves,* 223–225; and Brown, *Reaper's Garden,* 16.

female servants and housekeepers, who survived on £2 to £15 per annum, it was unimaginable.[26]

Access to African captives significantly amplified the wealth of Jamaica's free women. Nearly every female venture, from the small provisioning plot to the large mercantile operation, relied on enslaved laborers to function. As a group, female colonists made a considerable investment in slavery. Between the end of the seventeenth and the mid-eighteenth century, one of every ten slaveowners on the island was a woman, and an estimated 80 percent of all female property holders owned slaves. Female slaveholding patterns throughout British America require further investigation, but it is reasonable to assume that, given Jamaica's primacy in the Atlantic slave trade and the scale of its enslaved population, the free women who settled there reaped the greatest material benefits from slavery.[27]

In addition to economic gains, female colonists derived significant legal and social advantages from slaveholding. Just as local lawmakers sharpened the racial differences between servants and the enslaved, they also blunted the gendered distinctions between male and female slaveholders. Enslavers of both sexes wielded nearly unlimited juridical power over African captives. Although women throughout the Anglo-Atlantic world were expected to manage servants in their capacity as household heads, they exercised a dominion of an entirely different magnitude over slaves. Their command far exceeded the bounds of the domestic realm—the hearthstone of female authority. In sum, slaveholding counteracted the legal, material, and social disabilities and disadvantages that early modern women were typically subjected to. Yet it did not turn Jamaica into an egalitarian utopia for female

26. See Brown, *Reaper's Garden*, 16. Although indigent women who owned no property are difficult to track in the archives, comparatively, even the poorest female property holders in Jamaica survived on more than their British counterparts (Vickery, *Behind Closed Doors*, 130). Housemaids earned between two and eight pounds, while more skilled housekeepers could earn fifteen pounds per annum. See Clive Emsley, Tim Hitchcock, and Robert Shoemaker, "London History—Currency, Coinage, and the Cost of Living," Historical Background, London and Its Hinterland, *Old Bailey Proceedings Online* (www.oldbaileyonline.org, version 7.0, Mar. 20, 2014).

27. Nearly 80 percent of the estates owned by women that were probated between 1674 and 1765 included slaves. Of the 825 female-held estates that were probated between 1674 and 1765, 648 included slaves (Jamaica Inventories). Hilary Beckles offers a useful comparison of nineteenth-century Saint Lucia and Barbados indicating that white female slaveholders were normally urban dwellers who owned fewer than ten slaves, the majority of whom were female. See Beckles, *Centering Woman*, 62–65.

colonists. Men still controlled the lion's share of the money, land, slaves, and political power on the island. Moreover, women had no formal political rights and rarely held public office—nor did they anywhere else in the empire. The data collected from a survey of all 10,222 estates that were probated between 1674 and 1784 indicates that, although women held 12 percent of the estates, their holdings made up only 5 percent of the total value of the estates. The mean value is skewed, however, as it includes the outliers. The £360 median value of a colonist's estate is closer to the £285 median value of an ordinary woman's holdings.[28]

The material and social disparities between male and female colonists created distinctive forms of slaveholding wherein women enslavers who possessed fewer resources relied more intensively on individual captives for their labor and their monetary value as property. Women who operated taverns, shops, or small plantations, for instance, were more likely to work and live alongside the people whom they held in bondage than the male planters who controlled hundreds of slaves. *Jamaica Ladies* explores how the gendered dimensions of female slaveholding—its small-scale and intimate nature—shaped the lives of enslaved people in ways that are not well understood. Dependency and physical proximity personalized the relationships between women enslavers and enslaved people. Daily contact created ample opportunities for coercion and abuse. Indeed, captives who were held by female

28. My work focuses on a period before femininity was strongly correlated with domesticity and colonial circumstances required free and freed women to work outside the household. These characteristics distinguish Jamaica's female colonists from their later counterparts in the antebellum South, whose authority was primarily enacted in the plantation household. However, as Thavolia Glymph observes, the plantation household in the U.S. South was, in itself, both a public and a private space; see Glymph, *Out of the House of Bondage,* 43. My calculations of the mean and median values of estates suggest that Richard Dunn's analysis of Jamaica inventories may be on the high end. His study of 68 inventories made between 1699 and 1701 yields an average estate value of £825. My analysis of 126 inventories made during this period results in a mean value of £496 and a median value of £214. I have a more complete data set and have converted to pounds sterling, which may account for this variation. Nevertheless, my findings show that the average person's estate at the start of the eighteenth century was of a middling size. Yet, as Dunn notes, Jamaica appraisers did not include land in probated inventories, which means that estates were likely larger than the probates indicate. See Dunn, *Sugar and Slaves,* 266–267. Trevor Burnard determines the average wealth to be £466 between 1674 and 1699, £911 between 1700 and 1724, and £1,688 between 1725 and 1749. His estimate for the early period is closer to mine. His use of Jamaica currency and the mean versus the median may account for variations in our findings. See Burnard, *Planters, Merchants, and Slaves,* 179; and Jamaica Inventories.

owners might have struggled to maintain their anonymity and distance more than those who labored on large plantations.[29]

Despite the dramatic power differentials between enslavers and the enslaved, slavery was still a negotiated relationship that was influenced by captives themselves. As studies of baptism and manumission acts in later chapters of the book show, women treated slavery as a form of wealth building in people—thereby betraying the African influence on colonial practices of bondage. Enslaved people who navigated potentially treacherous relationships with their owners could pry concessions from them. Intimate connections might yield better living conditions, greater independence, powerful patrons, and sometimes even freedom. Although such actions may not reflect conventional examples of slave resistance, they still offer evidence of the ways in which the most marginalized members of colonial society sought to determine their own lives.[30]

29. Philip Morgan reaches a similar conclusion when he argues against Orlando Patterson's claim that authentic human relationships could not exist in dynamics predicated on violence. Morgan, on the other hand, contends that "an inhumane institution like slavery could still encompass within it warm and caring human relationships." See Morgan, *Slave Counterpoint,* 269–271. He finds ample evidence to contradict Patterson's generalization, as do I in this book.

30. Marisa Fuentes has made a powerful argument about the gendered and racialized structures of traditional archives, which are designed to silence enslaved people. However, I believe that it is still possible to read colonial sources against the grain and extract traces of enslaved people's actions. In doing so, we can resist the very terms of power with which the documents seek to inscribe themselves and that seek to commodify people as property. See Fuentes, *Dispossessed Lives,* 7. Chapters 6 and 7, below, describe the varied ways female slaveholders used baptisms and manumissions to enfold former slaves into their families while also explaining how women's motives and practices differed from those of male slaveholders in these contexts. For more work on different forms of slavery in Africa, see Suzanne Miers and Igor Kopytoff, eds., *Slavery in Africa: Historical and Anthropological Perspectives* (Madison, Wis., 1977); Paul E. Lovejoy, *Transformations in Slavery: A History of Slavery in Africa* (Cambridge, 2012); and Herman L. Bennett, *African Kings and Black Slaves: Sovereignty and Dispossession in the Early Modern Atlantic* (Philadelphia, 2019). Jennifer Palmer describes how the intimate bonds between slaveholding families and enslaved people shaped the lives of captives in significant and distinctive ways (Palmer, *Intimate Bonds*). Walter Johnson cautions us from interpreting all of the behavior of enslaved people as manifestations of "agency" (Johnson, "On Agency," *Journal of Social History,* XXXVII [2003], 113–124). The theorist Michel de Certeau provides an alternative model for interpreting the actions of enslaved people. Certeau argues that it is possible for disempowered people to co-opt the techniques and practices of the powerful and redefine them for their own purposes. Jamaica's captives exhibited the type of "intellectual creativity as persistent as it is subtle" that Certeau describes. See Certeau, *The Practice of Everyday Life,* trans. Steven

Atlantic slavery was never the sole concern of white men acting in isolation, nor were slave-based societies like Jamaica inhospitable and restrictive places for free women. On the contrary, as *Jamaica Ladies* demonstrates, colonial conditions created distinctive opportunities, especially in the form of slaveholding, for women who, in turn, commanded more affluence and authority than their counterparts living elsewhere in the empire. Of course, male colonists reaped even larger benefits from their positions in the Caribbean. But colonial advantages mattered more to female inhabitants, whose lives were otherwise legally, economically, and socially restricted in relation to men. In Jamaica, possessing other people who were both legal dependents and property significantly increased female sovereignty and financial independence. Slavery, therefore, provided women with an alternative to relying on men or marriage for support. In doing so, it altered the gendered and sexual relations between free people.

Attending to the varied lives of free and freed women, and revealing the advantages they gained from chattel slavery, challenges our fundamental understanding of how slave societies were constituted throughout the Atlantic world. When we shift our focus to female colonists, it becomes difficult to see how a remote and largely uninhabited island could have become the richest and the largest slaveholding colony in the British Empire without their involvement. Free and freed women participated in local and global markets, managed plantations, and directed the transmission of property from one generation to the next. Local actions had global consequences. Securing Jamaica—the fledgling empire's most lucrative possession—required the contribution of free and freed women in building a slave society.

Surviving, let alone succeeding, in Jamaica demanded nerve, adaptability, and ruthless pragmatism. Free and freed women exhibited all of these qualities, proving themselves to be every bit as calculating and brutal as the men with whom they shared the island. As critical members of a free minority, female enslavers engaged in the daily practices of management, negotiation, and violence that sustained slaveholder power in Jamaica and devised a range

---

Rendall, [I] (Berkeley, Calif., 1984), 38. Anthropologist Saba Mahmood goes one step further by asking us to move beyond a definition of agency that is rooted in emancipatory politics and hence understood to be resistance to relations of domination. Her account of agency as the "capacity for action that historically specific relations of subordination enable and create" offers an important lens for viewing the actions of both free women and enslaved people in the early modern era. See Mahmood, "Feminist Theory, Embodiment, and the Docile Agent: Some Reflections on the Egyptian Islamic Revival, *Cultural Anthropology*, XVI (2001), 203, 211.

of tactics to ensure the compliance of their captives. Women bought, sold, stole, and punished enslaved people and vociferously defended their rights to captives as property. Moreover, in their roles as wives, mothers, sisters, and aunts, women naturalized slaveholding practices within free families, ensuring the commitment of future generations of islanders to chattel slavery. By turning settler colonialism and slavery into opportunity, the first three generations of Jamaica's "ladies" charted the trajectory for an island that increasingly steered the course of the British Empire.

1. Port Royal

As Elizabeth Doddington sat amid the smoldering ruins of Port Royal writing her 1703 will, she decided to give her entire estate as charity to the town's "poor widows and orphans." The fire that burned Port Royal to the ground was not the first calamity to destroy the wealthiest port town in English America. A decade earlier, an earthquake and an ensuing tsunami had likewise devastated Port Royal. Doddington's life, it seems, was shaped by her unfortunate decision to settle in a place that attracted tragedies of epic proportions. Though Doddington's status as a widow indicates that she had either been married when she reached the newly acquired English colony of Jamaica or wed soon after her arrival, she made no reference to children—or, for that matter, to any other living relatives. Perhaps all of Doddington's kin had been killed by the disasters that had ravaged Port Royal or succumbed to the rampant diseases that plagued the island's inhabitants. Or, maybe the disastrous aftermath of the fire inspired her altruism toward a group of women and children caught in more dire straits than herself. In making her bequest, Doddington unwittingly disclosed the presence of a variety of female settlers on the island. Indeed, they were so noticeable that Doddington, herself a single woman without family in Jamaica, felt compelled to offer them all that she owned.[1]

A member of the pioneering generation of colonists who settled on the island after England captured Jamaica from Spain in 1655, Doddington had acquired land in Port Royal as well as in the embryonic town of Kingston,

1. Will of Elizabeth Doddington, 1703, Jamaica Wills, 1661–1771, X, Island Record Office (IRO), Spanish Town, Jamaica.

which was being built to replace a community that seemed destined for destruction. Modestly well-off but hardly affluent by local standards, she was also among the first generation of female settlers to survive off the labor of enslaved Africans. In addition to real estate, the widow owned a man, Tom, who worked as a bricklayer, a mother, named Rose, and her children, and seven other captives, whom she did not identify by name. These people composed a substantial portion of her estate. Instead of bequeathing them along with her land to Port Royal's "poor widows and orphans," however, she decided to manumit all of her slaves.[2]

As a slaveholder, Doddington treated her captives in a highly personalized manner. In the absence of family, she might have developed some of her closest relationships with the people whom she held in bondage. The widow offered Tom conditional freedom. He would enhance the worth of her charitable bequest, working for seven years to "help build on the land." She also promised to manumit Rose and her children after Rose served her friend for four years. Unlike Tom and Rose, Doddington's other slaves would be freed immediately on her death. The widow's motive for restricting the freedom of Tom and Rose, who might have been a couple, is unclear. Maybe she wanted to squeeze every last drop of labor out of her most skilled laborers. If so, Tom and Rose might have witnessed the manumissions of the rest of Doddington's slaves, who were likely their friends, with a mixture of joy and bitterness. Yet Doddington did not provide these people with money or land. They would join Jamaica's small community of free and freed colonists of African descent empty-handed. It is also possible that she wanted Tom and Rose to be held in a form of de jure captivity as a means of protecting them after her death. In reality, they would live as de facto freed people until they could save enough money to support themselves after being manumitted.[3]

Elizabeth Inglett, another member of the first wave of English colonists to settle in Jamaica, also developed ambiguous and complicated relationships with the people whom she held in bondage. Like Doddington, she found herself bereft of friends and family when she faced death in a foreign land. Enslaved people—two women and their children—approximated the closest kin she had on the island. Together, Inglett and her captives ran a small shop in St. Jago de la Vega (Spanish Town), the island's primary urban center under Spanish rule, which the English appropriated as the base for their colonial government. Inglett gave her modest estate to relatives in Brit-

2. Ibid.

3. Ibid.

ain in her 1689 will. Like Doddington, she also manumitted the women and children who had helped her to survive and served as her primary companions. Aside from distant relatives, her captives were the only people recognized in her will. She provided them with "the long yard and little houses southward of house I know dwell in" and £7. She also gave one of the women her "worster sort of waring cloaths." Her bequest of property, clothing, and money was worth the equivalent of £1,145 in today's currency and provided enough of a cushion to support their transition from enslavement to freedom. Nevertheless, these "gifts" were small recompense for women who had probably endured forcible separation from their own families in Africa and transportation across the Atlantic.[4]

As small-scale slaveholders who achieved moderate wealth and chose to manumit a few captives, Doddington and Inglett exhibited the attributes and the behaviors that would become characteristic of free and freed women in eighteenth-century Jamaica. Their wills reveal the central roles played by female colonists in constructing a particular kind of society, one that embodied the contradictory plans devised by the crown, the Lords of the Committee of Trade and Plantations (hereafter referred to as the Lords of Trade), and local governors during the seventeenth century. On the one hand, imperialists in London and Jamaica aimed to replicate an English model of a social order that idealized the independent patriarchal household. On the other hand, they quickly expanded the colony's—and in turn the empire's—interest in the African slave trade. As wives and mothers, English women were essential to these imperial plans, which hinged on the settlement and the reproduction of English families overseas. The rapid expansion of slavery and the ensuing slave revolts on the island during the late seventeenth century intensified, rather than diminished, the need for female colonists whose reproductive capacities could be harnessed to augment the free population, thus stabilizing the colony under English rule.

Women like Doddington and Inglett were driven by their own needs and concerns to migrate to Jamaica. They followed diverse paths to the island. Some traveled willingly with families while others went on their own, lured by government offers of cheap land and taxes or tales of quickly earned fortunes. Still others were forcibly carried to the colony as convict laborers and indentured servants. Though scant records make it difficult to determine how the majority of the first generation of female settlers arrived in Jamaica, a handful

4. Will of Elizabeth Inglett, 1683, Jamaica Wills, III–V; Measuring Worth, https://www.measuringworth.com/calculators/ppoweruk/.

of sporadic census records indicate that they soon formed an important contingent of colonial society. In 1662, just seven years after Oliver Cromwell's soldiers seized the island, 645 women and 408 children made up nearly one-third of the 3,653 free inhabitants living there. Enslaved people only composed 13 percent of Jamaica's inhabitants at this time. A decade later, 17,268 inhabitants lived in the colony. Of the 7,764 free people, 2,002 were women, 1,712 were children, and the remaining 4,050 were men. Though male colonists outnumbered their female counterparts, the presence of a considerable number of children suggests that families traveled to the island together and played a decisive role in shaping its early settlement.[5]

The few documents that have survived—male-authored narratives, probated inventories and wills, and court records—suggest that the first generation of female colonists adapted swiftly to the island's volatile environment. Devoted to commerce and increasingly invested in the African slave trade, Jamaica's heterogeneous society fostered more egalitarian gender dynamics. In the absence of entrenched institutions and customs, free and freed women carved out opportunities for themselves. Their presence was especially noticeable in the flourishing commercial hub of Port Royal, where women established a niche in the service industry. Those on the lower end of the social spectrum labored as domestic servants, cooks, and prostitutes. Middling women ran taverns, coffeehouses, and probably brothels. Wealthier women earned handsome estates working as merchants who imported a range of globally produced goods to the colony.

Doddington's and Inglett's bequests also highlight the early involvement of female colonists in Atlantic slavery. Probated inventories and wills show that, like Doddington and Inglett, the majority of Jamaica's free and freed women owned at least a few captives by the end of the seventeenth century. These early English settlers established a precedent that generations of islanders would follow. Women became slaveholders via inheritance. They

5. "List of Men, Women, Children, Negroes, Arms, Acres Land by Area on October 28, 1662, at Windsor's Departure," Collection of Papers Relating to English Affairs in the West Indies, and Chiefly in Jamaica, 1654–1682, Add MS 11410, British Library (BL), London. The population totals for 1673 are taken from Edward Long, *The History of Jamaica* . . . , I (London, 1774), 376. Of course, these figures are not entirely reliable. One colonial official claimed in 1671 that "no account" had been kept of "people arriving on island or dying" for seven years. See Author unknown, "An Answer to the Inquiries Given to Mr. Secretary Esq. Slingsby to Mr. Gaywood in the Pelican," Nov. 29, 1671, Collection of Papers Relating to English Affairs in the West Indies, Add MS 11410. The demographic information, however, is consistent enough to expose general trends.

also took advantage of England's growing involvement in the slave trade to purchase captive Africans themselves. Women of European, and, increasingly Euro-African and African descent, also established inheritance strategies that displayed their preference for devising enslaved people to other female kin. Altogether, these colonial practices aided in the development of a form of colonialism that was intensely reliant on slaveholding.[6]

By 1700, female colonists relied on the labor, monetary value, and sometimes the emotional companionship of captive Africans. They instituted a form of small-scale slaveholding that bound enslavers and enslaved in an uneasy closeness. Free women and the people whom they held in bondage weathered the volatile conditions of early English Jamaica, contending with the island's tropical heat, dense foliage, and mélange of unfamiliar sounds and smells. This forced intimacy with enslavers formed yet another aspect of the degradation experienced by enslaved people. But, in certain instances, the personalized nature of female slaveholding yielded benefits, especially in the form of manumissions. Doddington, Inglett, and other women slaveholders freed people on a regular basis, setting a trend that would persist well into the eighteenth century.

"SUCH AS ARE WILLING TO GO TO ENGLISH PLANTATIONS"

In comparison with older colonies in New England and the Chesapeake, Jamaica was a recent and unplanned addition to England's meager American holdings. Desperate to enhance his country's power and challenge Spanish hegemony across the Atlantic, Oliver Cromwell launched a secret military campaign called the Western Design in 1655. Hoping to gain a foothold in the Caribbean, he sent thirty-eight ships manned by three thousand soldiers to the Caribbean, where an additional fifty-two hundred men from Barbados and the Leeward Islands augmented the ranks. Aggressively imperialistic, the Design signaled England's shift from trade and piracy to outright conquest overseas. These lofty military ambitions, however, quickly crashed against the rocks of Spanish power in the region. The army's attempt to seize the well-guarded island of Hispaniola resulted in massive casualties. Poorly trained soldiers died in droves from dehydration and disease. Reeling from failure in Hispaniola but unwilling to return home empty-handed, Cromwell's military leaders made a last-minute decision to attack the poorly defended and

6. I study probated inventories and wills later in the chapter. They are drawn from: Jamaica Inventories, 1674–1765, Jamaica Archives (JA), Spanish Town, Jamaica; and Jamaica Wills.

sparsely settled island of Jamaica. England's capture of Jamaica gave the country a tenuous position in the Greater Antilles, a Spanish-controlled region of the Caribbean that was within striking distance of the territory where galleons laden with silver and gold set sail for Spain.[7]

In spite of Jamaica's strategic significance, its value to the fledgling empire was not apparent at first. The European public widely regarded the Western Design to be a fiasco, and English prospects remained bleak for several years following the conquest. Weakened by disease and starvation, Cromwellian soldiers scraped a meager living from the island. Their numbers dwindled rapidly, from seventy-eight hundred to fewer than three thousand men. The military also struggled to eradicate a collection of Spanish inhabitants who had fled to Jamaica's northern coast, where they continued to ambush English soldiers and challenge their occupation for the next five years. Aware of England's fragile control of the area, Spain was reluctant to hand over the territory, and the Spanish crown did not formally recognize its rival's right until 1670.[8]

Driven by the imperative to shore up England's weak hold on Jamaica, the crown, the Lords of Trade, and the early governors all envisioned the island as a settler colony. They hoped to attract families there and avoid the disasters that had unfolded in older colonies like Virginia, where a predominately male group of settlers barely survived their first years in America. English women who could perform essential reproductive and ideological functions figured centrally in early imperial strategies for the island. In addition to generating a self-reproducing population, wives and mothers would enable men to achieve the requisite markers of appropriate masculinity: marriage and family. According to early modern ideals, social order originated in the patriarchal household. Considered to be disorderly, the unmarried soldiers, privateers, political dissidents, and pirates who made up the majority of Jamaica's free society were viewed with suspicion and contempt.[9]

7. See Carla Gardina Pestana, *The English Conquest of Jamaica: Oliver Cromwell's Bid for Empire* (Cambridge, Mass., 2017); Abigail L. Swingen, *Competing Visions of Empire: Labor, Slavery, and the Origins of the British Atlantic Empire* (New Haven, Conn., 2015), chap. 2. Five thousand men from Barbados and twelve hundred more from the Leeward Islands joined the army. For more on the conquest of Jamaica, see Susan Dwyer Amussen, *Caribbean Exchanges: Slavery and the Transformation of English Society, 1640–1700* (Chapel Hill, N.C., 2007), 33–37.

8. Pestana, *English Conquest of Jamaica,* 157, 183–214.

9. After experiencing the unrest caused by a largely male group of colonists, Virginia Company officials adopted strategies for bringing English women to Virginia, sometimes by force, to create a more permanent settlement. Jamaican officials shared a growing belief that equated the

Metropolitan and local policymakers acted on these widespread gendered beliefs hoping to offset the prevalence of young unattached men on the island. When the military commander Edward D'Oyley began issuing marriage licenses to clergy in 1657, signaling his interest in creating a society of male householders, only a handful of women lived in Jamaica. Later governors treated marital status as a key qualification for colonial office holding. In 1672, for example, Governor Thomas Lynch invited John White, a "chief justice and lawyer" who moved to Jamaica with his family, to join the Jamaica Council, which acted as the governor's advisory board. White was not invited because of his legal training, rather, it was "because of his family," wrote Lynch, "wee thought fitt to add him." Although it is possible that the reference to "his family" related to White's rank and connections in England, the general preference for married men indicates that his position as a husband and father played an important role in establishing his fitness for a political post.[10]

James II also evinced a conviction that regulating marriage would establish order overseas. More importantly, he sought to ensure Jamaica's conformity to the official religion of England and the island's loyalty to the monarchy—both deeply contested and inseparable issues at the time of his reign (1685–1689). In 1680, James, then the presumptive heir to the throne, ordered Governor Charles Howard, first earl of Carlisle, to monitor marriage in Jamaica, instructing him to "take especial care that a table of marriages established by the canons of the church of England be hung up in every Church" and also "to endeavour to get a law pass'd in the Assembly for the strict observation of the said Table." Officials continued to favor married men as officeholders after the Glorious Revolution in 1688. In 1699, Governor William Beeston portrayed bachelors as untrustworthy and capricious figures. Nearly all of

---

family household with orderly colonial settlement, as efforts to attract families to the island reveal. For more on the gendered dimensions of colonization in Virginia, see Kathleen M. Brown, *Good Wives, Nasty Wenches, and Anxious Patriarchs: Gender, Race, and Power in Colonial Virginia* (Williamsburg Va., and Chapel Hill, N.C., 1995), 80–82. Similarly, the proprietors of Carolina established a headright system in which they offered land to attract male and female settlers to the colony. See Kirsten Fischer, *Suspect Relations: Sex, Race, and Resistance in Colonial North Carolina* (Ithaca, N.Y., 2002), 20; Brown, *Good Wives, Nasty Wenches;* and Alexandra Shepard, *Meanings of Manhood in Early Modern England* (Oxford, 2003).

10. "Extracts from Colonel D'Oyley's Journal, Relating to Jamaica, 1653–1661," Add MS 12410, BL, Sir Thomas Lynch to Lord Arlington, Jan. 24, 1671–Dec. 27, 1672, Collection of Papers Relating to English Affairs in the West Indies, Add MS 11410. In 1657, Governor D'Oyley offered a marriage license "to any minster to marry John Pearsicke and Judith Harper."

the men whom he recommended for political posts were married. One man, Major Halse, ran a tavern with his wife. Another man, "Mr. Moreton," was chosen because he had recently wedded a wealthy local widow "by whom he has a good estate." He also endorsed four other men who had "settled" families in the colony. Beeston considered these men to be strong candidates because their status as "housekeepers" signified their intention to stay on the island. He dismissed a captain and a merchant on the grounds that "neither of them are housekeepers, or like to settle here." Governor Beeston espoused an understanding of manhood that hinged on marital status. His preference for married men also made female colonists indispensable to local elites who hoped to advance their political careers.[11]

Beeston's statement inadvertently reveals the presence of women who had amassed considerable estates and industriously established businesses on the island by 1699. Either traveling with families or on their own, free women made their way to Jamaica soon after the English conquest. When Cromwell's military leader, D'Oyley, served as governor between 1661 and 1662, he specifically referred to families and single women in his endeavor to attract people to Jamaica. He sent a letter to Virginia offering generous land grants to colonists who relocated to the island. Single men would receive twenty acres, single women would be given ten acres, and married couples would be rewarded with thirty acres of free real estate. Similar attempts were made to recruit women and families from the English islands of Bermuda and Nevis. The results of these initial efforts to settle Jamaica with civilians were dismal. Governor D'Oyley reported that only eighty of the eighteen hundred people who relocated from Nevis in 1656 were still resident on the island four years later, blaming Jamaica's "unhealthy" environment and "poor soil" for the botched attempt.[12]

Offered the governorship of the colony in 1664, Thomas Modyford, an important planter and politician in Barbados, traveled to Jamaica to replen-

11. "A Collection of Tracts Relating to the Island of Jamaica, from 1503 to 1680," Add MS 12429–12430, BL; William Beeston, "A List of Persons to Fill up the Vacancies That May Happen in y' Council of Jamaica Recommended by Sir Will. Beeston," Feb. 1, 1699, CO 137/5, fol. 43, The National Archives (TNA), Kew.

12. Edward D'Oyley to Captain Francis Emperor, June 20, 1658, in "Extracts from Colonel D'Oyley's Journal, Relating to Jamaica, 1653–1661," Add MS 12410; Amussen, *Caribbean Exchanges,* 37; "A Relation of Collonell Doyley upon His Returning from Jamaica Directed to the Lord Chancellor," fol. 10, Collection of Papers Relating to English Affairs in the West Indies, Add MS 11410.

ish the flagging settlement with Barbadian families. According to some authors, the Barbadian migrants provided a much-needed boost to the population. Richard Blome, in his 1672 narrative *A Description of the Island of Jamaica,* claimed that 1,714 families and a total of 15,298 inhabitants resided on the island during Modyford's governorship. An eighteenth-century colonist, James Knight, confirmed Blome's figure in his 1743 historical account of Jamaica, possibly because he borrowed from Blome's work. According to Knight, the number of free "men women and children" tripled to roughly 11,000 colonists during Modyford's time in office. Other accounts disputed these positive figures. An unnamed official in 1671 portrayed the island as "vast" and "stragglingly" settled. Calling attention to the colony's critical labor shortage, he reported that there were "not enough hands to ship great quantities of sugar, cotton, ginger, cocoa or cattle." The same author described trade as "so uncertain that only logwood" had been exported over the past six months. He attributed Jamaica's failures to the Navigation Acts, which restricted trade with other empires and forced all imports and exports from the colonies to pass through England first.[13]

Citing Jamaica's numerous advantages to the English public, Blome contested this dismal account. He claimed that the "great encouragement of gaining Riches, with a pleasant life, doth invite every year abundance of People to Inhabite here, quitting their concerns at Barbadoes, and other our American Plantations." Blome portended a rosy future for Jamaica, boasting, "In a short time without doubt it will become the most potent and richest Plantation in the West-Indies." If some migrants were lured to the island by attractive land grants, tax relief, and the promise of easy wealth that publications like Blome's portended, others were coercively relocated to America. Imperial planners viewed the family household as the institution that would

13. Richard Blome, *A Description of the Island of Jamaica . . .* (London, 1672), 40–41; James Knight, "The Naturall, Morall, and Politicall History of Jamaica, and the Territories Thereon Depending, from the Earliest Account of Time to the Year 1742 . . . ," 1743, Add MS 12415, BL; "An Answer to the Inquiries Given to Mr. Secretary Esq. Slingsby to Mr. Gaywood in the Pelican," Nov. 29, 1671, Collection of Papers Relating to English Affairs in the West Indies, Add MS 11410; Richard Waterhouse, "England, the Caribbean, and the Settlement of Carolina," *Journal of American Studies,* IX (1975), 266; Mark G. Hanna, *Pirate Nests and the Rise of the British Empire, 1570–1740* (Williamsburg, Va., and Chapel Hill, N.C., 2015), 109. Eighteenth-century colonist James Knight claimed that there were seventeen hundred people on the island, one-third of whom were enslaved (Knight, "Naturall, Morall, and Politicall History of Jamaica," 1743, Add MS 12415).

stabilize overseas possessions. They devised forcible transportation as a form of judicial punishment that would further populate the colonies and address the critical labor scarcity in places like Jamaica. Apprehensions about political dissidents, impoverished people, and allegedly debauched women turned transportation into a means of enforcing social reform in England, moving undesirable members of society—the indigent, especially poor single women—to the colonies.[14]

Transportation had a long history in English imperial thought. During the Elizabethan era, before England even held any territory across the Atlantic, early proponents of the punishment—viewed as a humane alternative to hanging—reasoned that it would solve the overpopulation crisis in England while also establishing an English presence abroad. According to these types of plans, undesirable members of society would become useful laborers, consumers, and reproducers overseas. Imperialists put their plans into practice in Virginia. Members of the Virginia Company sent English women to the colony to increase the stagnant settlement. When Cromwell assumed power as lord protector in 1653, he enthusiastically adopted transportation as a means of social and political reform. To cleanse English society of disorderly members, he shipped political dissidents and criminals to Barbados and Jamaica, where they would ideally be transformed into useful plantation laborers. During the Interregnum, sending prisoners to Barbados became so common that people started using the phrase "to Barbados" as an active verb.[15]

Cromwell pursued decisively gendered transportation policies that tar-

14. Blome, *Description of the Island of Jamaica,* 41.

15. Edmund S. Morgan, *American Slavery, American Freedom: The Ordeal of Colonial Virginia* (New York, 1975), 95, 111; Hilary McD. Beckles, *White Servitude and Black Slavery in Barbados, 1627–1715* (Knoxville, Tenn., 1989), 53. Proponents of English expansion abroad proposed overseas transportation as a solution to overpopulation and poverty in England. At the end of the sixteenth century, vagrancy had become a significant problem there. The population in London grew from 120,000 to 200,000 between 1550–1600 and reached 375,000 by 1650. Domestic reform efforts, such as putting the poor in prison, failed. Colonization offered an alternative outlet for the numerous poor, specifically poor women. Richard Hakluyt the Elder argued that English women could be employed in making linen in Virginia to trade with England and the West Indies, "victuall and labour being so cheape there." See "Introduction: English Promotion and Settlement of the Americas," in Peter C. Mancall, ed., *Envisioning America: English Plans for the Colonization of North America, 1580–1640* (Boston, 1995), 13–14, and Richard Hakluyt (the elder), "Inducements to the Liking of the Voyage Intended towards Virginia in 40. and 42. Degrees," (1585), 42. Kathleen Brown also describes the shipment of English women to Virginia in *Good Wives, Nasty Wenches,* 80–83.

geted women. He had his soldiers scour the streets of London for "loose" women whom he could use to remedy the catastrophic losses caused by his Western Design in Barbados by compensating the island's planters who had supplied him with two thousand servants. Supposedly, he shipped twelve hundred of these "women of loose life" to Barbados and gave further orders for two thousand more English women to be sent there, generating rumors that they would be used for "breeding." These types of strategies identified female sexuality as a disruptive element in society that needed to be removed and harnessed. Cromwell imagined that "loose" women would serve multiple purposes for their country. Once they were transported to Barbados, the women would fulfill the needs of male colonists for domestic labor and sexual companions. They would also service the empire by reproducing the free population that had been decimated by Cromwell's own military activities in the region.[16]

Despite their radical political differences, Charles II readily adopted Cromwell's strategy of using transportation as a means of quelling the political unrest that flared up after the restoration of the monarchy. During the 1670s, the same decade when colonists began to settle in Jamaica, a series of political crises embroiled England. The Popish Plot (1679) and the Exclusion Crisis (1679–1684) threatened to unleash another civil war in the country. The crown treated the empire as a "corrective 'tool' of the state" and systematically punished criminals, political prisoners, nonconformists, and the poor by transporting them to America. In 1661, Charles II issued a proclamation to all of the unemployed people who were not legal inhabitants of London, ordering them to leave the city within two weeks or face arrest and whippings "(except such as are willing to go to the English plantations)." Whether they were "willing" to travel across the ocean or forcibly driven abroad, the crown's punitive policies brought settlers to Jamaica. Governor Lord John Vaughan disdainfully characterized the local populace as a set of unreconstructed Cromwellians, rebellious servants, and convicts "who chose transporting rather than hanging and Jamaica rather than Tyborn." His observation suggests that a considerable number of colonists chose transportation over the bleak prospect of being hanged at Tyburn, the location where the majority of London's criminals were executed.[17]

16. Beckles, *White Servitude and Black Slavery in Barbados*, 47.

17. Swingen, *Competing Visions of Empire*, 21; Charles II, *A Proclamation, for the Due Observation of Certain Statutes Made for the Supressing of Rogues, Vagabonds, Beggers, and Other Idle Disorderly Persons, and for Relief of the Poore* (1661), 12 Car. 2, cap. 37, quoted in Melissa M.

Aside from these scant references in government papers, little is known about the English men and even less about the women who were transported to the Caribbean. Male colonists certainly desired English women for the gendered and sexualized labor they could perform. Men in Barbados, for example, urged the crown to send over women who would serve as "domestics, wives, seamstresses and whores." The demand for women to perform these types of roles in the less-settled territory of Jamaica was probably even more intense. One scholar estimates that women made up one-quarter of the servants who either traveled to the island by choice or by force between 1683 and 1686. The journal kept by John Taylor, who personally oversaw the transportation of prison convicts to the colony in the 1680s, affords the most-detailed description of how destitute English women ended up in Jamaica as unfree laborers. Taylor, an ex-soldier who had become impoverished after being released from the army, found employment working as a middleman for the crown to transport convicts to Jamaica. He received the prisoners and paid for their food and passage. In return, Taylor kept the profits he earned when he sold them as indentured servants on the island.[18]

Mowry, *The Bawdy Politic in Stuart England, 1660–1714: Political Pornography and Prostitution* (Hampshire, U.K., 2004), 61–62; Vaughan to Sec. Coventry, May 28, 1677, Coventry Papers, LXX, 181, quoted in Richard S. Dunn, *Sugar and Slaves: The Rise and Fall of the Planter Class in the English West Indies, 1624–1713* (Williamsburg, Va., and Chapel Hill, N.C., 1972) 157. During the second half of the seventeenth century, transportation became a tool used by the Protectorate and then the crown to suppress political dissent. Melissa Mowry examines how emerging partisan political parties whipped up fears that current events threatened to reignite the Civil War (Mowry, *Bawdy Politic*, 44). Abigail Swingen states that transportation "represented the further intertwining of imperialism and violence." During the reigns of Charles II and James II, political prisoners were transported to America, including more than eight hundred men who were captured after the Monmouth Rebellion. See Swingen, *Competing Visions of Empire*, chap. 1, esp. 21.

18. Hilary MacDonald Beckles, "White Labour in Black Slave Plantation Society and Economy: A Case Study of Indentured Labour in Seventeenth Century Barbados" (Ph.D. Thesis, The University of Hull, 1980), 78; Beckles, *White Servitude and Black Slavery*, 45. A handful of scholars refer to the women who were transported to colonies in the Caribbean. More research remains to be done on this topic. The reference works that Beckles uses in *White Servitude and Black Slavery* include Michael Ghirelli, transcriber, *A List of Emigrants from England to America, 1682–1692* (Baltimore, 1968); Cregoe D. P. Nicholson, *Some Early Emigrants to America* (Baltimore, 1965); and John Wareing, "Some Early Emigrants to America, 1683–4: A Supplementary List," *Genealogist's Magazine*, XVIII (1976), 239–246. John C. Appleby writes that Port Royal's buccaneering culture fed the demand for the forced and voluntary migration of female servants and criminals, some of whom were prostitutes. See Appleby, *Women and English*

During one voyage, two of the four prisoners whom Taylor took charge of were women: Ann Sharp and Susanah Carslodon. He identified Sharp and Carslodon as "convicted felons" without elaborating on their crimes. All of his charges, irrespective of gender, went aboard the ship shackled in "irons" and were "secured" below deck, where they received a daily ration of bread. Once the journey began, the prisoners resisted their confinement. In one instance, they conspired to escape and "cut off their irons." Taylor retaliated, chaining all of the men below deck. On another occasion, the transports stole forty-six bottles of claret and "got drunk." As the trip across the Atlantic proceeded, they settled down, and Taylor relaxed his guard. He released all of the convicts from their chains except for a "Popish" man and an Irish boy named Trig, whom he claimed were "so disorderly" that he had them "chained down in a dark part of ship" to "resolve their stubborn spirits." Taylor viewed these two men, probably political prisoners, as the most threatening of his captives.[19]

The criminalized and impoverished status of the convicts blunted their gender differences. Aside from allowing the female transports to walk above deck during the voyage (though still in leg irons), Taylor made no effort to offer the women preferential treatment. When the ship reached Port Royal in Jamaica, both the male and female convicts were sold in a similar manner to enslaved Africans. Auctions took place in the evening to give potential buyers time to physically inspect the laborers. At the start of the sale, as was "the custom," the ship's captain raised his flag and fired a gun in the air. Buyers then raced aboard to choose their servants. Taylor reported that all of the prisoners aboard his vessel were sold except for one man who "fell overboard and drowned." It is possible that the convict had committed suicide, preferring death to years of hard labor in Jamaica. There were, of course, critical distinctions between indentured servants, prison transports, and captive Africans. Whereas the former were contracted to work for a fixed term, enslaved people labored in perpetuity.[20]

Piracy, 1540–1720: Partners and Victims of Crime (Suffolk, U.K., 2013), 93. Though Taylor's journal was edited and published by David Buisseret as *Jamaica in 1687: The Taylor Manuscript at the National Library of Jamaica* (Kingston, 2008), I have used the original manuscript journal for my study: John Taylor, "Multum in parvo or parvum in multo by John Taylor—Taylor's Historie of His Life and Travels in America and Other Parts of the Universe," 1683–1687, MS. 105, fol. 53, National Library of Jamaica (NLJ), Kingston.

19. Taylor, "Taylor's Historie," 144, 166.

20. Ibid., 166.

Nevertheless, Taylor expressed little interest in the humanity of his charges. He portrayed the sale of the prisoners as a strictly financial transaction, reporting that he received fifty-one pounds for the male servants and thirty-eight and thirty-four pounds, respectively, for the two female servants. Altogether, after paying the captain for the passage and food, Taylor made a profit of thirty-three pounds—less than he had anticipated. Taylor's journal makes no reference to the distress experienced by Sharp and Carslodon, who were shackled aboard a ship, fed enough to survive, and then sold to the highest bidder to perform arduous labor in a strange tropical land. Although no evidence exists of Jamaican colonists using female servants of European descent to work on plantations as they did in Virginia, the island's severe labor shortage and the contemptuous and callous treatment servants received suggest that indentured women could expect harsh futures there. Female migrants who arrived in desperate conditions faced a minimum of six years of servitude.[21]

When Sharp and Carslodon reached Port Royal in the 1680s, however, the colony was already heavily invested in using captive Africans as enslaved laborers, which might have improved the conditions of even the most degraded English women. Like the female transports who were shipped to Barbados, those sent to Jamaica could have occupied gender roles that were demeaning and exploitative but also familiar, acting as "domestics" and "whores" for the male populace rather than as field laborers. Because free women were thin on the ground, it is also possible that poor female servants and even prisoners like Sharp and Carslodon would have been viewed as marriageable partners. If they married, they might have gained a degree of financial security and social status that would have been unattainable for them in England.[22]

"FILLED WITH ALL MANOR OF DEBAUCHERY"

When Ann Sharp and Susanah Carslodon arrived in Port Royal, the burgeoning town, located on a thin strip of land that jutted out into the deep harbor on the island's south coast, afforded its female inhabitants a range of economic opportunities. After selling off his convicts, including the two

21. Ibid.

22. For a similar phenomenon in early Virginia, where English women of low social standing married well above their status in the colony, see Brown, *Good Wives, Nasty Wenches*, 82–83.

women, John Taylor filled his journal with some of the earliest and most vivid descriptions of the port. He characterized the town as a place that was abuzz with commerce, awash with money, and infested with vulgar women. Originally built by the Spanish and renamed Cagway Point by the English, the settlement was again renamed Port Royal after the Restoration of Charles II. Richard Blome portrayed the town in the 1670s as "unpleasant and uncommodious." According to Blome, the inhabitants of the sparse settlement had to import wood and fresh water, and everything was "very dear" there. Port Royal's strategic geographic location in the heart of the Caribbean Sea along the Spanish trade route, however, quickly changed the town's fortunes. It became the ideal gathering spot for English merchants, privateers, and pirates (who were often one and the same). Henry Morgan and his crew of pirates, whom Blome lauded as "lusty and stout *Fighting Men*" of "courage," launched their infamous raids on the cities of Portobelo, Panama, and numerous other territories in the Spanish Empire from Port Royal, and to Port Royal Morgan and his men triumphantly returned to spend the loot they acquired during their brutal raids.[23]

Although Port Royal's connection to piracy is well known, it was also the wealthiest and most important seaport in England's American empire at the end of the seventeenth century. Merchants throughout the Atlantic basin flocked to Port Royal to obtain tropical produce—sugar, rum, indigo, and cocoa. Ships from England carried over linen, silk, fruit, ironwork, pitch, tar, and rope, while others hailed from Dublin to retail Irish provisions—beef, pork, salmon, cheese, and butter. Jamaica also maintained strong trading ties to mainland North America, and New York merchants shipped food, provisions, and materials to the island for making rum and sugar casks. According to Taylor, local merchants extravagantly displayed their newly minted wealth, living "at the height of splendor." Their "sumptuously arrayed" tables groaned under the weight of a cornucopia of local and imported food, from "good and wholesome meats, fowls, fish and fruits" to "salt meats from England," along with cheesecakes, custards, and tarts. Indeed, the only thing Taylor found lacking on the island was "good soft bread." The merchants were served by "negro slaves, which always wait on them in livery"—living emblems of the sort of conspicuous consumption that England's expanding Atlantic trade made possible. Artisans, including mechanics, blacksmiths, carpenters, bricklayers, shoemakers, tailors, upholsterers, hatters, rope

23. Blome, *Description of the Island of Jamaica*, 30–31, 42; Hanna, *Pirate Nests*, 112–114.

makers, painters, combmakers, and washerwomen, also lived "very well, earning three times the wages in England," and were "able to maintain their families much better" in the colony.[24]

Completely devoted to commerce, Port Royal embodied a new type of Atlantic city for the English Empire. Unlike England, Jamaica established a policy of religious tolerance as a means of attracting more settlers. People of all faiths, from Anglicans and Presbyterians to Quakers, Catholics, and Jews, relocated to the colony. An estimated five thousand free English, Scottish, Welsh, Irish, and Spanish-Jewish inhabitants made Port Royal a multicultural and religiously diverse town. In addition to spiritual lenience, Port Royal's officials also adopted a lax approach toward the sexual behaviors of its inhabitants. English visitors like Taylor depicted it as a site of sexual and social disorder, a "loose place" that was "filled with all manor of debauchery." An early contributor to the trope of Caribbean degeneracy, Taylor portrayed the city as a "good times" boomtown, boasting an "abundance" of taverns, ordinaries, coffeehouses, and punch houses, which "may so fitly" be called brothels, where the local inhabitants lived in a boozy haze of excessive consumption, drinking wine, sangria, or a "jolly bowl of good punch" in one of the numerous taverns. They entertained themselves with bull-, bear-, and boarbaiting, cockfighting, billiards, and target shooting, visited music houses, and feasted on syllabub, cream, and tarts.[25]

Women featured prominently in Taylor's gendered and sexualized typography of Port Royal. He described "common" women who wore only smocks (undergarments) as halfdressed and "barefooted" adorned with manly hats and a "tobacco pipe in their mouths." Hardly the obedient wives and mothers that imperial strategists hoped to attract to Jamaica, the town's "common" women, who would "booze a cupp of punch" with anyone, defied gender norms. Taylor simultaneously masculinized and eroticized Jamaica's first female settlers, portraying them as "Creolian" and "warlike" "amazons." Disturbed by their independence, he linked female authority to subversive sexuality, labeling them as a "crew of vile strumpets, and common prostitutes," a "walking plague" that "infected" male islanders with venereal diseases. Taylor's misogynistic descriptions of local women complemented his

24. Taylor, "Taylor's Historie," 132–133, 135; Nuala Zahedieh, "The Merchants of Port Royal, Jamaica, and the Spanish Contraband Trade, 1655–1692," *WMQ*, 3d Ser., XLIII (1986), 570–593.

25. Taylor, "Taylor's Historie," 133–134; James A. Delle, Mark W. Hauser, and Douglas V. Armstrong, eds., *Out of Many, One People: The Historical Archaeology of Colonial Jamaica* (Tuscaloosa, Ala., 2011), 6.

severe treatment of female convicts. His journal also recycled themes from print culture that represented colonies like Virginia and Barbados as sites of "rampant prostitution." The author's characterization of "common," or poor, colonial women resonated with accounts of the English poor as well as indigenous women from Virginia and Africa. On the one hand, they were sexually alluring, scantily clad, and seemingly promiscuous. On the other hand, the masculine appearance and behaviors of Port Royal's female denizens, who wore hats, smoked pipes, and caroused in taverns, inverted gender roles and threatened male authority.[26]

Taylor's writings on Jamaica also helped to construct a distinctive colonial figure. The Creole, or "Creolian," as he described them, was a product of imperial expansion. A person of English descent, and eventually Euro-African descent, the Creole was born in America. Creoles who grew up in the Caribbean climate and had incessant contact with African slaves manifested physiological and ethnic differences from English people. According to the author, they reached maturity by age fifteen, began to decline at twenty, and rarely survived past thirty-five. "Creolians" had "thin bodies, pale complexions," and "light flaxen hair." They appeared as both wealthy and uncivilized, wearing "good linen but often barefooted without shoes or stockings." According to Taylor, the first generation of island-born colonists already ignored English legal and religious practices and preferred a more lenient approach toward family formation. He claimed that they eschewed English marital laws; the "common sort," he observed, "seldom marry according to the ceremony of church." Instead, couples "live together, and beget children, and if they fall out, or disagree, they part friendly by consent." Taylor, unsurprisingly, blamed the sexual excess of female colonists for these divergences, arguing that "neither the cage, whipping, nor ducking stools"—the standard means of punishing witches and wayward women in England—"would prevail" to control them. The unruly behavior of free and freed women on the island made it "almost impossible to civilize" Jamaica.[27]

Read against the grain, Taylor's text reveals an evolving sexual culture where men and women alike pursued intimate relationships outside the

26. Taylor, "Taylor's Historie," 134; Kathleen Wilson, *The Island Race: Englishness, Empire, and Gender in the Eighteenth Century* (New York, 2003), 144. These descriptions parallel Jennifer L. Morgan's account of the ways European visitors portrayed African and Amerindian women. See Morgan, "'Some Could Suckle over Their Shoulder': Male Travelers, Female Bodies, and the Gendering of Racial Ideology, 1500–1770," *WMQ*, 3d Ser., LIV (1997), 167–192.

27. Taylor, "Taylor's Historie," 134.

bounds of legal marriage as defined by the Church of England. What Taylor perceived as social degeneration reflected strategies that colonists were developing in response to local circumstances. Focused on trade, islanders displayed little desire to continue the religious and political strife that had roiled the British Isles for nearly two centuries. Nor were local officials interested in regulating people's sexual behavior. Aside from the preferential treatment shown by a few governors to married men, no laws were passed to discipline colonists for sexual misconduct. Couples also practiced self-divorce without facing legal restrictions or social ostracism.

Men like Taylor perceived all forms of female authority and independence—economic, legal, social, and sexual—as threatening. By inscribing a specific definition of femininity onto colonial women and presenting them only in sexualized terms, male authors could at least constrain female power on a discursive level. However, these types of accounts reveal little about how Jamaica's early female settlers actually lived. The handful of probated inventories, court records, and the odd mention in a government document that have survived from the seventeenth century tell a very different story about the first generation of free and freed women who helped to establish English Jamaica. Rather than drunkenly wandering from one tavern to the next, women were busy capitalizing on the economic opportunities that Port Royal's vibrant economy offered. Female settlers specialized in the service industry, laboring as shopkeepers, servants, washerwomen, barmaids, tavernkeepers, and prostitutes who earned a living from the thousands of transient men who worked in the maritime industry and circulated through Port Royal. According to Blome, three thousand *"Privateers, Hunters, Sloop and Boatmen"* visited the town, which was populated by five hundred families and thirty-five hundred permanent residents and slaves. Although Blome does not identify women in his description of eight hundred houses inhabited by *"Merchants, Storehouse-Keepers, Vinters, Alehouse-keepers,"* a 1671 census shows that free women and children made up just under half of Port Royal's permanent residents. Men composed only 35 percent, and the remaining 16 percent of the settlement were slaves.[28]

The high cost of goods and services in Port Royal benefited its female residents. The widow Ann Barnes operated a tavern and lodging house, a com-

28. Blome, *Description of the Island of Jamaica,* 30–31, 42. Port Royal's population was made up of 735 men, 539 women, 470 children, and 323 slaves. See "An Answer to the Inquiries Given to Mr. Secretary Esq. Slingsby to Mr. Gaywood in the Pelican," Nov. 29, 1671, Collection of Papers Relating to English Affairs in the West Indies, Add MS 11410.

mon occupation for early modern women. She provided rooms for guests, and the nineteen pots and drip pans, ten jugs, thirty-one pewter plates, and parcel of "old earthenware" itemized in the inventory of her estate suggest that she also served them food and drink. Barnes left behind numerous tablecloths and napkins, which added a degree of refinement to the dining room where customers ate, and their beds were furnished with "fine" sheets and "Spanish" pillowcases. Her home was decorated with pictures, maps, and mirrors and enlivened by the sound of a parrot in a cage. Three Bibles and "sundry" other books in her possession attest to her education. She died with a few hundred pounds and an impressive array of clothing, including silk petticoats and gowns, to her name. Barnes was, not the degenerate "Creolian" that Taylor described, but rather a successful and literate businesswoman.[29]

Other women were less successful than Barnes. They scraped by on the margins of the local economy. Widow Mary Cumberlidge survived by selling cider. She lived in a simple home furnished with an "old bedstead," a feather bed, and a few stools and chairs. The five "old sea trunks" in her house hinted at the journey that she had taken years earlier to reach the island. When she died, Cumberlidge's estate was valued at only twenty-two pounds. Her holdings were meager, but she, like Barnes, was also literate and kept a Bible and a "parcel of books" in her home. Elizabeth Gardner, whose occupation is not noted, was even poorer than Cumberlidge. With only a few pounds, a few pieces of furniture, some napkins, three "small pewter dishes," an iron pot, and a brass kettle to her name, she died impoverished in 1677. Nevertheless, her probated inventory offers a rare glimpse of how the first generation of free women who resided at the lower end of the island's social scale managed to survive and to save a few belongings of their own.[30]

Though Cumberlidge and Gardner did not grow wealthy in Port Royal, many others took advantage of a range of profitable opportunities in town. More successful female entrepreneurs worked as merchants who specialized in importing and retailing textiles and accessories. The widow Judith Jurdaine amassed an array of manufactured items in her home, which doubled as a shop. When she died in 1676, her stock included men's felt hats, "worsted" and woolen hose, "Irish" stockings, "ordinary" women's shoes, and serge and flannel fabric of "sober" colors intermixed with "callicoes" made in

29. Inventory of Ann Main als. Barnes, 1685, Jamaica Inventories, fol. 145.

30. Inventory of Mary Cumberlidge, 1685, Jamaica Inventories, fol. 136, Inventory of Elizabeth Gardner, 1677, I, fol. 145.

India. She also sold ribbon, knitting needles, horn and ivory combs, scissors, sewing needles, "casteel" soap, and waistcoat buttons together with nutmeg, aniseed, and pepper from the East Indies. Jurdaine extended credit to her customers, and she kept a careful record of her debtors. The majority of her clients (sixty-eight) were men, and she died with an estate valued at a respectable £364.[31]

Women like Jurdaine were a part of Jamaica's early mercantile community. They forged trading ties that funneled goods from across the globe to the island, selling textiles produced in Europe, the Middle East, and India. "Spinster" Mary Phillips retailed ribbons, silk stockings, fans, and muslins from a store alongside serge, "ghent Holland," and "scotch cloth." Her estate was valued at £609 in 1684, and her customers, including several men, owed her £552. Phillips was not fantastically wealthy, but she was certainly well-off. Eighteen years later, Johanna Armstrong operated as a "sole dealer" in Port Royal, where she purveyed luxurious imported fabrics. In addition to gloves and "hose" or stockings, Armstrong offered more luxurious textiles to her customers, including "holland" cloth from the Netherlands, Persian silk, and "garlix," "callico," "water bengall," chintz, printed linen, and flowered petticoats from India. Her goods by the time of her death, including the odd box of fishhooks and parcel of crucibles, had an estimated worth of £338—nearly identical to the value of Jurdaine's estate.[32]

In spite of Taylor's contention that colonists "seldom marry," a woman's marital status influenced her ability to engage in business on the island. The successful entrepreneurs—Barnes, Jurdaine, Phillips, and Armstrong—were all widowed or had never married. Without husbands to support them, they might have been especially motivated to earn an income. Being single also made it easier for women to facilitate marketplace transactions. During the early modern period, married women fell under coverture: a set of common law customs that prevented wives from extending credit, assuming debts, or signing contracts under their own names. But there were work-

31. Inventory of Judith Jurdaine, 1676, Jamaica Inventories, fol. 98. Only six women owed Judith money. The laws of coverture required married women to engage in credit and debt transactions under their husbands' names. Hence, it is possible that the list of men who owed Judith money included wives to whom she extended credit.

32. Inventory of Mary Phillips, 1684, Jamaica Inventories, fol. 55, Inventory of Johanna Armstrong, 1702, fol. 171. For more on cotton production and trade, see Giorgio Riello, *Cotton: The Fabric That Made the Modern World* (New York, 2013); and Beverly Lemire, *Cotton* (New York, 2011).

arounds to these restrictions. In Britain and the American colonies, wives could obtain the permission of their husbands to operate as independent, or feme sole, economic agents. This legal status overrode the restrictions that coverture impressed on married women, restoring their right to act as independent economic agents.[33]

Port Royal's early female settlers readily adopted the status of feme sole—one that did not always work to their advantage. As early as 1678, Alice Brocky, a "feme sole merchant," was taken to court for a debt of seven pounds that she owed to Thomas Boutwell. She had borrowed money from him and signed a "document," or a promissory note, vouching to repay her balance. Apparently, Brocky did not compensate Boutwell on time, and he pursued her for the money she owed him and the court costs. Though the outcome of the case is unknown, it reveals the myriad of small credit and debt dealings between male and female colonists that undergirded the local economy. The suit involving Brocky and a handful of other cases that have survived from the seventeenth century show that it was also commonplace for men and women to conduct business with one another. Men had no qualms about borrowing money from wives who were acting as "sole" dealers. When male borrowers failed to repay loans, women readily pursued them in court. Ann Inge, a wife "who tradeth by herself," sued Nicholas Law for eight pounds that he owed her. Gender was not a barrier to commercial partnerships on the island either. A "gentleman" named Edward Auerberrier and a "femme sole trader" called Judith Cook, for example, jointly acquired a debt of forty-nine pounds from another man, who then took them to court in 1681 when they defaulted on their shared loan.[34]

33. I offer the only comprehensive analysis of coverture in Jamaica in Chapter 4, below. For more on coverture in England and British America, see Marylynn Salmon, *Women and the Law of Property in Early America* (Chapel Hill, N.C., 1986); Amy Louise Erickson, *Women and Property in Early Modern England* (1993; London and New York, 1995); Linda L. Sturtz, *Within Her Power: Propertied Women in Colonial Virginia* (New York, 2002); and Carole Shammas, Marylynn Salmon, and Michel Dahlin, *Inheritance in America from Colonial Times to the Present* (New Brunswick, N.J., 1987). See also the discussion of feme sole traders in colonial America in Salmon, *Women and the Law of Property in Early America,* 44–53.

34. Thomas Boutwell v. Alice Brocky, 1678, Grand Court Records, 1680, I, JA, Ann Inge v. Nicholas Law, 1678, Charles Penhallow v. Edward Auerberrier, 1681. A Mr. Nevil reported in 1677 that the Grand Court "hath all the jurisdiction executed here in the king's bench, common pleas, and exchequer, and is held by way of grand sessions or terms at the town of St. Jago de la Vega." The court issued all writs and processes, and the governor acted as the chief justice. Nevil also referenced another court of common pleas, which was held in a town called The Point (prob-

As traders, retailers, moneylenders, and borrowers, free women played central roles in constructing Port Royal's marketplace. Though the majority of female settlers never accumulated the fantastical wealth of the settlement's most notorious pirates and its richest merchants, they ensured that local businesses could sustain these kinds of larger scale maritime ventures. Gleaned from starkly simple probate inventories, their business endeavors depict a town that was far more than a carnivalesque pirate's haven. Port Royal attracted a diverse crowd of migrants, many of whom were involved in illicit trade, but it was also a cosmopolitan city. Women merchants used their knowledge and connections to procure items from far-flung locations like India and Persia and retail those goods locally. Female retailers both catered to their customers' tastes and established fashion trends on the island. The economic activities of female colonists aided in the construction of a mini emporium that connected English Jamaica to the rest of the world. Their undertakings laid the groundwork for second- and third-generation free and freed women to cultivate a far more extensive and profitable trade network.[35]

The colony, however, was not hospitable for all the women who sought economic opportunities there. In 1671, several male merchants seized a ship laden with goods that was owned by an unnamed woman described as a "jewess" merchant; they then sought to bar her from trading in Port Royal. The group took her to the new Admiralty Court, claiming that she was a "foreigner," even though all of the "seamen and goods" on her vessel were English, indicating that she had not violated the Navigation Acts. One of the island's local officials, a "Mr. Ball of Plymouth," sympathized with the

ably Port Royal). This court tried cases for sums less than five pounds. Cases that occurred a few years before or after 1680 were still recorded in the first volume of the Grand Court Records, probably on a later date. The records from the Court of Common Pleas have not survived. See "The Present State of Jamaica, in a Letter from Mr. Nevil to the Early of Carlisle," in *Interesting Tracts, Relating to the Island of Jamaica . . .* (St. Jago De La Vega, 1800), 114. For more information on the condition of Jamaica's archival records, see James Robertson, "Jamaican Archival Resources for Seventeenth and Eighteenth Century Atlantic History," XXII, no. 3, *Slavery and Abolition* (December 2001), 109–140.

35. A shortlist of work on English piracy includes Hanna, *Pirate Nests;* Kris E. Lane, *Pillaging the Empire: Piracy in the Americas, 1500–1750* (New York, 1998); David Cordingly, *Under the Black Flag: The Romance and the Reality of Life among the Pirates* (New York, 1996); Marcus Rediker, *Villains of All Nations: Atlantic Pirates in the Golden Age* (Boston, 2004); Douglas R. Burgess, Jr., *The Politics of Piracy: Crime and Civil Disobedience in Colonial America* (Lebanon, N.H., 2014); and Kevin P. McDonald, *Pirates, Merchants, Settlers, and Slaves: Colonial America and the Indo-Atlantic World* (Oakland, Calif., 2015).

woman's plight, stating that Port Royal's merchants "were envious of the Jews." Indeed, the merchants had petitioned the crown to expel the town's Jewish residents, and Ball disagreed with their actions. He contended that the Jewish community on the island was so small that they hardly posed an economic threat to the merchants. Ball urged the crown to naturalize the Jewish and Dutch inhabitants who resided in Port Royal, for they were the most "profitable subjects" the crown could have.[36]

In the instance of the "jewess" merchant, a number of Port Royal men targeted her religion and ethnicity as the operative categories of difference that made her threatening. It is also possible that they pursued the woman because her status as a successful female merchant challenged their masculine prerogative to dominate trade. Although colonial institutions remained disinterested in enforcing English gender norms, certain women who posed economic threats to men could face censure for overstepping the bounds of an implicitly gendered hierarchy. Dorothy Petingall served as a local "Bayliff" for Port Royal, an unusually public governmental position for a woman to occupy. As bailiff, she might have been responsible for executing writs and even processing arrests. In 1680, John Fountaine sued Petingall for a sixty-five pound debt that she owed him for the "diverse goods and merchandise" that he sold her, alleging that he had "often requested that she pay" and that "she refused" to compensate him.[37]

Though her voice is mediated by the court clerk, Petingall appeared before the judge to defend herself, stating that she had given Fountaine "an account of the time that she was Bayliff and received of the moneys belonging to him total £89 [Jamaica currency]." She also declared her creditworthiness and financial integrity, claiming that she had "appeared and acknowledged herself accountable" to him. In Petingall's case, her role as bailiff was not at stake, as might be expected. Rather, the court was overwhelmed by the complex, entangled financial relationship between the plaintiff and defendant, describing the "accounts between them" as "difficult and tedious." It tasked two "impartial" men with the tiresome job of going through what must have been a large

36. Mr. Ball of Plymouth to Lord Arlington, Dec. 17, 1671, Collection of Papers Relating to English Affairs in the West Indies, Add MS 11410. A "Slingsby Esquire" made a similar argument for allowing the Jewish and Dutch communities to remain on the island. See Slingsby, Esq., to Lords Council, Mr. Gaywood in the Pelican, 1671, Collection of Papers Relating to English Affairs in the West Indies, Add MS 11410.

37. John Fountaine v. Dorothy Petingall, 1680, Grand Court Records, I; *Oxford English Dictionary*, s.v. "bailiff," http://www.oed.com.

stack of paperwork generated by a myriad of transactions between the bailiff and her creditor. Although the outcome of the Petingall case is unknown, it offers an extraordinary instance of the colonial government employing a woman in a typically masculine role. This shred of evidence suggests that a handful of women in Port Royal assumed exceptional positions of public authority. Indeed, Petingall, like the unnamed Jewish woman merchant, only appears in the archives for financial reasons. Quarrels over money, rather than gender transgressions, make them visible.[38]

Notably audacious and independent, Jane Trahorn also shows up in the government records as a result of a monetary conflict. Trahorn traveled from England to Jamaica by herself in 1699 to purchase the office of provost marshal general for her husband, named "Toplady." Conducting business on his behalf, she offered to pay a "considerable sum of money" for the lucrative colonial post. Viewing the couple as a political menace, local "Agents, Merchants and Planters" aimed to thwart her effort. When they were unsuccessful on the island, the assemblage appealed to the Lords of Trade in London to stop the couple from buying the post. Though Trahorn was presumably acting in her husband's interest, prominent colonists focused on her actions, writing that she "threatens" to return to Jamaica and "reimburse" herself for the sum that the couple paid for the provost marshal position. Apparently, Trahorn planned to use a form of extortion and extract "very large annual gratuities or rents from the deputies of the respective prisons," which would "cause miserable oppression to the poor prisoners" and "be a very great reflection and scandal to the said office." In other words, Trahorn would collect the bribes that the prison wardens themselves were extracting from prisoners. Even more outrageously, she intended to act as the de facto provost marshal in her husband's stead.[39]

Like the wealthy "jewess" merchant and the indebted female bailiff, Trahorn's proclamation of financial and political authority attracted negative attention from some local men. In an era where corruption was rife among prison officials and criminals were rarely considered to be objects of pity, the supposed concern expressed by the petitioners for oppressed prisoners was disingenuous. In an effort to buttress their case against the couple, the locals resorted to casting aspersions on the characters of "Toplady and Jane his wife." Alleging transatlantic knowledge of them, the group presented them-

38. John Fountaine v. Dorothy Petingall, 1680, Grand Court Records, I.

39. Memorial to the Board of Trade from Agents, Merchants, and Planters, Aug. 4, 1699, fol. 361, CO 137, The National Archives (TNA), Kew.

selves as "well informed" that the two were "persons of very mean reputations." Arguing that Toplady was not "quallifyed for an Employment: of so great a trust," they asked the Lords of Trade to "inform themselves" of the "character of Toplady as to his integrity and qualifications" before allowing him to assume the post. A handful of the island's elites objected to Toplady's serving as provost marshal. The feebleness of their reasoning suggests that ulterior motives were at play. Yet, rather than deploying the kinds of misogynistic attacks against Trahorn that men like John Taylor penned, the petitioners made an argument about her husband's character.[40]

Whatever sparked the local response to the couple, the petition offers yet another instance of a woman who not only acted with remarkable independence and influence on the island but, in this case, did so with the support of her husband. Instead of sending a male relative to act as his emissary, Toplady authorized his wife to cross the Atlantic by herself and transact political dealings for him. He placed a large sum of money in her hands and expected her to negotiate with Jamaica's leading men to obtain the political post. Trahorn proved herself to be more than her husband's representative. On reaching Jamaica, she attempted to exert political power in her own right. Whether Trahorn actually promised to return to the colony to act as provost marshal is irrelevant; local leaders perceived her as threatening enough to make this declaration and deemed it worthwhile to escalate the issue to imperial policymakers in the metropolitan capital.

The example of Trahorn illustrates how the construction of an empire—and the vast distance that it created between the colonies and England—modified women's roles within families. Husbands trusted their wives to handle local and even international business and political affairs. The first generation of male settlers also depended on female kin to operate family ventures. By the late seventeenth century, male planters regularly nominated their wives to be plantation managers when they died. Some specifically used the word "management" to describe the roles that widows would play in family-run agricultural enterprises. In his 1699 will, planter John Stretch noted that his wife "is to have management of whole estate during life." His contemporary Peter Demetris, another planter, also wanted his wife to have "management of whole estate till children come of age." Early planters like Stretch and Demetris probably sank all of their family capital into new sugar plantations, which made them especially needful of spouses. Plantations were long-term business ventures that took years to achieve profitability. This

40. Ibid.

also made plantations difficult to liquidate when husbands died. Planters began devising bequests that would incentivize their wives to successfully manage family estates. Samuell Philips gave his wife, Edith, a two hundred pound annuity in his 1700 will. The annuity was just one of several forms of property that he bequeathed to her. If Edith decided to manage the family estate, she would also receive all of the profits that it generated.[41]

As men's inheritance decisions show, the crucial roles played by female colonists extended far beyond the urban marketplace of Port Royal. They also aided in the construction of the island's lucrative agricultural economy. Though Trevor Burnard observes that the island did not experience a "sugar revolution" in the late seventeenth century, as earlier scholars have claimed, planters like Stretch and Demetris laid the groundwork for later developments. These men looked to their wives to continue their efforts. As plantation managers, plantation owners, and, increasingly, slaveholders, free and freed women helped to build the foundations of a colony that would become one of the most productive, and most exploitative, agricultural zones in the world.[42]

"MOST BARBAROUSLY MURTHERED BY SOME OF THEIR OWNE NEGRO SLAVES"

Rather than confine his wife, Edith, to a modest widowhood, Samuell Philips envisioned her publicly displaying the family's colonial riches after his death. She would inherit a coach and six horses: the ultimate early modern status symbol. She would also assume the legal ownership of two "negro women," Mall and Katy. Implementing a practice that was becoming commonplace on the island, Philips treated the women as moveable property and categorized them together with the horses that he gave to his wife. By using captive Africans to provide financial support for and enhance the social status of his spouse, Philips participated in an increasingly widespread inheritance custom in Jamaica, one that ensured that free and freed women had a vested

41. Will of John Stretch, 1699, Jamaica Wills, IX, Will of Peter Demetris, 1700, IX, Will of Samuell Philips, 1700, IX.

42. Trevor Burnard describes the transition to the large integrated plantation as slow in Jamaica during the seventeenth century. As he writes, no "big bang" or "sugar revolution" occurred. Instead, the island's plantation system did not develop until the 1710s. See Burnard, *Planters, Merchants, and Slaves: Plantation Societies in British America, 1650–1820* (Chicago, 2015), 23–25.

interest in slavery. Unlike the nameless people who labored on their plantation, Philips singled out Mall and Katy by name, signaling their importance to the couple. It is possible that his wife owned the women at the time of their marriage, at which point he claimed a legal right to them via the common law of coverture. Maybe the spouses had informally agreed that he would return Mall and Katy to Edith when he died. Whatever the circumstances, Edith wanted to maintain control of the two enslaved women. They would become part of her estate, serving important material and symbolic functions for the widow. As property, they constituted a portion of her wealth. As her personal servants, they performed valuable labor. On an island that was rapidly investing in chattel slavery, assuming command of the women solidified her status as a slaveholder, an increasingly important qualification for membership in free society.[43]

The Philipses participated in a colonial project initiated by the crown and imperial planners and carried out by the first wave of settlers that made Atlantic slavery essential to Jamaica's development. Unlike older colonies such as Virginia and Barbados, Jamaica did not go through a phase of employing indentured European servants as laborers before transitioning to enslaved people. From the start, captives from Africa were identified as the solution to the colony's labor needs, which were perceived as a severe setback for strategists who wanted to establish plantations there. After his stint as the first English governor of the island, Edward D'Oyley reported that planters were "forced to burn their cane for want of hands for harvesting" because colonists "scorn" the "dull tedious way of planting." Soon after the conquest, the governor already characterized enslaved Africans as ideally suited for Jamaica's climate and critical to its growth, describing the colony as "wonderfull healthfull for Negroes which are the life of the Plantations." D'Oyley acted on his belief that Africans were destined to perform agricultural work in the Caribbean. When he returned to London in 1661, he urged the crown to send five hundred slaves to the colony.[44]

43. Will of Samuell Philips, 1700, Jamaica Wills, IX. Amanda Vickery notes that a coach "was always ultra-expensive in itself, but the running of it demanded coachmen, postilions, horses, stables, feed, farriers. . . . In modern terms the coach's equivalent would be less the proverbial sports car than a helicopter." See Vickery, *Behind Closed Doors: At Home in Georgian England* (New Haven, Conn., 2009), 124.

44. "A Relation of Collonell Doyley upon His Returning from Jamaica Directed to the Lord Chancellor," 1661, fol. 10, Collection of Papers Relating to English Affairs in the West Indies, Add MS 11410. For more on the transition from servitude to slavery in other colonies, see Mor-

The first colonists either came as slaveholders or readily purchased African captives after relocating to Jamaica. In 1664, soon after Governor Thomas Modyford's arrival from Barbados, the number of enslaved inhabitants increased by tenfold to five thousand people—a group that was most likely augmented with captives who were transported to the new colony by their Barbadian owners. Modyford described an unsettled island populated by "old soldiers" who survived as hunters, selling game to the "seamen, merchants, and planters." But other soldiers were already establishing "brave plantations." Modyford, a planter and slave trader himself, admired these men, who "bought servants and slaves" to help them "settle" the land. During this gestational phase of expansion, the lineaments of the slave society that Jamaica would become were already apparent. Modyford treated enslaved people and servants interchangeably, mentioning in one document that a "negro, servant or horse" could be seized by the bailiff to pay off a debt. Borrowing liberally from Barbados law, he also devised the earliest slave codes, which were designed to police and punish captives who revolted. These laws deprived enslaved people of virtually any legal protection while ascribing a wide latitude of power to free colonists.[45]

In the 1670s, the Royal African Company (RAC) formalized the slave trade, increasing the current of captives from Africa to Jamaica. Founded by Charles II and governed by James, duke of York, who was also its largest shareholder, the RAC claimed crown control over English involvement in human trafficking, which grew considerably under its watch. Before the RAC's formation, free people outnumbered enslaved captives on the island. After the company's establishment, the enslaved population rapidly grew. By 1673, 7,764 free colonists had already imported 9,504 captives to Jamaica,

gan, *American Slavery, American Freedom;* and Hilary McD. Beckles, "A 'Riotous and Unruly Lot': Irish Indentured Servants and Freemen in the English West Indies, 1644–1713," *WMQ*, 3d Ser., XLVII (1990), 503–522.

45. Thomas Modyford, "A View of the Condition of Jamaica," Oct. 20, 1664, Collection of Papers Relating to English Affairs in the West Indies, Add MS 11410, Thomas Modyford, Orders for Court of Judicature, St. Jago, Oct. 20, 1664, Add MS 11410. The first English people to inhabit Jamaica unquestioningly viewed slave labor as an important component of colonization. Eighteenth-century colonist James Knight claimed that there were seventeen thousand people on the island, one-third of whom were enslaved. See Knight, "Naturall, Morall, and Politicall History of Jamaica," 1743, I, Add MS 12415. See also David Barry Gaspar, "'Rigid and Inclement': Origins of the Jamaica Slave Laws of the Seventeenth Century," in Christopher L. Tomlins and Bruce H. Mann, eds., *The Many Legalities of Early America* (Williamsburg, Va., and Chapel Hill, N.C., 2001), 82–83, 91–92.

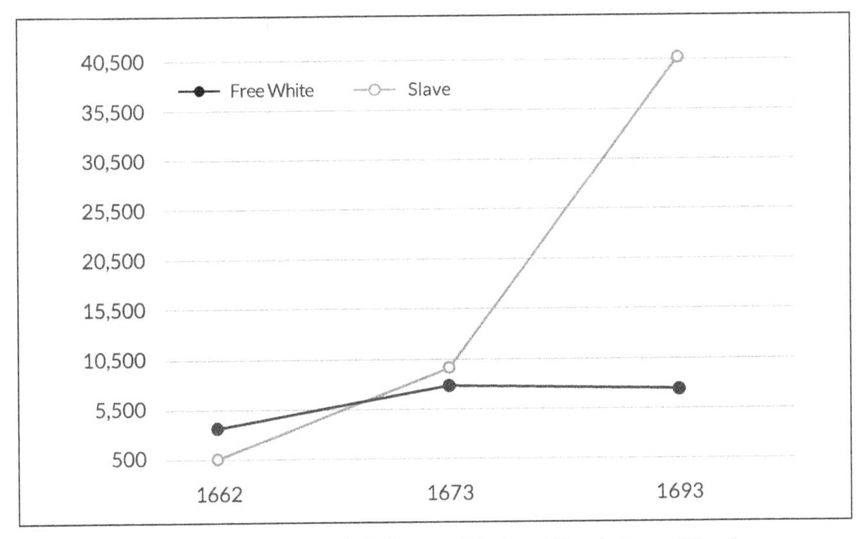

FIGURE 1. Growth of Jamaica's Free and Enslaved Populations, 1662–1693. Source: Trevor Burnard, *Planters, Merchants, and Slaves: Plantation Societies in British America, 1650–1820* (Chicago, 2015), 68–69.

creating a slave majority. The RAC's grip on the trade deteriorated in the 1680s, when James II left England. But the company's decline only encouraged free traders, who were already involved in the illicit slave market. In the absence of the RAC, the number of enslaved inhabitants further expanded. When John Taylor traveled to Port Royal to sell his prisoners in 1686, he reported that "an abundance of negro slaves daily" arrived there. During the twenty-year period between 1673 and 1693, colonists transported 33,000 captive Africans to Jamaica. At the turn of the century, there were roughly 7,365 free white people on the island, and the enslaved population had swelled to 48,000, outnumbering free people by six to one (Figure 1). The passage of the Africa Trade Act in 1698, which allowed all English citizens to participate in slaving, further opened the floodgates.[46]

46. Taylor, "Taylor's Historie," 135; William A. Pettigrew, "Free to Enslave: Politics and the Escalation of Britain's Transatlantic Slave Trade, 1688-1714," *WMQ*, 3d Ser., LXIV (2007), 5, 10–11. The activities of the RAC in Jamaica cannot account for the rapid growth of the enslaved population at the end of the seventeenth century. More work needs to be done on this subject. See also Pettigrew, *Freedom's Debt: The Royal African Company and the Politics of the Atlantic Slave Trade, 1672–1752* (Williamsburg, Va., Chapel Hill, N.C., 2013). Population figures for 1673 are taken from Long, *History of Jamaica*, I, 376; and Burnard, *Planters, Merchants, and Slaves*, 230.

The first female colonists who settled in English Jamaica readily exploited the financial, legal, and social opportunities that slaveholding offered. The small number of probate records that have survived from the seventeenth century indicate that not only did the number of women property holders increase during this period, so, too, did their investment in enslaved laborers. The majority of women (thirty-two out of forty-seven) whose estates were probated between 1674 and 1693 were slaveowners. Altogether, female property holders who died on the island had amassed 517 people, valued at £2,255. Yet the number of those who possessed slaves was larger than this figure suggests at first glance. An additional forty-eight women whose estates were not probated made wills during the seventeenth century (a person's estate was normally probated if he or she died intestate), and half of the them specifically mention enslaved people. Based on the pattern in the probated inventories, it is reasonable to conclude that women who only referred to "estate" or "real and personal" estates also owned captives. Altogether, approximately three-quarters of the ninety-five female property holders held enslaved people in bondage.[47]

Whether they lived in urban or rural areas, the majority of the island's free women devised a form of slaveholding that was small-scale and domestically oriented in nature. Those who settled in the towns of Port Royal and St. Jago de la Vega lived alongside a handful of captives—not hundreds of

47. I use Trevor Burnard's database of Jamaica inventories, which he collected from the Jamaica Archives and shared with me, to calculate larger trends that relate to property holding throughout the book. Probated inventories should be treated prudently though. First, they do not include all property holders on the island. Second, the records from the seventeenth century are especially inconsistent—no inventories, for example, exist for a five year period between 1694 and 1699. As a result, probated inventories suggest broad trends—they do not afford an entirely accurate account of colonial society. The probate records begin in 1674. Cumulatively, between the period of 1674 and 1699, women's estates only account for a tiny fraction (47) of the 780 estates that were probated. But the number of female property holders on the island grew along with the population of free settlers. In 1675, for instance, women held only 2 of the 55 estates that were probated, equaling 3 percent of the total. By 1693, women owned roughly 10 percent, or 13 out of the 112 estates that were probated. As stated above, no records have survived from 1694 to 1699. Hence, I use 1693 as my cutoff date for the seventeenth century. Between 1665 and 1699, a total of 59 women recorded wills; the estates of 11 of these women were also probated (this figure does not include the years 1694 to 1698, which are missing from the records). Therefore, a total of 95 women were identified as property holders (47 probated estates and 48 wills). See Jamaica Inventories; and Jamaica Wills.

people. Enslaved people accounted for a large portion of the total value of their middling and modest estates. Port Royal resident Martha Gray owned two captives and held property valued at £115. Dorcas D'Oyley commanded one enslaved woman. When she died, her small holdings were valued at £57. The free and freed women who helped to settle Jamaica's countryside also sank their money into African captives. Slaves composed the majority of Jane Robinson's £1,000 estate when she died in 1703. Her mixed-use venture typified the kind of agricultural operation that second- and third-generation women planters would manage. She cultivated crops and raised a herd of twenty-four steers and cows, twenty-seven mules, and three horses. Although Robinson commanded a middling fortune by local standards, she lived in a Spartan house furnished with four "old tables" and two beds made up with "old" sheets. Her contemporary, planter Ursula Kellway of Clarendon Parish, adopted a similar business model. She oversaw twenty-nine enslaved people on her ginger plantation, where she reared thirty-one head of cattle, nine horses, and twenty-six hogs. Her residence was scantily furnished with a simple bedstead, tables, and a chest. A handful of these female planters had grown immensely wealthy off the backs of enslaved laborers. Esther Cope commanded 165 slaves and possessed an estate valued at more than four thousand pounds. But Cope was exceptional. Women typically controlled far fewer captives in aggregate than men.[48]

Slaveholding offered women who were otherwise legally, professionally, and economically disadvantaged in relation to men significant qualitative and quantitative benefits. Jamaica's early female settlers readily capitalized on these advantages. Free and freed women protected their recently acquired colonial wealth with an impressive degree of legal savvy. When the widow Mary Freeman, for instance, bought land in 1678, she described the property as that "I have of my own industry purchased." Widows who had experienced the disabilities of coverture were especially careful to secure their wealth if they remarried. They used equity law to maintain exclusive control of their assets through the establishment of separate estates. In 1688, Mary Johnson of Port Royal gave her property to her grandchildren. Worried that

48. Inventory of Martha Gray, 1685, Jamaica Inventories, Inventory of Dorcas D'Oyley, 1686, Inventory of Jane Robinson, 1703, fol. 8, Inventory of Ursula Kellway, 1703, fol. 141, Inventory of Esther Cope, 1693. It is possible that Dorcas D'Oyley was related to Edward D'Oyley, the first governor of Jamaica. If she was connected to a prominent family, however, it is unclear why she died with such meagre holdings.

her daughter's current or future husband might "intermeddle with or alienate" the assets, she explicitly barred him from doing so in her will.[49]

The widow and planter Margaret Roe likewise moved to safeguard her assets by drafting a will before her remarriage in 1686. Though not a rich woman, she owned a few enslaved people, horses, and goats, most likely inherited from her first husband, which she protected by establishing a separate estate. She offered her future husband a mare, describing the gift as a small "token" of her affection, but asserted her "full liberty, sole power, and absolute authority" over the rest of her property. Yet, at the same time that she gave up her legal status as a widow, Roe did not relinquish her position as a slaveholder, and captives significantly enhanced the value of her otherwise meager estate. Women like Roe were legal innovators. Colonists would continue to use the kinds of legal strategies devised by early female settlers to protect married women's property in the eighteenth century.[50]

Unlike land, enslaved people constituted a new form of property—one that was particularly suited for female property holders. Traditionally, women received moveable or personal property such as cattle, furniture, or clothing, whereas men normally inherited real estate. More than a decade before the Jamaica Assembly formalized slavery as a legal institution, the island's first settlers already equated slaves with livestock and marked captives as a distinctively feminine form of property. Planter James Pennelerick, who was probably one of Cromwell's soldiers who received a land grant on the island, was also one of the earliest English slaveholders. In his 1668 will, Pennelerick gave "lands in St. Andrews," "one negro woman called Susanna," and "all my moveable goods" to his wife. It is not known how Pennelerick came to control the enslaved woman. What is clear from his bequest are the rudiments of a pattern to which colonial husbands would adhere for the next century. Men provided wives with generous bequests that often included real and movable property and also specified individual enslaved people by name whom they reserved for spouses. The same year Pennelerick made his will, Harstrian Hendrickson of Port Royal identified "negro slaves, servants,

49. Will of Mary Freeman, 1678, Jamaica Wills, IX, Will of Mary Johnson, 1688, III, IV, and V. For more on separate estates, see Salmon, *Women and the Law of Property;* Allison Anna Tait, "The Beginning of the End of Coverture: A Reappraisal of the Married Woman's Separate Estate," *Yale Journal of Law and Feminism,* XXVI (2014), 165–216; Erickson, *Women and Property in Early Modern England;* and Susan Staves, *Married Women's Separate Property in England, 1660–1833* (Cambridge, Mass., 1990).

50. Will of Margaret Roe, 1686, Jamaica Wills, III–V.

chattels" as half of his "personal estate," which he bequeathed to his wife. A decade later, Thomas Beend recorded separately "all lands, negroes, chattels, houses" that his wife would receive. Pennelerick also left his wife "£9 to buy one negroe for herself and children," thereby encouraging her participation in the nascent slave market and deepening her commitment to chattel slavery after his death.[51]

In addition to ensuring the involvement of their wives in slaveholding, the first generation of English colonists also identified enslaved people as a specifically suitable form of property for their daughters. In 1668, Robert Taylor gave his "great house" and half a share in a ship called the *Batchelor* to his wife; his daughter Sarah would inherit a "negro girl." Ten years later, the widow Mary Freeman transferred nine enslaved people whom she had hired out to earn an income to her daughters. The planter Joel White devised all of his plantations to two daughters, Mary and Elizabeth, in 1678. He also combined the "twenty and seven old and young negroes" with the "thirteen horses and mares and five colts" that he conveyed to them. Though White might have transferred his entire estate to his daughters because he lacked male heirs, his treatment of enslaved people as a form of movable property—one that he equated with livestock—is notable. His contemporary, Katherine Broone, did the same. Broone, a widow living in Port Royal, transferred all of the "horned cattle negro indian slaves horses, mares, goods, plate, money" to her children, whose gender she did not specify. White and Broone defined captive humans as a specific type of property—one that was not tied to land and that could easily be used as a form of currency in the marketplace. The distinction of slaves as movable goods would prove to be particularly beneficial to free and freed women.[52]

Colonial acts passed in 1683, which classified "Negroes" with cattle, horses, and "Utensils," codified these local inheritance practices into law. In 1684, the *Laws of Jamaica* listed slaves with "all other Goods and Chattels." By defining captives as moveable goods, the Jamaica Assembly turned them into flexible assets that could easily be sold for a profit or to pay off debts. Enslaved people became a form of currency on the island. Yet the legal definition of enslaved persons as "property" remained imprecise. Colonists exploited this ambiguity and tested the validity of each other's claims to captives. When

51. Will of James Pennelerick, 1668, Jamaica Wills, I, Will of Harstrian Hendrickson, 1668, I, Will of Thomas Beend, 1678, I.

52. Will of Robert Taylor, 1668, Jamaica Wills, I, Will of Mary Freeman, 1678, IX, Will of Joel White, 1678, IX, Will of Katherine Broone, 1681, III, IV, and V.

conflicts involving competing ownership claims to slaves escalated, they were tried at Jamaica's Grand Court. Located in Spanish Town, it acted as a type of small claims court. Even the most marginal members of free society—poor widows, freed women, and orphans—readily used the new legal system to uphold their rights as enslavers.[53]

Women's more tenuous claims to property made them especially motivated to safeguard their rights to enslaved people. Because of Jamaica's high mortality rates, female colonists cycled between marriage and widowhood. Each change in marital status triggered a considerable alteration in a woman's legal authority over her assets. When husbands died intestate, entitlements to estates, including enslaved people, were even more unsettled. Men, it seems, took advantage of the confusion caused by death, gendered property laws, and hazy definitions of slaves as property to claim valuable enslaved people for themselves. In 1680, for example, Thomas South challenged Elizabeth Walker's ownership of a man who had been "delivered" to her by the court in Port Royal "to be safely kept" when her first husband died. Apparently, Walker only had a right to the captive while she was "sole" or unmarried. By remarrying, South asserted that she had relinquished her stake in the man because she fell under coverture again. The outcome of this case, which was tried by a jury, is unknown.[54]

53. "An Act for Establishing Courts and Directing the Marshals Proceedings," in *The Laws of Jamaica, Passed by the Assembly and Confirmed by His Majesty in Council, Feb. 23, 1683 . . .* (London, 1683), 171–192; "An Act for the Better Ordering of Slaves," in *The Laws of Jamaica, Passed by the Assembly and Confirmed by His Majesty in Council, April 17, 1684 . . .* (London, 1684), 140–141; Thomas South v. William and Elizabeth Walker, 1680, Grand Court Records, I. Suits for theft of other forms of property must have been tried in a different court in the colony. A thorough scouring of court records from the seventeenth and eighteenth centuries, including the Grand Court, Supreme Court, and Chancery Court, failed to uncover criminal trials. The evidence collected from the Grand Court records for this project was gleaned from the only usable volumes at the Jamaica Archives. All other volumes of Grand Court (and Chancery Court) records have been deemed too fragile for public use and are inaccessible. This is unfortunate, as the few volumes that are fit for handling contain invaluable and virtually untapped information about colonial life. It is difficult to determine the exact date when the Grand Court was founded because most of the records from the seventeenth century have not survived. Cases that were tried in 1681 were still recorded in volume one of the court records under 1680 as the date. See Grand Court Records, 1680, I. A man named Mr. Nevil referred to the Grand Court operating in St. Jago De La Vega in 1677. See "The Present State of Jamaica, in a Letter from Mr. Nevil to the Early of Carlisle," in *Interesting Tracts, Relating to the Island of Jamaica,* 114.

54. Thomas South v. William and Elizabeth Walker, 1680, Grand Court Records, I.

In 1681, John Evans lodged a similar accusation against the widow Elaine Sympkins of keeping "one negro woman called Grace," who, he contended, belonged to him. Evans argued that he had given Grace to Sympkins's husband—when the husband died his widow then "denied to deliver" Grace to Evans. Sympkins, on the other hand, believed that Grace became her property on her husband's death. As a widow, she affirmed her prerogative as Grace's owner. The possible role played by Grace herself adds another dimension to the suit between Evans and Sympkins. Grace's enslaved status made her the weakest pawn in the power struggle between two free people who sought to exploit her labor and her monetary value. But Grace also had a limited capacity to influence and even instigate the conflict between Evans and Sympkins. Legally, her relationship with them was grossly unequal—but, in reality, the poor widow desperately needed Grace to survive. As the only enslaved person whom Sympkins owned, Grace might have established an uneasy, yet intimate, relationship with her. The women likely shared close living quarters, slept in the same room, and performed domestic chores together. This dynamic gave Grace a degree of sway over her enslaver. After living in Sympkins's household for years, she might have strongly opposed being handed over to a strange man. Or, perhaps the opposite was true. It is also possible that Grace sought out Evans's help and urged him to reclaim her when Sympkins's husband died in the hopes of improving her conditions.[55]

If colonists skirted the law, bending a weakly enforced system to serve their own interests in slaves as property, enslaved people likely took advantage of hazy legal situations to improve their circumstances and exert some degree of influence over who their enslavers would be. A remarkable suit between Elizabeth, a "negro woman," and planter John Rupert offers evidence of a woman of African descent using the court to defend her status as a legally free person against a man who claimed her as his property. Rather than punish Elizabeth as a runaway, Rupert, Elizabeth's purported owner, brought his complaint to the Grand Court and framed it as a property dispute, avowing that Elizabeth "unjustly detained" herself and her three children from him, depriving him of his right to his belongings. Though the details of the case are unclear, Elizabeth seems to have countered his statement by accusing Rupert of wrongfully abducting her. Elizabeth contended that he "did by force and with arms did take and carry away" her family against the "peace of the King." Though it is uncertain from the record whether Evans or Eliza-

55. John Evans v. Elaine Sympkins, 1681, Grand Court Records, I.

beth won the case, the court found one of the parties "not guilty." Regardless of the outcome, Elizabeth rejected her status as chattel and willingly went to court to defend her independence.[56]

Elizabeth's legally precarious position as a free woman of color might have made her vulnerable to Rupert's pursuit. Free people of African and Indian descent faced increasing animosity in the late seventeenth century. In 1671, less than a decade before Elizabeth appeared in court, one official reported to the Lords of Trade that colonists had treated him with "ill will . . . for favouring the Indians, Mulattos and Negroes that pretend to be free." The unnamed official "appointed special courts" to determine their cases because the "law and juryes" were "so unwilling to do them right." Frequent insurgencies by enslaved people generated acrimony toward free people of African and Indian descent. Colonists feared that they sympathized and colluded with enslaved people. There were six uprisings between 1673 and 1694 alone. In 1673, two hundred "Coromantee" slaves killed several white people in Saint Ann Parish and escaped into the mountains with weapons and ammunition. There were more revolts in 1678 and 1685–1686. In 1690, Governor William O'Brien, second earl of Inchiquin, reported the insurrection of four hundred enslaved Africans, whom he identified as "Coramantees," on Thomas Sutton's plantation in the middle of the island. The rebels killed one white man, seized fifty "fuzzess, blunderbuses and other arms, powder and ball," and then moved on to the next plantation, where they killed the overseer and tried to convince more captives to join them before dispersing into the woods. Armed and provisioned enslaved people, the governor believed, would continue to "pose a threat to mountain plantations." He stressed the "great want" of white men in more remote plantations. These insurgents joined the core members of the Leeward Maroons and came to dominate them. Uprisings occurred again in 1696, 1702, and 1704.[57]

Insurgents showed little regard for the gender of their captors during revolts. Female slaveholders exposed themselves to physical harm and some-

56. John Rupert v. Elizabeth "a negro woman," 1680, Grand Court Records, I.

57. Slingsby, Esq., to Lords Council, Mr. Gaywood in the Pelican, 1671, Collection of Papers Relating to English Affairs in the West Indies, Add MS 11410; Governor William Earl of Inchiquin to the Lords of Trade, Aug. 31, 1690, CO 137/2, fol. 134, TNA; Burnard, *Planters, Merchants, and Slaves,* 97–100. For an account of the Coromantee insurgency in 1673 that led to the formation of the Leeward Maroons, see David Barry Gaspar, "A Dangerous Spirit of Liberty: Slave Rebellion in the West Indies in the 1730s," in Laurent Dubois and Julius S. Scott, eds., *Origins of the Black Atlantic* (New York, 2010), 12.

times death. For example, the 1678 revolt, which occurred near Spanish Town, began on Edmund Duck's plantation, and Duck's wife was killed. As Richard Dunn observes, the violence of the event is carved into her tombstone for posterity. Still standing in the Spanish Town cathedral churchyard, it describes her as "BEING MOST BARBAROUSLY MURTHERED BY SOME OF THEIR OWNE NEGRO SLAVES." During the yearlong uprising from 1685 to 1686, the captives on the widow Guy's plantation stole weapons and killed several white people. Guy jumped out of a window, and one of her domestic captives hid her. Guy was fortunate. It is unlikely that the revolting enslaved people would have spared her. In 1711, another assembly of captives reportedly "committed [the] greatest villainy" and murdered their mistress. Governor Archibald Hamilton captured some of them, but others fled and avoided recapture. He hoped other slaves "will not follow their example." On the one hand, the rebels' violent treatment of women highlights in graphic terms the animosity that suffused the relationship between women enslavers and the enslaved. On the other hand, the effort of the unnamed "domestic slave" to protect Guy is suggestive of the intimacy that might have also existed between captor and captive, even if it was motivated by a shared interest in self-preservation.[58]

The colonial assembly sought to stamp out rebellion and uphold slaveholder power with brutal acts of retribution. The *Laws of Jamaica,* passed in 1684, were designed to terrify and subdue captives into compliance. Any challenge to the authority of a free person carried the whiff of rebellion and could elicit severe punishment. The constable whipped first-time offenders. Second-time offenders were subjected to bodily mutilations. Their slit noses and burned faces caused permanent disfigurements that carried symbolic meanings. In England, people who engaged in seditious behavior, acted as false accusers, or unworthily usurped authority also had their ears cropped or noses slit. Lifelong markers, these punishments were designed to incite public contempt, and they functioned in much the same way on Jamaica. Third-time offenders faced execution and further bodily dismemberment. Captives who participated in an "Insurrection" or "Rebellion," prepared arms, or held "Conspiracies for raising Mutinies or Rebellion" could be summarily executed. Servants who committed the same crimes, on the other hand, received punishments in the form of time being added to their indenture contracts.[59]

58. Dunn, *Sugar and Slaves,* 260, 261; Archibald Hamilton to the Lords of Trade, Jan. 13, 1711, CO 137/10, fol. 16, TNA.

59. "An Act for the Better Ordering of Slaves," in *Laws of Jamaica* . . . (London, 1684), 140,

Suffering from demographic and military weakness, the local government turned every free person into the judge, jury, and executioner of enslaved people. Colonial officials expected "mistresses" to control, compel, and coerce slaves with as much force as "masters" exerted and to contribute equally to the island's brutal system of repression. The laws charged both "Master[s]" and "Mistresse[s]" with the responsibility for uncovering plots among their slaves, instructing them to search the housing of enslaved people every two weeks for "Clubs, wooden Swords, and mischievous Weapons." The laws also sanctioned murder as a tool for controlling enslaved people. Colonists who killed slaves out of "wilfulness, wantonness, or bloudy mindedness" faced the comparatively light punishment of three months' imprisonment and a fine of fifty pounds to be paid to the owner to compensate for the loss of valuable property. In contrast, killing a servant was treated as a felony and was therefore punishable by death. Indentured servants who killed enslaved people could be disciplined physically with thirty-nine lashes on the "bare Back," whereas free people faced no legal charges for maiming or killing captives whom they accused of stealing or running away or who "refuseth to submit" to their authority.[60]

By authorizing every member of free society, from the lowliest indentured

---

142–143, 145, 146; Garthine Walker, *Crime, Gender, and Social Order in Early Modern England* (New York, 2003), 91–92. As scholars have observed, the laws governing slavery departed significantly from the laws governing servitude in the Americas. At the most basic level, servants were punished by extending the time of their indentures, whereas slaves, who were already held in captivity for life, received physical punishments. The Jamaican laws treated indentured servants as a distinctive class of persons with limited rights. For example, they needed the consent of their employers to trade and had to carry tickets when traveling. The laws also allowed for servants to be corporeally punished, but owners needed to obtain permission from the justice of the peace to have their servants "Whipt Naked." Servants who forged their identities were pilloried and had their ears chopped off. See "An Act for Regulating Servants," in *Laws of Jamaica* . . . (London, 1684), 4–9. For more on the distinction between servants and slaves in Virginia and Barbados, see Brown, *Good Wives, Nasty Wenches;* Morgan, *American Slavery, American Freedom;* Beckles, "A 'Riotous and Unruly Lot,'" *WMQ*, 3d Ser., XLVII (1990), 503–522; Jenny Shaw, *Everyday Life in the Early English Caribbean: Irish, Africans, and the Construction of Difference* (Athens, Ga., 2013); and Edward B. Rugemer, "The Development of Mastery and Race in the Comprehensive Slave Codes of the Greater Caribbean during the Seventeenth Century," *WMQ*, 3d Ser., LXX (2013), 429–458.

60. "An Act for the Better Ordering of Slaves," in *Laws of Jamaica* . . . (London, 1684), 142–143, 147.

servant to the wealthiest planter, male and female alike, to control, coerce, and even kill any enslaved person who was deemed unruly, the 1684 laws blunted the differences in gender, status, religion, age, and, increasingly, race between free people. The laws envisioned a starkly bifurcated society of legally free and unfree persons. They also began to correlate race with legal status by invoking the nascent racial category "white" when referring to servants in one clause. The slave codes invested nearly unlimited power in all free people—power that was monopolized in England by the crown, the court, and the church. The colonial transference of command from the institution to the individual marked one of the most significant departures from European legal tradition. In passing these acts, local lawmakers placed tremendous authority and responsibility in the hands of a wide range of ordinary colonists. Frequent outbreaks of violence justified slaveholder suspicions, making merciless retribution seem all the more necessary, especially in sparsely settled frontier regions.[61]

By 1690, according to eighteenth-century colonist and historian James Knight, Jamaica was "prosperous and flourishing," and people "flocked" there. The loosely regulated and profit-oriented town of Port Royal offered new economic opportunities and life possibilities for free and freed women. They lived in a multiethnic and multicultural place where local officials overlooked and often supported activities that skirted international treaties and imperial regulations. The frequency and violence of the insurgencies led by enslaved people also highlight the volatility of Jamaican society in the late seventeenth century. Eager to capitalize on unfree labor from Africa, the first wave of settlers, including women, surrounded themselves with a hostile captive population that quickly outnumbered them. Jamaica's legal codes recognized slaveholding to be a dangerous and even lethal practice. Yet the lure of profit enticed the majority of the colony's free inhabitants to participate in it anyway, and enslaved people came to comprise the majority of women's

61. "An Act for Regulating Servants," *Laws of Jamaica* . . . (London, 1684), 3–10, esp. 7, "An Act for the Better Ordering of Slaves," 140–148. The word "white" is used when referring to the amount of meat that should be given to a servant. Diana Paton makes the point that any violent act against a white person carried the "implicit threat" of slave rebellion. She contends that Jamaica's legal system "valorized the slaveholder's private penal power." It was a delegation of state authority. See Paton, "Punishment, Crime, and the Bodies of Slaves in Eighteenth-Century Jamaica," *Journal of Social History*, XXXIV (2001), 923, 927, 931.

wealth. In their eager adoption of slavery, female colonists contributed to the creation of a lucrative yet violent and unstable society.[62]

Natural disasters further threatened to upend English control of the island. On June 7, 1692, a terrible earthquake, followed by a massive tsunami, decimated the glittering wealth of Port Royal. Two-thirds of the thriving settlement sank into the sea. Dead corpses washed out from the graveyard and mingled with the thousands of inhabitants who were killed by the earthquake. Yellow fever epidemics followed, further reducing the surviving population. Governor William Beeston described the colony as being in a "disastrous state" after the catastrophe and the "sickness." Public buildings were destroyed and private houses reduced to huts. Twelve years after the earthquake, a fire burned down much of the remaining town, ringing the final death knell for the once flourishing Atlantic port.[63]

Even after all of these calamities, Port Royal's residents clung stubbornly to what, after the earthquake, had become a much narrower spit of land. Many did not want to relocate to Kingston, a more safely sheltered site inside of the harbor that was proposed as the new location for Jamaica's port town. Identified as "widows and orphans," free women were among the petitioners to the crown who protested their relocation after the Port Royal fire. Claiming that people who had an "interest" in building Kingston had "barred" them from resettling in Port Royal, they insisted on their right to stay in their hometown. Many of the women who signed the petition—Elizabeth Wood and two orphans, Ann Pallmer, and Mary Browne, for example—could not write but made their mark instead. However, they were no less determined to stay in Port Royal. Another petition sent by members of the Jamaica Council and the assembly echoed their complaints. Port Royal people, the petitioners claimed, were being discriminated against by the early settlers of Kingston. They alleged that the Kingstonians had quickly pushed through acts that forbade them from selling wine or liquor or from holding public office. These acts effectively destroyed Port Royal's economic and political viability, forcing the old town's inhabitants to relocate to the new settlement. The petitioners were loath to move to Kingston, which they described as "very unhealthy" and the "worst" place in Jamaica. Situated between a "great swamp" of "standing, stinking water," its inhabitants endured "noisome smells" and

62. Knight, "Naturall, Morall, and Politicall History of Jamaica," 1743, I, Add MS 12415.

63. William Beeston, 1693–1695, CO 137/3, TNA. The earthquake killed two thousand people. For more information about the earthquake, see Michael Pawson and David Buisseret, eds., *Port Royal, Jamaica*, 2d ed. (Kingston, 2000), 165–172.

"continual clouds of dust." The petitioners argued that Kingston's new residents had even fled to Port Royal to save themselves after a "multitude of people dyed" there.[64]

As the petitions show, many colonists continued to believe that Port Royal was the epicenter of the island's livelihood, in spite of its repeated destruction. Men and women alike wanted to rebuild the town that had brought such prosperity to the colony through maritime trade. Used to looking out to sea, they lived on a tiny island that was barely connected to the larger colony. In spite of the horrific catastrophes that Port Royal suffered, they viewed its location as a superior site for shipping and defense. Moving to Kingston would alter their lives, rooting the colonists in a swamp, entrenching them in the land, making them vulnerable to attack, and cutting them off from the sea and from trade. Ultimately, they lost out. Port Royal's former glory would never be restored. At the turn to the eighteenth century, Jamaica's future lay in the new town of Kingston. It was in the mucky morass of this settlement that the next generations of free and freed women would prosper, establishing a diversity of small businesses and large mercantile ventures that exceeded anything built by their predecessors in Port Royal. Moreover, the next generations of island-born women would capitalize on Kingston's ascendancy in the Atlantic slave trade, making ever-increasing investments in African captives to bolster their wealth, status, and authority.

64. "Petition on Behalf of the Freeholders, Inhabitants, . . . Widows, and Orphans That Reside on and Interested in Port Royal," 1703, fol. 26, CO 137/6, TNA, "Petition of Peter Beckford, Senr., Charles Knights, Charles Sadler, Charles Chaplin, John Walters, and Francis Rose, Six of the Council of Jamaica . . . to H. M. (Her Majesty)," 1703, fol. 31, CO 137/6.

2. Kingston

In November 1750, eighteen black horses adorned with black ostrich plumes paraded Anna Hassall's corpse through London to Westminster Abbey. The pages, coachmen, and porters attending the hearse wore funeral gloves and hatbands, and the female mourners were shrouded in black funeral gowns, scarves, and hoods. Hassall was buried in an opulent elm coffin with "best brass nails, double plate and four pairs gilt handles" and draped with the "best pall." A "fine shroud" covered her body inside. When her coffin was carried into Westminster Abbey, thirty-two men followed behind her pallbearers carrying branch lights to illuminate the cathedral. After the service, her casket was sealed inside a lead box and lowered into the ground in the Islip Chapel. Only five people were buried in this space in the eighteenth century. Hassall, a widow, "late of the island of Jamaica," was the sole woman in the group. The abbey's brief description of Hassall pays cursory attention to her life, incorrectly identifies her genealogy, and expresses bewilderment at her presence in the spiritual hearthstone of Britain.[1]

Hassall's burial in Westminster Abbey is puzzling indeed. How could an

1. Elizabeth Callender to John Trotter, Nov. 26, 1750, Miscellaneous Receipts, GD 345/1214, National Archives of Scotland (NAS), Edinburgh; Will of Anna Hassall, Feb. 15, 1741 (entered May 16, 1751), Jamaica Wills, 1661–1771, XXVIII, fol. 28, Island Record Office (IRO), Spanish Town, Jamaica; "Anna Hassall," Westminster Abbey, http://westminster-abbey.org/our-history/people/anna-hassall. Westminster Abbey's website incorrectly identifies Anna's husband, Arthur Hassall, as her father-in-law. His father, also named Arthur, was married to Mary Hassall. For the correct genealogical information, see Will of Arthur Hassall, Feb. 4, 1741, Jamaica Wills, XXV, fol. 16.

unknown and unimportant woman with no ties to the aristocracy be buried in the English pantheon of religious, political, artistic, and predominately male luminaries? To understand how a thirty-seven-year-old female merchant from Jamaica achieved such an elevated status, it is necessary to undo strong and gendered assumptions about who forged Britain's commercial empire in the eighteenth century. Hassall's death was a carefully orchestrated production that was designed to showcase her wealth, status, power, and taste. She left detailed instructions for her burial in her will, even going so far as to account for the cost of every mourning button and handkerchief that her guests would wear. Only a person with the shrewdest business sense and years of experience retailing textiles and manufactured items would attend to the ornamental details of her own funeral with such precision. Hassall mustered a lifetime of training to craft her magnificent final exit. Yet her ending had almost nothing to do with her origins. She died more than four thousand miles from her home. Her funeral was an act of skilled artifice, an effort to seamlessly produce a fashionable British woman out of a Jamaican colonist.

Hassall's lifelong involvement in Atlantic trade, slavery, smuggling, privateering, and moneylending generated the capital that funded her extravagant burial in Westminster Abbey. When her husband, Arthur Hassall, died in 1748, Anna, as his widow, assumed control of a vast mercantile enterprise valued at £21,429 (worth more than £2.6 million today), making her, at thirty-three, wealthier than most members of the English aristocracy. She also became one of the richest women in her hometown of Kingston. Her fortune dwarfed the estate of the average male resident, which amounted to around £2,345, and exponentially exceeded the assets controlled by ordinary women. The average woman's estate in the port city was worth an estimated £862. Significantly, thirty-nine enslaved men, women, and children both embodied and aided in the production of Hassall's affluence. Only a handful of her Kingston contemporaries commanded such a large retinue of captives. Most free women owned approximately eight slaves, whereas the average man owned twelve. Though men controlled the majority of the town's wealth, they were small-scale slaveholders compared to Hassall.[2]

2. Will of Arthur Hassall, Feb. 4, 1741, Jamaica Wills, XXV, fol. 16; Measuring Worth, https://www.measuringworth.com/calculators/ppoweruk/. The thirty-nine enslaved people listed in Arthur Hassall's will constituted a varied and highly skilled workforce valued at £651 (£91,000 in today's marketplace). The shortness of Arthur and Anna's marriage was not unusual in Jamaica, where mortality rates were high. Trevor Burnard calculated that the average marriage in the parish of Saint Andrew lasted a mean length of eight years. See Burnard, "A Failed Settler So-

Hassall's life was indelibly shaped by time and place. She grew up in Kingston at a moment when the new town had surpassed Port Royal's former eminence to become a major commercial and slaving hub in Britain's burgeoning commercial empire. By the 1730s and 1740s, when Hassall was a young woman, Kingston exerted a centrifugal force in the Atlantic basin, pulling in hundreds of ships hailing from Europe and Africa and numerous shorter hauling vessels from America to its harbor and supporting a large number of inhabitants whose livelihoods depended on licit and illicit maritime trade (Plate 2). Long-haul vessels were weighed down with European textiles and trinkets, North American flour and timber, and exotic items from the Far East. A large portion of the goods would be reshipped illegally to customers in Spanish territories. During Hassall's childhood, Kingston also became a vital node for the British slave trade. In 1714, the newly formed South Sea Company established a way station on the town's shoreline for enslaved people who had survived the Middle Passage. The majority of these captives were then reboarded onto ships and sent to Spanish territories, a process that Jamaica's colonists deeply resented and frequently complained about. Nevertheless, the island's slave population grew considerably after the company's arrival.[3]

Second- and third-generation female colonists formed a considerable contingent of Kingston's free society. These women maneuvered in colonial, circum-Caribbean, Atlantic, and increasingly global markets, acting as handmaidens for a valuable branch of trade that helped to secure Jamaica's rising

ciety: Marriage and Demographic Failure in Early Jamaica," *Journal of Social History*, XXVIII (1994), 67. Amanda Vickery notes that to achieve the "basic minimum of aristocratic lifestyle" in England in 1790 required an income of £5,000 to £6,000 per annum; "pretenders" to parish gentility lived on £300 or less (Vickery, *Behind Closed Doors: At Home in Georgian England* [New Haven, Conn., 2009], 130). Anna Hassall died forty years earlier, making the value of her fortune even larger. The average wealth of Kingston's male and female residents and the average number of slaves per owner were calculated based on the inventories of 264 women and 1,540 men whose estates were probated in Kingston between 1700–1765. Women's estates only account for 16 percent of those probated in Kingston. See Jamaica Inventories, 1674–1784, Jamaica Archives (JA), Spanish Town, Jamaica.

3. Edward Long estimated that 700 ships cleared Jamaican ports between 1769–1771. In 1774, 460 ships docked in Kingston alone. See Long, Add. MS. 12412, fol. 31, British Museum, cited in Edward Brathwaite, *The Development of Creole Society in Jamaica, 1770–1820* (Oxford, 1971), 112. Probated inventories indicate that 153 of the 298 men who were identified by occupation as mariners between 1675 and 1760 lived in Kingston. During the same period, 400 of the 623 merchants on the island also lived in Kingston. See Jamaica Inventories.

PLATE 2. *A Correct Draught of the Harbours of Port Royal and Kingston . . .*, by Richard Jones. [1756?]. Courtesy of the Library of Congress, Geography and Maps Division, G4964.P65P55 1756 .J6

commercial dominance. They leveraged ready access to imported goods and property to forge a range of ventures focusing on service and trade. Customers in the booming port town paid high prices for a suite of domestic services that were typically defined as women's work, from lodging and cooking to cleaning, laundry, and sewing. In addition to supporting a local service economy, female entrepreneurs strengthened a tendril of overseas trade, importing, retailing, and fashioning fabric, thread, buttons, ribbons, and lace for local consumption. Selling and bartering foreign goods, they filled a crucial and potentially lucrative niche in a marketplace that employed female inhabitants living in port towns throughout the Atlantic world.[4]

4. Similarly, Michael J. Jarvis shows that women dominated tavernkeeping as an occupation in colonial Bermuda (Jarvis, *In the Eye of All Trade: Bermuda, Bermudians, and the Maritime Atlantic World, 1680–1783* [Williamsburg, Va., and Chapel Hill, N.C., 2010], 294–295). As Kathleen M. Brown has observed, England laid the "material foundations" for its cultural empire through the exportation of manufactured goods to America (Brown, *Foul Bodies: Cleanli-*

Sarah Stubbick was one of Kingston's earliest female entrepreneurs She acquired and retailed a variety of imported and saleable manufactures. Her estate, probated in 1720, included numerous white, yellow, and colored gloves, bottles of "hungary" water and honey water, black silk shoes, rolls of tobacco, soap, toothbrushes, combs, and boxes of candles. She also imported and retailed barrels of pork, beef, herring, and biscuits. The remnants of calico, blue Holland cloth, and coarser ozenbrig, along with the thread and buttons in her home, indicate that she earned additional money as a seamstress or paid other women to do piecework for the customers who bought small trinkets, household goods, or a bit of meat from her shop. Stubbick also owned a number of books and "testaments" that attest to her literacy or to her customers' interest in reading.[5]

Living in Kingston before the South Sea Company opened the floodgates for the slave trade on the island, Stubbick and her contemporary the widow Mary Rich ran their businesses without the assistance of slave labor. Stubbick's investment in manufactures, rather than people, made up the bulk of her middling £304 estate. Her modest home was outfitted with a curtained bedstead sheltered by an essential mosquito net. A simple tea table and a water jar sustained her. Rich retailed groceries and basic commodities, including oatmeal, soap, currants, salt fish, candles, tobacco, onions, and lumber. Working as a shopkeeper, she amassed a respectable estate of £144. Though neither achieved affluence, the two women enjoyed comfortable livings plying imported goods to the town's growing community.[6]

Although Britain's commercial expansion abroad generated novel economic opportunities for women like Stubbick and Rich, commerce went

---

ness in Early America [New Haven, Conn., 2009], 100–101). Important studies have been done on women's engagement with the textile industry in early America and Europe. However, the activities of free and enslaved women who worked in this industry in the Caribbean have received little attention. See Kate Haulman, *Politics of Fashion in Eighteenth-Century America* (Chapel Hill, N.C., 2011); Laurel Thatcher Ulrich, "Wheels, Looms, and the Gender Division of Labor in Eighteenth-Century New England," *WMQ*, 3d Ser., LV(1998), 3–38; Marla R. Miller, "Gender, Artisanry, and Craft Tradition in Early New England: The View through the Eye of a Needle," *WMQ*, 3d. Ser., LX (2003), 743–776; Beverly Lemire, *Dress, Culture, and Commerce: The English Clothing Trade before the Factory, 1660–1800* (London, 1997); Clare Haru Crowston, *Fabricating Women: The Seamstresses of Old Regime France, 1675–1791* (Durham, N.C., 2001); and Jennifer M. Jones, *Sexing La Mode: Gender, Fashion, and Commercial Culture in Old Regime France* (Oxford, 2004).

5. Inventory of Sarah Stubbick, 1720, Jamaica Inventories, fol. 225.

6. Ibid.; Inventory of Mary Rich, 1720, Jamaica Inventories, fol. 215.

hand in hand with warfare. During the first half of the eighteenth century, rival European powers vied with each other for control of increasingly global empires. Nearly incessant imperial conflicts drew an unprecedented number of men into military service, placing new strains on families and increasing women's responsibilities in their absence. Tens of thousands of soldiers and sailors died overseas; many more spent years away from home. These developments reshaped the gender dynamics of maritime communities. In England, for instance, an estimated 20 percent of households in poor, port-city neighborhoods were headed by women. A significant number of domiciles in maritime communities in Rhode Island, South Carolina, Antigua, Barbados, Bermuda, and New York were also managed by women. With a large number of men either absent or dead, female kin acted as the legal heads of households and became the primary, if not the sole providers, for their families. Those who were either widowed or never married could assume debts, extend credit, and sign in their own names: all prerequisites for participating in the marketplace.[7]

As Kingston became a major entrepôt, it manifested gendered character-

7. Sarah M. S. Pearsall, *Atlantic Families: Lives and Letters in the Later Eighteenth Century* (New York, 2008); Margaret R. Hunt, *The Middling Sort: Commerce, Gender, and the Family in England, 1680–1780* (Berkeley, Calif., 1996), 38. Ellen Hartigan-O'Connor determined that women headed 17 to 21 percent of the households in Newport, Rhode Island, and Charleston, South Carolina (Hartigan-O'Connor, *The Ties That Buy: Women and Commerce in Revolutionary America* [Philadelphia, 2009], 40). Similar trends have been identified in Barbados, where white women outnumbered white men and many remained both unmarried and financially independent. See Hilary McD. Beckles, "White Women and Slavery in the Caribbean," *History Workshop*, no. 36 (Autumn 1993), 70–71. Natalie A. Zacek's study of a 1753 census from Antigua revealed comparable patterns (Zacek, "Between Lady and Slave: White Working Women in the Eighteenth-Century Leeward Islands," in Douglas Catterall and Jodi Campbell, eds., *Women in Port: Gendering Communities, Economies, and Social Networks in Atlantic Port Cities, 1500–1800* [Leiden, Neth., 2012], 130). Michael Jarvis also determines that women formed the majority of the free population in Bermuda and notes that female colonists headed a large number of households on the island (Jarvis, *In the Eye of All Trade*, 293–303). See also Serena R. Zabin, *Dangerous Economies: Status and Commerce in Imperial New York* (Philadelphia, 2009), chap. 2. Hunt contends that the massive demands of the army and the navy placed heavy burdens on the wives and mothers of many British families (Hunt, *Middling Sort*, 30–31). Sheryllynne Haggerty highlights this trend in British port cities. Sixty-three percent of the men in London's East End were absent at any one time as a result of sea-related occupations (Haggerty, "Women, Work, and the Consumer Revolution: Liverpool in the Late Eighteenth Century," in John Benson and Laura Ugolini, eds., *A Nation of Shopkeepers: Five Centuries of British Retailing* [London, 2002], 109).

istics similar to other maritime communities throughout the British Empire. The town's growth and stability depended as much on the women who remained ashore as it did on the men who climbed aboard ships and ventured out to sea. Strikingly, as Trevor Burnard has found, one out of every four households in town was legally headed by a woman, but, in reality, the number was probably even larger. The gender ratio between free men and women was also more balanced in Jamaica's maritime zone than it was in plantation-based parishes. A 1731 census—one of the few from this time period to survive—shows that female-headed families made up the majority of the free urban populace: 516 white women and 607 men lived in Kingston while an estimated 327 white women outnumbered the 199 white men who lived in Port Royal. These demographic patterns call into question a masculine narrative of colonialism featuring male merchants, pirates, privateers, and sailors. Families—many of them headed by women like Hassall—constructed Britain's commercial empire. A large portion of Kingston's male inhabitants were employed as merchants, sailors, ship's captains, sailmakers, and wharfingers. These husbands, fathers, brothers, and sons relied on female kin to manage their families' personal and financial affairs.[8]

In Jamaica, inheritance customs further enhanced the legal and material

8. Trevor Burnard found that 25 to 27 percent of householders in Kingston during the period 1745 to 1770 were white women (Burnard, "'Gay and Agreeable Ladies': White Women in Mid-Eighteenth-Century Kingston, Jamaica," *Wadabagei: A Journal of the Caribbean and Its Diaspora,* IX, no. 3 [Fall 2006], 31). Of the 706 wills made by women between 1665 and 1761, 698 listed their locations in Jamaica. Of those, 27 percent lived in Kingston, 16 percent in Saint Catherine, where Spanish Town was located, and 12 percent in Port Royal. The remaining 45 percent were spread very thinly over eleven other parishes and England (there are no wills from Saint Mary's Parish). Probated inventories yield similar results: 65 percent of the 825 women whose estates were probated between 1674 and 1765 lived in the three aforementioned urban areas. See Jamaica Wills, I–XXXVIII; and Jamaica Inventories. The probated inventories were recorded by Trevor Burnard and used with his permission. The 1731 census included masters, mistresses, and servants. The record takers grouped "white masters and mistresses" together, but, given the number of white children, it is safe to assume that the numbers of masters and mistresses were roughly equal. See "Jamaica to His Majesty, Relating to the Unhappy Situation of Affairs of That Island, by the Increase and Success of Their Rebellious Negroes," Feb. 11, 1731, CO 137/19, II, The National Archives (TNA), Kew. An estimated 15 percent of the men who made wills in Jamaica were mariners, merchants, ship's captains, sailmakers, and wharfingers. An even larger number (22 percent) who made wills and whose livelihoods depended on the sea had their estates probated. Calculations made using Jamaica Wills, I–XXXVIII; and Jamaica Inventories.

status of urban women. Seafaring husbands typically treated their wives—not male relatives—as the most suitable heirs of family estates. Nearly all of the mariners on the island transferred the entirety of their holdings to their spouses, even if they had children. Humphrey Ware of Port Royal, for example, gave his "real and personal estate" to his wife in 1710. Twelve years later, another mariner, John Bevis, bequeathed "all personal estate, house, lands, negro slaves male and female, and plate" to his spouse. Bevis's will reveals the rapid influx of enslaved people into ordinary colonial families. By the 1720s, even mariners like Bevis—who might have worked on a slave ship himself—were purchasing African captives. When men died, their widows assumed control of their enslaved people. One of Bevis's contemporaries, mariner James Neal of Port Royal, gave eight slaves, together with all of his "money land goods and estate," to his wife and daughter.[9]

Like Kingston's mariners, wealthier merchants also favored their wives. More than half of the husbands who engaged in overseas trade gave their entire estates to spouses outright. Others divided family property equally between wives and children (mainly daughters). John Gartbrand, one of Kingston's early traders, gave his wife "all personal estate rights and credits" owed to him and an annuity of £150 per annum. Additionally, she would assume possession of a plantation and all of the captives who labored on it, together with a 250-acre estate in the Blue Mountains. Gartbrand's wife was pregnant when he made his will in 1722, and he gave the remainder of the estate to their unborn child. Jamaica-based merchants like Gartbrand diverged from their counterparts in Britain, who increasingly named male relatives and business partners rather than wives as their executors. Gartbrand, in contrast, expected his wife to shoulder complex and sometimes contentious administrative duties, asking her to "execute seal and deliver" a "deed of release or conveyance if required" to his other legatees.[10]

9. Will of Humphrey Ware, 1710, Jamaica Wills, XIII, Will of John Bevis, 1722, XVI, Will of James Neal, 1722, XVI, Will of George Hall, 1748, XXVII, and Will of William Blackborn, 1749, XXVII. Fourteen of the seventeen mariners who were married bequeathed their entire estates to their wives. See Jamaica Wills, I–XXXVIII.

10. Will of John Gartbrand, 1722, Jamaica Wills, XVI. Nine of the seventeen merchants who were married bequeathed their entire estates to their wives. See Jamaica Wills, I–XXXVIII. Richard Grassby finds that men in England were adding other men to jointly administer their wills. See Grasby, *Kinship and Capitalism: Marriage, Family, and Business in the English-Speaking World, 1580–1740* (Cambridge, 2001), 125.

Local circumstances made it all but impossible, and certainly impractical, for Kingston traders to exclude women from mercantile activities. High mortality rates, chronic warfare, and the rapid expansion of slavery on the island increased, rather than diminished, men's dependence on wives and daughters to oversee business operations when they traveled abroad or died—both highly probable outcomes. Colonial trade was a family endeavor that involved all of the members in a kin group. These conditions subjected women, who became responsible for financially supporting their families in the absence of male kin, to hardships. Although it is difficult to uncover the struggles of impoverished female colonists who died without a penny to their names, they undoubtedly formed a contingent in Kingston. Other women, like Hassall flourished in Kingston's intensively commercial environment. For some, Jamaica became a place where the impetus for profit could blunt gender, status, or racial differences, affording novel financial possibilities for ambitious women.[11]

"I SHALL NOT PUT MY AFFAIRS IN ANY OTHER HAND"

Anna Hassall grew up in a maritime milieu of licit and illicit trade. As a female merchant, she followed in the footsteps of her mother, Sarah Shanks, who taught her how to operate in the shadowy world of smuggling and privateering. Though technically illegal, the activities of traders like Shanks and Hassall in Spanish territory strengthened the economic ties between countries with long-standing political animosities toward one another. The letters written by Shanks—one of the only surviving collections of female-authored correspondence from eighteenth-century Jamaica—provide a remarkable and rare account of an international trading operation that was headed by women. In the 1730s, Shanks and her sister Mary Skipp built ambitious mercantile and privateering enterprises in a town that was awash with money and slaves. Involved in the contraband trade, they acted as interlopers, or "rogue" colonists, and ignored Spain's severe trade restrictions, which forbade the inhabitants in Spanish territories from purchasing imports that were manufactured and sold by other European powers. Truly Atlantic and even global in scope, this female-run business drew on connections in Britain to ship a wide range of goods manufactured in Europe and Asia to Kingston. They

11. Linda L. Sturtz also stresses the importance of extended families and studies women who served as local representatives for kin-based trading networks in British North America. See Sturtz, *Within Her Power: Propertied Women in Colonial Virginia* (New York, 2002), 78–88.

then reshipped these items to eager Spanish customers, who were willing to pay black market prices for them.[12]

Shanks's family originated in Northumberland, England, where she and her husband, the Reverend Edward Shanks, baptized three children between 1712 and 1715. Edward Shanks was among the Anglican clergymen sent to America by the newly formed Society for the Propagation of the Gospel to strengthen the Church of England's anemic presence in Jamaica. He died soon after their arrival on the island, leaving his wife behind to support their family. Sarah's ambitions, however, drove her to accomplish far more than domestic management. Although the family earned money from a plantation they had mortgaged to a prominent planter, she was not content with surviving off the interest derived from the loan. Instead, Shanks determined to engage in overseas commerce. "While I am in this country am loath to have but 4½ cent when I can by trade make a great advantage," she wrote. When Shanks's Jamaica-based son fell ill while she was attending to business in Britain, she quickly returned to the colony, insisting "I shall not put my affairs in any other hand." The widow, who described herself as "hating idleness," found a cure for this malady in operating a mercantile business that tied transatlantic trade to the Caribbean contraband circuit, which she alluded to in references to the "Spanish Trade." Shanks planned to generate enough colonial profits to retire comfortably in England. "I shall hardly come empty handed," she confided to Ann Birkin—a single woman who lived in Bristol and acted as Shanks's metropolitan agent, acquiring British manufactures for Shanks to resell to Spanish customers from her trading base in Jamaica.[13]

12. Sarah Shanks identified Mary Skipp as her sister in her 1741 will and gave her one hundred pounds to purchase mourning clothes. See Will of Sarah Shanks, 1741, Jamaica Wills, XXIII. I borrow the term "rogue" from Shannon Lee Dawdy. Female smugglers in Jamaica shared much in common with Madame Real of New Orleans, who Dawdy uses as an exemplar of rogue behavior in the colonial zone. See Dawdy, *Building the Devil's Empire: French Colonial New Orleans* (Chicago, 2008), 19, 99–101.

13. Sarah Shanks to Ann Birkin, May 26, 1740, GD 1/32/33, NAS, Shanks to Birkin, July 26, 1740. Sarah Shanks's maiden name is unknown. Her husband, Edward Shanks, was christened May 29, 1683, in Alnwick, Northumberland. Sarah Shanks is also listed as Edward's wife at the christenings of three children: Richard (Dec. 23, 1712), Mary (June 22, 1714), and Anna (Dec. 8, 1715), in Lesbury, Northumberland. See "England, Births and Christenings, 1538–1975," www.familysearch.org. Anna Hassall describes herself as being from Stanwick and the daughter of "the Rev Shanks." On the title of her self-authored play, "Mrs. Hassals Tragedy," Anna Hassall described herself as the daughter of "the Rev Shanks" from Stanwick (England) ("Mrs. Hassals Tragedy," 1749, GD 345/1233, NAS). There is a record of an Edward Shanks traveling to

Alliances like the one forged between Shanks and Birkin undergirded the early modern world of trade. Rather than viewing commerce as impersonal and divorced from private life, people treated financial and personal interests holistically. Shanks and Birkin established a classic agent / principal merchandising arrangement that was characteristic of male traders. To import goods from Bristol, Shanks entrusted Birkin with a valuable five-hundred-pound bond and gave her permission to draw on it to pay for them. In return, Birkin received a commission for her service. The women were also intimate friends, and their emotional relationship inflected and strengthened their business partnership. On one occasion, Birkin told her partner that she would normally charge half a percent for negotiating Shanks's bills with her British merchants. Instead, Birkin only wanted a gift of a "pot" of green peppers—a Jamaican delicacy—in lieu of the commission. This type of bond did not feminize their economic connection. On the contrary, men also blended personal and financial concerns. Doing so was part and parcel of operating in an Atlantic marketplace and an Anglo-Atlantic culture, which, by the middle of the eighteenth century, was infused with the discourse of sentiment.[14]

Both Shanks and Birkin displayed shrewd expertise and familiarity with every detail of the textile trade, revealing their years of experience in that line of work. They possessed an exhaustive knowledge of cloth, its costs, and its producers. Shanks's meticulous descriptions of fabric indicate that she had

---

Jamaica in 1707 in "Anglican Servants in the Caribbean, c.1610–c.1740," at Lancaster University, http://www.lancaster.ac.uk/fass/projects/caribbean/ministers,%20working.pdf. It is possible that Edward Shanks traveled alone to Jamaica and then returned to England when his children were born. Then, he and his family might have either journeyed to the colony together, or Sarah possibly went there alone after his death.

14. Sarah Shanks to David Delany, Jan. 26, 1739, GD 1/32/33, NAS, Ann Birkin, "Anna Hassall Book of Receipts from Purchases in London," Oct. 8, 1739, GD 1/32/34. For more on the intertwining of personal and financial relationships during the early modern period, see Pearsall, *Atlantic Families;* Hunt, *Middling Sort;* Peter Mathias, "Risk, Credit, and Kinship in Early Modern Enterprise," in John J. McCusker and Kenneth Morgan, eds., *The Early Modern Atlantic Economy* (Cambridge, 2000), 15–35; Toby L. Ditz, "Shipwrecked; or, Masculinity Imperiled: Mercantile Representation of Failure and the Gendered Self in Eighteenth-Century Philadelphia," *Journal of American History,* LXXXI (1994), 51–80; David Hancock, *Citizens of the World: London Merchants and the Integration of the British Atlantic Community, 1735–1785* (New York, 1995); Hancock, *Oceans of Wine: Madeira and the Emergence of American Trade and Taste* (New Haven, Conn., 2009); Grassby, *Kinship and Capitalism;* and Alan L. Karras, *Sojourners in the Sun: Scottish Migrants in Jamaica and the Chesapeake, 1740–1800* (Ithaca, N.Y., 1992).

worked as a mercer, milliner, or seamstress before she moved to Jamaica. From the colony, she instructed Birkin to make bulk purchases for her at Bristol's "July Fair" of "rich" and "fashionable" items, including "rich porto bello flower silk," "rich hair cull damask," "silk hose," and "fashionable" wax necklaces, which were glass beads filled with wax to imitate the look and feel of pearls. She also ordered "fine white glaz'd lamb" gloves, gilt brushes, forehead combs, and "fashionable curls." Shanks further directed Birkin to order "fine Holland wale-bone hoop coats" from "Miss Gallbraith the person I used to buy them from," showing her familiarity with local retailers. Though Birkin found it "very difficult" to complete her friend's extensive order, she nevertheless vowed to make it her "whole study to get it all at the best rate."[15]

Shanks's instructions also disclose the aspirations and taste of her colonial clients, who desired "rich" fabric and "fashionable" items. She purchased silk stockings and white gloves for herself and dressed her daughter Anna in "genteel fashionable flowere'd silk" from Britain, advertising their superior fashion sensibility and overseas connections to the Kingston community. Some scholars contend that working with textiles consigned women to low-paying jobs. Yet this line of trade could also be very lucrative, as Shanks understood. In Jamaica, women who imported, retailed, and reexported foreign manufactures were not necessarily impoverished, nor were they reduced to surviving on the margins of the Atlantic economy. Female traders joined a varied mercantile community in Kingston. Between 1675 and 1760, four hundred men who lived there were identified as "merchants" in probated inventories. During this time, the average male merchant held a median estate worth an estimated £900 and a mean estate valued at £2,691. The gendered categorization of women by marital status—not occupation—in probate inventories makes it difficult to determine how many of them worked as merchants or retailers. Examples have been culled from the estates of women who were normally listed as "widows" but who also amassed numerous imported manufactures that they clearly either sold locally or reexported. The correspondence of Shanks and her daughter Hassall offers an exceptional level of detail about how female traders operated their ventures.[16]

15. Sarah Shanks to Ann Birkin, May 26, 1740, GD 1/32/33, NAS, Birkin to Shanks, September 1740. The *Oxford English Dictionary* defines a mercer as "a person who deals in textile fabrics, esp. silks, velvets, and other fine materials." See *Oxford English Dictionary,* s.v. "mercer, *n.,*" http://www.oed.com.

16. Shanks to Birkin, May 26, 1740, GD 1/32/33. Sheryllynne Haggerty contends that work-

Altogether, this fragmented evidence intimates that Kingston's women capitalized on both local circumstances and imperial developments. Living in or near the harbor gave female residents a direct line to the ships arriving laden with captive laborers, material objects, and consumables. By feeding the colonial demand for buttons, scissors, hats, gloves, stockings, and thread, they supported the British manufacturing industry. Women's business operations were more global in scope, though, reflecting Britain's enlarging empire. Female traders purchased Indian textiles such as "callico," "Indian calico," and "India chintz." These looser, lighter fabrics were more suitable for the hot, humid Caribbean climate than British-manufactured woolens. By importing and reexporting such goods, women merchants helped bind together the East and West and forge an international trading community.[17]

Shanks's sister Mary Skipp also established these types of commercial connections. Skipp accrued an impressive estate working as a textile merchant in Kingston. When she died in 1740, the trader left behind a vast quantity of imported cloth and manufactured items. Her storehouse was filled with cambric and Holland cloth, cherry- and rose-colored silk, green Venetian silk, black and white print calicoes, India chintz, and lawn as well as children's shoes, ribbons, and pins. The contents of Skipp's home were equally varied and globally produced, signifying her education, wealth, and cosmo-

---

ing with textiles provided low-paying jobs for women in Philadelphia. But Haggerty focuses on seamstresses and mantuamakers, whereas I discuss female merchants, mercers, and milliners. This may explain the disparity between women's financial success in Philadelphia and Jamaica. See Haggerty, "'Ports, Petticoats, and Power?' Women and Work in Early-National Philadelphia," in Catterall and Campbell, eds., *Women in Port,* 113–114. Of the 623 merchants on the island, 400 lived in Kingston during this time. See Jamaica Inventories. In his study of the probated inventories of Kingston's merchants during the second half of the eighteenth century, Douglas Mann determines that merchants made up 18 percent of Kingston's free population and controlled 30 percent of the town's total wealth. Interestingly, single women made up 11 percent of Kingston's property holders, and their estates represented 6 percent of the town's wealth. See Mann, "Becoming Creole: Material Life and Society in Eighteenth-Century Kingston, Jamaica" (Ph.D. Diss., University of Georgia, 2005), 45–46.

17. Inventory of Judith Jurdaine, 1676, Jamaica Inventories, fol. 98, Inventory of Dorothy Matson, 1734, fol. 16, Inventory of Mary Skipp, 1740, fol. 144, Inventory of Mary Martin, 1741, fol. 163. As Jonathan Eacott observes, English colonies in America were not subject to the Calico Acts, which, starting in 1696, prohibited the importation of dyed and printed cotton from Asia to Britain. Large quantities of these textiles continued to be imported to the Caribbean. See Eacott, *Selling Empire: India in the Making of Britain and America, 1600–1830* (Williamsburg, Va., and Chapel Hill, N.C., 2016), 89–90.

politan taste. Furnished with exotic "India prints" and "India" tea tables that had traveled from the Indian Ocean to the Caribbean, her household contained possessions that reflected her mercantile reach. Skipp's "scritore" or writing desk attested to her literacy and her engagement in an Atlantic epistolary culture, and her possession of whist and card tables evoked her sociability. When she entertained clients and friends over cards, Skipp truly glittered, adorning herself with diamond, emerald, garnet, and topaz rings, a diamond girdle buckle, a gold watch, and a pearl necklace.[18]

In addition to Indian furnishings and sparkling gems, Skipp also invested in people. When she died in 1740, Skipp owned two enslaved women, Celia and Amey, who helped to facilitate her affluent lifestyle. The captives likely performed the domestic work of cooking, cleaning, and washing as well as helping Skipp with her business operations, perhaps sorting, organizing, and keeping track of a myriad of valuable textiles and commodities arriving from overseas. Celia and Amey also served a symbolic function, signaling Skipp's status and belonging to a colonial mercantile community that increasingly relied on slaveholding. Living in Kingston during the first half of the eighteenth century, women like Skipp leveraged the labor of unfree people of African descent to construct profitable trading ventures.[19]

The volatile early modern marketplace created new forms of commerce that women throughout the Atlantic world participated in. Many came from cultures where it was commonplace for women to play prominent roles in the mercantile community. Dutch women, for example, worked as merchants and traders in New Netherland. Microhistories of traders like Esther Pinheiro—a Jewish widow from Nevis who assumed command of her husband's extensive mercantile network—or Jean d'Entremeuse—a Frenchwoman whose trading activities connected Portuguese, Spanish, and French colonies to the Indian Ocean—offer instances of women who operated thriving ventures in a globalizing and risky economy. Across the Atlantic, in the burgeoning port towns of Senegal and Madagascar, African and Afro-European women acted as influential merchants and slave traders. Their ties to both European and African communities made them important power brokers.[20]

18. Inventory of Mary Skipp, 1740, Jamaica Inventories, fol. 144. For a detailed study of the meanings conveyed by women's writing desks, see Dena Goodman, *Becoming a Woman in the Age of Letters* (Ithaca, N.Y., 2009).

19. Ibid.

20. Kim Todt and Martha Dickinson Shattuck argue that "gender did not determine participation" in trade for Dutch women. See Todt and Shattuck, "Capable Entrepreneurs: The

Shanks and Birkin operated in this broad network of female traders. Their ventures provide salient cases that make clear that the Atlantic marketplace was not sex segregated. Rather, male merchants were accustomed to transacting business with women. European colonial expansion scattered families throughout the world, deepening the importance of female involvement in economic activities. In an era before private banks, people obtained access to capital through individual and professional connections, which they used to establish creditworthiness. The personalized nature of the early modern economy created a space for women of all sorts to maneuver.[21]

As family members, friends, neighbors, and business owners, Jamaica-based women acted as moneylenders, creating intimate webs of credit and debt that greased the wheel of the colonial economy. Female islanders owned less property, but they tended to be cash rich, especially if they were involved in overseas trade. Male planters, in contrast, assumed large debt and depended on crops to pay their creditors. This distinction helps to explain why free and freed women operated as financiers to other women as well as men. Although Kingston shopkeeper Elizabeth Bucknor earned a living rearing horses and sheep and retailing goods worth two hundred pounds, the most valuable item she owned according to the 1719 probated inventory of her estate was a fifteen-hundred-pound mortgage made between two men. Bucknor probably received the mortgage in exchange for extending them credit. Even the most impoverished female colonists survived by acting as

---

Women Merchants and Traders of New Netherland," in Catterall and Campbell, eds., *Women in Port,* 184–185. For more on women traders, see Zacek, "Between Lady and Slave," in Catterall and Campbell, eds., *Women in Port,* 133, Ernst Pijning, "'Can She Be a Woman?' Gender and Contraband in the Revolutionary Atlantic," 215–250; and Wendy Wilson-Fall, "Women Merchants and Slave Depots: Saint-Louis, Senegal, and St. Mary's, Madagascar," in Ana Lucia Araujo, ed., *Paths of the Atlantic Slave Trade: Interactions, Identities, and Images* (Amherst, N.Y., 2011), 293.

21. For more on the history of women and work in early modern England, see Judith M. Bennett, *Ale, Beer, and Brewsters in England: Women's Work in a Changing World, 1300–1600* (New York, 1996); Patricia Crawford and Laura Gowing, eds., *Women's Worlds in Seventeenth-Century England* (New York, 2000); and Hunt, *Middling Sort.* In her study of eighteenth-century New York, Serena Zabin writes that "women and men wove trading webs across the Atlantic" (Zabin, *Dangerous Economies,* 36–37). Margaret Hunt describes a credit economy, which was predicated on personal connections (Hunt, *Middling Sort,* 31). Peter Mathias concurs that access to credit and cash in a hazardous and unpredictable marketplace was central to survival (Mathias, "Risk, Credit, and Kinship in Early Modern Enterprise," in McCusker and Morgan, eds., *Early Modern Atlantic Economy,* 23).

moneylenders. A poor widow who lived in Saint Andrew Parish on the outskirts of Kingston, for example, kept a modest estate of twenty pounds. Her house was furnished with a few bed linens, spoons, and a brass kettle. When she died in 1732, the fourteen-pound debt a man owed her was her most valuable asset.[22]

Sometimes the financial relationships between locals broke down. Disputes over unpaid debts, even for small amounts of money, were tried in Jamaica's Grand Court. Heavily trafficked by a broad swath of colonial society, its records offer a bird's-eye view of the range of islanders who were enmeshed in webs of credit and debt obligations to one another. Female creditors displayed little reserve about using the court system. Instead, they actively pursued delinquent male debtors. Elizabeth Hall appeared in court in 1743. A typical Kingston woman, Hall owned a house and two lots of land in the town, engaged in overseas trade, retailed imports to local customers, and commanded four enslaved people. Hall also extended credit to her customers, and she sued a male tavernkeeper for failing to pay for the twelve pounds in "diverse goods" and "merchandise she delivered to him." Hall won the case.[23]

Other women appeared as defendants in suits to collect unpaid debts. Kingston widow Elizabeth Bray owed a man sixty-seven pounds for "diverse goods wares merchandise"; she did not attend the 1743 session to defend herself. Another Kingston widow, Katherine Rutherford, owed a male shopkeeper a similar sum for the items she had purchased on credit but got lucky: the plaintiff did not appear, and she was acquitted. If defendants lost their cases, the penalties could be ruinous. Debtors faced property seizure and stiff fines that accrued interest at 4 percent. Lawsuits related to debt collection were so lucrative that people began to treat them as saleable assets.[24]

In addition to her trading venture, Shanks participated in Jamaica's dy-

22. Inventory of Elizabeth Bucknor, 1719, Jamaica Inventories, fol. 182, Inventory of Margaret Shellet, 1732, fol. 75. By the end of the eighteenth century, the start-up cost of establishing a sugar plantation ranged from £17,249 to £28,039—a considerable fortune. Few could afford such a staggering sum without assuming debt. See Trevor Burnard, *Planters, Merchants, and Slaves: Plantation Societies in British America, 1650–1820* (Chicago, 2015), 14, who obtains these figures from Edward Long and Bryan Edwards.

23. Will of Elizabeth Hall, 1747, Jamaica Wills, XXVI; Elizabeth Hall v. Henry Oburne, Grand Court Records, 1743, XLI, JA.

24. Charles Martin v. Elizabeth Bray, Grand Court Records, 1743, XLI, William Dallas v. Katherine Rutherford; James Robertson, "Jamaican Archival Resources for Seventeenth and Eighteenth Century Atlantic History," XXII, no. 3, *Slavery and Abolition* (December 2001), 119.

namic lending economy through the mortgage of her family's plantation land, which her husband might have purchased, to the wealthy planter, Richard Elletson. Although the records do not explain why she entered into this transaction, it was probably easier for Shanks to work as a trader in an industry that she displayed expertise in than to run a sugar plantation. While she was in Britain to oversee her family interests there, Shanks assumed responsibility for corresponding with Elletson about the mortgage arrangement. Her letters offer insight into the complex relationship between gender ideology and lived practice. Though Elletson owed Shanks money, their disparate gendered and social positions required her to treat him with deference. As a member of Jamaica's planter elite, Elletson enjoyed masculine privilege, an elevated social rank, and powerful political connections. The Elletson family were considerable landholders and slaveholders. Their estate included Hope Plantation in the foothills above Kingston, and their son, Roger Hope Elletson, was destined to become governor of Jamaica.[25]

Shanks's letters display her shrewd comprehension of the disparities in status and wealth between her family and the Elletsons. In contrast with the business confidence her letters to Birkin exude, Shanks assumed a submissive feminine posture and performed the requisite fealty to her social superior when writing to Elletson. In one letter penned in 1738, Shanks apologized to Elletson for being "too warm" and hoped that her outburst of emotion would not prevent him from "the dispatch of business in the beginning of the crop." On another occasion, Shanks adopted the typical female role of the poor widow in an effort to manipulate the delinquent debtor into paying her, demurely writing in 1738 that she was "more anxious than one of a liberall fortune" and needed to be "more exact" in collecting on the debt "than I could wish to be." Modulating between attempts to elicit his pity and flattery, she continued: "A short reflection must bring a gentleman of your understanding to be sensible my little fortune obliges me to keep it all in service to provide the common necessary's of life." Although Shanks was a successful merchant in her own right, she went so far as to claim that "I am a woman and unac-

25. When Richard Elletson's estate was probated in 1744, he owned 398 enslaved people. His estate was valued at an estimated £13,614. He owned a total of 5,495 acres on the island. See "Richard Elletson," Legacies of British Slave-Ownership, https://www.ucl.ac.uk/lbs/person/view/2146655563. This data is derived from Trevor Burnard's database of Jamaican inventories; and "A List of Landholders in the Island of Jamaica Together with the Number of Acres Each Person Possessed Taken from the Quit Rent Books in the Year 1754," CO 142/31, TNA, transcribed at http://www.jamaicanfamilysearch.com/Samples2/1754lead.htm.

quainted with the management of goods." Both parties understood that such statements were patently false.[26]

On a discursive level, Shanks's gendered position required her to adhere to certain conventions when discussing business matters. After her feminine performance of submission, Shanks could revert to financial dealings. During a temporary residence in Britain, she instructed Elletson to send her sugar from Jamaica "on the first ships for Bristol, consigned to my self; but not until you have advised me by some ship for London; or Bristol, that insurance may be made thereon." As this line suggests, though, the gendered nature of Shanks's business letters should not be overstated. As the language of feeling gained popularity in the mid-eighteenth century, new epistolary conventions influenced the correspondence between male merchants. Shanks's reference to being "too warm" shows her mastery of an emerging genre, rather than a feminine affect. Writing on the cusp of the cult of sentiment, her letters blended politeness and self-control with the newer language of sensibility that infused Atlantic epistolary culture. Her discursive abilities helped to establish her credibility—and her creditworthiness—in the Atlantic marketplace, just as it did for her male counterparts.[27]

There were also limits to the effectiveness of discourse. Ultimately, Shanks's skillful letters did not achieve the desired result—mortgage repayment—from Elletson. Four years after writing to him, she complained to Birkin that she had not received "a shilling" from him for the mortgage. El-

26. Sarah Shanks to Richard Elletson, Feb. 4, 1738, GD 1/32/33, NAS. Linda L. Sturtz identifies a parallel rhetorical strategy in Anna Eliza Elletson's letters. See Sturtz, "The 'Dimduke' and the Duchess of Chandos: Gender and Power in Jamaican Plantation Management—A Case Study; or, A Different Story of 'A Man [and His Wife] from a Place Called Hope,'" *Revista/Review Interamericana*, XXIX (1999), [1–15].

27. Shanks to Elletson, Feb. 4, 1738. For more on merchants and the discourse of feeling in business correspondence, see Ditz, "Shipwrecked," *Journal of American History*, LXXXI (1994), 51–80. Sarah Knott suggests that while polite modes of behavior stressed wit and self-mastery, sentimental writers used sensibility to engage the vicarious sympathy of readers (Knott, *Sensibility and the American Revolution* [Williamsburg, Va., and Chapel Hill, N.C., 2009], 55–58). The scholarship on epistolary writing and the republic of letters in the early modern period is extensive. See Pearsall, *Atlantic Families;* Goodman, *Becoming a Woman;* Gary Schneider, *The Culture of Epistolarity: Vernacular Letters and Letter Writing in Early Modern England, 1500–1700* (Cranbury, N.J., 2005); Eve Tavor Bannet, *Empire of Letters: Letter Manuals and Transatlantic Correspondence, 1688–1820* (New York, 2005); Anna Bryson, *From Courtesy to Civility: Changing Codes of Conduct in Early Modern England* (New York, 1998); and David S. Shields, *Civil Tongues and Polite Letters in British America* (Williamsburg, Va., and Chapel Hill, N.C., 1997).

letson's failure to pay his debt was a source of frustration for Shanks, but his reason for doing so is unclear. Perhaps he took advantage of his elevated standing or his position as a man, or perhaps he simply forgot. Shanks and Elletson operated in a marketplace that was simultaneously personalized and abstracted. This volatile economic environment created new opportunities for women to profit, but, as Shanks learned, it was also fraught with a high level of financial risk. As a widow, Shanks assumed responsibility for supporting her family. The struggle to collect mortgage payments from Elletson, combined with her pecuniary opportunism, spurred Shanks to explore new means of diversifying her sources of income.[28]

THE "SPANISH TRADE"

Sarah Shanks strategically leveraged her location in Kingston to generate new and technically illicit profits from the contraband trade to Spanish territories. Her location in the port town nurtured these kinds of endeavors. Spanish traders frequently visited the culturally and ethnically diverse urban area. Although slaves comprised the majority of the town's population, free people of African descent also formed a small contingent of a community that was comprised of English, Scottish, and Irish migrants and a small but prominent Jewish enclave. James Houston, a Scottish physician who spent time in Jamaica during his employment for the South Sea Company, published a disparaging account of Kingston's varied population, describing it as a "very odd Sort of Medley," the "Refuse of the *British Nation,* intermixed with some *Irish.*" Building on a discourse established decades earlier by men like John Taylor, Houston characterized locals as an "unruly, and ungovernable People, living almost like a Parcel of *Men-eaters* devouring one another." He then defined "all the Natives of his *Britannick* Majesty's Dominions in the *West-Indies,* of whatever Denomination or Colour" as *"Creols"* who were culturally, socially, and even ethnically different from Britons and colonists in mainland North America.[29]

28. Sarah Shanks to ? (most likely Ann Birkin), May 19, 1741, GD 1/32/33, NAS. Richard Elletson's mortgage debts to Shanks would be passed on to her daughter Anna when she died. Anna's husband, Arthur Hassall, pursued Elletson for four hundred pounds in debts. See Hassall v. Elletson, Grand Court Records, 1743, XLI.

29. Jacob Bickerstaff, comp., *Dr. Houstoun's Memoirs of His Own Life-Time . . .* (London, 1747), 276, 278. For a more detailed description of the emergence of the Creole type, see Chapter 1, above.

PLATE 3. *Harbour Street, Kingston.* Plate from James Hakewill, *A Picturesque Tour of the Island of Jamaica* . . . (London, 1825). Courtesy of the British Library, London

Although there is little to admire in Houston's contribution to an emergent discourse of ethnoracial difference, his experience of Jamaica as a culturally and socially distinctive space contains an element of truth. Kingston shared more in common with multinational, multiethnic, and religiously diverse cities like Rio de Janeiro, Brazil, Saint-Louis, Senegal, Le Cap, and Saint Domingue than it did with Bristol in England or Boston in mainland North America (Plate 3). Undoubtedly exaggerated, Houston's sneering comment that *"Money is Emperor of the World,* and I am sure that, it is the *Lord of Jamaica"* nevertheless conveys the port's entrepreneurial dynamism. Sarah Shanks joined a community of inhabitants who grew wealthy from the trade in contraband and African captives. Jamaica-based traders shipped loads of illegal European manufactures and enslaved people to Spanish customers. In the early eighteenth century, Kingston residents also made money from privateering, an officially sanctioned form of piracy that Jamaicans already had a long history of engagement with. Separated from imperial oversight by thousands of miles of ocean, smugglers and privateers easily maneuvered outside of ever-changing trade laws and regulations, acting on their own, familial, and communal interests.[30]

30. Bickerstaff, comp., *Dr. Houstoun's Memoirs,* 276–277. For descriptions of cities in Brazil, Saint Domingue, and Senegal, see James H. Sweet, *Domingos Álvares, African Healing, and*

All of these activities contributed to the development of the profiteering and materially focused culture that Houston critiqued and in which Shanks participated. After her husband's death, Shanks parlayed her trading connection with Ann Birkin to import manufactures to Jamaica that were desirable to Spanish, not local, customers. Her transactions did not end on the island. Shanks then reexported her goods as profitable and illegal contraband to Spanish colonies. Oblique references to the "Spanish Trade" in Shanks's writing shed light on the shadowy operations of Jamaica's import-export merchants and their illicit transactions with Spanish consorts. During the first half of the eighteenth century, women merchants like Shanks aided in the intensification of these activities. By 1740, Shanks was explicitly ordering items to smuggle into Spanish colonies. She sent a letter to one of her suppliers in Bristol, Fisher and Company, confirming that "you have all sorts of goods fitt for the Spanish trade." Shanks's understanding of fashion sensibility and taste, her Caribbean location, her connections to British purveyors, and her ties to local islanders made her ideally suited for participating in unlawful commerce.[31]

Contrabanding was a profitable business, but it was also fraught with risk. European powers continually vied for control over bullion, sugar, and the slave trade in the highly strategic Caribbean Sea, and Jamaica was situated in the crosshairs of these conflicts. Competition between colonists and South Sea Company employees added another level of tension to the marketplace. Locals believed that the company was monopolizing a lucrative branch of long-standing commerce between Jamaica and the Spanish Main. They also concluded that the company sent the healthiest African captives to Spanish customers, leaving children, elderly, and sickly people behind in Jamaica. Soon after the company's arrival on the island, the assembly began imposing duties on all slaves transshipped to Spanish colonies. The company retaliated, petitioning the crown to intervene and complaining about local officials who protected and even profited from illicit trade. The company was also at

---

the Intellectual History of the Atlantic World (Chapel Hill, N.C., 2011); Dominique Rogers and Stewart King, "Housekeepers, Merchants, Rentières: Free Women of Color in the Port Cities of Colonial Saint-Domingue, 1750–1790," in Catterall and Campbell, eds., *Women in Port*, 357–397; and Wilson-Fall, "Women Merchants and Slave Depots," in Araujo, ed., *Paths of the Atlantic Slave Trade*, 273–303. Douglas Mann characterizes Kingston in a similar fashion, describing it as a city that was of a "forward-looking nature" with an "entrepôt quality" connected to ports throughout Spanish America. See Mann, "Becoming Creole," 29–30.

31. Sarah Shanks to Fisher and Co., Jan. 6, 1740, GD 1/32/33, NAS.

odds with the Spanish for using the legal trade in people as a cover for the illegal trade in goods.[32]

Shanks built up her Jamaican enterprise in the 1730s, when friction between Spain and Britain was increasing. As a private dealer in contraband goods, Shanks contributed to the animosity between the two nations. Not only did she breach Spanish trade restrictions, her activities also challenged the official asiento contract, which promised the South Sea Company the exclusive right to send one ship per year to an annual fair at a Spanish port. By 1740, the tensions between interlopers like Shanks, the company, and the Spanish escalated into a full-fledged military conflict, the War of Jenkins' Ear, and halted the asiento trade. When the war threatened to spread to Europe, Shanks became anxious about its influence on business. Military conflicts shut down the watery highways that were the lifeblood of overseas commerce. Living in Kingston, Shanks already felt the effects of the expanding conflict. She closely monitored political and military developments, asking Birkin for "the exactest intelligence" on sugar prices in Britain. Birkin sent her newspapers and price lists to "amuse" her, she wrote wittily. Shanks used this information to determine whether it would be more profitable to offload her rum and sugar locally or wait to export it overseas. Birkin informed her that war between Britain and France was imminent and that the cost of sugar would rise, observing that the value of rum had already risen to "seven shillings a gallon" there. High prices reflected dwindling supplies.[33]

Shanks might have profited from the trade in illicit goods to Spanish America, but her business also suffered from the tensions and restrictions

32. Susan Dwyer Amussen, *Caribbean Exchanges: Slavery and the Transformation of English Society, 1640–1700* (Chapel Hill, N.C., 2007), 38–39. Military conflicts included: the War of Spanish Succession (1702–1713), the War of the Quadruple Alliance (1718–1720), the Blockade of Porto Bello (1726), the Anglo-Spanish War (1727–1729), the War of Jenkins' Ear (1739–1748), the War of Austrian Succession (1740–1748), and the Seven Years' War (1756–1763). For more on Jamaica's involvement in the slave trade with Spanish colonies, see Colin Palmer, *Human Cargoes: The British Slave Trade to Spanish America, 1700–1739* (Urbana, Ill., 1981), 65–68, 130; and Gregory E. O'Malley, *Final Passages: The Intercolonial Slave Trade of British America, 1619–1807* (Williamsburg, Va., and Chapel Hill, N.C., 2014), 224.

33. Sarah Shanks to Ann Birkin, Jan. 6, 1740, GD 1/32/33, NAS, Birkin to Shanks, Dec. 17, 1740, Shanks to Birkin, Jan. 27, 1740. As Abigail L. Swingen explains, Jamaican planters and privateers resented and resisted the South Sea Company's monopoly, which cut into their own profits from illegal trade. See Swingen, *Competing Visions of Empire: Labor, Slavery, and the Origins of the British Atlantic Empire* (New Haven, Conn., 2015), 193–194. See also Palmer, *Human Cargoes*, 9.

that these kinds of activities triggered. By 1740, military friction between Britain and Spain made shipping goods overseas hazardous. Privateers and enemy naval vessels seized merchant ships that ventured out in open water. To make matters worse, Parliament passed an act prohibiting the export of all provisions to Jamaica, except for the two staples of an enslaved person's diet: rice and fish. As the military conflict brought transatlantic travel to a standstill, Shanks expressed doubts to Birkin that she would ever return to Britain. In her mid-fifties or early sixties, Shanks was old by Jamaican standards, and perhaps she was ill. Birkin "longed to hear" from her friend and urged her to make the trip across the ocean aboard a ship armed with twenty guns that was bound for Jamaica, but she would never see Shanks in person again. Shanks died in 1741. In recognition of their strong personal and financial bond, Shanks nominated Birkin to be the executor of her British estate.[34]

Shanks also desired to keep her colonial trading enterprise in female hands, making her youngest daughter, Anna Hassall—the woman who would be buried a decade later in Westminster Abbey—the primary heir to her entire estate and the sole executor of the family's Jamaican holdings. Shanks's decision to hand the business over to her daughter was tactical. Anna Shanks had married a local merchant—Arthur Hassall—a few months before her mother's death. The marriage created a legal connection for the Shanks family to one of the wealthiest merchants in Kingston. Arthur Hassall was the sixth richest merchant to live in the town between 1700 and 1760. Before she died, Shanks nurtured her daughter's alliance with Hassall through her business dealings. Shanks and Hassall operated in an early modern economy that lacked the elemental preconditions, such as institutional banking, credit rating, and professional auditing, for the successful conduct of legitimate business. Britain's commercial empire was sustained by kinship connections through blood and marriage, and these conditions made women central to its economic stability. Mercantile families weathered an unstable and unregulated marketplace by interweaving personal and professional relationships, and intermarriage played a crucial role in establishing alliances and creating access to the lines of credit that made trade possible.[35]

34. Birkin to Shanks, Dec. 17, 1740, Shanks to Birkin, Jan. 6, 1740. Birkin brought Shanks's will to the Prerogative Court of Canterbury in November 1741. The document, "Mrs. Ann Birkin, Admin. of Mrs. Sarah Shanks Deceased," includes a list of expenses paid by Birkin related to the administration of the will. This document is filed under Arthur Hassall's "misc. receipts," October 1741, NAS.

35. Will of Sarah Shanks, Oct. 5, 1739, Jamaica Wills, XXIII; Shanks to Fisher and Co.,

Legally, wedlock subjected women to the common law of coverture and hampered their ability to transact business. In practice, female traders continued their activities after marrying. One scholar has argued that most male merchants never even inquired into a woman's marital status. References in literary works suggest that retailing goods, especially textiles, was a socially accepted and commonplace occupation for women like Shanks and her daughter Hassall. Female colonists from Jamaica, in particular, were strongly associated with trade. For instance, the dubious main character in William Pittis's *Jamaica Lady,* published in 1720, obtains smuggled "*India* Goods" in the form of cotton chintz in Britain by pretending to be a wealthy planter from Jamaica. Thirty years after Pittis published his work, the British courtesan Teresia Constantia Phillips, who achieved notoriety by publishing salacious memoirs about her life, moved to Jamaica. During her time on the island, Phillips, one of the only women to hold a political position in the colony, received an official government post as the "Mistress of Revels." When she returned to London, she allegedly opened a shop and "try'd her fortune in an India warehouse" as a means of repaying her creditors and was said "to have dealt in all manner of India goods." Both women, one real and one fictional, worked as importers or retailers of exotic India imports; their connections to Jamaica are not coincidental. Given the small size of the mercantile community in Kingston, it is even plausible that Phillips befriended female merchants like Hassall and learned how to import "India goods" from them while she was on the island.[36]

Jan. 6, 1740. Only five other men identified as merchants commanded fortunes larger than Hassall's. See Jamaica Inventories. Arthur Hassall was listed as a "merchant and factor" to Julines Beckford and William Willy in a suit filed at the Grand Court. Beckford was a member of one of Jamaica's wealthiest families. The Beckfords gained considerable political power in Britain. See Grand Court Records, 1743, XLI. Richard Grassby stresses the importance of marriage within Britain's merchant community while Peter Mathias contends that marriages "cemented alliances between families with close business interests." See Grasby, *Kinship and Capitalism,* 47; and Mathias, "Risk, Credit, and Kinship," in McCusker and Morgan, eds., *Early Modern Atlantic Economy,* 17, 19. In the absence of these institutions and systems, Mathias argues, people placed a high premium on personal trust and the "kinship nexus" where "reputation, standing, status in the trade depended upon the perceptions of others. . . . There was no distinction to be made between the firm and the person in this respect, as there was none in law" (Ibid., 17, 29).

36. W[illiam] P[ittis], *The Jamaica Lady; or, The Life of Bavia* . . . (London, 1720), 96–98; Teresia Constantia Phillips, *An Apology for the Conduct of Mrs. T. C. Philips* . . . , 3 vols., 2d ed. (London, 1748), III, 206; Zabin, *Dangerous Economies,* 34–37. Cotton textiles manufactured in India were prohibited in Britain at the time of the story's publication. Trevor Burnard and John

For Anna Hassall, who had been groomed by her merchant mother since childhood to manage the family's import-export business, marriage to Arthur Hassall amplified, rather than diminished, her endeavors. She continued to operate her mother's business independently after their wedding, an arrangement that was mutually beneficial to the couple. Hassall adeptly exploited her location in the epicenter of the slave trade, the contraband trade, and imperial warfare. Like her mother, she connected transatlantic trade to the Caribbean basin's brisk intercolonial market in smuggled imports, turning Shanks's venture into a far vaster enterprise. In 1743, she smuggled goods to Spanish territory amid the War of Jenkins' Ear, profiting from a market that reached its apogee in the 1740s. One contemporary account claimed that Jamaica's commerce with Spanish, French, and Dutch territories was worth £1,115,000 per annum, accounting for 80 percent of the empire's total trade with these regions in the Americas.[37]

Hassall typified the kind of colonial entrepreneur who built Britain's commercial empire. Unfettered by imperial politics or contracts, she was one of the creole merchants whose nimbleness and appetite for risk produced ample monetary returns. Hassall's varied contraband ventures brought in £327 of "Spanish coined silver" and forty ounces of "ball gold" along with other Spanish and Portuguese coin. She also took in French sugar and pimento as payments from incoming vessels, amassing her wealth out of illicit trade with Britain's enemies. Like other smugglers, Hassall also lost in the high stakes game that she was playing, but loss was already part of the calculation. New financial instruments enabled Hassall to offset some of the risk. On one voyage, she insured £140 worth of goods on her sloop the *Royal Ranger*, bound for the "Spanish Main." She took out insurance for £1,079 worth of items on another ship destined for Porto Bello just five years after Admiral Edward Vernon's capture of the city. Located on the Isthmus of Panama, Porto Bello was a hotbed of illicit trade. Though the *Royal Ranger*'s trip there proved a bust, Hassall received £63 in insurance compensation for the "loss." By the 1730s, Spanish officials were aggressively searching foreign ships for smuggled commodities. Perhaps a guarda costa or Spanish pirates captured

---

Garrigus refer to Phillips as the "Mistress of Revels" in Burnard and Garrigus, *The Plantation Machine: Atlantic Capitalism in French Saint-Domingue and British Jamaica* (Philadelphia, 2016), 72–77.

37. Kenneth Morgan, "Robert Dinwiddie's Reports on the British American Colonies," *WMQ*, 3d Ser., LXV (2008), 322.

the *Royal Ranger* and seized the contents on board. A year later, Hassall won a suit in the colonial Chancery Court to recover £165 in damages sustained by the *Royal Ranger* during yet another voyage to retail contraband goods.[38]

The world of imperial warfare was rife with perils, but conflict also generated commercial opportunities for traders with a keen eye for profit. During the War of Jenkins' Ear, British privateering increased significantly. More than one hundred ships manned by thousands of sailors were on the prowl for enemy vessels, primarily in the Caribbean. Privateering became a legitimate means of profiteering while also furthering the country's imperial aims. It was a pursuit that Hassall readily engaged in. Already well versed in maritime trade, she switched gears to take advantage of wartime ambiguity and regularly invested in British privateering ventures that set out to capture other European vessels and cargoes.[39]

Commandeering and outfitting a ship for a privateering trip required substantial capital, and few people were wealthy enough or willing to take on the risk of funding their own trips. Instead, Hassall and other private investors bought shares in expeditions. She spent a large sum outfitting a ship for one such trip: Hassall paid the crew's wages, repaired the vessel, and even supplied thirty gallons of rum to keep the sailors in good spirits at sea. She also gave one hundred pounds to the same captain, whom she regularly hired to transport her goods to Spanish territory. Like other colonial traders, Hassall probably outfitted her ship with cannon, running the risk of capture for the reward of inflated wartime prices for smuggled goods. Hassall's contrabanding and privateering activities offer evidence that female colonists were every bit as willing as their male counterparts to flout imperial laws and exploit imperial conflicts for their own profit. Moreover, Jamaica's merchant commu-

38. See "Anna Hassall Account Current with John Meyers," 1743, GD 345/1230, NAS. Work on entrepreneurial Jamaica merchants includes Hancock, *Citizens of the World;* Trevor Burnard, "'The Grant Mart of the Island': The Economic Function of Kingston, Jamaica in the Mid-Eighteenth Century," in Kathleen E. A. Monteith and Glen Richards, eds., *Jamaica in Slavery and Freedom: History, Heritage, and Culture* (Kingston, 2002), 225–241; Burnard, *Planters, Merchants, and Slaves;* and Mann, "Becoming Creole." The Hassall estate maintained a considerable sum of hard currency. Nearly two thousand pounds in cash was found when Arthur died in 1748. See Inventory of Arthur Hassall, 1748, Jamaica Inventories, fol. 164. Anna Hassall added to this monetary reserve through her own contrabanding and privateering activities. For more on privateering in the region, see Dawdy, *Building the Devil's Empire,* 114; and Palmer, *Human Cargoes,* 132–133.

39. Jarvis, *In the Eye of All Trade,* 242–243.

nity accepted women like Shanks and Hassall, rather than excluding them because of their sex.[40]

"AS GOOD AS THEY CAN GET FOR THE MONEY"

As a stakeholder in privateering expeditions, Anna Hassall received a portion of whatever prizes were seized during a voyage. During the first half of the eighteenth century, British prizes were usually Spanish or French ships and consisted of the value of the ship together with all of the cash, goods, and enslaved people that were found aboard. One of Hassall's investments paid off in 1745, when a privateering ship that she had hired brought a Spanish vessel, the *San José y las animas,* into port in Jamaica. As part of the prize, Hassall would obtain an estimated ninety-eight pounds in return for the sale of seven enslaved African, who had likely already endured multiple reshipments across the Atlantic and Caribbean. Rather than being treated as prisoners of war, enslaved sailors were handled as prize goods and sold. Another reference to "one third ransom of sundry negroe slaves takn by the ship tartar" demonstrates that stealing people was a strategy that Hassall deployed during the privateering ventures that she organized.[41]

Merging slavery with privateering and illicit trade, Hassall's schemes exemplified the high-risk and high-reward type of business that thrived in Kingston's exploitative commercial environment. Although she did not rely on hundreds of slaves to perform the kind of intensive agricultural labor sugar planters demanded, Hassall still maintained a sizeable retinue of captives. As an enslaver, Hassall diverged from her English-born mother, Sarah Shanks, who did not own any slaves when she died. Unlike her mother, Hassall came of age in Kingston—not Britain—during an era when the city's interests were profoundly intertwined with Atlantic slavery.

One of the earliest maps of Kingston, Michael Hay's 1740 plan of Kingston, provides a rare yet misleading depiction of Hassall's hometown (Plate 4). The map displays an orderly and flourishing port laid out in a grid of numbered lots. The properties increase in size as they move away from the harbor and from the noises, smells, and sounds that emanated from its busy

40. "Anna Hassall Account Current with John Meyers," Oct. 22, 1748, GD 345/1230, NAS. Jarvis describes Bermudian mariners taking similar steps to turn ships into privateering vessels (Jarvis, *In the Eye of All Trade,* 240).

41. Inventory of Arthur Hassall, 1748, Jamaica Inventories, fol. 164; "Anna Hassall Account Current with John Meyers," Oct. 22, 1745; Jarvis, *In the Eye of All Trade,* 247.

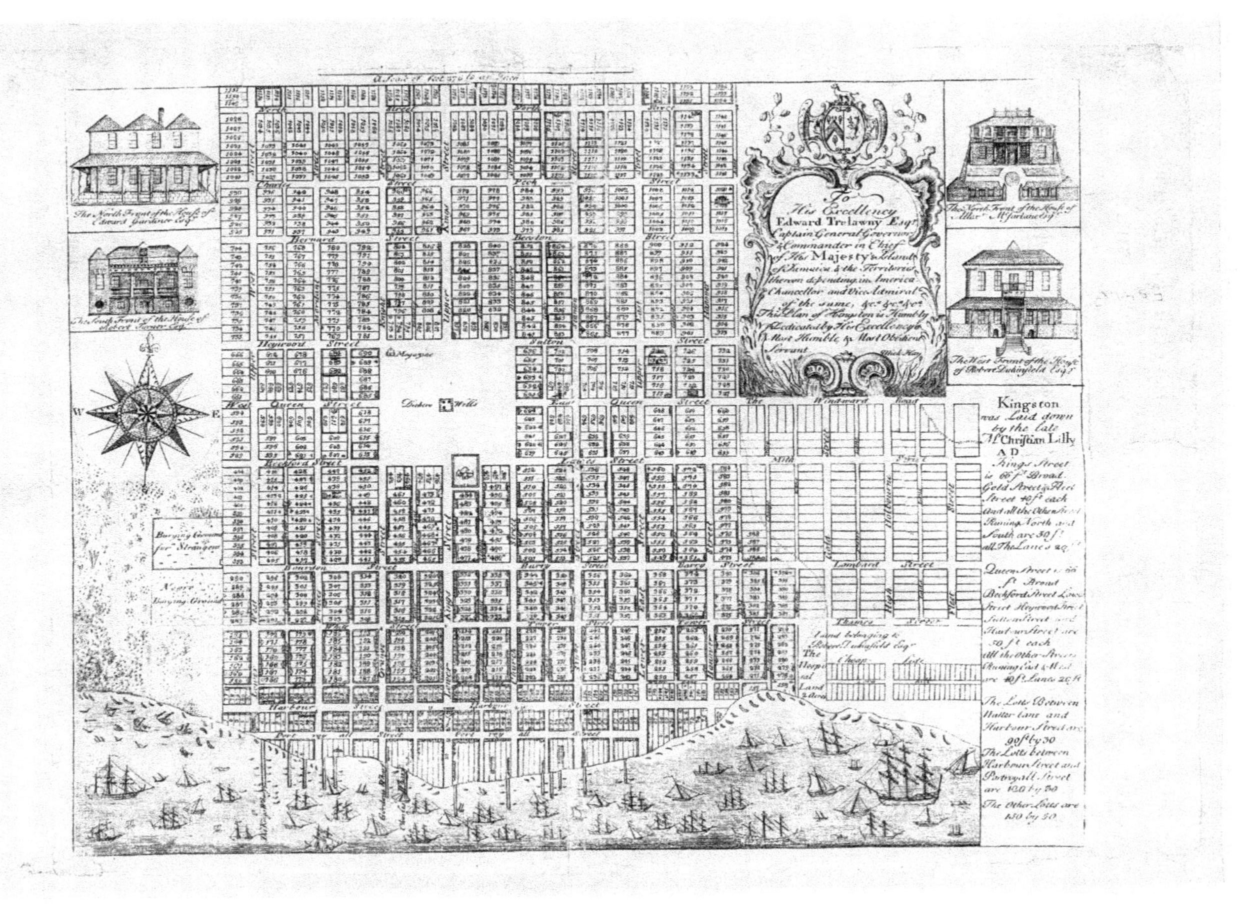

PLATE 4. [Plan of Kingston], by Michael Hay. [1745?]. Courtesy, Library of Congress, Geography and Maps Division, G4964. K5646 1745 .H3

Hay's 1740 map of Kingston features the houses of the town's most prominent residents, emphasizing Kingston's wealth, as well as the harbor teaming with the ships that produced its riches. The "Negro Burying Ground" on the left-hand corner next to the "Burying Ground for Strangers" is the only direct reference to slavery.

docks, where hundreds of ships were moored. The street names blend generic references to imperial Britain—"Charles," "Queen," and "Thames"—intermingled with local luminaries, such as "Beckford," "Lawes," and "Beeston." Four blocks inland, the Parade, or town square, flanked with the ornate homes of Kingston's wealthiest merchants and slave traders, forms the center of town. "Dickers Wells," located in the middle of the Parade and likely named after Samuel Dicker, one of Kingston's most affluent merchants, provided the town with its only source of fresh water. A magazine for weapons and gunpowder, built in the upper left corner of the Parade, underscores the need for constant vigilance against slave revolts and external attacks by European rivals and pirates.[42]

In their attempt to promote Kingston as an orderly and modern space, however, the mapmakers erased the town's biggest business. Though the harbor teeming with ships of all sizes emphasizes Kingston's prominence in overseas trade, the map offers no clues about the nature of this commerce. It cloaks the contents of many of the ships' cargoes, which were, not manufactured goods, but sick and terrified African people. The smaller canoes that appear on the map were probably used to ferry survivors of the Middle Passage from the dark and stinking hulls of slavers into the heat of the Caribbean sun. The mapmakers depicted the narrow lots that lined the harbor on Port Royal Street, but they did not identify these parcels of land, which would have been filled with people. Thousands of enslaved Africans were branded, sorted by perceived health, age, ethnicity, and gender, and seasoned in Kingston's yards. The lots were holding pens for these captives, most of whom would be forcibly separated from friends and shipmates, put aboard slavers again, and resold elsewhere in the Americas.[43]

What Hay's 1740 Map of King's Town leaves out and what Hassall's letters only refer to obliquely is Kingston's centrality to the British slave trade. In turn, these omissions belie the importance of the trade to Britain's growing economic and military dominance. When the War of the Spanish Succession

42. Samuel Dicker possessed a fortune of £30,014 when he died in 1762. See Burnard, *Planters, Merchants, and Slaves*, 285. Michael Hay's plan of Kingston, shown in Plate 4, is a more complete view of the same map that appears in the Introduction (Plate 1) and shows the location of Elizabeth Keyhorne's house.

43. Trevor Burnard refers to extensive slave yards on the streets adjoining Kington's harbor. More than three thousand captive Africans were held in the pens on Port Royal, Orange, and Harbour Streets, which he describes as "the most densely slave-populated streets in eighteenth century British America." See Burnard, *Planters, Merchants, and Slaves*, 205.

wound down in 1713, England wrested the asiento contract from France to act as the exclusive supplier of slaves to Spanish colonies as part of the Treaty of Utrecht. The crown then gave the nascent South Sea Company a monopoly on all trade to Spanish territories. By 1719, the company had closed down its factory in Barbados and transferred its operations to Jamaica, making the decades old "King's Town" its American headquarters. Like the Royal African Company in the seventeenth century, the constitution of the South Sea Company interwove Britain's national interest with Atlantic slavery. By 1729, the company gave up on sending its own ships to West Africa and began purchasing the majority of its slaves from the private traders who swarmed to Kingston. The privatization of the slave trade produced staggering results. Jamaica's involvement in slaving outstripped the activities of all of Britain's other colonies. Between 1711 and 1740, more than 140,000 captive Africans arrived in Jamaica. Nearly half of these people were then reshipped to Spanish territories. The island—and Kingston in particular—played a central role in circulating slaves throughout the Americas. As the only British colony located in the Greater Antilles, Jamaica's geographic location made it ideally suited for transshipping slaves from West Africa or elsewhere in the Caribbean to the Spanish Main. Sailing from Kingston to Cartagena, Veracruz, or Portobello took a few days. Throughout the eighteenth century, an estimated 37 percent of all British slave ships landed in Jamaica, and, until 1758, Kingston was their only port of entry. During the company's heyday, Jamaica's role was even more significant. Arnold Palmer determines that between 1714 and 1739, 59 percent of all slave ships that docked in Spanish America came from Kingston.[44]

The South Sea Company's presence in Kingston amplified the colony's involvement in Atlantic slavery. The surviving census taken in 1730 reveals with stark clarity the increasing influence of the slave trade on the island's urban areas. Enslaved people comprised an estimated two-thirds of Port Royal's

44. Palmer, *Human Cargoes,* 9–12, 15, 59, 98–99. Abigail Swingen makes the point about the relationship between the slave trade and imperial expansion in the seventeenth century (Swingen, *Competing Visions of Empire,* xxiv, 172–193). Gregory O'Malley estimates that 59,280 Africans (42 percent of the total slaves arriving in the colony) were reshipped to foreign colonies between 1711–1740, whereas departures from all Britain's colonies in the Lesser Antilles totaled 14,950 during the same period (O'Malley, *Final Passages,* Table 13, 222). See also Burnard and Garrigus, *Plantation Machine,* 80–82; and Mann, "Becoming Creole," 33. For the 1758 date, Mann cites Trevor Burnard and Kenneth Morgan, "The Dynamics of the Slave Market and Slave Purchasing Patterns in Jamaica, 1655–1788," *WMQ,* 3d Ser., LVIII (2001), 205–228.

and Kingston's populations: 1,562 slaves resided in Port Royal, and 2,724 captives lived in Kingston. The 1730 census was created during the Maroon War—a conflict between the African-descended inhabitants who lived in the island's mountainous interior and colonial slaveholders. The Maroon War, which was seen as the largest threat to the survival of British Jamaica during the first half of the eighteenth century, motivated Governor Robert Hunter (1728–1734) to order the census taken. The Maroons were numerous, highly organized, and successful. Some were the descendants of escaped or freed Spanish slaves who had inhabited the island long before English soldiers stepped foot on its shores. Others claimed Amerindian ancestry. Their numbers were bolstered with a steady stream of slaves who fled from a deplorable state of captivity.[45]

Describing the war as an "unhappy situation of affairs," the 1730 census takers attributed the "success" of the Maroons, whom they labeled as "rebellious negroes," to the growth of the island's enslaved population. In addition to emphasizing the disparity between free and enslaved people, they organized the members of free society into a hierarchy based on wealth, legal status, age, race, and, in some instances, gender. Free "masters" and "mistresses" were placed at the top rung. This select group, which included 185 residents in Port Royal and 504 residents in Kingston, was not categorized by gender or race (Figure 2). Instead, elite status was treated as the most salient feature of this group. In contrast, free "negro, Indian and mulatto" men, women, and children were distinguished from "white" male and female "servants." Though the census lumped boys and girls together as "children," it also separated them by racial descriptors. In Port Royal, 254 children were labeled as "white" and 27 characterized as "free" and "negro, Indian and

45. "Jamaica to His Majesty, Relating to the Unhappy Situation of Affairs of That Island," Feb. 11, 1731, CO 137/19, II. The Maroons divided themselves into two major groups: the Windward Maroons lived in the eastern mountains and the Leeward Maroons in the west. Together, they wreaked havoc in rural areas and halted the growth of the sugar plantation complex. As David Barry Gaspar has observed, slave revolts in antiquity and in the Americas suggest a strong correlation between "a low master-slave ratio and insurrection." This was exactly the kind of society built by settlers in Jamaica. See Gaspar, "A Dangerous Spirit of Liberty: Slave Rebellion in the West Indies in the 1730s," in Laurent Dubois and Julius S. Scott, eds., *Origins of the Black Atlantic* (New York, 2010), 13–15. See also Richard S. Dunn, *Sugar and Slaves: The Rise and Fall of the Planter Class in the English West Indies, 1624–1713* (Williamsburg, Va., and Chapel Hill, N.C., 1972), 259–262; and Kathleen Wilson, "The Performance of Freedom: Maroons and the Colonial Order in Eighteenth-Century Jamaica and the Atlantic Sound," *WMQ*, 3d Ser., LXVI (2009), 56–59.

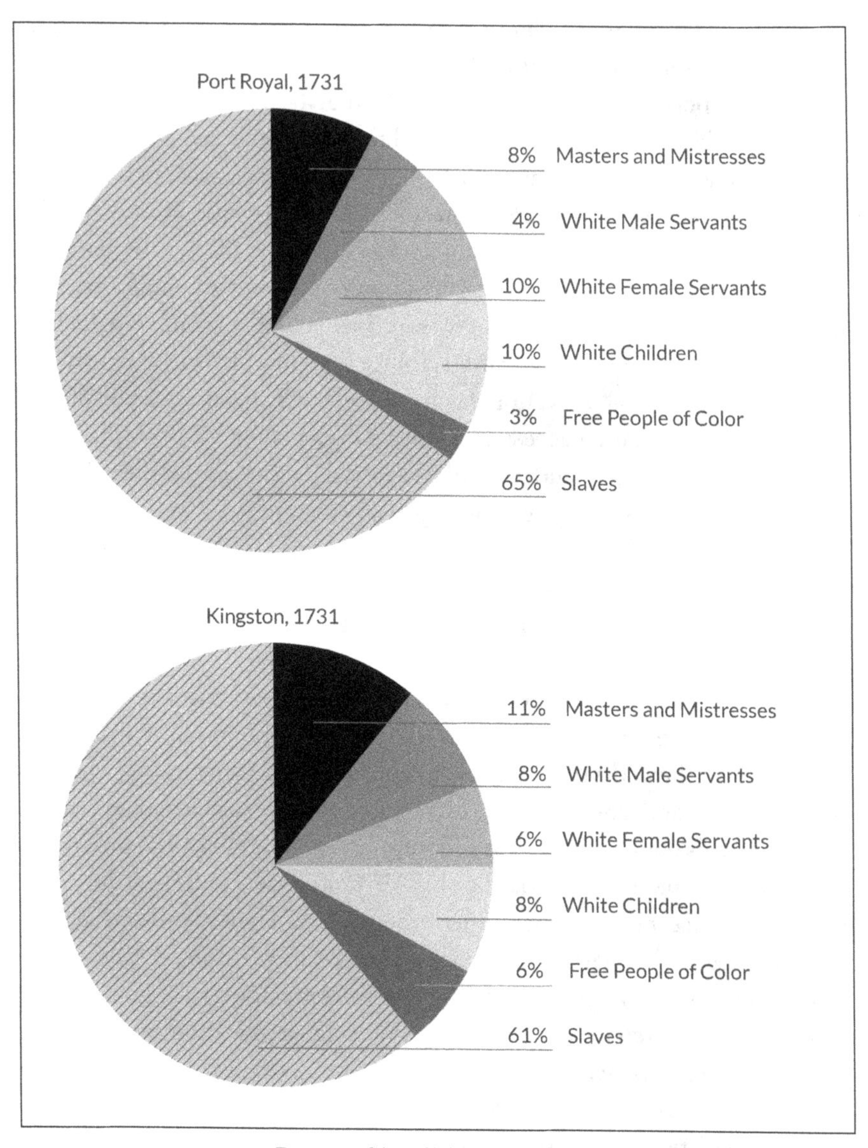

FIGURE 2. Demographics of Kingston and Port Royal, 1731.
Source: "Jamaica to His Majesty, Relating to the Unhappy Situation of Affairs of That Island, by the Increase and Success of Their Rebellious Negroes," Feb. 11, 1731, CO 137/19, II, NAE.

mulatto"; in Kingston 365 children were listed as "white" and 136 as "free" and "negro, Indian and mulatto."[46]

From the perspective of colonial officials, the Maroon War turned any free person of African descent into a potential threat. Their skin color connected them to a past marked by slavery, which implied, it was assumed, that they might harbor sympathies for and even aid the Maroon cause. By constructing race as a fixed and visible aspect of a person's identity, the census sought to assert control over a potentially unruly populace during a tumultuous time. In reality, these institutional efforts were ineffectual. Colonists paid little regard to the violence and social instability fomented by the expansion of slavery. The continual arrival of slaving vessels in Kingston harbor offered islanders unprecedented access to captive African laborers. Both the South Sea Company and independent traders labeled people whom they deemed to be less saleable to highly selective Spanish customers as "refuse negroes" and sold them locally—a practice colonists repeatedly complained about. But, by the early eighteenth century, second- and third-generation islanders were already deeply invested in slaveholding. They readily exploited the proliferation of captive Africans in Jamaica.[47]

Soon after the arrival of the South Sea Company, colonists began setting aside money in their wills to purchase African people directly from slave ships. Parents showed a particular preference for purchasing captive children as companions and assets for their own children. Thomas Cammack, for instance, gave his daughter a "negro girl Juno" in 1722; he also made provisions for "another to be bought aboard a ship" if Juno died. He treated Juno like an easily replaceable piece of property because he knew that his daughter had ready access to a market in affordable young African captives. The widow Mary Walker, another Kingston resident and a contemporary of Cammack's, also wanted to purchase African children for her family. She carefully distributed ten slaves between her son and daughter. Walker then asked her executors to collect nineteen pounds from the sale of an enslaved man that they were "immediately on receipt" to use to purchase two enslaved girls "out of the first Guinea" ship that arrived in Kingston's port "as good as they can get for the money." Walker treated the town's growing involvement in Atlantic slavery as an opportunity to furnish her own family with children who were

46. "Jamaica to His Majesty, Relating to the Unhappy Situation of Affairs of That Island," Feb. 11, 1731, CO 137/19, II. It is unclear why the census takers only sorted servants—not masters and mistresses or free people of African and Indian descent—by sex.

47. AGI, Indiferente, 2847, quoted in Palmer, *Human Cargoes*, 62.

abducted from Africa. Her reference to Guinea on the west coast of Africa signaled her awareness of the region where much of Britain's slaving activities occurred, and she probably attended the slave auctions that took place in Kingston (Plate 5).[48]

By the 1720s, women like Walker were already well versed in the parlance of the Atlantic slave trade. Urban residents were not the only ones who engaged in Kingston's slave market, though. Its reach was island wide. When Anne Barrow of Westmoreland Parish made her will in 1714, she offered seventy pounds to her daughter for the "purchase of negros to be markt A. B." Barrow wanted her initials to be inscribed on the bodies of Africans after her death, ensuring that her claim to them would endure beyond the grave. In 1729, Mary Hussey, a widow who settled in Hanover Parish, ordered two "negro women to be bought from on board of ship immediately after my death on the first opportunity." The women were to be given to her two daughters, and Hussey used them to influence the girls' relationship after her death, offering her elder daughter fifty acres of land and seven enslaved people if she gave "the negro woman aforementioned" to her younger sister. Another country dweller, Mary Cussans, distributed eighteen captives between her two daughters and set aside twenty-one pounds for her executors to "purchase" a "new negro girl" for one of them. As second-generation colonists, women like Barrow and Cussans were fully vested in slave labor. By either directly or indirectly involving their daughters and granddaughters in the slave market, they normalized slaveholding and strengthened the ties between female heirs and Atlantic slavery.[49]

Mothers and fathers who preferred to give enslaved children to their own children also shaped the demographic characteristics of Atlantic slavery. Slave traders alleged that their Spanish customers preferred to purchase adult men, and contemporary scholars generally accept this assumption. Jamaican parents, on the contrary, exhibited a strong interest in buying young Africans as gifts for their children. This unstudied local trend indicates that the buying preferences of customers in the Americas were more diversified than has

48. Will of Thomas Cammack, 1722, Jamaica Wills, XVI, Will of Mary Walker, 1718, XV.

49. Will of Anne Barrow, 1714, Jamaica Wills, XIV, Will of Mary Hussey, 1729, XVIII, Will of Mary Cussans, 1745, XXV. Trevor Burnard's sample of twenty-five slave voyages in which the purchaser's name was listed leads him to conclude that "women were not prominent as slave buyers." See Burnard, "'Gay and Agreeable Ladies,'" *Wadabagei* (2006), 34. The wills used in this chapter, however, suggest that women regularly purchased slaves directly from slave ships and exhibited detailed knowledge of the slave trade.

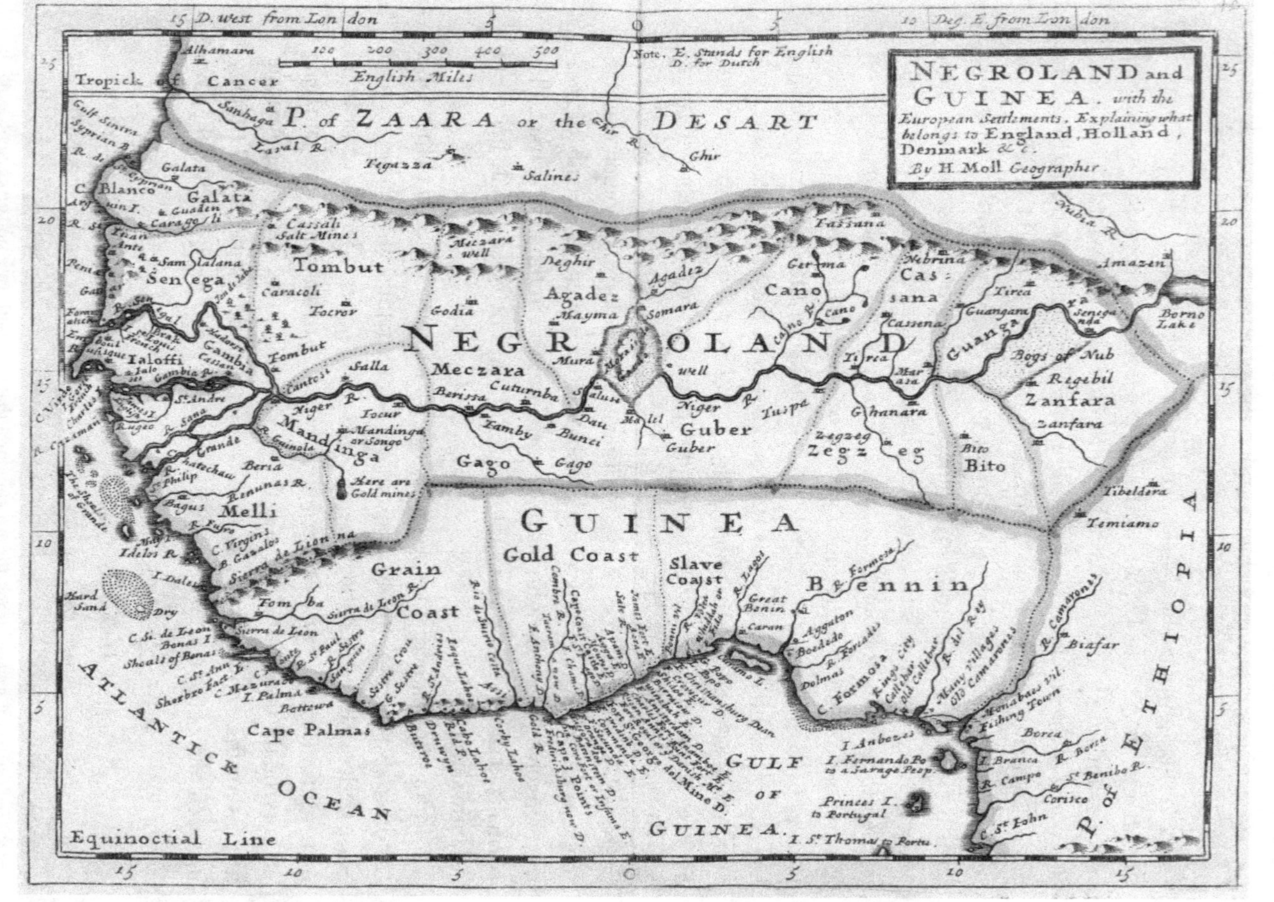

PLATE 5. *Negroland and Guinea,* by Herman Moll. 1736. Courtesy of David Rumsey Map Collection, https://www.davidrumsey.com/

been understood. Jamaican slaveholders created a demand for African children, viewing malleable youths as the ideal companions, laborers, and property for their own offspring. These perceptions rippled across the Atlantic, robbing African families of young people to fill colonial preferences.[50]

When Elizabeth Cross of Saint Ann Parish made her will in 1745, she owned an Atlantic portfolio of property that included land in Boston and Jamaica. She also controlled and planned to purchase more people. Her directives groomed the young members of her family to become slaveholders and participants in the Atlantic slave trade. In addition to bequeathing captives to her children, Cross set aside seven pounds for each of her granddaughters to purchase a "negro girl" on her tenth birthday. Planter William Farrell made similar plans for his infant daughter. Although she was "not christened" yet in 1740, the father set aside seventy-four pounds for his executors to buy "new negroes" from a slave ship for the child, involving her in the slave trade before she had even been named.[51]

By the 1740s, colonists like Cross and Farrell could not imagine a future devoid of slavery. They treated slave ships as repositories of valuable gifts, especially in the form of young people, for their own children and grandchildren. When the widow Jane Chisolm undertook the voyage from Jamaica to New York in 1748, she made this practice explicit, setting aside money for her father to "buy a negro girl and make a present of her" to her aunt and to "buy another girl and make her a present" to her nephew. Chisolm's bequests laid the groundwork for a series of transactions that would result in the abduction and transportation of children from Africa to Kingston and then to New York. Viewing young Africans strictly as "present[s]," Chisolm did not consider the profound trauma, loss, and disorientation that her instructions would cause them.[52]

The wills made by Chisolm and other colonists also divulge a connection

50. Spanish customers might have preferred male laborers along with some women and girls for the sex trade, making it plausible that more children were left behind in Jamaica. But colonists also actively sought to purchase children. In his study of the Portuguese slave trade, David Wheat shows that children comprised up to one-third of the migrants who were forced from West Africa to America. He attributes this trend to "slave production" in West Africa rather than Spanish demand. See Wheat, *Atlantic Africa and the Spanish Caribbean, 1570–1640* (Williamsburg, Va., and Chapel Hill, N.C., 2016), 72, 94, 97. Gregory O'Malley's work on the British slave trade in the eighteenth century also stresses the overrepresentation of male captives. See O'Malley, *Final Passages*, 237.

51. Will of Elizabeth Cross, 1745, Jamaica Wills, XXV, Will of William Farrell, 1740, XXII.

52. Will of Jane Chisolm, 1748, Jamaica Wills, XXVI.

between a woman's marital status and the slave market. Islanders viewed African captives to be an especially suitable form of support for widows and unmarried women. In 1739, Margaret Proudfoot of Port Royal wanted her entire "personal estate" to be liquidated and used "for purchasing negros" for her eldest daughter, Ann Prichard. Already widowed, Prichard would presumably buy the captives from a slave ship herself. The financial interests of Edward Phips and his widowed daughter, Ann Coles, to whom he was indebted, were also enmeshed in slaveholding. The father owed Coles for keeping in his "possession" a "negro wench named Progue" belonging to her. Exploiting his family's ready access to a market in enslaved people, Phips offered his daughter £222, instructing her to purchase "choice new negroes two men and two women" as well as "a new negro girl to wait on her" with the money. The father assumed that his daughter, whom he had raised to act as a slaveholder, had the necessary experience and connections to purchase a retinue of unfree laborers on her own.[53]

Rather than submit, enslaved people tested the strength of female rule. Three of the nine ads for runaway servants and slaves that appear in a 1718 edition of the *Weekly Jamaica Courant* were published by women. A captive woman named Nanne deserted her owner, a Mrs. Mary Hales from Kingston. Hales described Nanne as a "Creole Negro Wench," suggesting that she had been born in America. Nanne bore the imprint of slavery on her skin—her right shoulder was branded, which she might have covered up with the "Ozenabrig Jacket" that she wore with a white petticoat and a white handkerchief. Nanne was an urban dweller who probably worked as a servant or cook for Hales. Another woman, Rose, identified by her owner, Mrs. Drakes, as a "Yallow Negroe Wench," had also been branded on her right shoulder. Denigrated as "wenches" and racially typed by their owners as a "Creole negro" and a "yallow negro," Rose and Nanne might have absconded to escape the desperate conditions that their female owners subjected them to.[54]

53. Will of Margaret Proudfoot, 1739, Jamaica Wills, XXII, Will of Edward Phips, 1740, XXII.

54. "Run away from Mrs. Mary Hales," and "Run away from *Mrs. Drakes*," *Weekly Jamaica Courant* (Kingston), July 30, 1718. The newspaper was printed by R. Baldwin, who set up a print shop on Church Street in Kingston. Douglas B. Chambers has compiled and edited a list of the paid runaway slave ads that were published in Jamaican papers during certain months and years between 1718–1795. The records are sporadic until the 1770s, when they become far more comprehensive. See Chambers, ed., "Runaway Slaves in Jamaica (I): Eighteenth Century" (University of Southern Mississippi, 2013), http://docplayer.net/53138763-Runaway-slaves-in-jamaica-i-eighteenth-century-edited-by-douglas-b-chambers-university-of-southern-mississippi-february-2013-1.html.

Enslaved people like Rose and Nanne served economic, legal, and social purposes for free and freed women—objectives the two women challenged by running away. As a form of valuable movable property, captives fetched high prices in the local marketplace. As unpaid workers, slaves provided essential labor for female-run businesses. Free and freed women treated slaves as a form of currency in a variety of financial transactions, from financing debts and mortgages to funding their own funerals. In 1720, Mary Manton planned to sell a male captive, Robin, to pay off her debts and underwrite her burial expenses. Manton then ordered her executors to sell an enslaved boy if Robin's sale did not cover the costs. Similarly, when Dorothy Stout made her will in 1739, she planned to pay off her mortgage by selling eight of her slaves.[55]

Whether they operated taverns and shops or large mercantile outfits, women relied on African captives to perform the domestic tasks of cooking, cleaning, washing, and childcare. Enslaved people also served customers, loaded ships, and worked as sailors. Tavernkeeping, a commonplace occupation for women elsewhere in British America, was especially lucrative in Kingston, where the labor performed by enslaved people amplified the earnings of service-oriented establishments. Elizabeth Webster enjoyed a comfortable living from her tavern in the 1720s. Although she was married, Webster owned and operated the venture independently from her husband. Her tavern was a bustling multifunctional space where her customers sat on "thirty old chairs," ate off of pewter or china plates, drank from the ubiquitous silver punch bowl, and whiled away their time at three backgammon tables. Webster parlayed her proximity to a busy port to obtain a range of imports, which she also retailed, selling rolls of tobacco, candy, soap, split peas, and bitters to pipes and shoes. Located near Kingston's slave market, Webster's business also capitalized on the labor of seven captives. These people probably worked in the sweltering kitchen preparing food in iron and brass pots, saucepans, and dripping pans, boiling tea in the kettles, and making hot chocolate in a copper chocolate pot for Webster's customers.[56]

Webster's varied operation, which combined domestic service, retail, and

55. Will of Mary Manton, 1720, Jamaica Wills, XV; James Stout v. Thomas Verdon and wife (late Martha Stout), Sept. 28, 1739, Chancery Court Records, X, JA.

56. Inventory of Elizabeth Webster, 1733, Jamaica Inventories, fol. 119. Linda Sturtz studies women who operated taverns or ordinaries in colonial Virginia (Sturtz, *Within Her Power*, 89–110). Jarvis makes a similar point about trade in Bermuda (Jarvis, *In the Eye of All Trade*, 294–295).

slavery, proved to be profitable. When she died in 1733, her estate was valued at £418, placing the tavernkeeper firmly in Jamaica's middling echelon. Webster left behind silver girdle buckles, a pearl necklace, gold rings, gold buttons, and earrings—adornments that signified her success to locals, transient customers, and her enslaved workforce. A "parcel of old books" and a Bible attested to Webster's literacy; her small arsenal of guns, pistols, and swords hints at the violent society she was helping to construct, one that was continually threatened by slave revolts and imperial warfare.[57]

The widow Elizabeth Roach, a contemporary of Webster's, achieved a much vaster fortune than Webster, selling a larger array of British imports, from children's shoes, hornbooks, and silk to mourning buckles, looking glasses, shoe brushes, and spectacles. Roach also owned twenty-seven slaves who comprised a quarter of the value of her sizable £2,484 estate. The probated inventory of her estate provides no details about the nature of the labor that these people did. Some of the captives probably worked as servants who maintained Roach's large and well-appointed house. Two elbow chairs, ten cane chairs, a large oval table, a "scritore" or writing desk, a looking glass, clock, and six pictures adorned her hallway. The number of chairs suggests that the widow regularly entertained guests and clients, while her writing desk signifies Roach's education and her connection to an Atlantic epistolary culture. Roach slept on a luxurious featherbed, kept her gowns and petticoats in a mahogany dresser, and served her guests with a full tea set. She traveled around the island in a chaise coach driven by one of her slaves. Richer than the average West Indian colonist, Roach attained a vaunted social position. As a widow, she maintained legal control of her estate. As a slaveowner, she wielded absolute authority over the twenty-seven people who made her enterprise function on a daily basis.[58]

Anna Hassall capitalized on the business model established by women entrepreneurs like Roach, who effectively combined overseas trade with slave labor. Hassall and her husband lived in a household that merged their personal and professional interests. Captive Africans and young men from the

57. Will of Elizabeth Webster, 1733, Jamaica Wills, XIX. Though a girl's "satin" body coat was found amid Webster's possessions, she made no mention of a child and left her entire estate to her husband. In her will, Webster self-identified, first and foremost, by her occupation as a "tavern keeper." The recordkeepers likewise followed suit in her probated inventory. She named a male tavernkeeper living in Kingston, not a relative, to act as the executor of her estate.

58. Inventory of Elizabeth Roach, 1732, Jamaica Inventories, fol. 215. For more on the significance of correspondence in the Atlantic world, see Pearsall, *Atlantic Families.*

British Isles shared this domestic workspace. The "counting house stools" in Arthur Hassall's inventory indicate that the couple employed at least five clerks who operated in a large office that was likely in the back of the house. The couple probably tasked enslaved men, including Greenwich, Pompey, and Cuffee, with unloading and reloading ships that arrived in the harbor laden with imports destined for reexport. Female captives like Hannah, Bella, and Violet might have organized, sorted, and prepared the vast array of items stockpiled in the Hassall warehouse. The enslaved women, likely dressed in coarse ozenbrig linen, would have spent their days handling luxurious silver and gold silk, taffeta, lawn, and linen textiles. They likely used the "press for cambric and lawn" to iron the high-quality cotton before sale and counted boxes of candles, scissors, knives, and soap. An older enslaved woman or a child would have tended the herd of twenty-six goats and kids and sixteen sheep that the Hassalls kept on their property for meat and milk.[59]

Furnished to the hilt with exotic and luxurious imports, the Hassall home attested to the prosperity and status of Kingston's mercantile elite. Forty-four framed pictures and twelve "India prints" adorned the walls, visually linking the West Indian dwelling to a valuable line of trade with the East Indies. Several of the women and children whom Hassall owned would have been employed as domestic servants. They would have been tasked with maintaining the material emblems of the Hassalls' professional success, polishing the chairs and the two dining tables carved out of prized Jamaican mahogany. Perhaps they also handled the spits, frying pan, and stew pan to cook over an open fire in a kitchen building located outside of the dwelling house. They would have served meals on china plates to Hassall and her guests, poured them drinks in costly glasses, and emptied their bedpans and close stools.[60]

Though domestic laborers performed the essential tasks related to running a mercantile household, the Hassalls' large trading venture required a far more diversified workforce. The two enslaved men who were identified by their occupations in Arthur's 1748 estate inventory—London, a cooper, and Lorkra, a sailor—were indispensable and highly skilled laborers. An accomplished craftsman, London transformed wood into watertight con-

59. Inventory of Arthur Hassall, 1748, Jamaica Inventories, fol. 164. Scholarship on women's work during the early modern period in both Britain and America has been disassociated from slavery. Notable exceptions include Beckles, "White Women and Slavery in the Caribbean," *History Workshop Journal*, XXXVI (1993), 66–82; and Hartigan-O'Connor, *Ties That Buy*.

60. Inventory of Arthur Hassall, 1748, Jamaica Inventories, fol. 164. All of these objects are listed in the probated inventory of Arthur Hassall's estate, which his wife inherited.

tainers, which were crucial for carrying goods, especially sugar and rum, across the ocean. An able sailor, Lorkra probably manned Hassall's ship, the *Royal Ranger*, on smuggling voyages to the Spanish coast and on privateering ventures. These kinds of arrangements were commonplace in Britain's Caribbean colonies. In Bermuda, enslaved sailors supported white widows with the wages they earned. Lorkra's position as a sailor made him one of the most autonomous captives that Hassall commanded after her husband died. Aboard ships, free and enslaved sailors were treated with rough parity. As knowledgeable and experienced workers, London and, especially, Lorkra were likely more mobile and independent; they might have saved some of their earnings and stood a greater chance of purchasing their freedom.[61]

If Lorkra and London resided at one end of the spectrum of enslavement, enjoying a degree of mobility and even living as de facto free men, then Silvester, the man who was described as a "Spanish negro with one leg" in Arthur Hassall's inventory, occupied the other end of the continuum. Either born in a Spanish colony or in Africa, Silvester might have been a free sailor on a Spanish vessel who lost his leg and was then captured and enslaved on one of Hassall's privateering ventures. During wartime, the governor of Jamaica allowed British captains to impress Spanish prisoners into service, and colonial governments treated free men of African descent as slaves rather than as prisoners of war. Given that Hassall funded privateering ships, perhaps he acquired Silvester through similar mercenary activities. Silvester's limited mobility severely reduced his monetary value. He was appraised at just ten pounds, not much more than the child, Jone, who was valued at five pounds. Hobbling about the Hassall estate, Silvester stood little chance of escaping from bondage. Silvester was not the only one who suffered in the Hassall household. When Arthur Hassall's estate was probated, four slaves were listed as either sick or dead.[62]

61. London and Lorkra were valued at one hundred pounds (Ibid.). Michael Jarvis discusses the mobility of enslaved sailors and the reliance of households headed by widows on their wages. See Jarvis, *In the Eye of All Trade,* 148–149. See also Jane G. Landers, *Atlantic Creoles in the Age of Revolutions* (Cambridge, Mass., 2010); Peter Linebaugh and Marcus Rediker, *The Many-Headed Hydra: Sailors, Slaves, Commoners, and the Hidden History of the Revolutionary Atlantic* (Boston, 2000); W. Jeffrey Bolster, *Black Jacks: African American Seamen in the Age of Sail* (Cambridge, Mass., 1997); and Julius Sherrard Scott, III, "The Common Wind: Currents of Afro-American Communication in the Era of the Haitian Revolution" (Ph.D. diss., Duke University, 1986).

62. Inventory of Arthur Hassall, 1748, Jamaica Inventories, fol. 164. A woman named Phillis and her son as well as another woman, Celia, were dead at the time the estate was probated, and

Anna Hassall inherited her husband's holdings when he died in 1748. Soon afterward, she decided to move to London. Her plan prompted her decision to sell off several of the forty-two enslaved people over whom she had assumed control. The wealthy and prominent Kingston merchant Walrond Fearon purchased two men, Southampton and James. Another man, Tom, was also sold. Hassall leveraged the money that she earned from her dealings to help fund an expensive relocation to the imperial capital, leaving the Jamaica-based part of her business in the hands of her attorneys. When she died a few years after the move, another female slaveholder, Hassall's close friend Elizabeth Callender, inherited the remaining thirty-nine people whom Hassall owned.[63]

MONETIZING COLONIAL GAINS IN THE IMPERIAL CAPITAL

Comfortable in both Britain and Jamaica, Hassall was the sort of hybrid figure who both created—and was a creation of—Britain's rapidly expanding and largely unregulated commercial empire. Hassall's journey from the colony to the imperial capital signaled her fortune, status, and Atlantic cosmopolitanism. The merchant spent her childhood crisscrossing the Atlantic on voyages with her mother, Sarah Shanks, who died before she could return to Britain. By relocating to London, Hassall realized her mother's dream.

Hassall, however, did not travel to Britain on her own. She was accompanied by a close friend. Continuing in her mother's footsteps, she developed an intimate financial and personal relationship with another woman, Elizabeth Callender, the widow of a wealthy physician and planter, that resembled Sarah Shanks's rapport with her friend and factor, Ann Birkin. Hassall and Callender shared much in common. Both of the women controlled family estates, managed overseas trading ventures, and acted as slaveholders. When Callender moved to London, she received more than a thousand pounds in exchange for Spanish silver, showing that she, too, might have participated in the contraband trade. Given the personalized nature of early mod-

---

a "sick" slave was at "vendue" or being auctioned for five pounds. Zabin discusses the treatment of free soldiers of African descent as slaves (Zabin, *Dangerous Economies,* 118).

63. Anna Hassall, "Book of Receipts from Purchases in London," from John Hall, July 30, 1748, GD 1/32/34, NAS; Will of Anna Hassall, Feb. 15, 1741 (entered May 16, 1751), Jamaica Wills, XXVIII. Intriguingly, Fearon was listed as a "merchant, Kingston" and the acting executor for Mary Elbridge's estate when she died (Inventory of Mary Elbridge, 1745, Jamaica Inventories, fol. 132). For more on Elbridge, see Chapter 3, below.

ern business, it is likely that the two women engaged in illicit mercantile activities together in Jamaica. After establishing a strong bond in the colony, they determined to relocate to Britain. There, the pair set up house together and acted as intimate friends, business partners, and surrogate spouses. As joint householders, the women also shared a pecuniary interest. Between 1749 and 1750, Callender recorded thirteen entries with Hassall, ranging in value from paying her a little more than one pound for "gold lace bought for my under coat" to forty-five pounds on another occasion. The frequency of these monetary transactions attests to the familiarity and reciprocity of their relationship.[64]

Rather than severing their ties to the colony, settling in the metropole enabled colonists like Hassall and Callender to strengthen the British side of their transatlantic operations, and the women continued to manage their Jamaica interests from London. Hassall, for instance, attempted to collect from her British debtors in person. In 1749, she visited a man named Thomas Savill to demand repayment for a £179 bill of exchange he owed her. Savill had been stalling for time, claiming that he was waiting for a bill from Francis Sadler Halls, a wealthy Afro-European planter, to arrive on a ship from Jamaica to repay her. Like many planters who borrowed on future crops, Halls had assumed a sizable bond worth £3,500 from Hassall in 1746; perhaps she was awaiting payment on this debt as well.[65]

When Hassall arrived at Savill's London home, a scene worthy of an eighteenth-century comedy ensued. Savill cowered upstairs while his wife informed her that he was suffering from gout. Undeterred, Hassall demanded the money. Hearing the fracas below, Savill sent word downstairs that if either of his ships were lost at sea, he would pay her with the insurance money that he received. Of course, there was nothing entertaining about the episode for either Hassall or Savill. Like her mother, Hassall extended credit to men, but their similarities ended there. Whereas Shanks cautiously and ineffectively

64. "Mrs. Callenders New Journal London in Great Brittain," July 11, 1749 (Spanish currency), Dec. 1, 1749, Mar. 2, 1749 (two transactions with Hassall listed), Mar. 21, 1749 (three transactions with Hassall listed), Apr. 12, 1750, May 21, 1750, June 16, 1750 (four transactions with Hassall listed), Sept. 2, 1750, GD 345/1214, NAS.

65. "Account of Notes and Bonds Left by Mrs. Hasall with the Honorable Charles Dawes Esq. and John Hall Esq. in June 1748; With Observations Taken by Alex. Grant This 15th Feb. 1752," GD 1/32/34, NAS. Sadler Halls was the son of Mary Rose, who owned vast sugar plantations in the colony. For reference to Hals, see Anne M. Powers, "The Maroon War Settlement of 1739," A Parcel of Ribbons: Eighteenth-Century Jamaica Viewed through Family Stories and Documents, http://aparcelofribbons.co.uk/2011/11/the-maroon-war-settlement-of-1739/.

sought repayments from Richard Elletson on his mortgage with her, Anna Hassall wielded the wealth and status to treat Savill as her social inferior.[66]

Callender displayed an equally intrepid attitude in her commercial dealings with men. After moving to London, she assumed control of the importation side of her sugar plantation business. She diligently calculated the customs duties on her imported goods and the fees for landing and wharfing the ships and paid to have the sugar weighed and stored in warehouses while awaiting sale. As an absentee planter, it made sense for Callender to hire a colonial manager, Edward Wilson, to handle the daily operations of her Jamaica plantation. Wilson recognized Callender's sophisticated knowledge of the sugar business, writing in one letter, "As you know sugars are ultimately a Legall Tender . . . and you know what a chance a man stands to take sugars valued by two fisherman who never sees any but what they buy to make chocolate with, I thought it best to take them at market price." Wilson did not condescend to Callender because she was a woman. In an effort to justify his decision to sell her sugar at "market price," the employee acknowledged her expertise in the industry, implying that she was fully aware of the value and quality of the sugar that her plantation produced. She also understood the Jamaican custom of using sugar as a form of currency.[67]

Hassall and Callender also remained involved in slavery from their new home in Britain. Callender's disparate relationships with two women—Lucy and Sukey—provide a detailed portrait of the variable dynamics that characterized the relationships between female enslavers and enslaved people. Though Lucy, an enslaved woman, was identified callously as "a negro wench Lucy and her children" in a list of debts owed to Callender's husband, she forged an intimate albeit grossly unequal relationship with Callender. Callender never labeled Lucy as a "negro" or a "slave," calling the woman instead by her name or describing her as a "servant." When Callender decided to move to London, she negotiated the terms of the relocation with Lucy, whom she wanted to accompany her. Lucy, who had children of her own in Jamaica, was reluctant to leave them behind. The two women agreed that Lucy would travel with Callender to Britain, and the slaveholder would then pay for Lucy's voyage home. Callender's attachment to Lucy, her de-

66. Anna Hassall, "Book of Receipts from Purchases in London," unsigned "memorandum" in back of book, Jan. 9, 1749, GD 1/32/34, NAS.

67. Edward Wilson to Elizabeth Callender, Dec. 1, 1749, NAS, Wilson to Callender, Apr. 30, 1751. Callender frequently recorded the shipments of sugar that she received from Jamaica in her account books.

scription of Lucy as a servant, and her willingness to deal with the woman implies that the two might have grown up together, or at least spent years in each other's company.[68]

During the weeks at sea, Lucy probably dressed Callender, arranged her hair, cared for her daughter, and acted as her companion. Though Lucy's role as a domestic servant spared her from the grueling and dangerous labor of sugar cultivation, this does not imply that Lucy's life was qualitatively better. Enslaved people who worked as maids, cooks, and laundresses in their owners' homes endured greater isolation from family and friends than field laborers who lived together in villages on plantations. Some female owners subjected household slaves to chronic physical and emotional abuse. The scant records do not indicate whether Callender mistreated Lucy, but she displayed a level of consideration for the enslaved woman's comfort and health, which indicates that the two shared an asymmetrical yet privileged bond. When they reached Britain, Callender bought Lucy "warm cloths" and paid for a doctor and medicines for her. In turn, Lucy manifested a sense of herself and of her position within the Callender family that superseded her status as a slave.[69]

Once Lucy returned to Jamaica, Callender anxiously asked Edward Wilson, her attorney-manager on the island, for news about her. Wilson's reports back to his employer convey Lucy's displeasure at finding herself in reduced circumstances on the island. Accustomed to enjoying more independence, she chaffed under Wilson's management and signaled her dislike of the man by treating him "indifferently." Though it was a common practice for female slaveholders to earn extra income by hiring slaves out, Lucy bitterly resented Wilson's decision to employ her as a servant in other households. She probably found the work—and the change in her status in Callender's absence—to be demeaning. Though Lucy's actions are highly mediated by Wilson,

68. A separate paper titled "A List of Debts Outstanding on Account of Estate of James Callender Dec., in Jamaica," found in Account Book, no. 3, of Anna Hassall's estate, undated, GD 345/1220, NAS.

69. "Mrs. Callenders New Journal in Great Brittain," Nov. 12, 1748, GD 345/1214, NAS, "Elizabeth Callender's Account Current with Edward Wilson," August 1750, GD 345/1230. Beckles asserts that captives who lived with urban small-scale slaveholders might have experienced greater isolation. See Hilary McD. Beckles, *Natural Rebels: A Social History of Enslaved Women in Barbados* (New Brunswick, N.J., 1989), 55–68. Thavolia Glymph has demonstrated that white women in antebellum North American used terror and violence to control household slaves under their management. See Glymph, *Out of the House of Bondage: The Transformation of the Plantation Household* (Cambridge, 2008), 32–62.

his letters offer rare glimpses of the conduct of an enslaved woman who rejected the terms of her captivity. In turn, her behavior exposes the fissures between Jamaica's rigid slave codes and lived experience. Lucy was described in racialized, gendered, and sexualized terms as a "negro wench" in official documents, but she did not adhere to these categories. Her status as an enslaved woman constrained her capacities, yet Lucy's privileged relationship with Callender empowered her to exercise a modicum of authority in her dynamic with Wilson—a white man who was her superior in every respect in Jamaican society.[70]

Lucy understood that Callender ultimately wielded more power, and commanded more wealth, than her male employee, and she leveraged this knowledge to her advantage. Rather than asking Wilson to discipline the enslaved woman, whom he accused of disobedience, Callender fretted over Lucy's unhappiness. Longing to be reunited with her favorite "servant," Callender attempted to convince Lucy to relocate permanently to England. Lucy, in turn, used her connection with Callender to negotiate the terms of her move across the Atlantic. She would only travel to London, she bargained, if she was accompanied by her child. Wilson reported: "I have told your maid Lucy your intentions of sending for her which she seems well pleas'd with, but at the same time hopes you'l permit her Child to come with her." A vast chasm of social and financial disparities distinguished Lucy from her enslaver. But their relationship also shows the power of emotional bonds to mediate these differences. Though Lucy was legally defined as Callender's property, she asserted a degree of personal authority over her owner, who, desperate for her company, sought to placate and parley with a woman whom she held in bondage. It is unclear whether these negotiations resulted in Lucy and her child sailing across the Atlantic to Britain, but the records suggest that this plan did not come to fruition. In 1750, nearly a year after Wilson relayed Lucy's request to her owner, he recorded the "cash" that he received at "sundry times" for the "hire" of "Lucy" and an enslaved man named Bristol in his account book, indicating that Lucy could have still been in Jamaica and that she was being hired out as a servant.[71]

In contrast, Callender's callous and abusive approach toward another enslaved woman whom she owned, Sukey, emphasizes the role of intimacy in

70. John Hall to Elizabeth Callender, 1749, GD 345/1230, NAS.

71. Edward Wilson to Elizabeth Callender, July 12, 1749, GD 345/1230, NAS, "Elizabeth Callender's Account Current with Edward Wilson," August 1750. Lucy and Bristol earned roughly forty-two pounds in wages.

yielding protection and preferential treatment from enslavers—a dynamic that Lucy effectively utilized and Sukey did not. In the absence of these bonds, enslaved people could be subjected to a high degree of instability and severe treatment. Like Lucy, Sukey was probably a domestic servant in Callender's household. She had children to care for, and, when one of them fell ill with smallpox, John Hall, Callender's other Jamaica manager, accused Sukey of "making excuses" to nurse her sick child instead of working. Sukey also suffered from poor health. In their letters to Callender, Wilson and Hall characterized Sukey as deceptive, lazy, and disobedient, portraying her actions as ruses to avoid work. Wilson described Sukey as "very idle" and "pretending [to] so much sickness." In her responses, Callender displayed little concern for Sukey, whom she viewed as a slave, not a beloved "maid" like Lucy.[72]

Rather than sympathize with Sukey, Callender exercised the full range of her authority as a slaveholder over her. First, she ordered Wilson to send her to the jail in Kingston, a common penalty for enslaved people who were accused of defiance. The crowded, filthy, and pestilent prison must have been a terrible place for a woman who already suffered from poor health. Worse was yet to come. Callender's other attorney manager reported that "Sukey is in Gaol and I believe the best way will be to ship her off . . . she has not brought a farthing this great while." Locals used transportation to other colonies as another means of harshly disciplining enslaved people who were identified as rebellious. Defined as insubordinate, charged with failing to provide income for the Callender estate, and imprisoned for her alleged intransigence, Sukey was then sold. In 1750, Wilson recorded a payment to a man for selling "a negroe woman suckey (Sukey)" and her "child." The records do not mention whether the mother and child were sold to the same owner or if they faced a traumatic separation from one another.[73]

Lucy operated within Jamaica's evolving slave system, strategically calling on her intimacy with Callender to keep her family intact. Alternatively, Sukey's lack of a relationship with her owner had devastating consequences. The dynamics between Callender, Lucy, and Sukey were not unique. Strong interpersonal ties between enslavers and slaves shaped the nature of bondage. The dissimilar life outcomes for Lucy and Sukey illustrate this point. Some captives, like Lucy, lived as de facto free people while others, like Sukey, ex-

72. Hall to Callender, 1749, [John] Hall and Edward Wilson to Elizabeth Callender, Jan. 24, 1750, GD 1/32/34, NAS.

73. "Elizabeth Callender's Account Current with Edward Wilson," August 1750.

perienced the severe restrictions their status as property imposed on them. Their divergent experiences portray slavery as intimate relationships that assumed varied forms. The brief references to Lucy and Sukey in a few letters also reveal the extent to which the lives of free women and enslaved people were entangled. Colonists like Hassall and Callender relied on captives to provide labor for their Jamaican enterprises. Both women received money from the sale of enslaved people. Callender continued to earn an income from hiring out slaves on the island after she moved to London. Women did not divest themselves from their involvement in slavery when they moved to Britain. Instead, they continued to carefully manage the actions—and earnings—of enslaved people who lived across the Atlantic.[74]

The relationships forged between Sarah Shanks and Ann Birkin, Anna Hassall and Elizabeth Callender, and Callender and Lucy reveal broader truths about the nature of Britain's growing commercial empire. Personal connections, including the close ties between female friends, male and female merchants, and enslavers and the enslaved—rather than the abstract and impersonal operations of the market—made the empire function. Before her death, Hassall paid doctors on "account of sickness" as well as apothecaries and surgeons, who bled her "several times." She died at the age of thirty-seven, just one year after her move to London. Hassall left her entire fortune to her friend Callender, emphasizing the importance of intimate relations. Imperial expansion made it possible for a woman like Hassall, who had no titles, connections, or estates in Britain, to propel herself into the most rarefied space of Westminster Abbey. When she died in 1750, imperial strategists ranked Jamaica as the most valuable of Britain's twenty-three American colonies.[75]

Kingston's female inhabitants lived at the center—not the periphery—of the developing Atlantic world. Their economic activities show that Jamaica was far more than a sugar island. Kingston's mercantile connections with the

74. Chapters 5 and 6, below, show, for instance, how captives who forged close connections with owners obtained better living conditions and, sometimes, freedom. Jennifer L. Palmer makes a similar observation about the varied nature of slavery in context of the eighteenth-century French Empire. Her book explores how the "intimate bonds" that connected enslaved people to families "led to different experiences within slavery." See Palmer, *Intimate Bonds: Family and Slavery in the French Atlantic* (Philadelphia, 2016), 2–3. See also Philip D. Morgan, *Slave Counterpoint: Black Culture in the Eighteenth-Century Chesapeake and Lowcountry* (Williamsburg, Va., and Chapel Hill, N.C., 1998).

75. "Account Book: 1748–1750, Kept by Anna Hassall while in London," Aug. 13, 1750, GD 345/1220, NAS.

Spanish Empire, its strategic military importance, and its centrality to the British slave trade all made the port town as crucial to Jamaica's meteoric rise in the 1740s and 1750s as the expansion of sugar planting. Britain's emphasis on open trade as the cornerstone of its imperial project created space for women like Shanks, her daughter Hassall, and Hassall's friend Callender to play central roles in commerce, especially on an island where few colonists survived to operate business ventures. For both free and freed women, Jamaica was a seedbed of unprecedented commercial opportunity. It was a place where Shanks, the wife of an English minister, could gather textiles and paintings crafted on the other side of the globe and disperse them to Spanish customers in the Caribbean. It was also a site where her daughter, Hassall, could nimbly skirt around imperial law, adding wartime profiteering to a female-built enterprise.[76]

Between the 1720s to the 1740s, women merchants like Shanks, Hassall, and Callender benefited from smuggling and military conflicts. All of their maritime activities—from contrabanding to privateering—relied on slave labor. African captives aided in the production of considerable mercantile fortunes, which enabled Hassall and Callender to join a cadre of elite male merchants as well as to fund their relocation to London. Once there, these women further capitalized on their colonial gains by investing in the British stock market. Hassall and Callender both reinvested their Jamaican wealth in the very company that had turned their hometown of Kingston into the center of the transatlantic slave trade. From 1750 to 1751, Callender purchased twelve hundred pounds in South Sea Company stock; Hassall also purchased fourteen hundred pounds worth of stock in the company. By reinvesting colonial proceeds in the stock market, Hassall and Callender increased their fortunes while obscuring and abstracting their connections to slavery, illicit trade, and sugar planting. As Hassall and Callender demonstrate, the women who actively advanced colonialism and slavery also bought shares in the East India Company and annuities in the Bank of England, lending further support to institutions that financed the empire. Strategic outlays of colonial capital in British joint-stock companies and banks aided the mone-

76. Kingston's wealthiest merchants earned fortunes of one hundred thousand pounds. For assessments of Jamaica's value to the empire in comparison with the other twenty-three colonies, see Burnard and Garrigus, *Plantation Machine,* 78, 80. In her study of imperial New York, Serena Zabin observes that Britain's emphasis on trade created opportunities for women. See Zabin, *Dangerous Economies,* 33.

tization of the financial market in the eighteenth century. In turn, these practices extended the profitability of plantation agriculture and the life of plantation slavery. The counting house was built by the slave trade, and colonial women, acting alongside men, aided in the construction of these imperialist institutions and processes.[77]

77. "Anna Hassall Account Current with John Meyers," 1748, GD 345/1220, NAS, "Mrs. Callenders New Journal London in Great Brittain," 1749, GD 345/1214, June 20, 1751, GD 345/1214, "New South-Sea Annuities at Ten Per Cent, Received of Mrs. Anna Hassall," Miscellaneous Receipts, Sept. 14, 1750, GD 345/1220 (fourteen hundred pounds). Hassall purchased one thousand pounds in bank annuities, earning a generous 9 percent return on the Royal Exchange. Callender's annuity in the bank was worth two thousand pounds.

3. Plantations

When Mary Elbridge wrote to her relatives in Bristol, England, in 1737, she described her dealings with enslaved people as the most demanding part of her role as the manager of Spring Plantation—a middling sugar estate located in Saint Andrew Parish in which she and her in-laws in Britain owned shares. Elbridge complained that she "was quite tired" from dealing with captives and cited them as the source of "much vexation." Two years later, Elbridge expressed similar grievances, stating that she was "tired with the fatigue of negroes" and reiterating her "vexation" with them. She urged the Bristol-based Elbridges to sell Spring, threatening that she would "have no more to doe with the plantation." In an effort to elicit pity, she asked her brother-in-law John Elbridge, who acted as her business partner in Britain, to "consider how hard I have laboured" for the plantation and "what I have gone through in my Body and Mind and the troubles wth. these negroes." Elbridge portrayed herself—not the people who performed the relentless and exhausting work involved in sugar production—as bonded to the plantation. A few years later, Elbridge was aging, dispirited, and ill. She made the analogy between herself and her captives more explicit, writing: "Realy I have bin a tru Slave to the plantation and ought to have any advantage." She died one year later.[1]

In her correspondence, Elbridge moderated between casting herself as the victim and acting as the supreme arbiter of "justice" on Spring. As an en-

1. Mary Elbridge to Rebecca Woolnough, July 29, 1737, Woolnough Papers, Ashton Court Archives, AC/WO/16/15, Bristol Record Office (BRO), U.K., Mary Elbridge to John Elbridge, Jan. 29, 1739, AC/WO/16/22b, Mary Elbridge to Thomas Elbridge and Henry Woolnough, Nov. 22, 1739, AC/WO/24g, Mary Elbridge to Henry Woolnough, Feb. 18, 1743, AC/WO.

slaver and a plantation manager, she wielded nearly unlimited authority over more than one hundred people. Yet her increasingly desperate letters expose the fissures in her power. Elbridge engaged in a continual tug-of-war for mastery with her captives. She did not specify what particular enslaved people on Spring did to provoke her. Perhaps they deserted the plantation, refused to work, or committed theft. Whatever their actions, she retaliated with harsh punishments, which including selling those she found insubordinate. She announced her intention to "endeavour to dispose of the negros to the best advantage I can . . . with all the justice as lys in my power." Elbridge equated "justice" with authority and financial concerns, claiming to execute "justice" on behalf of her distant relatives in Britain so that their "interest may not suffer." Anyone who challenged her power or failed to meet her labor demands met with swift reprisals.[2]

Elbridge viewed her life through the prism of slavery because slaveholding was a defining feature of her experience and enslaved people comprised the majority of her wealth. Elbridge grew up in Jamaica during the early decades of the eighteenth century, when slavery was becoming a pervasive feature of island life. In addition to managing 123 captives on Spring Plantation—51 one of whom made up part of her one-third share in the estate—Elbridge held 25 people in bondage outright. Altogether, between her portion of the property and those Elbridge came to own herself, she was responsible for 76 enslaved men, women, and children. Like many female slaveholders, Elbridge acquired her captives through inheritance and direct purchases. Her husband bequeathed 9 people to her when he died in 1726, and an inventory taken nineteen years after his death listed 16 more enslaved people, indicating that Elbridge acquired them during her widowhood.[3]

Though she projected mastery over an unfree labor force, Elbridge struggled to maintain control of the captives on Spring during a volatile time in Jamaican history. The plantation manager rightfully identified the

2. Mary Elbridge to Henry Woolnough, Dec. 14, 1737, Woolnough Papers, Ashton Court Archives, 19a, John Elbridge to Mary Elbridge, July 19, 1727, AC/WO/16/8a.

3. Will of Robert Elbridge, 1726, Jamaica Wills, 1661–1771, XVII, Island Record Office (IRO), Spanish Town, Jamaica; Inventory of Mary Elbridge, 1745, Jamaica Inventories, 1674–1784, fol. 132, Jamaica Archives (JA), Spanish Town, Jamaica. According to both her late husband's will and the probated inventory of her estate, Mary was "entitled" to 11/32 parts of Spring Plantation. Her brother-in-law and her niece, who lived in Bristol, owned the remaining shares in the estate. When her estate was probated in 1745, Mary's portion was calculated to include fifty-one enslaved people on Spring. Additionally, she possessed six adult men, six adult women, five of whom were mothers, and seven children. She also claimed six "boys."

rapid growth of the island's enslaved population—a development she herself contributed to—as the primary source of social instability in the colony. Jamaica was faltering, she wrote, and "times is so hard" because "every body has negros that hear is more then the place wants." Elbridge both witnessed and contributed to the rapid growth of plantation slavery on the island. In 1730, there were 429 sugar plantations and nearly seventy-five thousand captives in Jamaica, 70 percent of whom were employed on sugar plantations. Even the smallest planters held at least a few people in bondage. Moreover, Elbridge sought to compel people to labor in the middle of a military conflict. In 1737—the year when she urged her British relatives to sell the plantation—British troops, the local militia, and enslaved soldiers were fighting a losing guerilla war against the Jamaican Maroons. Large numbers of enslaved people deserted their owners to join these independent groups, and colonists fled from more remote settlements that had experienced slave uprisings for decades. The conflict might have emboldened the captives on Spring to defy Elbridge's authority. The fragility of local and imperial authority was obvious, and the plantation's location in the foothills of the Blue Mountains offered temptingly easy access to thick forests and rugged terrain.[4]

In spite of her complaints and concerns, Elbridge and other women planters and plantation managers helped to maintain stability in Jamaica's hinterlands during a time of intense upheaval from the 1720s to the 1750s. Women planters balanced the complexity of cultivating, producing, and shipping tropical produce abroad while also compelling a resistant, unfree labor force to perform backbreaking work. Their efforts aided in securing the colony against the Maroons. Yet, despite the critical roles played by female agriculturalists such as Elbridge, almost nothing is known about their contribution to the plantation economy. Aside from occasional and largely hearsay refer-

4. Mary Elbridge to Rebecca Woolnough, July 29, 1737, Woolnough Papers, AC/WO/16/15. The population figures are drawn from Trevor Burnard's use of the 1730 survey of the island's inhabitants. See Burnard, *Planters, Merchants, and Slaves: Plantation Societies in British America, 1650–1820* (Chicago, 2015), 64–65. For more on slave revolts and the Maroon War in Jamaica, see David Barry Gaspar, "A Dangerous Spirit of Liberty: Slave Rebellion in the West Indies in the 1730s," in Laurent Dubois and Julius S. Scott, eds., *Origins of the Black Atlantic* (New York, 2010), 11–25. See also Helen McKee, "From Violence to Alliance: Maroons and White Settlers in Jamaica, 1739–1795," *Slavery and Abolition,* XXXIX (2017), 27–52; Richard S. Dunn, *Sugar and Slaves: The Rise and Fall of the Planter Class in the English West Indies, 1624–1713* (Williamsburg, Va., Chapel Hill, N.C., 1972), 259–262; and Kathleen Wilson, "The Performance of Freedom: Maroons and the Colonial Order in Eighteenth-Century Jamaica and the Atlantic Sound," *WMQ,* 3d Ser., LXVI (2009), 45–86.

ences to planters' wives, scholars have presented the Jamaican plantation as a masculine site. Mary Elbridge's role as a plantation manager and slaveholder disrupts a historical narrative that, unsurprisingly, relies on the material left by an elite group of absentee male planters. These men—many of whom lived during the latter part of the eighteenth century—are the people who inherited, rather than built, the colony's enormously valuable plantation zone. During the first half of the eighteenth century, second-generation poor and middling islanders, including women like Elbridge, laid the groundwork for what was to become the most profitable—and the most exploitative—agricultural economy in the British Empire.[5]

5. Cecily Jones argues that the lack of attention to female planters and slaveholders in the Anglo-Caribbean stems from a larger tradition in Caribbean historiography of dismissing "white female agency." According to Jones, they remain "shadowy figures" who are treated as "victims" of colonialism rather than agents (Jones, "Contesting the Boundaries of Gender, Race, and Sexuality in Barbadian Plantation Society," *Women's History Review,* XII [2003], 204). Hilary McD. Beckles raises a similar critique of the victim approach to the study of white women in the formation of slave societies. See Beckles, "White Women and Slavery in the Caribbean," *History Workshop,* XXXVI (Autumn 1993), 69. A few notable exceptions include Aleric Josephs, "Jamaica Planter Women and the Challenges of Plantation Management," *Journal of Caribbean History,* XLIX (2015), 9–12; and Linda L. Sturtz, "The 'Dimduke' and the Duchess of Chandos: Gender and Power in Jamaican Plantation Management—A Case Study; or, A Different Story of 'A Man [and His Wife] from a Place Called Hope,'" *Revista/Review Interamericana,* XXIX (1999), [1–15]. Scholars typically attribute the growth of the plantation system in English colonies throughout the Atlantic world from Virginia and South Carolina to Barbados and Jamaica to the actions of elite white men like William Byrd II, Landon Carter, William Beckford, Simon Taylor, and Thomas Jefferson. See Trevor Burnard, *Mastery, Tyranny, and Desire: Thomas Thistlewood and His Slaves in the Anglo-Jamaican World* (Chapel Hill, N.C., 2004), 84; Burnard, "Evaluating Gender in Early Jamaica, 1674–1784," *History of the Family,* XII (2007), 81, 85, 90; Christer Petley, *Slaveholders in Jamaica: Colonial Society and Culture during the Era of Abolition* (New York, 2009); Philip D. Morgan, *Slave Counterpoint: Black Culture in the Eighteenth-Century Chesapeake and Lowcountry* (Williamsburg, Va., and Chapel Hill, N.C., 1998), 273–296; Robert Olwell, *Masters, Slaves, and Subjects: The Culture of Power in the South Carolina Low Country, 1740–1790* (Ithaca, N.Y., 1998), 191–200; Anthony S. Parent, Jr., *Foul Means: The Formation of a Slave Society in Virginia, 1660–1740* (Williamsburg, Va., and Chapel Hill, N.C., 2003), 197–209; and Kathleen M. Brown, *Good Wives, Nasty Wenches, and Anxious Patriarchs: Gender, Race, and Power in Colonial Virginia* (Williamsburg, Va., and Chapel Hill, N.C., 1996), 322–366. As Lucille Mathurin Mair points out, women were scarcer higher up on the socioeconomic ladder, whereas women and children were far more prominent on middling plantations and small farms (Mathurin Mair, *A Historical Study of Women in Jamaica, 1655–1844,* ed. Hilary McD. Beckles and Verene A. Shepherd [Kingston, 2006], 108–109). In contrast, Cara Anzilotti reaches a similar

At first glance, Jamaica's rural parishes appear to be male-dominated spaces. According to a 1739 survey made during the time that Elbridge managed Spring, only one out of the sixteen sugar holdings in Saint Andrews Parish was held by a woman. Similarly, only four of the forty-five sugar plantations in Westmoreland Parish had female owners. However, official records obscure the extent of female participation in plantations as proprietors and managers, sometimes listing "heirs" or deceased husbands as the holders of land that was in actuality overseen by women. The 1739 survey identifies the owners of Spring Plantation as "John Elbridges heirs"—there is no reference to Mary, who possessed a third of the estate, which she was also single-handedly managing, at the time of the survey's creation. Likewise, the surveyors determined that Barbican Plantation—also located in Saint Andrews Parish near Spring—belonged to "Chas. Chaplain heirs in England." When Charles Chaplain died in 1742, a few years after the survey was taken, his widowed mother inherited Barbican. In addition to large plantations in other parishes, the widow Priscilla Guy also appears on the 1739 survey as the owner of land in Saint Andrew's Parish (still called Guy's Plantation on a 1763 map [Plate 6]) located next to Snow Hill, owned by Elizabeth Lawes (née Gibbons). A 1750 survey reveals that Catherine Boone oversaw the modest 79-acre Boone's Plot, while Sarah Williams held the more extensive 426-acre Williams Plantation. Altogether, women administered a small but noticeable cluster of sugar plantations in Saint Andrews Parish, where Spring Plantation was located. As these instances show, surveys can disguise female ownership of, and contribution to, agricultural enterprises.[6]

---

conclusion about the enhanced freedom women experienced in colonial South Carolina, where husbands nominated wives to be plantation managers to stabilize family property holding, just as they did in Jamaica. See Anzilotti, "Autonomy and the Female Planter in Colonial South Carolina," *Journal of Southern History*, LXIII (1997), 239–241.

6. "Sugar Plantations in Jamaica, with the Quantities of Sugar Made for Some Years Past," 1739, Add MSS 12434, British Library (BL), London. Charles Chaplain was the son of Anne Saunders. See Will of Charles Chaplain, 1741, MS 1570, National Library of Jamaica (NLJ), Kingston. The will is also enclosed in a letter written by Edward Chaplin in 1757. See "Copy of Will of Charles Chaplain," Oct. 2, 1742, in Edward Chaplin to Rose Fuller, Mar. 22, 1757, Jamaica Correspondence of Rose Fuller and Stephen Fuller (1746–1775), SAS/RF 21/106, Deeds and Documents Relating to Lands Formerly Belonging to the Family of Fuller of Brightling, East Sussex Record Office (ESRO), Lewes, U.K. Susannah Elletson managed Hope plantation. See "Susannah Elletson to James Ord, May 1758, Stowe Brydges Correspondence, Box 25, Huntington Library (HL), San Marino, Calif. For the "widow Guy" and her holdings, see Will of Priscilla Guy, 1748, Jamaica Wills, XVII; Inventory of Priscilla Guy, 1749, Jamaica Invento-

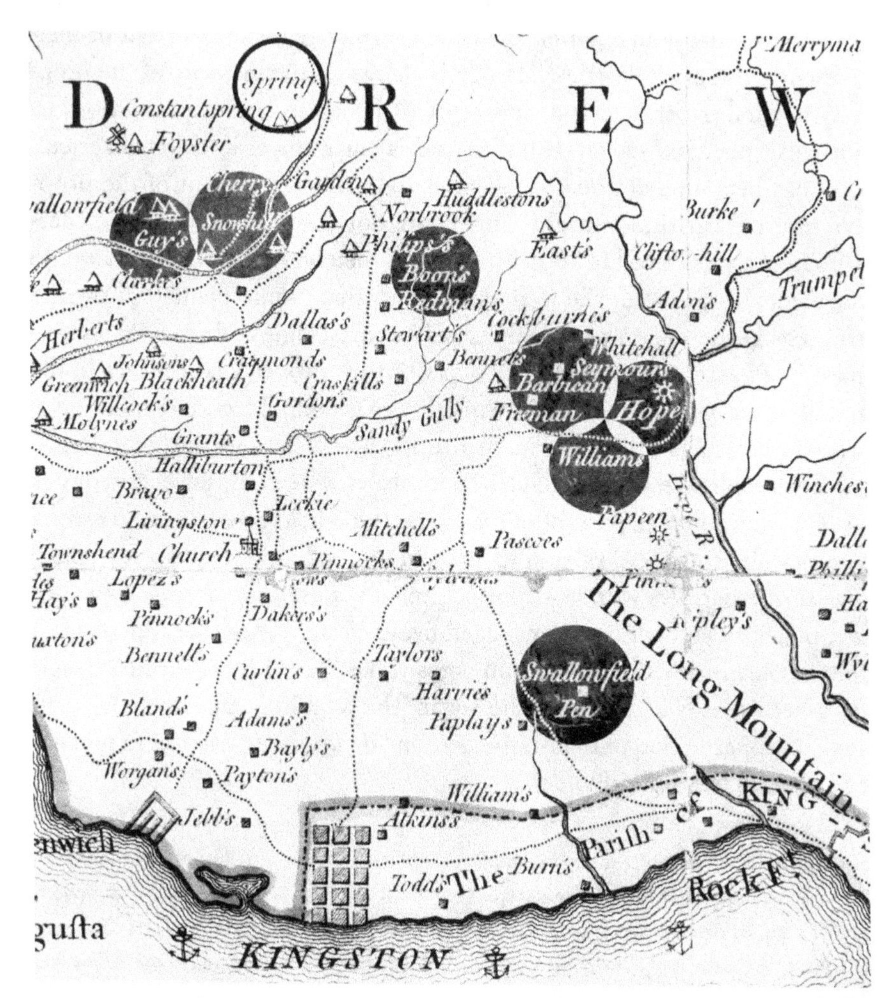

PLATE 6. Detail from *This Map of the County of Surry in the Island of Jamaica*, by Thomas Craskell. 1763. Courtesy, Library of Congress, Geography and Maps Division, G4963.S9 1763 .C7

This detail shows plantations that were administered or owned by women living in Saint Andrew Parish, near Spring Plantation.

Although the above examples focus on women who oversaw sugar plantations, widening the lens to include other types of agricultural and ranching enterprises that flourished on the island further reveals the extent of their presence in these industries. Though men owned the majority of the property in rural parishes, a 1750 survey of all Jamaican landowners—not just the sugar planters—suggests that women's engagement in colonial agriculture has been underestimated. Women controlled 11 percent of the property in rural parishes outright. This figure does not include female owners who held estates "for life" or who were grouped with "heirs," which would augment this portion. The findings suggest that, while plantation ownership was gendered, it was not an exclusively masculine endeavor. At an estimated 445-acres, the average size of a woman's property placed her in the middling category of the majority of Jamaica's landholders, including men, who owned tracts that were less than 1,000 acres. If a 140-acre plot constitutes the median, then most female landholders were in the lower end of this group. Altogether, 42 percent of the women who held estates in 1750 owned between 100 to 500 acres, and 37 percent controlled fewer than 100 acres. The smaller farmers with less acreage probably raised provisions, grew ginger, pimento, and cotton, or managed livestock pens. Another 9 percent of these women owned 500 to 1,000 acres. Like Mary Elbridge, they would have been more likely to cultivate sugar. The wealthiest planters who controlled properties larger than 1,000 acres made up the remaining 12 percent of Jamaica's female landholders.[7]

---

ries. The holdings of Catharine Boone and Sarah Williams appear in "A List of Landholders in Jamaica Together with the Quantity of Acres Land Each One Possesses and Quantity Supposed to Be Occupied by Planter," circa 1750, in Add MS 12436 (information probably recorded from CO 142.31 in Calendar of State Papers, 1754), BL. My findings draw attention to the overlooked presence of women as managers and owners of plantations. But more work needs to be done on female landholding practices in Jamaica. To determine all of the estates owned or administered by women in Saint Andrews Parish, one would need to conduct a study of land deeds from the parish, carefully review all of the wills that were made by the men and women who lived there, and study the Chancery Court records, which are very difficult to gain access to, for additional information about any disputes over landownership in the parish.

7. All my figures are drawn from "A List of Landholders in Jamaica Together with the Quantity of Acres Land Each One Possesses and Quantity Supposed to Be Occupied by Planter," circa 1750, in Add MS 12436. The 1750 survey offers a snapshot of the gendered dimensions of landholding on the island. It is not a comprehensive study of the subject. To undertake such a project, one would need to conduct an analysis of land-related transactions, including a review of all of the deeds of transfer, sale, and mortgage as well as land plats and surveys, which are held in the IRO,

During the first half of the eighteenth century, second- and third-generation women like Mary Elbridge who were born in Jamaica, accustomed to the tropical environment, and comfortable with slaveholding readily exploited the varied agricultural opportunities afforded by Jamaica's mild climate and diverse topography. Unlike Britain's other Caribbean colonies, Jamaica never became a sugar monoculture. Nor did the island experience a sugar revolution in the first half of the eighteenth century. Instead, the transition to sugar occurred slowly and haphazardly. A large number of planters who lacked the capital or the connections to fund the construction of expensive sugar

---

the JA, and the NLJ—a project that is beyond the scope of this book. But the 1750 survey still provides a useful starting point for considering how gender influenced landholding patterns in Jamaica. From the survey, I have determined that women made up 11 percent of the landholders in the colony in 1750, a higher percentage than the estimates proposed by other scholars. In 1750, 175 of the 1,596 landowners were women, and the mean average size of female-held estates was 456 acres; the median size, at 145 acres, was considerably smaller. However, the 1750 survey does not include Kingston, for instance, where women's wills indicate a high level of real estate holding. Furthermore, the names of women who acquired real estate through inheritance were not necessarily added to the original land deeds for estates. Altogether, these discrepancies may indicate that 11 percent is a low approximation. Linda L. Sturtz notes that Kathleen Butler estimates that women held 5 percent of the land in Jamaica at the time of emancipation, suggesting a possible decrease in female landownership. Another set of scholars conclude that women only made up 7.7 percent of the sellers and 4.1 percent of the buyers outside of Kingston. They also determine that women typically purchased only 7 acres. See Kathleen Mary Butler, *The Economics of Emancipation: Jamaica and Barbados, 1823–1843* (Chapel Hill, N.C., 1995), 92–95; Sturtz, "'Dimduke' and the Duchess of Chandos," *Revista/Review Interamericana,* XXIX (1999), [1–15]; and Ahmed Reid and David B. Ryden, "Sugar, Land Markets, and the Williams Thesis: Evidence from Jamaica's Property Sales, 1750–1810," *Slavery and Abolition,* XXXIV (2013), 15. Scholars have reached different conclusions about the distribution of landholdings in the colony by the 1750s. There are discrepancies in the findings of Trevor Burnard and Verene A. Shepherd, who both use the same return of landholders as I do. Burnard concludes that 1,000-acre tracts accounted for more than 78 percent of claimed land. Shepherd shows that only 28 percent of these tracts were more than 1,000 acres while 52 percent were 500 acres or less. Although both interpretations stress the transition to large-scale sugar planting, they provide different portraits of how land was being used in the colony. I am primarily concerned with female-held property. If Shepherd's analysis is accurate, then half of the island's landowners fell into this category. Burnard describes a dramatic increase in the price of land after 1690. Yet he also observes that landownership was never out of reach for "ordinary white men." It was also not out of reach for ordinary women of European and Afro-European descent, who purchased property in the island's urban and rural regions. See Shepherd, *Livestock, Sugar, and Slavery: Contested Terrain in Colonial Jamaica* (Kingston, 2009), 18; and Burnard, *Planters, Merchants, and Slaves,* 77–78.

works focused on other crops. More than half the colony's agriculturalists, and women in particular, worked as ranchers and livestock, or they grew provisions or minor staples and cultivated small cash crops like ginger, cocoa, indigo, and cotton.[8]

Jamaica's sprawling and ecologically abundant landscape supported these differentiated farming ventures. An extensive mountain range with elevations reaching seven thousand feet cuts across the island from east to west, creating deep, forested valleys and dividing the northern from the southern parishes. Large tracts of land remained uncultivated well into the eighteenth century, and planters lived in frontier-like conditions that bore a greater resemblance to early settlements in Georgia or Carolina than to Barbados or Antigua. Visitors to the colony marveled at its agronomic variety rather than its uniformity. In 1727, one anonymous author waxed lyrical about the proliferation of Amerindian, European, and African produce in Jamaica, a place where English herbs and peas, African eddoes, plantains, and yams grew together with soursops, custard apples, star apples, avocados, guavas, bananas, coconuts, melons, and "fields of pine-apples, the most delicious fruit under heaven."[9]

Mary Elbridge's correspondence—one of the only collections of letters authored by a woman who lived in eighteenth-century Jamaica to survive—tells how female planters contributed to the creation of this heterogenous agricultural world. Her communications offer unique insight into the lived

8. Sugar, rum, and molasses made up three-fourths of the colony's exports. See Jack P. Greene, *Pursuits of Happiness: The Social Development of Early Modern British Colonies and the Formation of American Culture* (Chapel Hill, N.C., 1988), 160. Edward Brathwaite describes smallholders and pen-keepers as "the most numerous and important group" of white colonists aside from sugar planters. He calls them the "pioneers" of Jamaica and suggests that they were not "all men." However, he then dismisses the importance of female farmers by stating that agriculture was "naturally, mainly a man's world." See Braithwaite, *The Development of Creole Society in Jamaica, 1770–1820* (Oxford, 1971), 146–150. Richard S. Sheridan's study of Saint Andrew in 1753 supports this finding. Of 154 estates in the parish, only 26 were devoted to sugar. The others grew provisions, coffee, ginger, livestock, and cotton. See Sheridan, *The Development of the Plantations to 1750: An Era of West Indian Prosperity, 1750–1775* (Barbados, 1970), 45.

9. Anon., *Some Observations on Jamaica, as to Its Natural History, Improvement in Trade, Manner of Living, etc.* (London, 1727), 13. Peter H. Wood's description of the involvement of enslaved Africans in managing herds of livestock in Carolina bears a striking resemblance to pen-keeping in Jamaica. See Wood, *Black Majority: Negroes in Colonial South Carolina from 1670 through the Stono Rebellion* (New York, 1974), 28–31. For descriptions of women's economic activities in rural Georgia, see Ben Marsh, *Georgia's Frontier Women: Female Fortunes in a Southern Colony* (Athens, Ga., 2007), 47–50.

experiences of this neglected yet instrumental group. Elbridge was one of many commercially oriented slaveholding women who aided in the construction of a form of colonialism that blended a multiplicity of rural agricultural and urbanized maritime activities. Elbridge, for instance, owned a home in Kingston, which she inherited from her "merchant" husband, Robert Elbridge, in 1726, but she also acquired a one-third share in Spring Plantation, which she became the official manager of when he died. As a planter, Elbridge coerced enslaved people to cultivate crops and produce sugar and kept the estate's account books in order. She then used her Atlantic connections to ship sugar overseas for a profit. And that profit could be considerable. Successful sugar planters like Elbridge earned the highest amounts, which ranged between 10 and 13 percent per annum, but agriculturalists of all sorts reaped financial benefits from their engagement in the increasingly gainful plantation business. Jack P. Greene estimates that the net worth of a free white person living in Jamaica was nine times that of someone in the wealthiest colonies in mainland North America.[10]

Free islanders produced these earnings off the backs of enslaved laborers. The same anonymous author who waxed lyrical about the diversity of the Jamaican countryside also identified slavery as its sinister underbelly in 1727, describing "gentlemen" who enjoyed "country lives" in a "glorious lovely scene of nature" and who also wielded "absolute dominion" over their slaves. The slaveholder's power extended "to every thing but taking away their lives; nor would that be very difficult, if a master were bent upon it." But it was not only "gentlemen" who controlled an enslaved labor force. Women planters like Mary Elbridge proactively asserted their rights as slaveholders to exert unlimited authority over captives.[11]

Nevertheless, the slave codes, passed at the end of the seventeenth century, empowered all slaveholders, irrespective of gender, to physically abuse,

10. Will of Robert Elbridge, 1726, Jamaica Wills, XVII. Trevor Burnard and Verene Shepherd both provide brief overviews of Spring Plantation's profitability. Neither of them studies Mary Elbridge's life or her activities as a plantation manager nor do they consider her gendered position. See Burnard, *Planters, Merchants, and Slaves*, 176–177; and Shepherd, *Livestock, Sugar, and Slavery*, 32–36. Jack Greene calculates the annual rate of profit on a sugar estates in *Pursuits of Happiness*, 160. See also J. R. Ward, "The Profitability of Sugar Planting in the British West Indies, 1650–1834," *Economic History Review*, XXXI (1978), 207–209. For a detailed overview of how to determine the profitability of a sugar plantation, see David Hancock, *Citizens of the World: London Merchants and the Integration of the British Atlantic Community, 1735–1785* (New York, 1995), app. IV, 411–418.

11. Anon., *Some Observations on Jamaica*, 14, 16.

imprison, sell, transport, and, in some cases, even execute their captives. Female violence was not necessarily considered abnormal in the early modern era. English women disciplined dependents within their household, including children and servants. They were expected to defend their homes, and print culture touted positive models of women who used physical force, especially in self-sacrificing or defensive acts. However, according to British standards, colonial women who publicly claimed and performed masculine forms of authority, which included aggression, exceeded the bounds of acceptable feminine force.[12]

In addition to participating in these overt displays of brutal mastery, women planters engaged in the more insidious but no less deleterious degradations of slavery. On the whole, enslaved people who labored on plantations endured extremely high mortality rates resulting from malnutrition, exhaustion, disease, and unsanitary living conditions. Because women planters generally oversaw middling or small estates, they were more likely to be directly involved in plantation management than male planters who controlled thousands of acres and could afford to delegate this work. The economic activities of these women far exceeded the bounds of the domestic realm. They exhibited the same entrepreneurially minded zeal that has been attributed to the male planters who strove to maximize production. Female planters coerced enslaved laborers to use both rudimentary farm tools as well as technologically advanced machinery to produce exotic products from crops not grown in Europe on an industrial scale that they then exported abroad. Altogether, the actions of female planters were crucial to the advancement of a plantation system that demanded flexibility, innovation, and ruthlessness.[13]

12. Ibid.; Garthine Walker, *Crime, Gender, and Social Order in Early Modern England* (New York, 2003), 76, 79–80, 85–90. For more on the seventeenth-century slave codes, still in place in the early eighteenth century, and how they distinguished between servants and enslaved people, see Chapter 1, above.

13. Vincent Brown summarizes the scholarship on slave mortality rates, revealing the devastating toll suffered by field-workers and jobbing gangs in particular. He notes that slaves who held higher-status positions on plantations "could enjoy more food, rest, and longevity." See Brown, *The Reaper's Garden: Death and Power in the World of Atlantic Slavery* (Cambridge, Mass., 2008), 50–55. The assumption that slaveholding societies were patriarchal or paternalistic has obscured women's roles as plantation managers in early America. Scholars who study enslaved people who worked in the household bring free women into view as managers of domestic workers, not field slaves. See, for instance, Hilary McD. Beckles, *Natural Rebels: A Social History of Enslaved Black Women in Barbados* (New Brunswick, N.J., 1989), 56–69; and Thavolia Glymph, *Out of the House of Bondage: The Transformation of the Plantation Household* (Cam-

HER "PRUDENT AND FRUGAL MANAGEMENT"

In an unpublished work "The Islanders; or Mad Orphan," written during the early eighteenth century, Jamaican author John O'Kelly offered a contemptuous portrait of plantation life. He described free women as being "buried" alive in the countryside on plantations that were isolating and grim working environments. Echoing Mary Elbridge's equation of herself with a slave, he represented the planter's wife in the story as being enslaved to the plantation. Although the wife's captives labored in the fields, she was "employ'd all day in making Breeches and Pettecoats" for them. In addition to performing customary domestic work like sewing, her involvement in the plantation business compelled her to labor at jobs that fell outside of the usual feminine province, such as "taking an Account of the weight of sugar; which goes out of the plantation, with the quantity of Rumm," while also operating "a Hucksters Shope" that sold "drams and Tobacco" to enslaved people.[14]

In return for her labor, the wife in "The Islanders" is rewarded with tawdry symbols of luxury marred by their association with the plantation economy. Rather than being pulled by fancy carriage horses, her "coach and six" was driven by the workhorses used to grind sugarcane. Similarly, a "negro coachman, with a pair of ozzenbrig breeches, a half hat, and livery coat . . . with two or three naked negro wenches be hind" were used to "compleat the equipage," not proper servants. Like Elbridge, O'Kelly did not perceive of enslavement as degrading for those who were being held in captivity. Instead, he portrayed slavery as a practice that debased free women. Living in Jamaica forced them to serve—and to be served—by ill-dressed men and "naked," sexualized female slaves. Furthermore, not only were wives in Jamaica degraded by their participation in slavery, they were also treated like slaves by their husbands, who, as one character observes, "look upon their Wives, as very little above their Slaves, nay very often treat'em worse." According to the playwright, immersion in a slave society turned husbands into absolute rulers and reduced wives to a state of bondage.[15]

---

bridge, 2008), 51–53. See also Laurel Thatcher Ulrich's concept of the "deputy husband" in *Good Wives: Image and Reality in the Lives of Women in Northern New England, 1650–1750* (New York, 1982), 35–50. Women also contributed to the development of the "expansive, flexible, and innovative" eighteenth-century Jamaican plantation that Trevor Burnard describes in *Planters, Merchants, and Slaves,* 20, 22, 24.

14. John O'Kelly, "The Islanders; or Mad-Orphan," [before 1727], Kings MS 301, 19, BL.

15. Ibid., 19, 29.

Reading O'Kelly's negative expository of Jamaica against the grain offers an alternative perspective on the roles played by free and freed women—both married and unmarried—in developing Jamaica's plantation zone. Though O' Kelly portrayed their work as demeaning and unfeminine, he showed them to be actively involved in the domestic and business activities on the plantation, from sugar production and account keeping to retailing goods to free and enslaved customers. Elbridge's role as a plantation manager provides a rich counterpoint to depictions like O'Kelly's. Whereas he characterized planters' wives as weak and ineffective victims of an intensively patriarchal society, Elbridge, despite her battles with her enslaved laborers, exuded the competence of a highly skilled agriculturalist and proved herself to be an adept businesswoman. A second-generation colonist, she considered Jamaica her home. Though no record exists of her baptism, Elbridge's knowledge of sugar planting and her familiarity with slave management suggest that she was either born on the island or grew up in Jamaica. Rather than aspiring to return to Britain, she focused on colonial enterprises.[16]

For the families who built the foundations of the colony's agricultural industry, however, the path to plantation profit was neither linear nor obvious. The Elbridges, a well-established merchant family in seventeenth-century Bristol, for instance, followed a circuitous route to Jamaica. Lured by new entrepreneurial opportunities in America, a few family members crossed the Atlantic. But, whereas brothers Aldworth and Robert went immediately to Jamaica, a third brother, Thomas Elbridge, and his wife, Rebecca, initially moved with their five children to a location that was as far from the balmy tropics as possible: Bristol, Maine—the town's name signaling its connection to their place of origin. The couple purchased land there and attempted to profit from the cod fishing trade in the cold Atlantic waters. It was only with the failure of this venture that they decided to leave New England in search of more favorable colonial ventures. The potential for earnings in Jamaica, where Aldworth and Robert had taken control of Spring Plantation in the 1670s, prompted Thomas to join them. He died in 1682, and his wife followed him to the grave soon afterward. At some point in the 1710s or 1720s, Robert Elbridge married a woman named Mary, a local widow.[17]

16. Will of Mary Elbridge, 1744, Jamaica Wills, XXV, fol. 3. Mary Elbridge's recognition of a man named Robert Cooke as her brother in her 1744 will suggests that Cooke might have been her maiden name.

17. The Elbridge family's settlement in Jamaica in the late seventeenth century offers one example of the varied migration paths followed by colonists during the early period of English rule

The plantation business faltered under Robert Elbridge's management. As Mary's husband's efforts show, producing a profit from sugar planting took years. In a 1719 letter to a fourth Elbridge brother, John, who had stayed in Bristol, Robert described the colony as "quite spoyld" and urged John, who had also inherited a share in the plantation, to travel to Jamaica to "see yr interest." Seven years after writing to his brother, Robert was dead. Widowed for the second time in 1726, Mary Elbridge became the only surviving Elbridge relative who lived in Jamaica. Elbridge had a vested interest in its success. In addition to providing his widow with nine enslaved people and a house in Kingston, Robert had bequeathed his one-third share of the plantation to Mary during her lifetime.[18]

All of the other Elbridges lived in Britain and expressed no interest in traveling to a foreign colony with a notoriously unhealthy climate. The metropolitan relatives determined to place a female in-law, Mary Elbridge, in charge of Spring Plantation. Located in Liguanea in Saint Andrew Parish, Spring was built in the foothills of the Blue Mountains, overlooking Kingston and its deepwater harbor. The moderately sized, six-hundred-acre estate held a land patent issued by Charles II that dated back to 1665. Spring's profits fluctuated significantly during the first half of the eighteenth century. On good

---

on the island. There was nothing unusual about the Elbridge connection to both New England and Jamaica. As Wendy Warren reminds us, a large number of New England colonists had family in the Caribbean and owned property there. See Warren, *New England Bound: Slavery and Colonization in Early America* (New York, 2016), 11–12. The Elbridges also aided in establishing the local custom of bequeathing plantations to female heirs. When Aldworth Elbridge died in October 1703, he gave his one-third share in Spring Plantation to his two daughters, Mary and Rebecca, before sending them to England to be educated. Neither of the girls would ever return to the colony, and Mary sold her share in the estate to her uncle, Robert. See Calculations of the Partition of Aldworth Elbridge's Estate in Jamaica between His Heirs, Woolnough Papers, Ashton Court Archives, AC/WO/16/25a–f; and Charles Francis Jenney, "The Fortunate Island of Monhegan," *Proceedings of the American Antiquarian Society,* XXXI (1921), 324–328. As Chapter 4, below, demonstrates, it was common for fathers on the island to provide daughters with generous bequests.

18. Robert Elbridge to John Elbridge, Mar. 19, 1719, Woolnough Papers, Ashton Court Archives, AC/WO/16/6a–c, Draft Power of Attorney John Elbridge, Esq., Thomas Elbridge Merchant; and Mary His Wife; Rebecca Elbridge, Spinster, to Michael Atkins, of Kingston, Jamaica, Merchant, to Account with Mary, Widow of Robert Elbridge, January 1727, Woolnough Papers, Ashton Court Archives, AC/WO/16/9. Robert Elbridge died in 1726. See Woolnough Papers, Ashton Court Archives, AC/WO/16/25a; and Inventory of Robert Elbridge, 1727, Jamaica Inventories, fol. 113.

years, it produced around ninety hogsheads of sugar and earned roughly fifteen hundred pounds per annum; on bad years, the numbers for production and profits were halved. Prudent management and favorable weather significantly influenced the amount of money the plantation generated. Mary Elbridge would prove to be its most effective administrator.[19]

Mary Elbridge's assumption of the role of plantation manager for her family was not unusual in Jamaica. During the early decades of the eighteenth century, it became commonplace for free women to oversee agricultural operations. The plantation was a family-run enterprise that linked colonial and metropolitan relatives. Local circumstances—the extreme demographic disparity between the free and enslaved population and high mortality rates—made colonists especially reliant on kinship connections. This was particularly true on an island where husbands often predeceased wives and many free couples either had no surviving children or only daughters. Imperial expansion further scattered kin throughout the Atlantic basin, increasing the reliance of planter families on women to run colonial ventures. The nature of the plantation business also necessitated the contribution of every relative. Plantations were multigenerational endeavors that required experience with cultivating finicky tropical crops and Atlantic mercantile connections for retailing products overseas. Costly equipment and a large enslaved labor force made sugar production markedly expensive. Planters took out considerable loans or mortgages to finance their endeavors, and debt made these agricultural ventures risky. If a husband died before paying off his loans, he exposed his family to financial loss and possibly destitution.[20]

In this context, legally independent widows and women who never married became logical candidates to administer Jamaican holdings. They could sign contracts and engage in commercial transactions. Widowed mothers

19. Shepherd, *Livestock, Sugar, and Slavery*, 32.

20. Aleric Josephs's description of the planter Jannet Hynes, who managed several large estates in Westmoreland Parish, bears a striking similarity to Mary Elbridge. As Josephs observes, Hynes was never "upbraided" by the men with whom she worked nor did they ask her to hire a male attorney or manager. Jannet's management of the plantations was considered to be normal and skillful, enough so for her to save £5,000 in earnings. See Josephs, "Jamaica Planter Women and the Challenges of Plantation Management," *Journal of Caribbean History*, XLIX (2015), 9–12. The influence of high mortality rates on the gendered nature of colonial inheritance practices is explored in much greater detail in Chapter 4, below. Trevor Burnard describes the considerable start-up cost of a sugar plantation, which, by the end of the eighteenth century, ranged from £17,249 to £28,039, in Jamaica. Most planters needed to assume debt to establish sugar plantations. See Burnard, *Planters, Merchants, and Slaves*, 14.

who had children to support were particularly motivated to earn a living from plantations, more so, colonists probably concluded, than far-flung male heirs who had no roots in Jamaica. Mary Elbridge, for example, needed to provide for her daughter, Elizabeth, the child from her first marriage. When her second husband, Robert Elbridge, made his will, he described Elizabeth as a "poore spinster," giving her a gold watch and erasing any debts that she owed to him for "lodging and washing." Elizabeth was probably an adolescent when her stepfather died. Lacking an inheritance from her biological father, the daughter depended on her mother, which probably intensified Elbridge's desire to improve Spring Plantation.[21]

All of these factors made female heirs significant participants in agricultural enterprises. Recognizing colonial circumstances, families professionalized women's managerial roles on plantations, paying them annual fees and offering them partial ownership of estates. This is exactly what occurred in the Elbridge family, when Mary Elbridge's husband made her the manager and partial owner of Spring—a decision her British kin, who held the remaining shares in the plantation, supported. Relying on the professional capacities of female relations enabled local families to cope with island and imperial conditions while also earning an income from highly capital-intensive ventures that took years to produce a return.

By the 1740s, planters expected wives and daughters to undertake the command of cultivation and livestock rearing on their estates. John Campbell, for instance, gave his wife, Elizabeth, a handsome annuity of £407, a furnished house, eighteen slaves, a coach, and eight horses. He also insisted that Elizabeth serve as his executor, to ensure that his "debts and greatest part of legacies are paid." Like other colonial husbands, Campbell envisaged his spouse working after his death—not retiring to an idle life of pleasure. He stressed her right to graze a herd of livestock, including goats, hogs, and "all manner of poultry" on the property—an enterprise she was likely involved in before he died. Additionally, she would oversee the "provision ground" where captives grew their own produce. Campbell also planned for her to advance the plantation's operations, instructing Elizabeth to "fell" and "clear woodland." Emphasizing Elizabeth's authority, Campbell sternly reminded his "children and relations" to "distinguish themselves by a dutiful and respectful behavior to her."[22]

Families like the Campbells placed a premium on kinship connections

21. Will of Robert Elbridge, 1726, Jamaica Wills, XVII.

22. Will of John Campbell, 1740, Jamaica Wills, XXII.

and colonial experience. They often preferred to place agricultural ventures in the hands of female relatives who possessed the knowledge, the contacts, and the desire to live in Jamaica. Mary Elbridge's Bristol-based in-laws made such a calculation when they nominated her to become Spring's manager. No references were made to Mary's gender. On the contrary, the Elbridges voiced high expectations about her abilities and professionalized her role by offering her an annual fee. In 1730, she received £146 from Spring's profit. The widow's brother-in-law, John Elbridge, who acted as Elbridge's agent in Bristol, made glowing predictions about her capacity to improve the business. He went so far as to claim that Mary would outperform the family's male relatives. "You'll live on the plantation," he informed her, "and manage it better to advantage than it has been done since my brother Aldworth's death." When Mary shouldered responsibility for Spring in the 1720s, the Elbridges desperately needed her to succeed. Half a century of planting had depleted the land, the buildings were falling apart, and profits were dwindling.[23]

John Elbridge's estimation of his sister-in-law's abilities proved to be accurate. As plantation administrator, Mary Elbridge quickly put Spring's accounts in order, collected on debts, including payments in the form of slaves, and remitted bills of exchange. All of these transactions reveal her connection to local credit networks, one of the factors that made her the most suitable person for the job. After cleaning up the plantation's finances, Elbridge turned her attention to its aging infrastructure, writing to John that she intended to build a new still house and a curing house. As Elbridge understood, sugar plantations were small factories. During harvest time, the still house and the curing house would have operated twenty-four hours a day. These buildings contained an array of machinery and equipment that transformed green sugarcane into sugar. In the still house, large metal rollers crushed the juice out of the sugarcane, which then needed to be processed quickly before it spoiled. The sugarcane liquid was boiled in copper stills until it crystalized. The crystals were then packed into clay pots and left to dry in the curing house before further processing or shipping overseas.[24]

23. Spring Plantation Account with Gale and Co., Agents for John and Rebecca Elbridge, 1730, Woolnough Papers, Ashton Court Archives, AC/WO/16/10, BRO, John Elbridge to Mary Elbridge, July 19, 1727, Woolnough Papers, AC/WO/16/8a. In addition to the £146 Mary received from the plantation's income in 1730, she also sent the two overseas owners, John and Rebecca Elbridge, £139 each.

24. John Elbridge to Mary Elbridge, Jan. 4, 1727, Woolnough Papers, Ashton Court Archives,

In addition to updating the worksite infrastructure, Elbridge also set about improving the dilapidated family home on the estate, which was furnished with a cane couch and chairs, a broken elbow chair, an "old bed," and four guns (three "unfit for use") along with seventeen "small pictures" and a "large" map. She requested bricks, window sashes, and new furniture from England. Perhaps planning to host more guests at Spring, she ordered twelve new chairs, two tables, and a couch for the house as well. Rather than trying to direct his relative, John Elbridge characterized her as the most qualified person to oversee the plantation. Her expertise earned his admiration, and he readily agreed with her proposal to make costly improvements, "not questioning" her "prudent and frugal management."[25]

The plantation was a multipurpose operation that demanded the manager's continual attention. To make these alterations, Elbridge needed to understand the entire sugar production process from start to finish. Even the term "sugar plantation" belies the agricultural diversity of ventures like Spring. Agricultural heterogeneity—rather than homogeneity—sustained sugar plantations, and Elbridge grew a variety of crops in addition to raising livestock. Sugarcane only took up one-sixth of Spring's total acreage. The rest of the property was comprised of "mountain land," where enslaved laborers cultivated their provisions. Cattle, mules, and horses grazed in the "pasture land," flocks of chickens, ducks, and geese pecked for insects, and hogs rooted for food around the kitchen gardens captives planted outside of their dwellings. When she determined to clear more forest and plant it in sugar in 1729, Elbridge displayed a holistic understanding of tropical agriculture, also increasing the number of livestock on the land, purchasing mules, and renting a cattle pen.[26]

AC/WO/16/8d. For more on the operations of Caribbean sugar plantations, see Burnard, *Planters, Merchants, and Slaves;* Richard S. Dunn, *A Tale of Two Plantations: Slave Life and Labor in Jamaica and Virginia* (Cambridge, Mass., 2014); and Dunn, *Sugar and Slaves.*

25. John Elbridge to Mary Elbridge, July 20, 1730, Woolnough Papers, Ashton Court Archives, AC/WO/16/8l, John Elbridge to Mary Elbridge, July 19, 1727, AC/WO/16/8a.

26. John Elbridge to Mary Elbridge, Dec. 15, 1729, Woolnough Papers, Ashton Court Archives, AC/WO/16/8h. In Trevor Burnard's study of Saint Andrew Parish, where Mary Elbridge lived, only one sugar property produced sugar alone. The rest of the estates grew provisions and raised livestock. Furthermore, though fifteen estates concentrated on sugar, the remaining seventy-three properties cultivated coffee and ginger. As Burnard's sample shows, large sugar plantations did not dominate the landscape (Burnard, *Planters, Merchants, and Slaves,* 178–179). My findings reveal that women must be included in this complex agrarian world. Roderick A. McDonald provides a detailed description of the variety of livestock and produce that slaves

Mary Elbridge was a skilled planter, but she was not provincial. On the contrary, the plantation's success relied on her overseas connections, and she moved fluidly between Spring and her house in the busy port of Kingston. Located close to the harbor, Elbridge's urban abode provided her with a venue for socializing with the mercantile community and maintaining valuable business ties to ship's captains, factors, and British creditors. Her residence projected wealth, genteel status, and cosmopolitan taste. It was illuminated by mahogany and gilt sconces and furnished with imported elbow and Windsor chairs. Elbridge served her guests on china with ivory-handled cutlery. Proximity to the port allowed Elbridge to monitor sugar prices and determine where to sell Spring's produce. Two years after taking over the oversight of the property, she reported to John Elbridge that the crops were "good." At first, she retailed sugar and rum to local buyers and sent the profits in the form of 729 ounces of "Spanish money" to Bristol. By 1729, Elbridge was sending sugar directly to her brother-in-law in England.[27]

Spring Plantation connected two people who never met in person—the colonial woman and the metropolitan man—across a vast ocean. This distance augmented—rather than diminished—the importance of nurturing kinship connections. Mary and John Elbridge sent each other gifts to strengthen their economic bond. When her husband died, Mary shipped John his brother's gold-headed cane. She then sent him local delicacies, like rum and pots of ginger. John reciprocated, mailing her British newspapers, plant seeds, butter, and cheese. These actions helped to sustain the rapport essential for facilitating commercial transactions.[28]

John Elbridge rarely complained about his sister-in-law's performance on the plantation. Although he told his local agent in Jamaica on one occasion to ensure that the sugar they shipped to him was "well cured," instructing him to fill the large hogshead barrels "gradually" to "calm the sugar," he did not fault Mary Elbridge for the issue. In another letter, John described ten hogsheads of sugar he received as being of "middling" quality, informing Mary that there was a glut of sugar from Jamaica and Barbados in Bristol,

---

cultivated in their gardens and provisioning grounds on sugar plantations. See McDonald, *The Economy and Material Culture of Slaves: Goods and Chattels on the Sugar Plantations of Jamaica and Louisiana* (Baton Rouge, La., 1993), 18–25.

27. John Elbridge to Mary Elbridge, Aug. 30, 1729, Woolnough Papers, Ashton Court Archives, AC/WO/16/8h.

28. John Elbridge to Mary Elbridge, Oct. 27, 1727, Woolnough Papers, Ashton Court Archives, AC/WO/16/8a.

more than it "wanted or will sell to advantage either w. you or here." Aside from these minor quips, the Bristol factor's appraisal of her efforts was overwhelmingly positive. Elbridge lauded his sister-in-law's "good management" and described Spring as "flourishing" under her care. He even observed that her abilities as a planter surpassed those of her late husband, writing that he wished that his "Brother had prevailed" on Mary "to have lived on the Plantation in his time wch. would have been not only for yor health but the interest of the concerned in the Plantation."[29]

If John Elbridge subscribed to beliefs about feminine vanity, calculating that flattery would be the most effective way to motivate a woman, the correspondence between the two does not support such an interpretation. Similarly, Mary Elbridge's responses to the man did not adhere to prescriptions for feminine comportment. Rather than treating him with deference, Elbridge readily concurred with her brother-in-law, boldly yet accurately proclaiming that she could "prove by the accounts" that she had "made more mony for it [Spring] and saved more than ever was under any persons management," particularly "considering that the land was very much worn out [and] the seasons more uncertain." Elbridge had the figures to back her claim. Under her management, Spring's total value nearly doubled from £2,571 to £5,714. It was worth more than the median value of £3,819 for estates inventoried in Jamaica between 1741 and 1745. Exuding pride in the plantation's economic success and keenly aware of her own financial stake in the endeavor, Elbridge estimated her total investment in Spring over thirteen years to be worth £1,396 (£175,000 in today's economy).[30]

29. John Elbridge to Mary Elbridge, Aug. 30, 1729, Woolnough Papers, Ashton Court Archives, AC/WO/16/8f, John Elbridge to Mary Elbridge, Oct. 1, 1729, AC/WO/16/8g, John Elbridge to Mary Elbridge, Oct. 31, 1730, 16/8n, John Elbridge to Mary Elbridge, Dec. 15, 1729, 16/8h.

30. Mary Elbridge to Henry Woolnough, June 19, 1739, Woolnough Papers, Ashton Court Archives, 24e, Mary Elbridge to John Elbridge, Jan. 29, 1739, AC/WO/16/22a. It is useful to compare Mary Elbridge's tone in her correspondence with John Elbridge to the letters written by Sarah Shanks to Richard Elletson, which are analyzed in Chapter 2, above. Whereas Shanks deemed it necessary to adopt a feminine posture of subordination in her business correspondence with a man, Mary Elbridge did not. The two women were contemporaries, and Shanks's connection to Arthur Hassall—one of the wealthiest merchants in Jamaica—indicates that she, like Mary Elbridge, enjoyed connections to local elites. Perhaps Shanks viewed Elletson as her social superior whereas Elbridge did not consider Woolnough, a British merchant whom she had never met, to be of higher rank than herself. Or perhaps their difference in tone might be attributed to personality. For plantation values, see Burnard, *Planters, Merchants, and Slaves,*

Mary Elbridge and the other women who actively built Jamaica's plantation economy were central, rather than peripheral, figures of empire. Elbridge projected agricultural expertise, financial acumen, and professional confidence in her letters to her brother-in-law. Her skill as a plantation manager and the willingness of her male relatives to support her endeavors unsettles the ubiquitous characterization of plantation slavery as a masculine creation. Elbridge and other women like her played decisive roles in developing Jamaica's incredibly lucrative, yet profoundly exploitative, agricultural industry. As her correspondence suggests, possessing colonial knowledge and experience, especially in relation to planting and slaveholding, could counteract the gendered or racialized dimensions of a person's status in colonial and Atlantic hierarchies. Elbridge herself comprehended and sought to use this dynamic to her advantage, wielding plantation productivity to assert authority within a British kin network in which she would have otherwise exercised minimal influence.

SPANISH TOWN AND WOMEN RANCHERS

Unlike Mary Elbridge, the majority of Jamaica's free and freed women lacked the capital, land, and workforce to cultivate sugar. But the urban landscape of Spanish Town and its surrounding hinterland afforded its inhabitants, and women, especially, with other lucrative means of making a living that did not require the same initial outlay as sugar planting. Founded by the Spanish in 1534 as the Spanish capital of Jamaica, St. Jago de la Vega, or "Spanish Town," in the parish of Saint Catherine, remained the seat of government after the British conquest of the island. Home to the Jamaica Assembly, the governor's mansion, and the courts, it was distinctive from the maritime center of Kingston. Removed from the busy wharves, the slaving ships, and the throngs of transient arrivals, Spanish Town retained a rustic character and a Spanish imprint, preserving, as James Robertson has observed, a truly indigenous and "locally rooted" creole culture. Whereas Kingston's streets were carefully laid out in a grid, visitors described Spanish Town, which had been designed two centuries earlier, as bucolic, open, and village-like. Rather than demolishing the original buildings and layout, residents adapted to its

---

247; Richard B. Sheridan, *Sugar and Slavery: An Economic History of the British West Indies, 1623–1775* (Kingston, 1974), 229–231; and Measuring Worth, https://www.measuringworth.com/calculators/ppoweruk/.

spacious lots, narrow side streets, blocks organized around squares, and central plaza (Plate 7).[31]

Spanish Town's inhabitants were as eclectic and creolized as its architecture. According to the 1754 survey of landowners in the town, 405 free colonists of African descent resided alongside 866 people who were identified as "white." Though the surveyors did not record the number of slaves who lived there in 1754, it is reasonable to estimate that they comprised at least an additional two-thirds of the population, increasing the total number of occupants to 3,600. The religiously assorted group of Catholics, Quakers, and Jews added to the community's ethnic and spiritual multiplicity. Some British visitors experienced the town's diversity as disorderly and threatening. The merchant James Houston, who critiqued Kingston society, also disparaged Spanish Town's social milieu, portraying its Jewish residents as "*low-life Thieves,* (as bad as the *Negroes* themselves, who are all naturally *Thieves*)" and claiming that Jewish people and people of African descent worked together to fence "stolen Goods."[32]

Houston's unsavory representation unwittingly betrays the existence of a vibrant marketplace where local residents ignored ethnic, racial, and religious divides. One-third of the white female "proprietors" or property holders who had Christian names either shared or rented their lodgings to Jewish men, including Emanuel Mendes, Moses DeCordova, and Solomon Correa. Jewish men, in turn, extended credit to women of African descent. For example, Dorothy Plummer owed ten pounds to the shopkeeper Isaac

31. James Robertson, "Late Seventeenth-Century Spanish Town, Jamaica: Building an English City on Spanish Foundations," *Early American Studies,* VI (2008), 387, 388, 350.

32. "Census of St Jago de la Vega [Spanish Town] undertaken by Charles White, gent, in July and August 1754," Feb. 19, 1754, SAS/RF 20/7, Jamaica Papers of Rose Fuller (1729–1763), Removal Acts, Deeds and Documents Relating to Lands Formerly Belonging to the Family of Fuller of Brightling, ESRO; Jacob Bickerstaff, comp., *Dr. Houston's Memoirs of His Own Life-Time . . .* (London, 1747), 276–277; Robertson, "Late Seventeenth-Century Spanish Town, Jamaica," *Early American Studies,* VI (2008), 362. Although Spanish Town was not a port, a varied population of free and enslaved people lived there. In 1731, enslaved people formed roughly two-thirds of the populations of Port Royal and Kingston. Given the similar demographic makeup of Port Royal, Kingston, and Spanish Town, it makes sense that a comparable portion of the population in the latter would have been enslaved. Numbers for the 1731 census are taken from: "Jamaica to His Majesty, Relating to the Unhappy Situation of Affairs of That Island, by the Increase and Success of Their Rebellious Negroes," Feb. 11, 1731, CO 137/19, II, The National Archives (TNA), Kew.

PLATE 7. *King's Square, St. Jao de la Vega.* Plate from James Hakewill, *A Picturesque Tour of the Island of Jamaica . . .* (London, 1825).
Courtesy of the British Library, London

Desilva. When he sued her for the money, she did not to appear in court to defend herself.[33]

The presence of independent, property-holding women of European, Euro-African, and African descent added to Spanish Town's distinctive character. By 1754, female "proprietors" controlled one-third of the 499 "tenements" that made up the community. Though Kingston, the busy new port, would, at first glance, seem to afford the most lucrative ventures for women, Spanish Town, the colony's political capital and the meeting point of the island's road network, attracted more elite clientele than the sea captains, slave traders, and sailors who stopped over in Kingston. Islanders who made Spanish Town their temporary home, often for months at a time during the season when the assembly and courts were in session, paid high rates for lodging, cooking, and washing—rental and domestic services monopolized by free and freed women.[34]

Some of Spanish Town's female residents made small fortunes by engaging in these pursuits. When Mary Hutchinson died in 1740, just five years before Mary Elbridge, her estate was valued at twenty-seven hundred pounds. Hutchinson operated a transportation, tavern, and lodging house business with the labor of thirty-one enslaved people. Her ferry service shepherded passengers from Kingston to the boarding house that she owned at Passage Fort—a small outpost between the harbor and Spanish Town—where her customers dined on pewter and "blue and white" china dishes and drank tea, coffee, chocolate, or brandy at a large mahogany table. One of Hutchinson's three "coaches and six," which were lined with red and blue fabric, then drove her clients to her lodging in Spanish Town. Once there, guests could play whist at a mahogany card table or an exotic "eight square japan table," lounge in a "yellow room" at a mahogany table decorated with "money seals," or sleep on one of the proprietor's imported featherbeds. Ever the interminable entrepreneur, Hutchinson was still devising plans to expand her busi-

33. Isaac Desilva v. Dorothy Plummer, May 1761, Jamaica Grand Court Records, LXI, JA. The majority of Jewish people in the colony were descendants of the Jews who fled Portugal and Spain in the sixteenth and seventeenth centuries to escape persecution. Jews were granted religious freedom in Jamaica, but the local government imposed a higher tax on them early in the eighteenth century. For more on this subject, see the correspondence to the Lords of Trade and Plantations, including 1690–1691, CO 137/2, fol. 209, TNA, 1699, CO 137/5, fol. 55, 1715, CO 137/10, fol. 355, 1721–1722, CO 137/14, fol. 6.

34. "Census of St Jago de la Vega [Spanish Town] undertaken by Charles White, gent, in July and August 1754," Feb. 19, 1754, SAS/RF 20/7.

ness when she made her will in 1740, transferring her operations to her sister and instructing her to add "a piazza and a balcony" to the new house that she was constructing.[35]

Hutchinson's venture relied on skilled enslaved laborers. Eleven captive men worked in "boat gangs" that ferried her patrons in wherries across the harbor from Kingston to Passage Fort. Spending most of their time on the water, these men would have been expert mariners who maintained a degree of independence, a cosmopolitan outlook, and perhaps pocketed a bit of extra income from tips offered to them by customers. Hutchinson's coach drivers, Cudjoe, London, and Hannibal, would have established a similar degree of independence, sophistication, and savings, whereas the enslaved women who used the "coffee grinder" and "chocolate grinding stone" in Hutchinson's Passage Fort tavern or the domestic servants in her Spanish Town lodging house probably led more restricted lives under her scrutiny.[36]

Hutchinson's neighbor, Anne Merrick, who lived in a large house across the street from Spanish Town's Jewish synagogue, also controlled a retinue of professionally trained captives. Merrick earned wages from the enslaved cook, carpenter, and barber whom she hired out. Both she and Hutchinson further increased their wealth by acting as moneylenders and offering loans to a range of men. Hutchinson, for example, extended bonds worth upward of twelve hundred pounds to male borrowers, while Merrick provided credit to planters and pursued them in court when they defaulted on their loans.[37]

Whereas Hutchinson and Merrick amassed fortunes from urban pursuits, other female residents of Spanish Town took advantage of their location situated in the midst of rolling savannah land to merge urban and agrarian endeav-

35. Will of Mary Hutchinson, 1739, Jamaica Wills, XXII.

36. Inventory of Mary Hutchinson, 1740, Jamaica Inventories, fol. 43; Jane G. Landers, *Atlantic Creoles in the Age of Revolutions* (Cambridge, Mass., 2010); Peter Linebaugh and Marcus Rediker, *The Many-Headed Hydra: Sailors, Slaves, Commoners, and the Hidden History of the Revolutionary Atlantic* (Boston, 2000); W. Jeffrey Bolster, *Black Jacks: African American Seamen in the Age of Sail* (Cambridge, Mass., 1997); and Julius Sherrard Scott, III, "The Common Wind: Currents of Afro-American Communication in the Era of the Haitian Revolution" (Ph.D. diss., Duke University, 1986).

37. Will of Ann Merrick, 1745, Jamaica Wills, XXV; Ann Merrick v. Roger Ormond, 1743, Jamaica Grand Court Records, XLI, Ann Merrick v. Charles Kelsall and His Wife, Rebecca; Inventory of Mary Hutchinson, 1740, Jamaica Inventories, fol. 43. Merrick divided her slaves between her sister-in-law and cousins and gave the rest of her estate to her nieces. Hutchinson and Merrick typify wealthy urban women in the colony. They operated sophisticated businesses that relied on slave labor.

ors. They diversified, growing cotton, pimento, ginger, cacao, and provisions alongside raising livestock. Even the island's poorest free women scraped by on meager incomes from slave-based agriculture. Catherin Custis, a widow who died in 1739, relied on the labor of an enslaved girl and an elderly blind man to rear milk goats and cultivate corn. Custis's decision to bequeath her assets to the son of Elizabeth Thomas, a free woman of African descent, and to manumit the elderly man whom she owned suggest that she might have had African ancestry herself. Custis did not, however, liberate the girl whom she held in bondage. As Custis's will shows, nearly all of the island's female planters were slaveholders, irrespective of the size of their operations.[38]

In contrast with Custis's cottage-scale operation, the widow Elizabeth Collier, who was also a contemporary of Mary Elbridge's, ran a middling plantation. Collier owned a few small parcels of land, ranging from nineteen to fifty acres in size. Her venture was supported by the labor of twenty-four enslaved people who helped her to raise grain, corn, and cotton and also maintain a pen of sheep and horses. Planters like Collier shared more in common with farmers in mainland North America than they did with Jamaica's elite minority of large-scale sugar planters. Gritty and shrewd, these women probably spent a large portion of their time outdoors to monitor the weather, examine their crops, tend livestock, and maintain control of their slaves.[39]

Small and middling agricultural ventures of the kind managed by women like Collier were essential to the development of Jamaica's distinctive plantation economy. Jamaican planters constructed a more heterogenous agriculture landscape that differed from the models constructed in older English sugar colonies such as Barbados. These variations influenced the lives of enslaved people. Whereas 75 percent of the captives in previously established colonies labored on sugar plantations, a considerable portion of the enslaved population on Jamaica worked on smaller diversified plantations performing a variety of tasks, rather than focusing on a single job. Some were employed as ranch hands who managed herds of livestock while others grew crops of ginger, tended cocoa walks, and raised flocks of poultry. Not beholden to the demands of a onetime, sensitive crop, enslaved people who labored on these kinds of estates also exercised greater control over their daily lives. These conditions led to better health and higher survival rates.[40]

38. Will of Catherin Custis, 1739, Jamaica Wills, XXII, fol. 45.

39. Will of Elizabeth Collier, 1737, Jamaica Wills, XXII.

40. Although sugar plantations occupied a significant, and certainly prosperous, space in Jamaica's agrarian economy, planters and ranchers also established varied agricultural operations

By the early eighteenth century, some women planters were earning considerable returns on their holdings. In 1716, for instance, Anne Rennalls ran a profitable middling agricultural endeavor and commanded thirty-three enslaved people who cultivated corn and pimento on her plantation. Engaging in what became a specialized female niche in the agricultural industry, Rennalls also raised livestock, including horned cattle, mules, horses, turkeys, hogs, chickens, ducks, and goats. Though Rennalls earned a livelihood in the seven-hundred- to one-thousand-pound range—achieving respectable status—she still maintained a modest home, eating at an "old" table and sleeping on an "old" bed covered in "coarse sheets." A few opulent items enhanced her rustic existence, including brass candlesticks, a punch bowl and glasses, and pudding dishes, attesting to her access to imported manufactures.[41]

During this era, women ranchers began congregating in Spanish Town and the neighboring parishes, including Vere and Clarendon (Vere is now merged with Clarendon). Their cohort included islanders like Anna Woodard, one of the wealthiest women of African descent in Saint Catherine, who made her fortune from two livestock pens: Dirty Pit and Hoghole. Other women similarly prospered. Though Frances Curtis did not achieve Woodard's level of wealth, she still owned a house in Spanish Town and even expanded her holdings in 1728, purchasing one hundred acres in Saint Catherine, where she relied on six enslaved people to raise provisions and "stock and cattle." Abigail Cole followed a similar path. She likely rented out her Spanish Town property and chose to live in another abode on her "pen land" in the parish. During her widowhood, Cole augmented her ranching business, purchasing sixty acres at one time and one hundred acres at another in grazing land. A "negro woman named Diego"—perhaps signaling Spanish origin—probably worked as Cole's enslaved domestic servant while helping with the

on the island, which have received far less attention. Using Barry Higman's work on nineteenth-century Jamaica, Trevor Burnard estimates that only 52 percent of Jamaica's enslaved population were employed in sugar production. See Burnard, *Planters, Merchants, and Slaves,* 18, citing B. W. Higman, *Slave Populations of the British Caribbean, 1807–1834* (Baltimore, 1984), 46–71. Brathwaite, referencing Edward Long, estimates the presence of 680 sugar estates, 110 cotton works, 100 pimento walks, 30 ginger plantations, and, of particular importance to this chapter, 500 livestock breeding pens and 600 polinks and provision places as well as 150 coffee plantations on the island in the late eighteenth century. See Edward Long, *The History of Jamaica,* 3 vols. (London, 1774), I, 495–496, cited in Brathwaite, *Development of Creole Society,* 120–121. See also Shepherd, *Livestock, Sugar, and Slavery;* and Brown, *Reaper's Garden,* 52.

41. Inventory of Anne Rennalls, 1716, Jamaica Inventories, fol. 31.

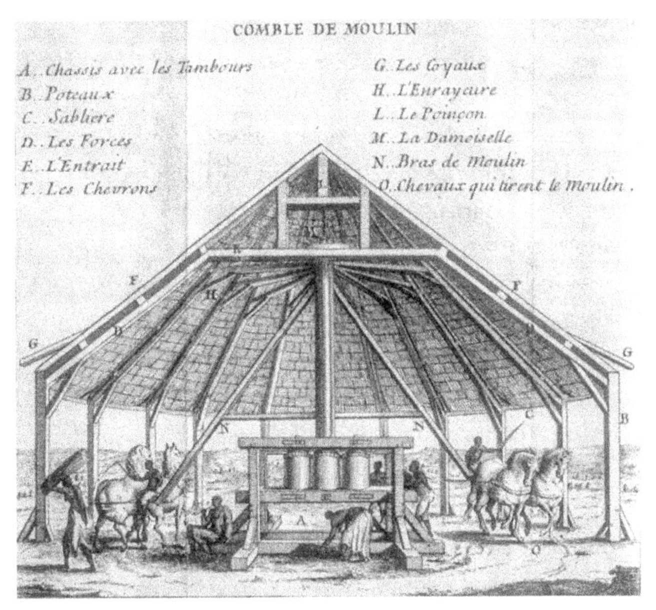

PLATE 8. Sugar Mill, French West Indies, circa 1700.
Plate from Jean Baptiste Labat, *Nouveau voyage aux Isles de l'Amerique,* III (Paris, 1722).
Courtesy of the John Carter Brown Library

daily chores involved in livestock care. Cole carefully distributed her cattle to her children and grandchildren in her 1739 will.[42]

By 1754, 11 percent of the sixty white women who owned real estate in Spanish Town identified themselves as "planters"—a profession that included pen-keeping. These women specialized in animal husbandry—a form of agriculture that has received far less attention than sugar planting despite that livestock were essential to the creation of Jamaica's plantation economy. Every step in the sugar cultivation and production process relied on domestic animals. Cattle, mules, and horses supplied the manure to fertilize soil that would have otherwise been rapidly depleted from repeated planting. Cattle and mules also provided essential muscle for plantations, where they moved heavy cartloads of cane to the mills and powered the large grinding stones that crushed the cane to squeeze out the juices (Plate 8). Draft animals then hauled hogsheads of sugar from the countryside to the seaports for shipment abroad. In essence, planters could not produce sugar without domes-

42. Will of Frances Curtis, 1728, Jamaica Wills, XVII, fol. 22, Will of Abigail Cole, 1739, XXII, fol. 28. Verene Shepherd refers to Anna Woodard. See Shepherd, *Livestock, Sugar, and Slavery,* 85.

tic animals. Yet they also devoted most of their land to cane fields, preferring to purchase livestock rather than raise them on their own. This created an opportunity for women ranchers, who capitalized on the symbiotic relationship between pen-keeping and sugar cultivation.[43]

Ranching was both more accessible and more suited to female agriculturalists. With lower start-up costs, raising livestock offered an alternative to women who lacked the capital or the lines of credit required to establish a sugar plantation (Plate 9). Ranchers could generate profits quickly. As Verene A. Shepherd observes, they stood to earn upward of one thousand pounds per year with a 300- to 500-acre farm planted in guinea grass for grazing. Developing a sugar plantation, in contrast, cost ten thousand pounds. Working with farm animals also connected free and freed women to agricultural pursuits typically identified as feminine in Europe and Africa. English women worked in dairying while African women oversaw herds of cattle. Communities in both parts of the world treated livestock as a specifically feminine form of property. Domestic animals were often included in a woman's dowry in Europe or bride-price in Africa. Perhaps influenced by these practices, Jamaican colonists also preferred to pass pen-keeping operations along female lines. In 1748, Priscilla Guy offered her daughter and granddaughter more than 780 acres of land in Saint Elizabeth Parish together with 183 acres of "pen land" in Saint Catherine that she had purchased during her widowhood. Similarly, Guy's contemporary Frances James transferred land and cattle to her daughter and granddaughter.[44]

43. Thirteen of the women listed as proprietors in the 1745 Spanish Town census identified themselves as "planters" under "occupation." But this census only listed female planters who lived in one town; the numbers were larger for the entire colony. See "Census of St Jago de la Vega [Spanish Town]," Feb. 19, 1754, SAS/RF 20/7. With few exceptions, little work exists investigating the involvement of women of European and African descent in expanding the plantation system throughout the Atlantic world. The scholarship on antebellum North America is richer, but it is an inadequate model for understanding the distinctive gendered dynamics of labor in eighteenth-century Jamaica. A century later in the southern states, white women's lives were more restricted and their roles more limited. Work on antebellum America includes Glymph, *Out of the House of Bondage;* Deborah Gray White, *Ar'n't I a Woman: Female Slaves in the Plantation South* (New York, 1985); Elizabeth Fox-Genovese, *Within the Plantation Household: Black and White Women of the Old South* (Chapel Hill, N.C., 1988); and Catherine Clinton, *The Plantation Mistress: Woman's World in the Old South* (New York, 1982). Verene Shepherd's detailed study of livestock on the island emphasizes the importance of this industry to sugar cultivation (Shepherd, *Livestock, Sugar, and Slavery,* esp. 23–31).

44. Will of Priscilla Guy, 1748, Jamaica Wills, XXVI; "A List of Landholders in the Island of

PLATE 9. *A View in the Island of Jamaica, of the Spring-Head of Roaring River on the Estate of William Beckford Esqr.* Engraving by James Mason, after painting by George Robertson. 1778. Courtesy of the John Carter Brown Library
This engraving shows enslaved people herding cattle. It also foregrounds a female figure, hinting at her possible involvement in managing the livestock.

These colonial customs turned pen-keeping into a profitable profession for women. By the middle of the eighteenth century, Spanish Town's female pen-keepers, like those engaged in more urban pursuits, were furnishing their homes with elegant and expensive imports and luxury items. Elizabeth Wheeler owned a house and a plot of land in Spanish Town "where the beef market is now kept," a prime location for a woman who raised cattle at "savanna pen." She also held three women in captivity who probably labored as domestic servants. The majority of her slaves worked as ranch hands. As a property holder and a slaveholder, Wheeler achieved the requisites for prestige and status on the island, which she further amplified with her chariot,

Jamaica Together with the Number of Acres Each Person Possessed Taken from the Quit Rent Books in the Year 1754," CO 142/31, TNA, transcribed at http://www.jamaicanfamilysearch.com/Samples2/1754lead.htm; Will of Frances James, 1748, Jamaica Wills, XXVI, fol. 123; Shepherd, *Livestock, Sugar, and Slavery*, 92.

jewels, rings, and plate. Another Spanish Town widow, Mary Baldwin, owned two pens where she raised 203 sheep alongside 128 cattle and steers as well as numerous horses, cows, mules, and asses. Baldwin amassed a fortune worth approximately £1,850 and furthered her profits by acting as a money-lender. She listed numerous people in her 1760 will who owed her sums ranging from £20 to £2,000. Her three homes (one in town and two ranches) embodied her success. Baldwin's guests enjoyed silver cutlery, china, and a tea table at which they drank expensive Madeira and European brandies.[45]

As Baldwin prepared for her demise, she carefully distributed livestock to the most important people in her life, offering to return the "note" that Moses Affalo had given her for two mules. She also provided heifers to Jane Lewis and the children of another woman, her "black horse coal" to a man, and her riding horse to Mathew Gregory, a wealthy and prominent member of Spanish Town's community. Rearing and selling horses, mules, and cattle produced considerable riches for Baldwin, who then used these animals to recognize her intimate ties to her kin and close friends. But Baldwin could not have achieved her wealth without the labor of the sixty-four enslaved people whom she held in bondage. As Baldwin's business shows, slaveholding was an intrinsic dimension of every type of female-run agricultural enterprise, from the small provision plot to the ranch to the sugar plantation.[46]

"IN IRONS TILL THE FIRST OPPORTUNITY SERVES TO SEND HIM OFF TO BE SOLD"

To prosper from their planting and ranching ventures, women enslavers engaged in a range of coercive behaviors toward their captives. By the time that Mary Elbridge assumed control of Spring, planting on Jamaica had become synonymous with a brutal form of slaveholding, a dynamic the Elbridge family participated in constructing. At the end of the seventeenth century, they sank all the venture's capital into African captives. By 1712, the Elbridges had assembled a complex labor force of free and unfree workers on Spring and in Kingston. In addition to an overseer named Kenny and eight white servants, Mary oversaw a group of seventy-four enslaved people—twenty-eight men,

45. Will of Elizabeth Wheeler, 1750, Jamaica Wills, XXVII, fol. 211, Will of Mary Baldwin, 1759, XL, fol. 10.

46. Will of Mary Baldwin, 1759, Jamaica Wills, XL, fol. 10; "Dr. Mathew Gregory," Legacies of British Slave-Ownership, https://www.ucl.ac.uk/lbs/person/view/2146650711; Inventory of Mary Baldwin, 1760, Jamaica Inventories, fol. 10.

including "5 negro men very old," thirty-six women, and ten children—who were valued at £1,254, comprising 75 percent of the total value of the property. A large portion of her work as a plantation manager involved either directly or indirectly purchasing, coercing, and disciplining enslaved people.[47]

When Elbridge took over Spring's management, its captives were aging and afflicted with a host of physical ailments, likely resulting from the harsh labor conditions, malnourishment, and disease characteristic of sugar plantation labor. Whereas Mary issued her white servants shoes and blankets and in all probability shared with them the food supplies that she ordered for the estate—which included pepper, nutmeg, bacon, oatmeal, cheese, rice, and onions—she expected her captives to feed themselves from the provisioning grounds they cultivated after toiling in the fields all day. This practice was in keeping with other planters on the island. Enslaved people were customarily granted the right to kitchen gardens, provisioning grounds, and animals, and they grew plantains, yams, cocoas, and corn as well as reared chickens, hogs, goats, and cattle. Though owners allowed them to sell extra produce and meat at the island's Sunday markets and keep the proceeds from these sales, such arrangements were not always enough to maintain a healthy diet. The colony's provisioning system also created high food insecurity on plantations, as frequent natural disasters and military conflicts led to suffering and starvation.[48]

In addition to chronic malnourishment, enslaved people on plantations were subjected to a punishing labor regime. Field laborers or "gangs"—the majority of whom were women—performed the backbreaking work of hoeing, planting, and cutting sugarcane while elderly people and children cleared the fields of weeds and brush. Men occupied the higher status positions: they managed the field gangs as drivers and operated the boiling houses and still houses. Elbridge's purchase of "coars hats" and stockings

47. When Aldworth Elbridge died, Spring Plantation was estimated as worth £1,630. See Inventory of Aldworth Elbridge, 1712, Jamaica Inventories, fol. 127.

48. Enslaved people came to control a considerable portion of the silver coin circulating on the island, much of which they earned by retailing produce and meat grown on provision grounds. Sunday—the one day off per week for enslaved people—provided them with a respite from drudgery, time to travel to town, socialize, spend money, and the chance to distance themselves from the plantation. For a detailed overview of enslaved people's agricultural activities and Jamaica's informal economy, see McDonald, *Economy and Material Culture of Slaves,* 16–30. For more on the mortality rates of enslaved people who labored on plantations, see Dunn, *Tale of Two Plantations;* Kenneth Morgan, "Slave Women and Reproduction in Jamaica, c.1776–1834," *History,* XCI, (2006), 231–253; and Jennifer L. Morgan, *Laboring Women: Reproduction and Gender in New World Slavery* (Philadelphia, 2004).

for twelve enslaved people hints at the dangers faced by the workers who processed scalding liquid. During harvest time, all of her captives worked around the clock to process the temperamental sugarcane before it spoiled. As Sasha Turner notes, the "unrelenting" labor demands on a sugar plantation made it difficult for enslaved women to conceive and bear children, for they often performed the most grueling tasks. Rather than fostering conditions conducive to fertility and reproduction, most planters preferred to replenish their enslaved workforce with new captives.[49]

Elbridge supported this severe ethos. She projected a utilitarian and profit-oriented view of the elderly and sick people on Spring, describing them as "worn out," "so old and past labor," and "not valued at anything." From her perspective, they were a drain on the plantation's resources. "The taxes and cloaths and other things for them when often sick," Elbridge explained in one letter to a relative in Britain, "is more than any manner of service they can do for it." The planter made arrangements to sell one woman, "bety," who was "sickly," and another, "hanah," whom she described as "a very lazy creture," writing, "hir work will scarce maintain" her. She urged her relatives with ruthless pragmatism to sell the venture before "any of the negroes dye or cattle," which would compromise a large portion of the plantation's value.[50]

Elbridge assumed sole responsibility for purchasing captive Africans to replace the people whom she defined as useless to Spring. Her Kingston-based home afforded her direct access to the slave market at a time when the South Sea Company's arrival had significantly bolstered the number of slave ships traveling there (Plate 10). When John Elbridge informed her that she could "have negroes at reasonable rates, there being many ships-going to the coast-that you may purchase what you want" in 1730, such advice would have been obvious to a woman who spent part of her time in a house located a few blocks away from one of the busiest ports in the Atlantic slave trade.[51]

Elbridge also exploited her proximity to Kingston's slave market to acquire African captives for herself. Some of these people probably worked for

49. Spring Plantation Account Current with Gale and Co., Agents for John and Rebecca Elbridge, 1730, Woolnough Papers, Ashton Court Archives, AC/WO/16/10; Sasha Turner, *Contested Bodies: Pregnancy, Childrearing, and Slavery in Jamaica* (Philadelphia, 2017), 12–13.

50. Mary Elbridge to Rebecca Woolnough, July 29, 1737, Woolnough Papers, Ashton Court Archives, AC/WO/16/15, Mary Elbridge to John Elbridge, Jan. 29, 1739, AC/WO/16/22b; Brown, *Reaper's Garden,* 50–55.

51. John Elbridge to Mary Elbridge, Oct. 31, 1730, Woolnough Papers, Ashton Court Archives, AC/WO/16/8n.

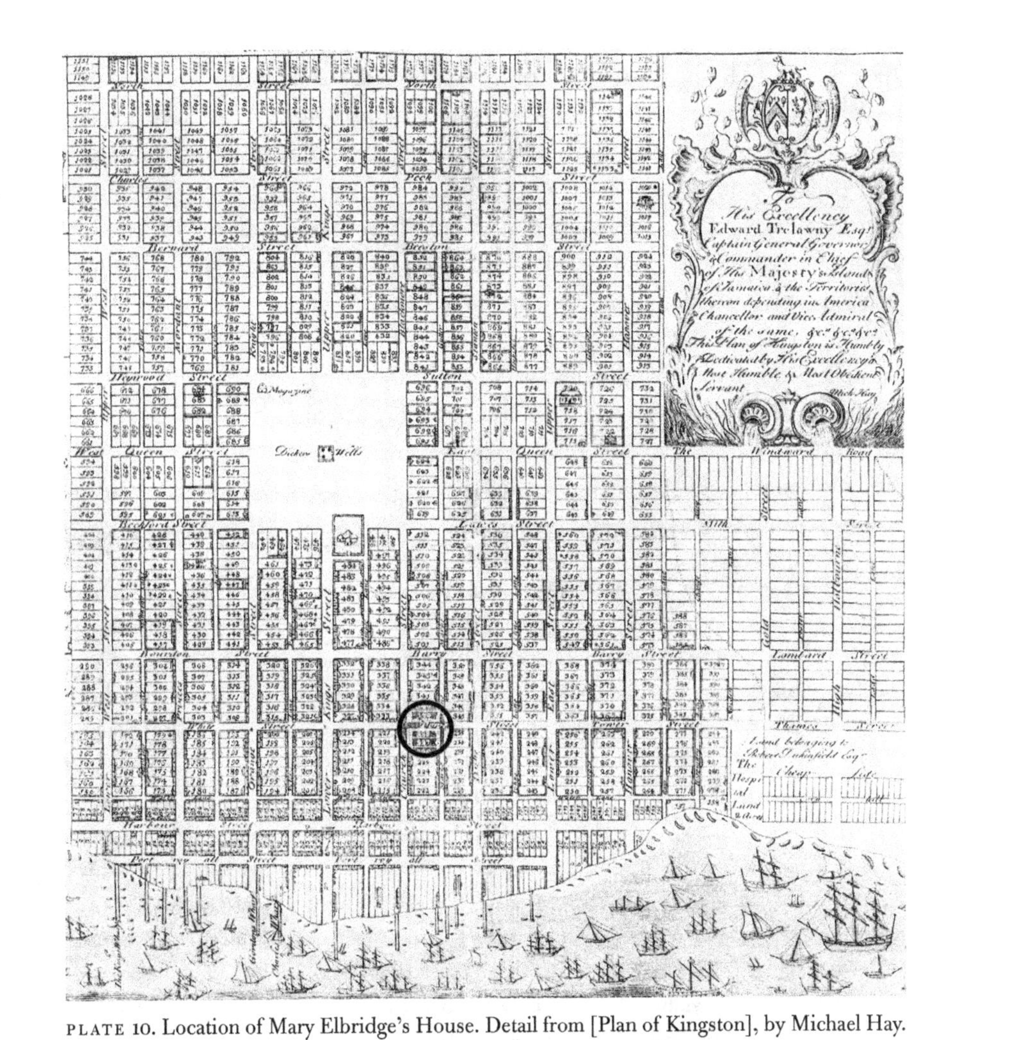

PLATE 10. Location of Mary Elbridge's House. Detail from [Plan of Kingston], by Michael Hay. [1745?]. Courtesy, Library of Congress, Geography and Maps Division, G4964.K5646 1745 .H3

Robert Elbridge listed the cross streets for the property in his 1726 will (Will of Robert Elbridge, 1726, Jamaica Wills, 1661–1770, XVII, Island Record Office, Spanish Town, Jamaica).

her as domestic servants, sleeping on the four "old Spanish mats" that lay on the floor or in the "old straw hammock" in her Kingston home. In contrast, Elbridge rested in a bedstead with curtains and mosquito netting worth fourteen pounds. Her bed was the most expensive piece of furniture she owned.[52]

If Elbridge aimed to project discursive authority in her letters to Britain, she wielded a form of colonial authority as a slaveholder that was immediate, visceral, and absolute. Although the nature of the type of sugar planting Elbridge engaged in is well known, the complicity of free and freed women in the systemic brutality of plantation slavery has received less attention. Though scholars have studied female violence in the antebellum South in the U.S., similar work has not been done for early British America.[53] The scarcity of records for the colonial era might account for this lacuna. Eighteenth-century Jamaican sources are especially sparse. Yet there are some oblique references in women's letters and account books that offer clues about how free and freed women treated their captives. Mary Elbridge's correspondence, for instance, contains shadowy allusions to her reactions toward enslaved people

52. Inventory of Mary Elbridge, 1745, Jamaica Inventories, fol. 132.

53. Payment to catch a "run away negro," Spring Plantation Account Current with Gale and Co., Agents for John and Rebecca Elbridge, 1730, Woolnough Papers, Ashton Court Archives, AC/WO/16/10. Barbara Bush briefly references the sadistic satisfaction that white women derived from physically and psychologically punishing slaves. See Bush, "White 'Ladies,' Coloured 'Favourites,' and Black 'Wenches': Some Considerations on Sex, Race, and Class Factors in Social Relations in White Creole Society in the British Caribbean," *Slavery and Abolition*, II, no. 3 (December 1981), 256, 258. Hilary Beckles briefly summarizes eighteenth- and nineteenth-century literature referencing white women's acts of "extreme cruelty" toward black women. See Beckles, "White Women and Slavery in the Caribbean," *History Workshop*, XXXVI (Autumn 1993), 76–77. Lucille Mathurin Mair references a few episodes of female owners beating and whipping their slaves in *Historical Study of Women in Jamaica*, ed. Beckles and Shepherd, 176–177. None of these authors, however, investigates female violence in depth. Terri L. Snyder's study of cases involving violence in colonial Virginia households is a useful starting point for thinking about how and when gender differences shaped legal and social responses to household violence in colonial societies. See Snyder, "'As If There Was Not Master or Woman in the Land': Gender, Dependency, and Household Violence in Virginia, 1646–1720," in Christine Daniels and Michael V. Kennedy, eds., *Over the Threshold: Intimate Violence in Early America* (New York, 1999), 225. For the colonial period, see also Kirsten Fischer, *Suspect Relations: Sex, Race, and Resistance in Colonial North Carolina* (Ithaca, N.Y., 2002), 166, 173–174; and Beckles, *Centering Woman: Gender Discourses in Caribbean Slave Society* (Kingston, 1999), 66–68. Although Thavolia Glymph offers a comprehensive study of white women's abuse of enslaved people, her work focuses on antebellum America. See Glymph, *Out of the House of Bondage*, chaps. 1–2. My work highlights a much longer tradition of female brutality toward enslaved people.

who challenged her authority. Although Elbridge did not discuss her own use of force directly, she did list payments for "catching a run away negro" and the "prison charges for a run away negro" in her account book, intimating the power struggle she engaged in with her captives. The entries do not explain why these people risked severe punishments to escape from Spring. Perhaps the abysmal conditions there made the gamble worthwhile.[54]

It is possible that Elbridge's slaves, especially the men, tested her authority because she was a woman. But, from an African perspective, female slaveholders were not unusual. Women living in port towns along the West African coast and in Madagascar played important roles in facilitating the domestic slave trade. Numerous captives passed directly through female hands on their forced journeys across the Atlantic, and they circulated rumors about these powerful women. Memories and stories about female slave traders in Africa likely informed enslaved people's views of slaveholding.[55]

On arriving in Jamaica, however, the extreme demographic differences between free and enslaved and men and women in rural areas might have emboldened some male captives to challenge female enslavers. Perhaps these gendered dynamics explain why enslaved men continually absconded from the widow Hannah Jacobson, a contemporary of Mary Elbridge's. Under "Sundry Charges attending the negroes" in her account book, she recorded payments for administering nearly thirty whippings to slaves who were recap-

54. Female-authored journals and diaries from eighteenth-century Jamaica have not survived. Moreover, criminal court records and slave court records from the early colonial period are not available. The dearth of manuscript sources has resulted in scholarly emphasis on a handful of accounts published in the late eighteenth and early nineteenth centuries. Two of these narratives—*Journal of a Lady of Quality, Being the Narrative of a Journey from Scotland to the West Indies, North Carolina, and Portugal, in the Years 1774 to 1776,* ed. Evangeline Walker Andrews and Charles McLean Andrews (Lincoln, Neb., 2005), kept by Janet Schaw in 1774–1776, and *Lady [Maria] Nugent's Journal of Her Residence in Jamaica from 1801 to 1805,* ed. Philip Wright (Kingston, 2002), chronicling the first five years of the nineteenth century—offer British women's observations about the colony. Alongside these, Edward Long's monumental three-volume *History of Jamaica,* first published in 1774, has become a dominant source of information about the social and sexual mores of colonists. Though fascinating in their own rights, Schaw and Nugent, both outsiders, only lived on the island briefly, while Long's perspective—admittedly extensive as a planter, slaver, lieutenant governor, and vice-admiralty judge—is notoriously racist and misogynistic.

55. Wendy Wilson-Fall, "Women Merchants and Slave Depots: Saint-Louis, Senegal, and St. Mary's, Madagascar," in Ana Lucia Araujo, ed., *Paths of the Atlantic Slave Trade: Interactions, Identities, and Images* (Amherst, N.Y., 2011), 277–279, 292–295.

tured, including fees for "whipping Tom, whipping Adam, ditto Darby, catching Chaplin, and whipping him." On another occasion, she paid for "catching, imprisoning and whipping four negroes, d. for Cambridge and Chaplin and whipping them, whipping Jonathan, prison fees for six negroes."[56]

Free and freed women willingly disciplined male and female captives alike for the slightest infractions. They used the threat of sale or transportation from the island as a form of punishment. In her 1727 will, Elizabeth Turnbridge ordered her executors to put an enslaved man "in irons till the first opportunity serves to send him off to be sold." Jamaica's legal codes required male and female slaveholders alike to punish enslaved people who challenged the authority of free society. In Britain, transportation to the colonies was a severe form of punishment the courts administered as an alternative to execution. Colonial laws, in contrast, empowered individual slaveholders with the right to transport captives off the island at their discretion. Women like Turnbridge readily enacted this form of retribution, which permanently separated enslaved people from their family and friends. The "spinster" Ann Perrin asked her executors to transport a woman named Nancy off the island in her 1746 will. Colonists generally transported people whom they considered to be too rebellious, which suggests that Nancy might have challenged Perrin's command. Perrin, in turn, planned to profit from the disciplinary action. She ordered her estate to use the money that was collected from Nancy's forcible exile and sale to fund the purchase of a "negro boy" for her own illegitimate son.[57]

In addition to whipping, jailing, and transporting captives, female slaveholders also abducted or "detained" them. Mary Elbridge herself was accused of engaging in this form of coercive behavior. She appeared in court in 1746 (the same year that Perrin ordered Nancy to be transported off the island), to defend herself against a man named James Edwards. Edwards claimed £214 in damages in return for Elbridge's taking two adult women, Venus and Obbah, along with Obbah's children, from him at Halfway Tree on the outskirts of Kingston. Elbridge argued that she was not guilty and put herself "on the country," asking to be tried by a jury: they found her guilty. The record does not reveal how Elbridge came into possession of the women and children. Perhaps she forcibly assumed control of them, or perhaps they

56. James Stout v. Thomas Verdon and Wife (Late Martha Stout), Sept. 28, 1739, Jamaica Chancery Court Records, 1738–1744, X, JA.

57. Will of Elizabeth Turnbridge, 1727, Jamaica Wills, XVII, Will of John Stoddard, 1730, XVIII, Will of Ann Perrin, 1746, XXVI. For a more detailed analysis of Jamaica's slave codes, see Chapter 1, above.

conspired with her to leave Edwards. Whatever the case, Elbridge strongly believed that she was their rightful owner. A jury of her peers did not. The fates of Venus, Obbah, and Obbah's children—the people whose lives were the most influenced by the trial's outcome—are unknown.[58]

The intensive reliance of women like Elbridge on slavery contributed to Jamaica's culture of violence, transforming agricultural regions into battlegrounds between planters, enslaved people, and, until 1739, the Maroons. Free women formed a small portion of the population in rural areas. Female aggression might have been intensified in plantation parishes where women, conscious of their minority status, felt compelled to defend their precarious positions. Elbridge's contemporary Jannet Hynes oversaw four properties in Westmoreland Parish, where she handled the shipment of her sugar from Jamaica to Bristol. After her husband's death, a neighboring planter tried to seize control of one of Hynes's properties: a six-hundred-acre plot "containing milk house, boiling house, [and] 100 cottages." Hynes and her daughters disputed his claim to the property, and, when they found him there, the daughters "with force of arms, ejected him" from the land. Though the court decided against the young women, who were categorized as "spinsters" and "infants," the actions of the Hynes women hint at both the tenacity and the tendency toward violence of Jamaica's female planters, who readily took up arms to safeguard their interests.[59]

Thomas Thistlewood's descriptive account of life on a sugar plantation offers further evidence of free and freed women's contributions to the colony's violent culture. Infamous for his own sadism, Thistlewood also recorded the abusive behaviors of neighboring women. On one occasion, he noted that "Mrs. Anderson" placed a chain around the neck of an enslaved woman named Sarah for "not Coming to Work last Week." Mrs. Anderson also hired out her captives to work on the plantation where Thistlewood was employed as an overseer, and he whipped them for arriving late. When Thistlewood punished one of Anderson's slaves, Coffee (Cuffee), for stealing a drink of rum from the distillery, Cuffee threatened to "complain to his mistress" about his treatment. Though the overseer belittled the threat, Cuffee's

58. James Edwards v. Mary Elbridge, 1743, Jamaica Grand Court Records, XLI.

59. John Doe v. Elizabeth and Hellen Hynes, 1743, XLI, Jamaica Grand Court Records. Doe would later claim in court that the property had been conveyed to him by William Beckford, one of the island's most powerful and wealthy figures. Aleric Josephs discusses Jannet Hynes in greater detail in "Jamaica Planter Women and the Challenges of Plantation Management," *Journal of Caribbean History*, XLIX, no. 1 (2015), 9–12.

words demonstrate his awareness of Mrs. Anderson's superior economic and social position in the community in relation to the overseer.[60]

Mrs. Anderson and other planters not only disciplined their captives themselves, they relied on a host of individuals and colonial institutions to enforce Jamaica's severe slave regime. Like Mrs. Anderson, Mary Elbridge employed a "M.[Mr.] Kenny" to work as an overseer on her plantation, and he probably performed similarly ruthless acts on her direction. Elbridge also used local establishments like the jail in Spanish Town to enforce compliance among her captives. Additionally, by the early eighteenth century, each parish on the island hired a "common Whipman" to flog enslaved people.[61]

Despite the violence of plantation life, when read together, Mary Elbridge's will, probated inventory, letters, and account books offer a more nuanced portrait of a woman enslaver's divergent and sometimes contradictory treatment of her captives. As noted above, Elbridge viewed the majority of the enslaved people whom she managed as disposable assets whom she readily sold when they grew ill or old. By purchasing African adults and children in the local slave market to labor on Spring Plantation, she increased the demand for more people to be forcibly shipped to the Americas. These are the familiar behaviors of a slaveholder, albeit one who is typically portrayed as male.

"MY NEGRO BOY NAMED HARDY"

If Elbridge treated most of her captives with calculated brutality, however, she singled out certain people of African descent for more favorable treatment. For example, Elbridge paid a "negro carpenter" the considerable sum of thirty pounds per annum to repair Spring's buildings and employed sawyers of African descent to make wooden boards. Their connection to the plantation hints at the presence of free people of color in the hinterlands, away from the urban areas of colonies with which they are normally identified. The enterprising planter then selected an "ingenious Negro Man and a Boy belonging to the plantation to work with the Hired negro." By as-

60. Thomas Thistlewood, Diary, Aug. 14 and 26, 1754, box 1, folder 5, Feb. 12, 1755, box 2, folder 7, Feb. 12, 1756, box 2, folder 6, Ser. I: Diaries, 1748–1786, Thomas Thistlewood Papers, OSB MSS 176, Beinecke Rare Book and Manuscript Library, Yale University, New Haven, Conn.

61. Spring Plantation Account Current with Gale and Co., Agents for John and Rebecca Elbridge, 1730, Woolnough Papers, Ashton Court Archives, AC/WO/16/10; Diana Paton, "Punishment, Crime, and the Bodies of Slaves in Eighteenth-Century Jamaica," *Journal of Social History,* XXXIV (2001), 927.

sisting the artisan, Elbridge hoped that these people would "learn the carpenter's trade." She also directed two other captives to work with the free sawyers and "learn to saw boards." John Elbridge, pleased with her plan to train Spring's enslaved workforce, encouraged her to have another enslaved child instructed to be a cooper and make barrels for the sugar shipments. Yet her distant brother-in-law did not manage the plantation's daily operations. Elbridge's right to select a few fortunate people whom she identified as "ingenious" emanated from her immersion in the business and her familiarity with its captive laborers. These people, in turn, benefited from forging close ties to owners and managers like Elbridge. They received specialized training, and, as skilled artisans, they would be spared from a lifetime of arduous agricultural labor. In addition to enjoying better health, enslaved artisans were commonly hired out by owners, which afforded greater independence, mobility, and sometimes extra money.[62]

Elbridge's preferential treatment of certain people was informed by intimate contact with, rather than distance from, them. Her decision to manumit a boy named Hardy together with two women, Peggy and Phillis, reveal the closeness that Elbridge perceived to exist between herself and a few of the people whom she held in bondage. As she faced her own death, Elbridge was preoccupied with the fates of these three individuals. She devoted the first section of her 1745 will to outlining plans for their future, underscoring their importance to her. The child, whom she described as "my negro boy named Hardy," received the majority of her attention. Elbridge wanted Hardy to be placed in the custody of her friend Catherine Feake, a widow who lived in Kingston, when she died. The planter gave Feake money to apprentice Hardy to "learn such trade as she (Feake) shall think proper." He would then be freed when he turned twenty-one.[63]

Living in a society that defined the majority of its inhabitants as property, Elbridge stressed her right to free people just as she did to consign others to a lifetime of toiling in captivity. With a few lines in her will, Elbridge

62. John Elbridge to Mary Elbridge, Jan. 4, 1727, Woolnough Papers, Ashton Court Archives, 16/8d. Manumissions, apprenticeship training, and free communities of color are discussed in greater detail in Chapters 5 and 6, below. Philip D. Morgan describes enslaved master carpenters in Virginia as the most skilled craftsmen. Their work commanded the highest prices. The man hired by Mary Elbridge seems to have been a free man of African descent, as she makes no reference to his owner. Sawing boards was the least valued skill, and sawyers were typically equated with field hands. See Morgan, *Slave Counterpoint,* 227–228.

63. Will of Mary Elbridge, 1745, Jamaica Wills, XXV.

altered Hardy's life trajectory. He would join a free family, be educated as a skilled artisan, and then possibly earn a steady income. The boy's experience would differ vastly from two other enslaved children, Barton and Clary, whom Elbridge bequeathed to her overseer and his daughter. Hardy's improved circumstances might have come at a cost though. It is possible that he was an orphan when Elbridge made her will and that she viewed him as a sort of surrogate child. Women preferred to manumit children whom they informally adopted. If Hardy had parents, Elbridge made no mention of them, affirming her prerogative to determine the child's future without consulting his mother and father. If this was the case, then even the act of freeing Hardy underscored her unconditional possession of the boy. There is also a third possibility. Hardy might have been the son or the grandson of one of the two women, Phillis and Peggy, whom Elbridge also manumitted. Perhaps his mother urged Elbridge to place Hardy under the care of a wealthy woman who would act as a powerful patron for him after the planter's death.

Though Peggy received fewer advantages from Elbridge than Hardy, Elbridge's treatment of the woman, whom she had inherited from her husband in 1726, further demonstrates how attachments to owners could result in material and immaterial rewards. In addition to freeing Peggy, Elbridge provided her with three and a half pounds, a copper kettle, and some iron pots. She signaled Peggy's elevated, yet still inferior, status by offering her "such part of my wearing apparel as my friend shall refuse to have." Peggy probably acted as Elbridge's closest domestic servant, and it is possible that she already maintained a degree of independence. Peggy lived in her own house on Elbridge's Kingston property; she also received the house for use during her lifetime along with a four-pound annuity when her owner died. These were paltry gifts for a woman who, by 1745, would have been elderly by local standards. Still, the bequest enabled Peggy to live out the remainder of her life as a free woman with a modest income in her own household.[64]

In a transaction that was commonplace by the 1740s, Elbridge also tied Peggy's free status to slaveholding. On being manumitted, Peggy would become the owner of an enslaved boy, Scotland. As Elbridge and Peggy understood, possessing someone else would bolster Peggy's fragile status as a freed person after her owner's death. Scotland might have been related to Peggy, though Elbridge's decision to transfer him to her own daughter after Peggy's death shows that she planned to keep him enslaved. The planter's generosity toward Peggy did not extend to the woman's children, who were listed years

64. Will of Robert Elbridge, 1726, Jamaica Wills, XVII, Will of Mary Elbridge, 1745, XXV.

earlier in the inventory for Robert Elbridge's estate as "Mulatto Betty" and "Cesar." If the "Betty" who appeared in the inventory for Mary Elbridge's property was the same woman, then she remained enslaved. Cesar's fate is unknown.[65]

By freeing and financially supporting Hardy and Peggy, Elbridge acted as their patron and treated the two people as inferior members of her extended kin group. She did not display this type of limited munificence to everyone. Rather than manumitting other people outright, Elbridge required some of them to pay for their liberty. At the very end of her will, in a codicil, Elbridge transferred a man named Selvin to her brother and included a proviso allowing Selvin to "purchase" his own freedom if he was "minded" to pay her executors the hefty sum of seventy pounds. As her handling of Selvin suggests, Elbridge was by no means a benevolent owner. The planter only manumitted an estimated 5 percent of the sixty-seven enslaved people whom she controlled at the time of her death.[66]

Mary Elbridge's uneven treatment of enslaved people exemplifies the arbitrary and sometimes contradictory nature of colonial slavery. Free and freed women had no qualms about using violent means to coerce and discipline enslaved people. They handled the majority of their captives like property, which women bought, sold, and transferred via inheritance. Yet, like Mary Elbridge, female slaveholders also forged close connections with certain captives. As their actions show, islanders developed a harsh form of enslavement that relied on government-sanctioned violence; but it was never an absolute system, and certain people escaped from bondage because of the rapport they established with their enslavers.

"I HAVE LABOURD AND FITEAGUED MY SELF FOR THIS TWELVE YEARS"

When Mary Elbridge wrote her will in 1745 and elected to manumit Hardy and Peggy while keeping the majority of her slaves in captivity, she was worn

65. Inventory of Mary Elbridge, 1745, Jamaica Inventories, fol. 132.

66. Inventory of Robert Elbridge, 1727, Jamaica Inventories, fol. 113; Will of Mary Elbridge, 1745, Jamaica Wills, XXV; Inventory of Mary Elbridge, 1745, Jamaica Inventories, fol. 132. Interestingly, of the people whom she manumitted, only Scotland appears in the inventory, not Hardy, Clary, Barton, or Peggy (Phillis was listed as belonging to Spring Plantation). Their omission might indicate that her directives had already been executed. See Chapter 4, below, for a table charting the average number of slaves owned by women between 1675–1769.

down by her incessant struggles with enslaved people. Years earlier, Elbridge had sought to divest herself of the responsibility of managing Spring to no avail—her British relatives had grown too reliant on a distant female kin member to allow her to relinquish her role in the business. In 1730, Elbridge placed her son-in-law, Samuel Dicker, in charge of daily operations. Though Dicker was one of the wealthiest merchants in Kingston, the Bristol-based Elbridges did not take kindly to the change in management. Financial results—rather than ideological beliefs about masculine superiority—continued to be their yardstick for the plantation's success. John Elbridge believed that the quality of Spring's produce deteriorated under Dicker's watch and reproached him with producing "common sugars." Blending emotionally charged attacks with business, Elbridge characterized the matter as a personal insult, demanding, "Can you think that I will bear such usage without shewing my resentment of it?" Elbridge supported his accusation with his sales records, showing that he had lost eighteen pounds on one shipment, accusing Dicker of negligence, and threatening to replace him: "As you have no regard to my interest nor to what I write, I will endeavor to get one that will."[67]

Though Elbridge called himself an "employer" and labeled Dickson his "factor," he viewed economic transactions through a lens of familial obligation and reciprocity. Operating in a moral as well as a financial economy turned financial shortcomings into personal failings. From this vantage point, matters like sugar quality became individual affronts. It was "unjust," he claimed, for Dicker "not to follow his orders." John Elbridge's conflict with Dicker typifies the predicament faced by family-run operations in the Atlantic world, where distant kin coordinated business operations across thousands of miles with rudimentary technologies. He was completely reliant on the colonial members in his kin group to produce and ship sugar and rum to Britain. The interdependency of far-flung relatives and friends to operate in the marketplace heightened each member's sensitivity to one another's performance. Mary Elbridge was effective in her role as plantation manager. Her letters established her trustworthiness, which she validated with the sugar that arrived in Britain. Consequently, John Elbridge described his "sister" as

67. John Elbridge to Mary Elbridge, Oct. 31, 1730, Woolnough Papers, AC/WO/16/8n, John Elbridge to Samuel Dicker, September 1732, Woolnough Papers, Ashton Court Archives, AC/WO/16/12 a–c. John referred to the nuptials of Mary's daughter in a letter. The newlyweds might have moved into the plantation house that Mary had so painstakingly repaired while she returned to her abode in Kingston. Trevor Burnard estimates that when Samuel Dicker died in 1762 he possessed a fortune of £30,014. See Burnard, *Planters, Merchants, and Slaves,* 285.

the paragon of professional virtue, contrasting her skill with Dicker's: "[I] expect that you would consistently have complied with the orders I have from time to time given sister Elbridge." He then claimed that his "sister" "would do every thing that is right and honest" in relation to Spring.[68]

Apparently, the complaints from Bristol compelled Mary Elbridge to remain involved in Spring. Nine years after Dicker was brought into the running of the plantation, Elbridge sought to separate herself entirely from the role. In 1739, she urged her British in-laws to sell Spring to another woman planter in the neighborhood, Elizabeth Lawes (née Gibbons), with whom she had devised a real estate deal. Elizabeth, who went on to become the Countess Dowager of Home in England, was the thirty-three-year-old widow of James Lawes, son of Sir Nicholas Lawes, lieutenant governor of Jamaica (1718–1722). In addition to Snow Hill Plantation, which she inherited from her husband, Lawes also acquired extensive plantations from her father elsewhere in the colony. Lawes planned to expand her holdings and cast her eye on Spring. Exhibiting expertise in the local property market, Elbridge proposed that the family sell Spring to Lawes for a down payment of £3,000 and a mortgage. The transaction would net them the equivalent of £1,000,000 pounds in today's currency. Elbridge herself stood to earn £1,785 from her share—enough to make her wealthier than the vast majority of British subjects.[69]

In comparison with her metropolitan relatives, Elbridge possessed superior knowledge of the plantation business and the colonial property market. She reasoned that the deal with Lawes would enable the buyer to easily move sugarcane from Spring to her sugar mill, "which would render both estates in one owner each the better for the other." Well versed in the island's property market, Elbridge also stated confidently, *"According to my notion of it is as nigh as can be computed the just valuation to be paid in money according as estates are now valued in Jamaica."* Projecting the wisdom of an island-born inhabitant, she augured a gloomy future for the plantation if it remained in Elbridge hands. She stated that the land was "worn out from constantly planting it for fifty years" and forecast a future of "dry weather"

68. John Elbridge to Samuel Dicker, September 1732, Woolnough Papers, AC/WO/16/12 a–c.

69. "Sugar Plantations in Jamaica, with the Quantities of Sugar Made for Some Years Past," 1739, Add MS 12434, BL; Measuring Worth, www.measuringworth.com. For more on Elizabeth Lawes (Gibbon), see Anne M. Powers, "The Queen of Hell in Portman Square," A Parcel of Ribbons: Eighteenth Century Jamaica Viewed through Family Stories and Documents, http://aparcelofribbons.co.uk/tag/sir-nicholas-lawes). In 1739, Spring Plantation was valued at £8,000.

and droughts. Enslaved people also factored into her calculation. Like the land, the property's captive artisans were "worn out." She averred it would cost £178 to purchase replacements for the men.[70]

Years of positive encouragement from her brother-in-law and factor John Elbridge led Mary Elbridge to conclude that she wielded influence in decisions related to the plantation. Yet John's death in 1739, at the very moment that she was trying to settle the sale, revealed the limitations of a colonial woman's authority in Britain. Correspondence sustained Atlantic trade networks, but, as Mary bitterly discovered, discursive relationships did not necessarily translate into authentic connections. When John died, he made no mention of his Jamaica relative in his will. Though he was "vastly rich and left long legacies," Mary did not even receive a symbolic token—a mourning ring or a handkerchief—to recognize their tie. Smarting from the slight, she sent outraged letters to the Bristol Elbridges: "[I] do not hear that he (John) has in the least remembered me who was his brother's widow and have served him faithfully as a sister and friend." Despite her dedication to the family and the business, she had engaged in a performance that was ultimately hollow.[71]

Adding insult to injury, the Elbridge family deferred the decision to sell Spring, causing Lawes to grow wary and withdraw her offer. Mary Elbridge experienced firsthand the strains wrought by imperial expansion on families, separating colonial and metropolitan members who often had distinctive experiences and interests. The inconsistent flow of letters across the Atlantic aggravated these tensions. Elbridge used declarative language to bridge this distance and assert her influence overseas. She mailed a stream of angry missives, writing in one letter: "For what reason you doe not comply I cannot imagine I am sure it is neither my principall nor for any advantage I can reap that I give you this advice." Unwilling to accept the letdown of her botched property sale, Elbridge quickly recovered and changed tactics, offering to buy the shares her Bristol relatives held in the plantation herself. If the family declined the sale, she demanded they pay her a higher commission as Spring's manager. They chose the latter option.[72]

70. Mary Elbridge to John Elbridge, Jan. 29, 1739, Woolnough Papers, AC/WO/16/22a (emphasis in the original letter).

71. Mary Elbridge to Henry Woolnough, May 17, 1739, Woolnough Papers, Ashton Court Archives, AC/WO/d, BRO.

72. Mary Elbridge to Thomas Elbridge and Henry Woolnough, Nov. 22, 1739, Woolnough Papers, Ashton Court Archives, AC/WO/24g, BRO, Mary Elbridge to Henry Woolnough, July 23, 1740.

As Elbridge's experience reveals, colonial circumstances foisted new demands—and new opportunities—on free women. But colonial sway did not, in Elbridge's case, translate into imperial power. Her provincial position was more limiting than her gender. Elbridge's relatives did not replace her with a male manager. They valued her local expertise and continued to pay her for her work. The family also increased her authority by granting her power of attorney for her niece's share of the estate. Comfortable in Britain, the Elbridges did not want to dispense with the colonial revenue they received from their Jamaican holdings. Defeated yet unwilling to give up her position and the income she earned as Spring's manager, Elbridge agreed to continue on in her role.[73]

Elbridge's later letters manifest a striking change in tone, as commercial confidence and financial pragmatism gave way to resentment and disillusionment. In her correspondence with her niece's husband, the merchant Henry Woolnough, who became her new Bristol factor, Elbridge sought to elicit pity rather than admiration, casting herself as a feeble elderly widow: "I think it very hard to be made so uneasy in my old days and in the latter part of my life." Rather than cite her earnings, as she had done earlier, Elbridge emphasized her colonial poverty in comparison with the wealth held by metropolitan men. "You are both gentlemen of fortune" she wrote in one letter, "and it is a trifle to you [;] but it is all the support I have and what I have labourd and cared for." She transitioned from a poised planter to a self-sacrificing and impoverished widow whose efforts for her family wore her out, lamenting "I have labourd and fiteagued my self for this twelve years." She also claimed that her late brother-in-law failed to pay her, leaving "no mony in my hands." Her correspondence with Woolnough displayed her mastery of eighteenth-century gender conventions. Perhaps recognizing that her earlier projection of more masculine assuredness did not yield results, she switched her discursive strategy, hoping the figure of the pitiable widow would be more affective.[74]

Elbridge was not the only female planter to adopt this approach in her correspondence with men. Years later in 1758, a dispute between Susannah Elletson, another widow who managed Hope Plantation in Saint Andrew Parish, and her son-in-law over mortgage rates led Elletson to portray her-

73. Will of Mary Elbridge, 1744, Jamaica Wills, XXV.

74. Mary Elbridge to Thomas Elbridge and Henry Woolnough, Nov. 22, 1739, Woolnough Papers, Ashton Court Archives, AC/WO/24g, Mary Elbridge to Henry Woolnough, May 17, 1739, AC/WO/d.

self in similarly gendered terms as a pitiable old widow. Elletson, who was "just able to walk about the house" with her walking stick, reminded him of the "difficulties I have laboured under since a Widow." She also recalled her son-in-law's promise to "serve myself and family," which meant not charging "more than five percent interest" on the mortgage he extended her. The planter then wryly informed him that "actions to me are the only proof, words I have long found to bear very little meaning." Mary Elbridge had learned this lesson years earlier when she discovered that John Elbridge's praise for her efforts turned out to be empty. Elbridge and Elletson sought to influence male relatives by adhering to familiar feminine tropes, stressing their age, status as widows, and their selfless nature. Aware that she operated in a gendered moral economy, Elbridge stressed her upstanding character, thanking God that she had "always discharged an honest consince and what other people wod have made an advantage of I scruple to doe." When referencing her niece, Rebecca, who had moved from Jamaica to Britain when she was a child, Elbridge described the "care and motherly kindness" she had shown to her female relative. Such correspondence turned the gritty business of running a plantation and coercing enslaved people into a form of family care.[75]

When Mary Elbridge died in 1745, Jamaicans had garnered a reputation for excessive cruelty and arbitrary brutality. An anonymously authored play—*The Fancy: or, A Voyage to London,* first published in London in 1744—perpetuated these emerging tropes. In a scathing critique of empire, the playwright uses the interactions of two Jamaican families with their English servants on a visit to London to contrast the corrosive influence of colonial slavery with a patriotic celebration of British liberty. When the character Lady Fancysick struggles to gain mastery over servants who refuse to submit to her will, she complains, "I wou'd be glad to be served by my own Negroes, and not by these Servants, who will do what they please, they have given me Warning;

75. Elletson to Ord, May 1758, Stowe Brydges Correspondence, Box 25, HL; Mary Elbridge to Henry Woolnough, June 29, 1739, Woolnough Papers, Ashton Court Archives, AC/WO/e. Hope Plantation was established by Major Richard Hope, a member of Cromwell's army who participated in the seizure of Jamaica. Elletson married into a prominent Jamaican family, and she oversaw Hope Plantation for decades following the death of her husband. Hope was primarily a cattle pen until the early eighteenth century, when Susannah's husband, like many other planters, began to cultivate sugar. Susannah's son, Roger Hope Elletson, would go on to serve as the governor of the island for a year in 1766.

I'm now troubled to look out for new ones." Referring to her abusive behavior, one servant states that she "D[am]ns and C[urs]es" and "threaten to use us" as she did with her captives. Another character, a colonist named Mr. Miser, exclaims that he longs to "live my own way," which means "have 'em [the slaves] at Command." When a servant urges him to "Take Care of what you say, Sir, you are now in a Christian Country, and not amongst your Black Slaves," Miser responds, "I don't know who can live in this Country, I'm sure I can't, I wish I was amongst my Blacks."[76]

The Fancy identifies the desire to "command" and "threaten" enslaved people as the definitive characteristic of colonials like Mary Elbridge. According to the author, slaveholding turned people into tyrants who refused to relinquish their increasingly ingrained impulse to dominate others. This trait prevented them from assimilating into a more allegedly egalitarian and polite British society. The author critiques the "transculturated customs," as Kathleen Wilson describes them, of white colonists, thereby emphasizing the cultural distance between the two places and containing slavery in Jamaica. In *The Fancy,* islanders mimic and appropriate the taste, speech, and manners of their captives. Lady Fancysick fails to adopt a genteel persona. She disparages British taste, claiming that she "can't eat the meat" prepared for her by her English servants. Instead, she longs for the African-influenced cuisine of Jamaica—plantains, yams, salt fish, cassava, pepper pot, bananas, and cashews—exclaiming, "I like them better than your varieties." Unable to appreciate polite society, Lady Fancysick also disparages London's social offerings in favor of African performance, yearning to "see the negroes dance" in Jamaica. Portraying creolized and Africanized colonists as foreigners in their own country enabled literary productions like *The Fancy* to distance metropolitan people from their own complicity in—and the benefit they derived from—slavery.[77]

The Fancy is also a gendered critique of powerful colonial women like Mary Elbridge who acted as slaveholders and planters. The author neutralizes the threat posed by female colonists who unsettled metropolitan stan-

76. Anon., *The Fancy: A Comedy as It Was Acted between Two Jamaica Families, during the Time They Resided in London, until They Returned into Their Own Country* (London, 1744), HL, act 5, scene 12, act 3, scene 4, act 4, scene 1.

77. Ibid., scene 4, act 1. Kathleen Wilson describes transculture as "the violence, creativity, and mobility that characterized Jamaican . . . cultural interchange." She uses this term to emphasize the operation of power in creolization. See Wilson, "Performance of Freedom," *WMQ*, 3d Ser., LXVI (2009), 51n.

dards of gendered propriety and challenged masculine authority by casting the character of Lady Fancysick in a patronizing light. *The Fancy* disparaged women like Elbridge because they wielded considerable social, legal, and financial authority. But, on the island, women's activities as planters and slaveholders overrode their gendered status.

At the end of her life, Mary Elbridge's power was waning, rather than waxing. After her brother-in-law's death in 1739, she managed Spring for six more years. During this period, she buried a grandchild and bid farewell to her daughter, who moved to Britain. Afflicted with "grief" after "parting with her daughter," Elbridge was plagued by a "distemper" for three weeks and then died in 1745. Shorn of sentimentality and ostentation, her funeral directives were simple. She asked to be buried in a "plain cedar coffin" in the Kingston churchyard next to her grandson. Unlike John Elbridge, Mary Elbridge carefully remembered her relatives and friends in her will, setting aside money for her brother, her niece, and her "dear friend," another local widow, to buy mourning clothing. Though she emphasized her poverty, Elbridge also left behind a sizable estate valued at twenty-two hundred pounds, which she gave to her beloved daughter.[78]

Mary Elbridge envisioned a radically different end to her life from the one planned by her contemporary Anna Hassall (the woman merchant from Kingston whose commercial activities are detailed in Chapter 2). Whereas Elbridge chose a modest burial, Hassall orchestrated a grand funeral procession that ended with her entombment in Westminster Abby. It would seem, from their contrasting endings, that the two women occupied opposite ends of the fulcrum—one was considerably wealthier than the other, and one relocated to Britain while the other was buried in Jamaica. Yet an entangled community of kin, friends, and business associates connected Elbridge and Hassall to one another, underscoring the importance of local ties in Jamaica. Elbridge's niece—one of the three people whom she offered money for mourning clothes—was Elizabeth Callender, Hassall's intimate friend who moved with her to London and then inherited Hassall's fortune. Further emphasizing the strength of colonial associations, Mary Elbridge also nominated the Kingston merchant Alexander Grant to be one of her executors. A

78. Thomas French to Henry Woolnough, June 4, 1744, Woolnough Papers, Ashton Court Archives, AC/WO/16/28a; Christening of Samuel Dicker, Mar. 2, 1732, Kingston, "Jamaica Church of England Parish Register Transcripts, 1664–1880," Family Search, www.familysearch.org; Will of Mary Elbridge, 1744, Jamaica Wills, XXV, fol. 3; Inventory of Mary Elbridge, 1745, Jamaica Inventories, fol. 132.

few years later, Grant married Elbridge's niece, Elizabeth Callender, in Britain. As Callender's husband, he then assumed control of the legacy Hassall had bequeathed to Callender.

If Mary Elbridge stayed in Jamaica, her British relatives could contain her influence, as her experiences after John Elbridge's death illustrate. Once her wealthier contemporaries like Hassall and Callender moved to Britain, they brought colonial fortunes and colonial customs, including a steadfast commitment to slavery and practices that enhanced female autonomy, to the heart of the empire. The majority of Jamaica's female colonists did remain on the island though, and British observers increasingly identified women like Mary Elbridge as disturbing figures of empire. The power they exercised over African captives exceeded the bounds of feminine propriety according to British gender norms that associated womanhood with weakness, delicacy, restraint, and sensibility. If actions of women planters unsettled British writers, Elbridge's letters indicate that metropolitan family members were also deeply reliant on the colonial knowledge and skill of Jamaica-born women. British critics of empire might have considered Elbridge's actions to be aberrant, but free and freed women like her were essential participants in mercantile and plantation ventures that revolved around slaveholding. Islanders could not afford to consign their few free female kin to domestic roles. Women, too, needed to play a role in coercing a large population of captive laborers to perform grueling tasks in towns and on plantations. As imperial strategists recognized, female colonists and the families they maintained helped to establish what was, at the time of Elbridge's death, the most productive and exploitative agricultural economy in the British Empire.[79]

79. Kathleen Wilson, *The Island Race: Englishness, Empire, and Gender in the Eighteenth Century* (New York, 2003); Sarah E. Yeh, "'A Sink of All Filthiness': Gender, Family, and Identity in the British Atlantic, 1688–1763," *Historian*, LXXVIII (2006), 66–88; Melissa K. Downes, "Ladies of Ill-Repute: The South Sea Bubble, The Caribbean, and *The Jamaica Lady*," *Studies in Eighteenth-Century Culture*, XXXIIII (2004), 23–48; Erin Mackie, "Jamaican Ladies and Tropical Charms" *ARIEL*, XXXVII (2006), 189–219; Vickery, *Behind Closed Doors;* Dror Wahrman, *The Making of the Modern Self: Identity and Culture in Eighteenth-Century England* (New Haven, Conn., 2004); Richard Godbeer, *Sexual Revolution in Early America* (Baltimore, 2002); Anthony Fletcher, *Gender, Sex, and Subordination in England, 1500–1800* (New Haven, Conn., 1995); Tim Hitchcock, *English Sexualities, 1700–1800* (New York, 1997).

4. Inheritance Bequests

Though Sarah Harrison was "sick" and "weak of body" when she made her will in 1737, she painstakingly outlined plans for the distribution of her modest estate. Harrison was not wealthy by Jamaican standards, but she carefully set aside a white waistcoat and a red striped petticoat for her sister Nanny and the sentimental gift of a silver spoon for each of her great-granddaughters. Harrison also left her "large Mahogany chest with a drawer in it and one small Iron Pott" to one of the girls. She had even acquired enough property to offer a small gold "finger ring set with a stone" to her friend Elizabeth Moore. Most of Harrison's family members were still enslaved, which indicates that Harrison, who self-identified as a "free negro woman," had also spent part of her life in captivity. Yet, by 1737, she had achieved the status of a legally free female property holder.[1]

Harrison's will is an extraordinary document. Only 12 of the 706 female colonists who recorded wills between 1665 and 1761 were identified as being "free negro" or "free mulatto" women. She made her will in the midst of the Maroon War, when free and freed people of African descent were viewed with increasing suspicion by colonial authorities. Although this charged climate might have deterred some property-holding women of color from declaring their racial status, Harrison either chose to categorize herself as a "free negro woman" or someone else who recorded the will did so for her. Whatever the case, her racialized legal categorization and her meager estate relegated Harrison to the lowest echelon of free society, making her will even more rare.

1. Will of Sarah Harrison, 1737, Jamaica Wills, 1661–1771, XXI, Island Record Office (IRO), Spanish Town, Jamaica.

Harrison recorded her will during an era when inheritance, not wage labor, provided people with the most considerable resources they would have in their lifetime. Wills dictated how vital assets would be distributed, making them essential family documents. As Amy Erickson states, wills also "reveal personal intentions," in contrast with the "impersonal operation of the law." These records yield glimpses of the plans and desires of people like Harrison, who otherwise leave few traces in the archives.[2]

Local conditions in Jamaica intensified the importance of inheritance. The island's lethal environment wreaked havoc on its human inhabitants. Still pools of water in towns and on plantations created breeding grounds for the mosquitos that carried malaria and yellow fever. Free and enslaved inhabitants were also plagued by smallpox and dysentery. Virtually incurable with early modern medicine, these viral and bacterial infections caused traumatic and painful deaths. Victims experienced black vomit, organ failure, swollen pustules, and diarrhea. Facing such pestilence, free settlers who moved to the island rarely lived more than thirteen years. Jamaican-born people who were classified as white commonly died before the age of forty. Aware of the terrible odds of survival, colonists understood that their marriages were likely to be short-lived and their children, who were especially susceptible to infection, illness, and disease, would probably not grow up to reach adulthood. In Kingston, white infants only had a 33 percent chance of surviving past age five. At the same time that free islanders struggled with Jamaica's toxic epidemiological conditions, they also contended with chronic warfare between European rivals, attacks by privateers and pirates, slave revolts, and, until 1739, the Maroon War, which began in 1728 as an outgrowth of previous guerilla warfare. Additionally, the island was ravaged by natural disasters, including hurricanes and earthquakes.[3]

2. Jamaica Wills, I–XXXII; Amy Louise Erickson, *Women and Property in Early Modern England* (London, 1993), 3, 33. Vincent Brown describes inheritance as one of the strongest "social currents" shaping colonists' lives. See Brown, *The Reaper's Garden: Death and Power in the World of Atlantic Slavery* (Cambridge, Mass., 2008), 92, 93.

3. J. R. McNeill, *Mosquito Empires: Ecology and War in the Greater Caribbean, 1620–1914* (New York, 2010), 48–49, 51–52; Richard S. Dunn, *Sugar and Slaves: The Rise and Fall of the Planter Class in the English West Indies, 1624–1713* (Williamsburg, Va., and Chapel Hill, N.C., 1972), 301–303; Brown, *Reaper's Garden*, 17. Trevor Burnard calculates that the average marriage in the parish of Saint Andrew from 1666 to 1731 lasted between six to eight years. See Burnard, "A Failed Settler Society: Marriage and Demographic Failure in Early Jamaica," *Journal of Social History*, XXVIII (1994), 67, 69–70; and Burnard, *Mastery, Tyranny, and Desire: Thomas Thistlewood and His Slaves in the Anglo-Jamaican World* (Chapel Hill, N.C., 2004), 16.

The colonial instabilities caused by demographic disaster and chronic warfare had imperial implications. Britain needed a sufficient free population to defend the increasingly important and valuable colony from enslaved inhabitants, the Maroons, and European rivals. The inheritance customs established by ordinary islanders—rather than imperial policies originating in the metropole—proved essential for securing Jamaica under British rule. Confronted with demographic crises, colonists devised inheritance strategies that enabled them to secure family property. By their actions, they aided in upholding Britain's interest in Jamaica. The wills recorded on the island between 1661 and 1761 show how free and freed people accomplished this feat. In spite of the decisive role played by inheritance in the development of Jamaica, colonial wills have received scant attention. Very little is known about inheritance patterns on the island during the seventeenth and eighteenth centuries. The existing scholarship, based on small samples of wills, emphasizes the masculine character of property holding, thereby overlooking the possibilities local conditions generated for free and freed women like Harrison to own property, especially in the form of enslaved people.[4]

Drawing on 1,210 wills held by the Island Record Office (the modern iteration of the Island Secretary's Office, where they were originally recorded), this chapter offers the first comprehensive overview of inheritance patterns in colonial Jamaica. All 706 wills made by female colonists between 1665 and 1761 are examined as well as a sample of the wills left by men who gave legacies to female kin (which show how husbands and fathers distributed resources to women) in one-year sequences for every decade between 1661 and 1770. The scarcity of census records combined with the categories devised by census creators obfuscate, rather than reveal, the numbers of free male and female colonists in Jamaica, making it difficult to determine the ratio of free and freed women who made wills on the island. A 1731 survey of Kings-

4. Based on a study of the wills of a handful of free colonial elites, Vincent Brown, for instance, contends that "white women were rarely recognized as vital participants" in Jamaica (Brown, *Reaper's Garden,* 92, 93, 100). Analyzing the wills made by 183 men in Saint Andrews Parish between 1667 and 1734, Trevor Burnard determines that husbands were reluctant to "assign significant economic authority to their wives" (Burnard, "Inheritance and Independence: Women's Status in Early Colonial Jamaica," *WMQ*, 3d Ser., XLVIII [1991], 106). Lucille Mathurin Mair's older work agrees with my determination about the importance colonists attached to enslaved people as a form of property in bequests to free and freed women. However, she claims that the law of primogeniture limited land transference to most women. She studies a sample of forty wills and eighteen probated inventories. See Mathurin Mair, *A Historical Study of Women in Jamaica, 1655–1844,* ed. Hilary McD. Beckles and Verene A. Shepherd (Kingston, 2006), 132.

ton's population, for example, lumps 504 "masters and mistresses" and 269 free people of African descent together in their respective categories without distinguishing between men and women. Altogether, 773 free and freed people lived in Kingston in 1731. During the five-year period after the census was taken, 25 Kingston women either had their wills recorded or estates probated. These female residents comprised a varied group that included a "free mulatto woman," a "tavern keeper," "spinsters," and several "widows." With estates worth a mean value of £700 and a median value of £300, these women joined Kingston's middling class. Yet their fortunes varied more considerably than these averages suggest: the poorest woman's property was appraised at £31 while the wealthiest was worth £2,361.[5]

Distinctions also emerge between inventories and wills. Inventories include people who died intestate or who possessed very meager resources. Hence, this type of source captures a broader cross section of colonial society. Female will makers, on the other hand, normally referred to "real" and "personal" property, indicating that the majority might have possessed middling to large fortunes. Nevertheless, inventories are standardized documents that lack the richly detailed and personalized descriptions conveyed by wills. Additionally, as legal scholar Lee B. Wilson points out, unlike colonies in mainland British America, such as New York and Pennsylvania, Jamaica did not have an intestacy statute, which meant that colonists followed common law and English statutes when someone died without making a will. The absence of a clear intestacy process and the limited data related to intestacy cases enhances the value of surviving colonial wills.[6]

5. This chapter draws on colonial wills and inventories taken from Jamaica Wills, I–XXXVIII; and Jamaica Inventories, 1674–1784, Jamaica Archives (JA), Spanish Town, Jamaica. Of the 503 wills made by men between 1661–1770 in my sample, 374, or three-quarters, identified themselves as husbands or widowers. The remainder in the group, who did not refer to wives, still left property to female heirs. Chapter 2, above, includes a more detailed study of the gendered and racialized dimensions of the categories in the 1731 census: "Jamaica to His Majesty, Relating to the Unhappy Situation of Affairs of That Island, by the Increase and Success of Their Rebellious Negroes," Feb. 11, 1731, CO 137/19, II, The National Archives (TNA), Kew, U.K. Ten women recorded wills and thirteen different women had their estates probated between 1731–1736 (I have excluded the probated inventories for the five women who also made wills). Since wills were descriptive documents that rarely listed total estate values, I only use the total estate values from inventories here.

6. As Lee B. Wilson notes, the colonial governor in Jamaica had the power to oversee the probate of wills and issue letters of administration—an authority colonists contested. It is not easy to calculate how many property holders in the colony died intestate. Trevor Burnard concludes

Read together, these records capture the views and practices of a variety of free and freed people, including women with modest possessions like Harrison. Although Harrison's racialized and gendered identity renders her appearance in the archive significant, these features had little bearing on her actions. Harrison's inheritance decisions reflected practices in wide use among free and freed Jamaicans by the 1730s. Islanders lived in a rapidly developing region that produced vast riches. Yet high mortality rates stripped families of male heads of household and heirs, making it impractical, if not impossible, to favor male property holders. To cope with dire circumstances, free and freed people modified and adapted British inheritance laws to suit local needs. These alterations benefited female heirs, who were often the only family members to survive to inherit colonial capital. The average free woman owned an estate with a median value of £285 and a mean worth of £803. Women acquired much of this wealth through local inheritance customs. With an estate valued at £28, Harrison was more impoverished than most of the women in this group, but she still adhered to island practice in her handling of property. Harrison, like most female property holders, preferred to transfer her estate to other women. This custom directed family resources, especially in the form of enslaved people, along female lines. In Harrison's case, this local inheritance custom also provided vital support to women who were still enslaved.[7]

Though Harrison was a freed woman who likely spent part of her life in bondage, she was also a slaveholder. In addition to bequeathing familiar feminine goods—clothing, furniture, and jewelry—to her heirs, Harrison also made plans to sell an enslaved woman named Flora when she died. Valued at twenty pounds, Flora represented her most expensive asset. Referencing the

---

that intestacy was high in Jamaica. However, as Wilson argues, the estates of people who died intestate were subjected to an escheat process. Wilson has found escheat lists from 1702–1703, 1709, and 1712, but, as she explains, it is difficult to quantify the number of escheats in the colony owing to the absence of data and the lack of clarity as to how the escheat process actually worked there. See Wilson, "A 'Manifest Violation' of the Rights of Englishmen: Rights Talk and the Law of Property in Early Eighteenth-Century Jamaica," *Law and History Review,* XXXIII (2015), 553–556; and Burnard, "Inheritance and Independence," *WMQ,* XLVIII (1991), 95–96.

7. Inventory of Sarah Harrison, 1739, Jamaica Inventories. The median and mean values of the average free woman's estate are based on my analysis of all 915 of the probated inventories of women's estates made between 1674 and 1770 (Jamaica Inventories). For a detailed account of the average value of a woman's probated estate and how her wealth compared to the resources of Britons who lived elsewhere in the empire, see Introduction, above.

"money thereby arising from the sale of my said negro woman slave," Harrison viewed Flora as an exchangeable commodity whose worth might yield enough of a return to purchase the freedom of her own children, who were still enslaved. In her handling of Flora, Harrison expressed the localized definition of slaves as a form of movable goods. Enslaved people commanded a high monetary value in the British Caribbean—the average price of a captive ranged from eighteen to thirty pounds between 1700 and 1750. Eager to liquidate these costly human assets, Jamaica's lawmakers and colonists regularly categorized African-descended captives as movable or personal property rather than defining them as real or landed estates, as they were identified in Barbados. The Jamaica Assembly also diverged from a 1696 statute that classified enslaved people as real property. Instead, both officials and ordinary colonists followed the inheritance customs associated with common law, classifying slaves as chattel that could be sold to repay debts.[8]

The first generation of English settlers in the late seventeenth century equated slaves with furniture, livestock, and plate, and second- and third generation colonists intensified the trend. A few years after Harrison's death in 1740, the Jamaica Assembly affirmed local practice, passing acts stating

8. Will of Sarah Harrison, 1737, Jamaica Wills, XXI; David Eltis, Frank D. Lewis, and David Richardson, "Slave Prices, the African Slave Trade, and Productivity in the Caribbean, 1674–1807," *Economic History Review*, VIII (2005), 679. Colonial lawmakers and colonists handled enslaved people as fungible assets. Richard Sheridan estimates an average value of thirty pounds per slave (*Sugar and Slavery*, 252–253). Personal property included movable goods such as household furnishings and clothing. Real estate meant land. As Edward B. Rugemer points out, enslaved people were considered real or landed property in Barbados, which protected them from debt collection. This definition made captives a less fungible type of asset and, hence, more difficult to transfer to women. However, he observes that the Jamaica Assembly did away with this distinction in 1684. Additionally, Rugemer finds that the Jamaica Assembly handled slaves as personal property. This conflicting treatment of slaves as real and personal property likely points toward the broader confusion and contests related to property transmission in Jamaica. See Rugemer, "The Development of Mastery and Race in the Comprehensive Slave Codes of the Greater Caribbean during the Seventeenth Century," *WMQ*, 3d Ser., LXX (2013), 429–458. Wilson describes this conflict in relation to escheats. Wilson determines that colonists used escheats to obtain slaves from estates where the decedents died intestate. Referring to "An Act for the Better Order and Government of Slaves" passed by the Jamaica Assembly in 1696, Wilson contends that slaves were defined as real estate on the island. See Wilson, "A 'Manifest Violation' of the Rights of Englishmen," *Law and History Review*, XXXIII (2015), 553–554. Here, however, my findings diverge from Wilson. Colonists' grouping of captives together with other movable goods in their wills indicates that they also handled slaves as personal, rather than real, property.

that enslaved people could be "accounted" for and sold as chattel to pay debts. Colonists took advantage of this definition of slaves as personal property, which made captive Africans easier to use in marketplace transactions. By handling enslaved people as movable goods, islanders made them a fundamental type of currency on the island—one that could easily be passed from one generation to the next. Captives were also distinguished as an especially suitable form of property for female heirs, who traditionally inherited movable goods.[9]

Jamaica's demographic conditions, inheritance practices, and the local handling of slaves as movable property were especially advantageous to free and freed women. Colonists devised pragmatic approaches to transferring assets that overrode gendered legal handicaps, even for married women. In British territories, wives were subjected to the common laws of coverture, which placed a woman's property under her husband's control. Under coverture, married women could not testify for themselves in court, author wills, sign contracts, assume debt, or extend credit in their own names. These kinds of restrictions proved to be unwieldy and unpopular in Jamaica, where families that lacked male heirs—and even families with sons—instead regularly transferred significant holdings to women. Colonists then took legal measures to preserve married women's property, establishing trusts and separate estates. In the first half of the eighteenth century, these family-oriented strategies became widespread, enhancing the capacities of female kin to hold property irrespective of marital status.[10]

9. [Charles Leslie], *A New History of Jamaica: From the Earliest Accounts, to the Taking of Porto Bello by Vice-Admiral Vernon*... (London, 1740), 218. Mathurin Mair makes the point that Jamaica lawmakers readily defined slaves as moveable property for the settling of debts and even applied this principle to the widow's dower, which was normally protected from debt collection. See Mathurin Mair, *Historical Study of Women in Jamaica,* ed. Beckles and Shepherd, 154.

10. Marylynn Salmon offers an overview of coverture in colonial America. See Salmon, *Women and the Law of Property in Early America* (Chapel Hill, N.C., 1986), 14–15. For more on women and inheritance in Britain and early America, see also Erickson, *Women and Property;* Linda L. Sturtz, *Within Her Power: Propertied Women in Colonial Virginia* (New York, 2002); and Carole Shammas, Marylynn Salmon, and Michel Dahlin, *Inheritance in America from Colonial Times to the Present* (New Brunswick, [N.J.], 1997). For a discussion of how the common law of coverture treated marriage as an ideal unity of person while giving the husband the legal power to act for the couple, see Joanne Bailey, "Favoured or Oppressed? Married Women, Property, and 'Coverture' in England, 1660–1800," *Continuity and Change,* XVII (2002), 351. Salmon identifies a similar pattern in colonial South Carolina, where high mortality rates also created opportunities for women to receive larger marriage settlements and control more property than they

Unlike the southern colonies in mainland British America, Jamaica did not limit the shares of personal property, which included slaves, that women could receive. Consequently, islanders turned enslaved people into a particularly valuable form of inheritable property for female heirs, who regularly acquired captives from parents and husbands and then bequeathed them to future generations. These familial actions aided in the commodification of slaves as a particular type of property and ensured the commitment of free and freed women to slaveholding as a primary means of amassing material wealth. More than half (452) of the 706 women who made wills between 1665 and 1761 specifically mentioned slaves whom they owned. Given the high saturation of slavery on the island, it is reasonable to conclude that a considerable portion of the women who only referred to "real and personal" estate also possessed enslaved people. Overall, three-quarters of Jamaica's female property holders were likely enslavers.[11]

Slaveholding offered female colonists an unprecedented means of accumulating and transmitting expensive property on a larger scale than would have been possible elsewhere in the empire. The addition of captive people to female-owned estates nearly doubled the value of women's holdings. Though comprehensive studies of women enslavers in other British colonies have yet to be done, Jamaica's primacy in the Atlantic slave trade and the massive size of its enslaved population indicate that free and freed women living on the island profited the most from Atlantic slavery. As colonial wills show, inheritance was a crucial means through which they derived this profit. Once in command of enslaved people, women preferred to bequeath their captives to female heirs, thereby further entwining the interests of all free people—not just men—in slaveholding.

---

did elsewhere in America or England. See Salmon, "Women and Property in South Carolina: The Evidence from Marriage Settlements, 1730 to 1830," *WMQ*, 3d Ser., XXXIX (1982), 655-685. John McNeill observes that early modern doctors perceived men as being more susceptible than women to yellow fever. McNeill suspects that this was probably owing to women's not being exposed to the disease as much as men (McNeill, *Mosquito Empires*, 35-36). Dunn makes a similar point about women outliving men in the Caribbean (Dunn, *Sugar and Slaves*, 332).

11. Jamaica Wills, I-XXXII. Kirsten E. Wood observes that widowed mothers in Virginia and North Carolina divided personal property equally with children but that widows in South Carolina received one-third irrespective of whether they had children. Furthermore, widows in Virginia and North Carolina only claimed slaves, defined as real estate, for life, whereas those in Georgia and South Carolina received absolute title to enslaved people. See Wood, *Masterful Women: Slaveholding Widows from the American Revolution through the Civil War* (Chapel Hill, N.C., 2004), 16-17.

Localized inheritance customs enabled free families to survive and accumulate riches amid appalling mortality rates, slave insurgencies, and military conflicts. As wives, mothers, grandmothers, and aunts, women played vital roles in familial property transactions, which often involved enslaved people. Their actions aided in securing Jamaica's slave system. By classing captives as movable goods, male and female testators engaged in a subtle yet fundamental act with significant colonial and imperial consequences. The interest in slaveholding originated in the free family. As families grew more reliant on enslaved people as both laborers and assets, they increased demand for more captives to be shipped from Africa to the Caribbean, spurring the rapid growth of the island's enslaved population, which, in turn, made free and freed women even more critical to sustaining Jamaican slavery.

"THE FEMALE ART OF GROWING RICH HERE"

Jamaica's free inhabitants were resourceful, pragmatic, and opportunistic in their usage of metropolitan legal precedents. Both islanders and the colonial court system acted in concert to appropriate British laws designed to regulate movable property and applied the concepts to enslaved people. In addition to defining slaves as a form of movable property—an alteration with specific benefits for free women—locals also used equity measures to override the conservative and punitive handicaps that coverture impinged on married women. Colonists were reluctant to subject family resources to the caprices—and debts—of male in-laws. Equity, an alternative set of procedures to common law custom, provided free people with a means of preserving married women's material wealth. Islanders adopted British equity procedures such as the trust and the separate estate to maintain the holdings of female kin, a large portion of which was comprised of enslaved people. These measures further deepened women's dependency on captive Africans, who were already used as one of the chief means of supporting female heirs.

Equity, or Chancery, courts were established in England in the fourteenth century to provide a remedy to the oppressiveness and inequity of common law customs. Common law required individuals to adhere to a set of precedents when handling property. Equity ceded greater power to the individual. At the end of the sixteenth century, equity courts began to administer separate estates for wives. Also called marriage settlements, separate estates enabled women to maintain control over resources during marriage by holding it in trust. The separate estate circumvented coverture, thereby posing a challenge to the common law definition of marriage as a unity of persons, with the wife subsumed under her husband's legal identity. As one scholar argues, this legal instrument laid the groundwork for the married women's property acts, which were passed later in the nineteenth century. But advancing women's rights was not the goal for most people in the early eighteenth century. Instead, families established trusts to shield assets from current or future spendthrift husbands.[12]

Jamaica's colonists participated in an Atlantic legal culture that was accessible to anyone who could get a hold of a conveyance manual, but they also innovated, using equity procedures and courts to further commodify enslaved people. The actions of husband and wife Richard and Anna Owen show how islanders devised multigenerational inheritance strategies to keep wealth under family control. The Owens used equity to shield their Jamaica fortune of £11,000 for their married daughter and her children. To accomplish this, Richard Owen transferred half of his property to his wife and the other half to his daughter in his 1730 will. He also returned "all personal estate," which he held under coverture, that his wife "was possessed of or entitled to" when they married. He offered to give back her holdings, which included slaves and £2,222, in "full barr lieu and compensation of her dower." Owen also instructed his executors to sell the family estate and the "profits divide between wife and daughter Judith equally." In addition to half the pro-

12. Common law courts emerged from feudal customs that prevailed during the Saxon and Norman periods of English history and subsequently reformed and improved over time. Common law covered a broad range of legal subjects, from individual rights to criminal law, and tended to follow precedent instead of statute. Generally, common laws limited the legal rights of women, children, and servants. The Court of Chancery, or equity, was a newer system of judicature jointly approved of and established by the crown and the church. Chancellors, rather than juries, decided cases in equity courts, which gained jurisdiction over trusts, land law, fraud, security for moneylending, charities, the administration of estates imperiled by mental illness, and the guardianship of infants. See "Proceedings in the Courts of Equity," in William Blackstone, *Commentaries on the Laws of England* (London, 1765–1769), Book 3, Chapter 27, Lonang Institute, http://www.lonang.com/exlibris/blackstone/bla-327.htm. During the Elizabethan era, the popularity of equity grew, and the operation of two competing legal systems created conflict in Britain. Equity and common law were still widely perceived in the eighteenth century as oppositional, with equity acting as an abatement of the "rigor" of the common law, a belief Blackstone sought to dispel in his work. Alison Anna Tait's study of Chancery cases from eighteenth-century Britain reveals the power of the separate estate. It "introduced the idea of divided household sovereignty" and was a "marker of destabilized gender roles" that forwarded women's property rights. See Tait, "The Beginning of the End of Coverture: A Reappraisal of the Married Woman's Separate Estate," *Yale Journal of Law and Feminism*, XXVI (2014), 216.

ceeds from the sale of the property, Judith would receive another £1,400. In contrast, Owen only left his son, who lived in Bristol, £200.[13]

When Anna Owen made her will three years later, she placed all of the "legacies bequeathed to me by my late husband," including five hundred acres of land, thousands of pounds, enslaved people, and the "bonds mortgages debts due to me," into a separate estate for her daughter, belaboring Judith's exclusive right to the trust. The money could only "be paid into her hands . . . for her sole separate and peculiar use benefit and disposal exclusive of her husband," who had no authority to "intermeddle or have any power or control over" it. Captives comprised a considerable portion of this trust. The ten people whom Owen's husband returned to her on his death were placed under Judith's control, and Judith would maintain the legal right afforded her by equity to "dispose, hire employ and enjoy the wages and their future increase" during her lifetime. They would then be passed on to Anna Owen's grandchildren. Although the distinctions between common law and equity might seem arcane, they were of great consequence to colonial families like the Owens. As Richard and Anna Owen understood, slaves substantially altered the value of female-held assets, which intensified the need to preserve married women's resources. Equity offered them the measures to accomplish this.[14]

Equity was designed to shield individual property rights. It is not surprising then that the colonies in British America that invested the most heavily in chattel slavery also established Chancery Courts. Access to equity benefited the free and freed women who lived in these regions. They inherited more resources and commanded greater financial and legal authority than female inhabitants living in colonies without equity courts. Second- and third-generation female islanders displayed an impressive degree of legal competency, and they adeptly established trusts and separate estates to secure married women's property. Marriage patterns on the island necessitated these Jamaican adaptations. Free and freed women married at a younger age than men, whom they also tended to outlive. As a result, female colo-

13. Inventory of Richard Owen, 1731, Jamaica Inventories; Will of Richard Owen, 1730, Jamaica Wills, XVIII; Tait, "Beginning of the End of Coverture," *Yale Journal of Law and Feminism,* XXVI (2014), 172–174. It is possible that Owen gave his son, whom he did not name in his will, an inter vivos (lifetime) gift, which negated the necessity of providing him with a large legacy. But it seems more likely that the two were either estranged or that his son had received money from another relative.

14. Will of Anna Owen, 1734, Jamaica Wills, XIX.

nists often wed more than once and subsequently inherited multiple estates. Sir Nicholas Lawes, governor of Jamaica from 1718 to 1722, wryly observed, "The female art of growing rich here in a short time was comprized in two significant words, '*marry* and *bury*.'" Edmund Morgan's glib description of seventeenth-century Virginia as a "widowarchy" echoes Lawes's characterization of eighteenth-century Jamaica. Although such depictions acknowledge the presence of formidable female property holders throughout the Anglo-Atlantic world, the principle slaveholding colonies on the mainland slowly restricted widows' legacies and limited their access to the executorship of estates. This change did not occur in Jamaica.[15]

15. Equity offered families a means of shielding assets for female heirs. The author would like to thank David Ryden for drawing her attention to this Nicholas Lawes quote in Edward Long, *The History of Jamaica. . .*, 3 vols. (London, 1774; rpt. 1970), II, 286. Edmund S. Morgan has argued that marriage became a "principal means for the concentration of wealth" in Virginia (Morgan, *American Slavery, American Freedom: The Ordeal of Colonial Virginia* [New York, 1975], 166). An equity jurisdiction was established in colonies in the West Indies and colonies settled later in the American South from their founding. See B. H. McPherson, "How Equity Reached the Colonies," *Queensland University of Technology Law and Justice Journal*, V (2005), 112–113. See also Salmon, *Women and the Law of Property;* and Lorri Glover, *All Our Relations: Blood Ties and Emotional Bonds among the Early South Carolina Gentry* (Baltimore, 2000). Richard Grassby reaches a similar conclusion from his study of twenty-eight thousand business families in Britain (Grassby, *Kinship and Capitalism: Marriage, Family, and Business in the English-Speaking World, 1580–1740* [Cambridge, 2001]). A handful of scholars have examined the influence of equity in reshaping gender relations. Marylynn Salmon describes equity as "the most significant change in the legal status of women until the advent of the married women's property acts in the nineteenth century" (Salmon, *Women and the Law of Property*, 81). Allison Tait identifies the separate estate, which was handled in Chancery Courts, as providing real practical and economic benefits to women (Tait, "Beginning of the End of Coverture," *Yale Journal of Law and Feminism*, XXVI [2014], 166–215). See also Erickson, *Women and Property in Early Modern England;* Susan Staves, *Married Women's Separate Property in England, 1660–1833* (Cambridge, Mass., 1990); Amy M. Froide, *Never Married: Singlewomen in Early Modern England* (New York, 2005), 117–128; and Sturtz, *Within Her Power.* Lois Green Carr and Lorena Walsh argue that planters' wives in seventeenth-century Maryland received larger shares of their husband's estates because they were widowed at younger ages with more dependent children. See Carr and Walsh, "The Planter's Wife: The Experience of White Women in Seventeenth-Century Maryland," *WMQ*, 3d Ser., XXXIV (1977), 542–71. See also Salmon, *Women and the Law of Property;* and Glover, *All Our Relations.* Though Jamaican marriage settlements have proven difficult to locate, wills refer to their existence. This trend in Jamaica mirrored patterns in mainland America, where widows regularly instigated their own settlements prior to remarriage. See Salmon, *Women and the Law of Property*, 89; and Wood, *Masterful Women*, 17.

Women continued to receive substantial bequests of real and personal property, including enslaved people, well into the eighteenth century. Indeed, the willingness of female islanders to use the courts to protect their claims has led one scholar to characterize them as "spoilt beneficiaries and litigious dependents." But such portrayals diminish the brittleness of women's property claims under common law. Female colonists were legally crafty and litigious because English legal precedents drove them to be. They used every weapon in the arsenal of property law to protect claims that were always vulnerable and subject to contestation. Unlike Governor Lawes, Jamaican-born author John O'Kelly recognized the weak legal positions of female colonists vis-à-vis property. In his early eighteenth-century play "The Islanders, or Mad-Orphan," O'Kelly casts the men—not the women—as fortune hunters. Describing marriage as a form of piracy, one character states that men seek to "plunder the Widdow, and ruin the Orphan." In Jamaica, widows are viewed as objects themselves, and "a rich widdow is as much gap'd after; as the guardianship of a good sugar work." Exploiting female islanders to gain control of their estates through coverture is described as the "laudable Custom of the Country."[16]

As O'Kelly understood, gendered laws made marriage a far riskier proposal for women than it was for men, who married wealthy widows in fact and fiction for their own benefit. The career of Sir Hans Sloane, the celebrated pioneer in natural history, a member of the Royal Society, and a founder of the British Museum, offers one example of a man who acquired his fortune from a Jamaican widow. Sloane traveled to the island as the personal physician of Christopher Monck, second duke of Albemarle, when Monck was appointed lieutenant governor there in 1687. While in Jamaica, Sloane befriended the physician Fulke Rose, who made the bulk of his fortune importing captive Africans and cultivating sugar. Sloane married Rose's widow in 1695, soon after his friend's death, and gained control of the substantial inheritance she received from him. A widow's Jamaica riches, produced from plantation slavery and the slave trade, provided the start-up capi-

16. John O'Kelly, "The Islanders, or Mad Orphan," [before 1727], Kings MS 301, British Library (BL), London. Lucille Mathurin Mair disparagingly described white women's legal activities in the following manner: "Having little other means of livelihood than what their menfolk handed out, maiden sisters, aggrieved wives, determined widows were prepared to harass the estate for legacies and allowances." See Mathurin Mair, *Historical Study of Women in Jamaica,* ed. Beckles and Shepherd, 167.

tal for Sloane's popular medical practice and the publication of his scientific findings in Britain.[17]

By the eighteenth century, Scottish merchants were following in Hans Sloane's footsteps. They traveled to Jamaica with the express purpose of marrying local widows and leveraging common law, bypassing "the standard way" to earn fortunes "by attention to business." Remarriage, however, was not a one-sided act that only benefited men. For some women, remarrying promised greater financial security and an improved social standing. Others showed an acute awareness of the threat posed by remarriage. Widowhood "gave a woman power, a legal identity, and independence." Unlike spinsters, widows garnered social respect for having once been married; most also gained a separate income after their husbands' deaths. A large number of men vested wives with absolute control over family wealth. Widows who acted as sole heirs and executors could divvy up property as they chose, which often meant sheltering resources for children.[18]

17. Fulke Rose imported large numbers of Royal African Company slaves to Jamaica during the 1670s. See James Delbourgo, "Slavery in the Cabinet of Curiosities: Hans Sloane's Atlantic World," *British Museum,* 2007, https://www.britishmuseum.org/PDF/Delbourgo%20essay.pdf. See also Delbourgo, "Sir Hans Sloane's Milk Chocolate and the Whole History of the Cacao," *Social Text,* XXIX, no. 1 (106) (Spring 2011), 75; and *Oxford Dictionary of National Biography,* online ed., s.v. "Sloane, Sir Hans, Baronet (1660–1753), Physician and Collector," by Arthur MacGregor, https://doi-org.proxy.wm.edu/10.1093/ref:odnb/25730. The match with a colonial woman proved to be profitable for Sloane. Fulke Rose left his wife, Elizabeth, one-third of the family estate for life and two thousand pounds as well as plate, jewels, and furniture. Given that Elizabeth Rose was also pregnant when Fulke authored his will, he strove to follow the common law of primogeniture, offering his unborn child the majority of the family property if it was a boy. He provided each of his three living daughters with her own plantation together with property in Spanish Town. In addition to inheriting from her late husband, Elizabeth was the coheir of her father's estate. See Will of Fulke Rose, June 17, 1691, Abstracts of Jamaica Wills, 1625–1792, Add MS 34181, BL.

18. Alan L. Karras, *Sojourners in the Sun: Scottish Migrants in Jamaica and the Chesapeake, 1740–1800* (Ithaca, N.Y., 1992), 158; Grassby, *Kinship and Capitalism,* 150. Amanda Vickery observes that the "spinster and the wife were divided by a chasm of status. Upon marriage a woman renounced her legal personality in common law . . . but acquired significant social credit in compensation . . . . A wife had a prominent position in the fundamental institution of society, the male-headed household family." See Vickery, *Behind Closed Doors: At Home in Georgian England* (New Haven, Conn., 2009), 193. Spinsters also had the legal right to make wills, but fewer chose to do so. The disparity between widows and spinsters suggest free women were to marry at least once in the colony, leaving fewer spinsters. Or perhaps spinsters' resources were

Last wills and testaments created a contested terrain where the friction between common law and equity—masculine privilege and colonial reality—played out. If they married, women relinquished their power over property. They also stood to lose control of their children. Only fathers were considered to be legal guardians. This is why Francis Palmer insisted on his wife's sole guardianship of their children in his 1710 will. She alone would assume the "management of whole estate" during their "minority" and could "not be removed from guardianship by any person." Other husbands manipulated their patriarchal privileges to separate mothers from offspring. Joseph Dickson asserted "above all things that the hand of my wife may be totally unconcerned in every thing or anything that concerns her [the daughter Mary] either as to her interest education or otherwise." Dickson granted his wife a £350 annuity, but the money was more of a bribe than a gift. If she rejected the annuity, it would "be void and not effect" the "guardianship and care of my daughter," whom the father placed under the control of two male executors. Dickson's will does not explain why he sought to divide mother and daughter, but his actions expose the raw legal authority husbands exercised over their wives.[19]

Infrequently, men also added punitive clauses to their wills, threatening spouses with the seizure of children and estates to dissuade them from remarrying. Mariner Daniel Cornelius's wife would possess his houses and slaves during her widowhood, but, according to his 1710 will, if "my wife do marry again . . . she shall have only her third part." In other words, her more generous portion would be reduced to the customary dower allotment. Men like Cornelius might have aimed to guard their property and children from the exploits of new husbands. Similarly, the planter John Curle, a contemporary of Cornelius's, made his wife sole executor, giving her five acres of land along with the use of his holdings during her lifetime. If she had a "desire" to remarry, however, Curle required the new husband to agree to a marriage settlement and offer "good and sufficient security" that his estate would not be "wasted or embezzled." She would also be compelled to relin-

---

more meager, although the considerable legacies parents gave to daughters does not support such a conclusion. Twenty women identified themselves by their occupations rather than marital status. They worked as tavernkeepers, midwives, planters, schoolmistresses, and seamstresses. Amy Froide also shows that spinsters, or single women, in early modern England received considerable legacies from parents and continued to prosper throughout their lives. They were not pauperized, as has been assumed (Froide, *Never Married*, 118).

19. Will of Francis Palmer, 1710, Jamaica Wills, XIII, Will of Joseph Dickson, 1730, XVIII.

quish the guardianship of their son on remarriage. A little more than a decade later, Daniel Lopez Laguna, a member of the colony's Jewish community, provided his wife with a plot of land and a house "rent free." He then stipulated that if she remarried, "I leave her no house or anything." Likewise, in 1730, tavernkeeper Thomas Webb awarded his wife all of his property for life; her remarriage would reduce the share to her widow's "third," or dower. John Harding adopted a harsher measure, transferring two enslaved girls, a horse, saddle, and an annuity of thirty-seven pounds to his spouse, but, if she wed again, she "was to have nothing to do with the estate nor to have care of my children any longer till they are fit to be put to school either here or in England." Regardless of their motives, husbands' instructions show how they exerted influence over widows from beyond the grave, either reducing or severely restricting women's rights to material resources and children.[20]

The above instances, however were unusual. Islanders generally sought to shelter, rather than undermine, female property claims. By the 1720s, they used wills to establish trusts and estates for female heirs while expressly denying husbands the "authority" and the "power" they claimed through coverture. Thomas Hals, Jr., created a trust for his "dear and honored" mother to ensure that it would not "be subject to the power control or debts of her said husband or any future husband but to be enjoyed by her and to be disposed of . . . notwithstanding her coverture." Similarly, Barnart Woodstock set up a trust for his "beloved sister" and ordered her trustees to only accept receipts in her handwriting, "notwithstanding her coverture." Barnart wrote that it was his unequivocal "will and meaning" that his sister's spouse could not "receive take or intermeddle" with her income, which was solely for her "separate use and benefit."[21]

Separate estates or trusts were of great consequence for married women. Those who had them acquired an independent source of income as well as the right to devise assets and to appear in Chancery Court as litigants. In an era when obtaining a legal divorce was rare and costly, the trust also provided women who separated from dissolute or violent husbands with a means of supporting themselves. Few colonists who created stipulations or established

20. Will of Daniel Cornelius, 1710, Jamaica Wills, XIII, Will of John Curle, 1710, XIII, Will of Daniel Lopez Laguna, 1722, XVI, Will of Thomas Webb, 1730, XVIII, Will of John Harding, 1740, XXII. An estimated 17 out of the 330 men with living wives placed restrictions on the inheritance of their spouses if they remarried. See Jamaica Wills, I–XXXVIII.

21. Will of Thomas Richard Hals, 1748, Jamaica Wills, XXVII, Will of Barnart Andriess Woodstock, 1753, XXIX.

trusts for kinswomen overtly referred to marital strife as a reason for doing so, but some implied it. When Elizabeth Taylor offered her daughter a £2,536 legacy, she stressed that the money was a "separate estate" from her husband and hence "not subject to his debts." Maynard Clarke was more explicit about the purpose of the £214 he bequeathed to his "dear unhappy and much injured niece." Openly expressing contempt for her husband, whom he described in his 1759 will as his "profligate abandoned nephew," Clarke wanted his niece to use the funds to travel to England and see her children. Clarke recognized that women like his niece who married tyrannical or "profligate" spouses had few legal options for dissolving their marriages. By establishing separate estates, they at least provided female kin with independent income.[22]

Wives who held property in separate estates could act as autonomous economic agents who could extend credit or assume debts. Lady Mary Molesworth, for instance, placed £308 in a trust to pay off the debts of her niece in 1721. She also gave her an annuity of £46, insisting that her niece's husband "shall have no power thereof . . . notwithstanding her coverture." When she made her will eight years later, Priscilla Saunders mentioned "considerable sums of money" that she had paid toward her husband's debts "out of my own separate estate and effects." Married women could also subvert common law and bequeath property that they held in trusts. The widow Elizabeth Hargrave referred to an agreement with her future husband that, "notwithstanding . . . coverture," "empowered" her to write her own will in 1744, which she used to bequeath the substantial sum of £7,142 in a trust for her daughters. Aware of the power of equity, Hargrave also wanted the inheritance for her married daughter to be kept "separate" from her husband and "not subject to his control during her life."[23]

22. Will of Elizabeth Taylor, 1752, Jamaica Wills, XXVIII, Will of Maynard Clarke, 1759, XXXII. Alison Tait discusses the benefits that the separate estate offered to married women in Britain. Married women in Jamaica also enjoyed these advantages. See Tait, "Beginning of the End of Coverture," *Yale Journal of Law and Feminism,* XXVI (2014), 205–208. Divorce could only be granted by an act of Parliament. A couple could seek a judicial separation from an ecclesiastical or a Chancery Court, but Jamaica did not have an ecclesiastical court. Chancery would have been the only option for women to seek legal separation and financial support. For more on Chancery and separation in Britain, see ibid., 184–189.

23. Will of Mary Molesworth, 1721, Jamaica Wills, XV, Will of Priscilla Saunders, 1729, XVIII, Will of Elizabeth Etough [Hargrave], 1744, XXIV (Hargrave remarried). Women circumvented the rules related to real estate by conveying real property to themselves before remarry-

Women like Hargrave who had experienced the limitations of coverture in previous marriages were particularly anxious to shield legacies for female kin. Another widow, Priscilla Guy, employed equity to manipulate her granddaughter's marriage. She placed 780 acres of land in trust jointly for her daughter and her granddaughter "exclusive" of the latter's husband, who would "not have or interfere with it." Additionally, Guy offered to make her granddaughter her sole heir if she agreed not to "cohabit" with her spouse. Perhaps the grandmother was a family meddler, or maybe she dangled the offer of a larger inheritance in front of her granddaughter as a means of persuading her to leave a bad marriage.[24]

Equity also provided colonists with a means of strengthening women's claims to enslaved people as property, which advanced their interest in slaveholding. According to the 1741 will of Martha Hughes, a widowed mantua-maker from Kingston who possessed three "Indian and negro slaves," she had set up a trust that asserted her full ownership of the captives and the right to bequeath them when she remarried. Mothers showed particular concern for daughters' claims to enslaved people. When Margaret Tenticow left ten captives and the rest of her property to her daughter in 1741, she barred her son-in-law "from having any right title or claim" to the legacy, ordering that "he shall have no authority to sell or alienate her inheritance." That same year, the widow Charity Butler also placed ten enslaved people in a trust for her daughter, "for her sole and separate use," stating that it was her "express will" that her son-in-law would have "no power to intermeddle with the said negro slaves and that he do not receive any benefit from them." The trust, in effect, enabled Tenticow and Butler to uphold their daughters' rights as slaveholders.[25]

The overlapping—and often competing—aims of coverture and equity placed wives in ambiguous legal positions. Colonists brought the more serious conflicts that were generated by this uncertainty to the island's Chancery Court. British Chancery Courts drew criticism for lengthy and expensive cases, involving the settlement of numerous accounts, inquiries into debts, and a "hundred little facts to be cleared up" before a decree was issued.

---

ing. See Tait, "Beginning of the End of Coverture," *Yale Journal of Law and Feminism,* XXVI (2014), 201.

24. Will of Priscilla Guy, 1748, Jamaica Wills, XXVI. If Priscilla's granddaughter remained with her spouse, then her daughter would inherit the property.

25. Will of Martha Hughes, 1741, Jamaica Wills, XXIII, Will of Margaret Tenticow, 1752, XXVIII, Will of Charity Butler, 1744, XXIV.

Jamaica's Chancery Court offered locals the only legal venue for resolving disputes over substantial amounts of real and personal property. Elizabeth Eaton initiated a suit against the friends of her second husband to Chancery in 1739, claiming that they had all conspired to embezzle her estate. Eaton alleged that she was "in good circumstances," having "by her labour and industry saved a considerable sum of money" when she decided to remarry. Attracted to the wealthy widow, her late husband, who was "pleased" with her fortune, "induced her to become his wife" and promised to bequeath land and slaves to her, which the couple agreed to in a marriage settlement.[26]

When her new spouse died, the widow Eaton discovered that the deed devising his property to her had never been proved. She believed that the paperwork error resulted from her husband's "contrivance," their attorney's "negligence," or the connivance of his friends. Eaton's case underscores the influence of common law principles to determine property rights. Though she had carefully designed a marriage settlement, the absence of an official document threatened her claim to her husband's estate. The Eaton suit also illuminates how remarriage sparked a host of thorny conflicts over resources for women as they cycled between the legal independence of widowhood and dependency of wedlock. During the early decades of the eighteenth century, slaveholding augmented the value of family holdings, making the stakes of inheritance even higher.[27]

Remarriage and slaveholding likewise shaped the dispute between William Martin and his mother Elizabeth Bows. When Martin sued his mother in Chancery in 1709, she had been married four times. Bows's first husband bequeathed a large plantation and enslaved people to her. A year later, Bows married William's father, who "seized in right of his wife several parcels of land" that she brought to the marriage. The couple then sold nineteen captives along with the real estate. William's father also devised six of Elizabeth's

26. "Of Proceedings in the Courts of Equity," in Blackstone, *Commentaries on the Laws of England*, Book 3, Chapter 27, Lonang Institute, http://www.lonang.com/exlibris/blackstone/bla-327.htm. Access to the Chancery Court records in Jamaica is limited, which makes it difficult to work with these cases and to determine their outcomes. The island's Grand Court handled disputes over smaller sums. When her husband fell ill at their friends' house during a visit, Elizabeth Eaton (Godin) claimed they took advantage of his "weak and infirm" condition to coerce him to change his will and convey the land and slaves to them. See William and Mary Hall v. Elizabeth Goodin, Aug. 24, 1739, Jamaica Chancery Court Records, 1738–1744, JA.

27. See William and Mary Hall v. Elizabeth Goodin, Aug. 24, 1739, Jamaica Chancery Court Records, 1738–1744.

slaves to their son, another right that he claimed by coverture. He then died, and Bows remarried again. Her third husband convinced her to petition for a reconveyance of the land and enslaved people, which they recouped. Bows then conveyed all of the captives to her son. When her third husband died, she remarried yet again, and her fourth husband issued a "writ of judicature" against William to reclaim the slaves she had given him. At this point, William brought the case to Chancery Court.[28]

Martin v. Bows exemplifies the disruption and confusion remarriages caused to families. Each time Bows remarried, her new husband proclaimed his right under the law of coverture to sell, convey, and reclaim her holdings. During her second and third marriages, Bows sought to make her son the legal owner of enslaved people. Her fourth time at the altar triggered a challenge to her actions, which was probably instigated by her new husband. Bows and her son ended up in court because her claim to property—as a wife and a mother—was weak. In the absence of a trust, Bows exerted no control over her estate when she remarried. The suit was a struggle between men—her husbands and her son—who made varying demands on holdings she did not command. The outcome of the suit involving Bows is unknown. It is possible that she won it by default because all of her son's witnesses were "dead" or "gone off the island." Regardless of the outcome, the suit highlights the precariousness of married women's property in the absence of equity measures. Caught in the middle of these legal skirmishes, the instability of female holdings disturbed and dislocated enslaved people who, defined as objects, were subjected to multiple moves and transfers of owners.[29]

By investing men in their familial roles as husbands and fathers with the sole authority to devise family property, English common law aimed to uphold a patriarchal social order. As the above cases illustrate, colonial men certainly invoked these gendered laws to gain control of resources held by women. The friction between common law and equity was one symptom of the broader tensions surrounding female authority within and outside of marriage on the island. Free and freed women occupied a contested legal status in Jamaica. Men depended on mothers, wives, and daughters to preserve family resources, to manage households, to oversee family ventures, and to maintain control of enslaved people, but it was an uneasy dependency. Women also relied on men to confer assets on them—and the legal capaci-

28. Suit brought by William Martin, July 18, 1709, Jamaica Chancery Court Records, 1707–1709, III.

29. Ibid.

ties related to property ownership. Once widows became sole heirs of family estates, they could allocate resources as they thought best. Female colonists who attained this position proactively directed the flow of material wealth to the next generation of free islanders.

"ALL REAL AND PERSONAL ESTATE"

Although court cases offer up instances of conflicts between men and women over estates, a survey of the wills authored by husbands and widowers indicates that most men desired to improve, rather than diminish, women's holdings. Even as these second- and third-generation islanders were driven by pragmatism, rather than an interest in gender parity, their actions still enlarged the material holdings of female heirs. Nearly half of the 330 men studied here who identified themselves as husbands of living wives left them all of their real and personal estates. Of these, almost three-quarters bequeathed "all real and personal" holdings, including the right to devise property, to spouses in perpetuity. The remainder enabled their wives to maintain possession of family estates during their lifetime.[30]

Men sought to strengthen the material and legal command of their female kin who held the greatest interest in conserving and increasing family holdings, particularly if the couple had children to support. Recognizing that island-born women possessed the indigenous experience, knowledge, and connections necessary for overseeing family businesses, including plantations and mercantile ventures, husbands viewed wives as indispensable estate managers, business partners, property owners, and household heads. If they believed in patriarchal ideology, men's inheritance choices acknowledged the actualities of colonial life, displaying realism rather than dogmatism.

A little more than 80 percent of the 330 husbands who made bequests to their wives further augmented the legal authority of their spouse by nominating them to serve as their executor, and just under 65 percent of those named

30. An estimated 374 of the 503 men whose wills were sampled for this chapter identified themselves as husbands or widowers (the remainder did not refer to wives). Of these, 330 men had wives who were still living. One hundred forty gave the majority of their estates to their wives, while the remainder offered their spouses an assortment of property, including annual annuities, "half" or a "third" of their estates, houses, specific parcels of property, household goods, and enslaved people. Of the 140 men who gave "all real and personal" property to their wives, 102 (73 percent) made the bequests permanent, but the other 38 (27 percent) only granted them their estates for life. See Jamaica Wills, I–XXXVIII.

TABLE 1: *Husbands' Bequests to Wives, 1661–1770*

BEQUESTS	NUMBER	PERCENTAGE
Wives left the majority of their husband's estate	140	42
in perpetuity	102	31
"for life":	38	12
Wives charged with settling their husband's estate	274	83
as co-executors	96	29
as sole executors	178	54

Source: Jamaica Wills, 1661–1771, I–XXXVIII, Island Record Office, Spanish Town, Jamaica.
Note: Of the 503 men whose wills were sampled for this chapter, 330 identified themselves as husbands with living wives. Percentages in this table are based off N=330.

their wife as sole executor (see Table 1). Assuming the role of executor was no small matter. The death of a spouse triggered a myriad of financial and legal transactions that the executor was responsible for handling. A widow tasked with this role had to organize her husband's funeral, distribute the legacies in his will, and settle any lingering debts on the family's estate. Successful executors possessed the skills of attorneys, bookkeepers, and plantation overseers while often caring for young children. Executors "stood at the center of transfers of wealth and, therefore, of status and social continuity" within families, and relatives, friends, and business partners could not interfere with their actions.[31]

Given the manifold responsibilities involved in settling an estate, wives did not necessarily want to serve as executors. Husbands expected, coaxed, and sometimes compelled their spouses to perform the role. In his 1740 will, John Campbell provided handsomely for his wife. He also insisted that she could not "on any pretense whatsoever relinquish or refuse acting as executor until all my debts and greatest part of legacies are paid." Men like Campbell assumed the competency of wives to manage legal and financial affairs. Indeed,

31. Of the 330 men who named wives in wills, 274 appointed them as executrices. Although men normally nominated grown children or male friends to act as executors alongside their wives, 178 designated wives as "sole executrixes." See Jamaica Wills, I–XXXVIII; and Brown, *Reaper's Garden*, 102. Grassby observes that, "liquidating a working business in seventeenth-century England demanded skill and knowledge" (Grassby, *Kinship and Capitalism*, 133).

Campbell's reliance on his spouse's capabilities drove him to compel her to undertake the duties of executor, whether she wanted to or not.[32]

The preference for electing wives to manage family property and offering them generous bequests was widespread on the island. Husbands from all walks of life, including doctors and surgeons, mariners, merchants, tavernkeepers, "gentlemen," and "esquires" as well as artisans—such as blacksmiths, bricklayers, carpenters, coopers, cordwainers, millwrights, shoemakers, and tailors—made wives their sole executor and transferred considerable portions of family property to them. When Hugh Perrott, a cooper who lived in St. Jago de la Vega made his will in 1699, he bequeathed "all real and personal" estate to his wife. Perrott made no mention of children; his spouse might have been the only person who survived to inherit. A few decades later, James McDaniel, a Kingston joiner, made provisions for his wife and daughter to share his assets equally.[33]

The practice of transferring entire estates to wives also cut across emergent racial categories. Artisan Goody Jacobson, a Port Royal butcher who identified himself as a "free negro" in his 1724 will, gave his wife, Esther, two enslaved women and "all the rest of my real and personal estate." Two of the Jacobsons' four children were sons, and the butcher could have bequeathed his middling estate, which included nine captives, money, and horses, to his eldest son while offering a smaller legacy to his spouse. Instead, Jacobson chose to allot enslaved people and cash to his children while designating his wife as his primary heir. Jacobson also inveighed her with the legal right to devise the family holdings as she saw fit.[34]

32. Will of John Campbell, 1740, Jamaica Wills, XXII.

33. Will of Hugh Perrott, 1699, Jamaica Wills, IX, Will of James McDaniel, 1722, XVI. Men who identified their occupation as planter comprised only 38 percent of the will makers in my sample. It is possible that some of the eighty men who identified themselves as "esquire" or "gentleman" in my sample of men's wills also owned plantations. Both of these terms had various meanings in the early modern period, which makes it difficult to determine the occupations of these men (who probably applied the titles to themselves). It was used to describe men of "gentle" birth, officers in service of the king, landed proprietors, and those of the higher order of the English gentry. "Gentleman" was equally nebulous, indicating a person of higher rank or one who was a member of a certain society or profession. See *Oxford English Dictionary*, s.v. "esquire" and "gentleman," http://oed.com. Gentlemen and esquires accounted for 28 percent of the men whose estates were probated and whose occupations were identified. Artisans made up roughly 17 percent of the men in my sample of wills. See Jamaica Inventories; and Jamaica Wills, I–XXXVIII.

34. Will of Goody Jacobson, 1724, Jamaica Wills, XVI.

Viewing estates as long-term investments, men like Goody Jacobson made their immediate kin responsible for estate management irrespective of gender. Colonial husbands and fathers disavowed patrilineal common law practices such as dower, primogeniture, and entail, which associated property with masculine prerogatives, through their actions. The stingy common law custom of dower entitled a widow to the use of one-third of her family's estate during her lifetime—she had no right to devise the estate under dower. Primogeniture and entail, customs that supported elder sons who inherited entire estates to the disadvantage of their mothers and siblings, were also unpopular. In a place where the deaths of young boys winnowed males from the ranks of inheritors, gender restrictive inheritance laws were impractical, if not impossible, to follow. Jamaica's colonists devised alternative strategies to survive a continual demographic crisis. Husbands defined property as a family resource rather than a masculine prerogative. Some men explicitly rejected dower's limitations, including phrases such as "in lieu of" or "in bar of" dower when describing legacies for spouses. Edith Philips's husband asked her to "discharge in law" her dower—that is, relinquish her right to the third of the property—in his 1700 will. She would then receive a more substantial and permanent right to his land, money, and slaves.[35]

The individualized nature of colonial bequests makes it more difficult to discern a singular gendered pattern in the types of assets offered by fathers

35. Will of Samuell Philips, 1700, Jamaica Wills, IX. Husbands could not convey or sell the protected dower portion of property without obtaining their wife's permission, and courts privately examined wives to ensure that husbands were not coercing them to sell property. See Erickson, *Women and Property in Early Modern England,* 25. The common law customs of primogeniture and entail dictated, respectively, that land and estate would pass to the eldest living son or eldest sons born to future generations. As a result of these practices, widows regularly received far less than they had brought to the marriage, and their incomes were for life. Christer Petley has described primogeniture "as a guiding principle rather than as a rigid rule" in early nineteenth-century Jamaica. He bases this claim on three examples: John Cunningham (who died in 1812), who gave sugar plantations to his sons and ten thousand pounds Jamaica current to each of his daughters; John Coates, who divided his estate equally between six children; and Charles Gordon Gray, who divided his property equally between his wife and children. See Petley, "'Legitimacy' and Social Boundaries: Free People of Colour and the Social Order in Jamaican Slave Society," *Social History,* XXX (2005), 494. My findings differ from Petley's analysis. My study of more than one thousand eighteenth-century wills made by men and women shows that primogeniture was rarely practiced in Jamaica. Out of 330 men who left legacies for their wives, 34 specifically stated that their bequests were in lieu of dower. See Jamaica Wills, I-XXXVIII.

to children than it is to identify patterns in husbands' bequests to wives. Although it would be fruitful to compare wills with probated inventories and land deeds, in many cases estates were only probated when someone died intestate. Analyzing colonial land deeds is beyond the scope of this project. Some general tendencies do emerge from men's wills, however, in relation to the allocation of wealth to children. Overall, men's inheritance bequests exhibit a preference for keeping Jamaican prosperity in local hands, which enabled free families to survive and sometimes prosper in a volatile environment. Male colonists favored island-born female kin over distant male heirs who lived overseas. Parents participated in an Anglo-Atlantic trend by allocating resources more equitably between sons and daughters, but the colony's higher mortality rates and rapidly growing enslaved population amplified this development. As suggested by both men's and women's wills, daughters were also more likely than sons to survive to adulthood, and families appear to have had more daughters than sons; hence girls received larger legacies in families that had only daughters to provide for. Of the 387 bequests made by men to their children, 44 percent (170) referred to sons, and 56 percent (217) named daughters. Women's wills show identical gender ratios between siblings (Table 2). Of the 425 women who devised legacies to children, 44 percent (185) referred to sons, and 56 percent (240) to daughters.[36]

Contending with colonial circumstances, fathers strove to support all of their children. Instead of adhering to a single inheritance practice such as primogeniture, men tailored children's legacies to meet the specific demands of their families. Overall, the majority of fathers (61 percent) who had both daughters and sons chose to divide family resources equally among siblings regardless of gender or age. When parceling out his estate in his 1710 will, the self-titled "gentleman" James Parker, who lived with his family in Half-

36. Jamaica Wills, I–XXXVIII. Amy Froide points out that the "focus on primogeniture" has led to the assumption that men inherited real estate over women in Britain. Although the aristocracy tended to employ primogeniture and entail, the majority of British families sought to provide sons and daughters with equal portions in the form of land and moveable goods. See Froide, *Never Married,* 124; Vickery, *Behind Closed Doors,* 130; and Erickson, *Women and Property,* 68–71. Michael J. Jarvis has shown that in eighteenth-century Bermuda fathers regularly provided their daughters with generous allotments of land and slaves (Jarvis, *In the Eye of All Trade: Bermuda, Bermudians, and the Maritime Atlantic World, 1680–1783* [Williamsburg, Va., and Chapel Hill, N.C., 2010], 265–266). For more on parents' inheritance practices in early America, see Glover, *All Our Relations;* and Jean Butenhoff Lee, "Land and Labor: Parental Bequest Practices in Charles County, Maryland, 1732–1783," in Lois Green Carr, Philip D. Morgan, and Jean B. Russo, eds., *Colonial Chesapeake Society* (Chapel Hill, N.C., 1988), 306–341.

TABLE 2: *Parental Bequests to Children by Gender, 1661–1771*

	FATHERS		MOTHERS	
BEQUESTS	NUMBER	PERCENTAGE	NUMBER	PERCENTAGE
To sons	170	44	185	44
To daughters	217	56	240	56
Total	387	100	425	100

Source: Jamaica Wills, 1661–1771, I–XXXVIII, Island Record Office, Spanish Town, Jamaica.
Note: Of the 503 men who made wills from 1679 to 1770 sampled for this chapter, 387 left property to children. Of all 741 women who made wills between 1665 and 1761, 321 left property to children. I have separated bequests to children of different sexes who were named in the same will. The nearly identical proportions of the bequests made by mothers and fathers to sons and daughters show that parents were in agreement about how to distribute family property between sons and daughters. Although it is possible that some fathers offered sons intro vivos gifts and did not mention them in their wills, this practice was not popular on the island.

way Tree on the outskirts of the newly built town of Kingston, provided for all of his heirs on both sides of the Atlantic. But whereas he might have been expected to privilege his sons, then living in England, he did the opposite, favoring his wife and daughter who resided in Jamaica as the most suitable heirs to his colonial holdings. Although his sons stood to inherit the family house in England, Parker gave his daughter £210 and an enslaved boy. She would also receive all of the family holdings on the island when her mother died. Furthermore, Parker expected his daughter to handle the estate's financial dealings with her brothers, instructing her to send them £140 to discharge the mortgage, likely on the Jamaica property, which they held. In distributing his colonial and metropolitan holdings evenly, or possibly offering more to his daughter, Parker ensured that his children would take over the management of the family property on both sides of the Atlantic. This type of family arrangement was increasingly common. Even if sons and daughters often received different types of resources, the majority of men distributed roughly equal portions among their children, regardless of gender.[37]

By the 1730s and 1740s, second- and third-generation colonists from all

37. Will of James Parker, 1710, Jamaica Wills, XIII; Sarah M. S. Pearsall, *Atlantic Families: Lives and Letters in the Later Eighteenth Century* (New York, 2008); Daniel Livesay, *Children of Uncertain Fortune: Mixed-Race Jamaicans in Britain and the Atlantic Family, 1733–1833* (Williamsburg, Va., and Chapel Hill, N.C., 2018).

walks of life had larger fortunes to offer children. The practice of divvying up assets more equitably between sons and daughters was widespread. John Jones, a blacksmith by trade, gave his "stock, mares, horses, a negro boy," and household goods to his daughter. Jones also referred to four enslaved people his wife had set aside for her son, indicating that she maintained the captives in a separate estate during the marriage. In addition to receiving enslaved people from his mother, Jones's son would share the family land equally with his sister. Though planter Robert Cole operated in a more elite echelon of colonial society, he also allotted equal portions of his estate to both his son and daughter.[38]

Sometimes fathers favored daughters over sons outright. Harding Goodin, a planter in Westmoreland, appointed his widowed daughter as his executor in 1740. He showered her with a generous inheritance of £370, furniture, bonds, cash, and the profits from his plantation. He also released her from all debts she owed him and made her the sole executor of his estate. In stark contrast, Harding only left fifteen pence to his two sons and did not invite either of them to act as his executors. The father's exclusion of his sons seems acrimonious and likely hints at family conflict.[39]

Although the majority of Jamaica's fathers might have intended for daughters to marry, they still furnished female heirs with the financial means to live independently. Women who received land, cash, and enslaved persons were less pressured by economic need to enter wedlock when they came of age. Overall, the remaining 39 percent of the men who left bequests to both sons and daughters reserved the majority of their property for sons while also providing handsomely for their daughters. Few fathers made references to marriage in their bequests to their daughters. However, "Gentleman" Caleb Dickson's restrictive actions toward his daughters offers a notable exception to the island norm. Dickson promised each of his two girls a fortune of five thousand pounds when they turned twenty-one or married. But they would only receive their inheritance if his executors approved of their future suitors. Dickson further attached another string to his daughter Mary's legacy, offering her an additional one thousand pounds if she accepted the "proposal of marriage" from one of his executors, a merchant from Bristol who was most likely Dickson's business partner.[40]

38. Will of John Jones, 1730, Jamaica Wills, XVIII, Will of Robert Cole, 1748, XXVII.

39. Will of Harding Goodin, 1740, Jamaica Wills, XXII.

40. Will of Caleb Dickson, 1730, Jamaica Wills, XVIII. In Jamaica, parents set different ages as the age of maturity in wills: some allowed children to inherit at sixteen and some at twenty-

In contrast with Dickson, most fathers did not place restrictions on the property they reserved for girls. Men who gave family estates to sons still left daughters money, annuities, and enslaved people. In 1710, planter Thomas Waite set aside £370 and a "negro girl" for his daughter while reserving the family estate for his son. George Raastead, another planter who made his will in 1710, also endowed his daughter with personal goods—a feather bed, two slaves, and thirty heifers—and left the land to his son. Planter Philemon Dunn adopted a similar strategy, willing his daughter cash, chattel, and slaves, which he lumped together. She would receive £140, a cow, a calf, six "able" captive adults, and an enslaved girl named Mimbo. Dunn also wanted his daughter to be "maintained" and "educated according to her quality."[41]

Charles Price, the owner of Rose Hall, a plantation that exists today as a resort, provided handsomely for his daughter Sarah in his 1730 will. She would inherit land and eight slaves, including two "Indian" captives named Dobake and Maria. Her brothers, who were to receive the rest of his property, would have to pay her thirty-three hundred pounds out of the profits from Rose Hall and another plantation. Colonial fathers like Price created situations where sons might end up land rich and cash poor; plantations were expensive and often required years of investment before producing a profit. Daughters like Sarah, on the other hand, gained readily disposable income in the form of cash. They also received enslaved people, who further enriched female holdings as salable assets.[42]

When fathers transferred captives to their daughters, they ensured the commitment of the next generation of female islanders to chattel slavery, a trend mothers also followed. Between 1665 and 1761, the majority of the 706 women who made wills were widowed mothers. Nearly half of the 101 mothers who had sons and daughters to provide for divided family estates equitably among them. For example, the widow Elizabeth Dodd, who established a ferry service in Port Royal, equally divided her wealth, the bulk of which constituted twenty-seven enslaved individuals between her sons and daughters.[43]

---

one. Gender generally did not play a role in determining the age of maturity. Amy Froide describes personal property as a more "flexible and practical inheritance." See Froide, *Never Married,* 128–129.

41. Will of Thomas Waite, 1710, Jamaica Wills, XIII, Will of George Raastead, 1710, XIII, Will of Philemon Dunn, 1710, XIII.

42. Will of Charles Price, 1730, Jamaica Wills, XVIII.

43. Will of Elizabeth Dodd, 1728, Jamaica Wills, XVII. Dodd's enslaved people likely

Strikingly, only one-quarter of the widowed mothers who made wills favored male heirs. Women might have transferred larger shares to female heirs as a means of offsetting the inter vivos or lifetime gifts offered by men to male heirs. If this was the case, then mother's bequests offer an incomplete picture of the size of family holdings. Trevor Burnard finds that gifts made inter vivos, however, were not popular in Jamaica. Furthermore, even mothers who preferred their sons still offered daughters personal items in the form of movable property, specifically captive Africans, just as fathers did. Mary Tuckey furnished her daughter with an enslaved girl named Halfpenny in 1705; her son inherited the rest of the estate. Similarly, Ann Hansis offered her daughter a "mulatto girl"; the rest of the family holdings went to her son. Some of the mothers in this category might have bequeathed the majority of their fortunes to sons because daughters were already married. Perhaps this is why Elizabeth Price transferred enslaved people together with livestock, "money," and "jewels" to her sons in 1692 while only giving her daughter seven pounds. The daughter was married to Peter Beckford—a member of the prominent Beckford family—and probably stood to inherit a substantial bequest from her husband.[44]

Acrimony between mothers and sons might have also motivated the inheritance choices of certain women. Elizabeth Scott only left "the sum of one hundred shilling and three pence" to her son in 1714 "because of his undutyfullness to me"; she conveyed the bulk of the family holdings to her daughter. Another woman, Judith Pestana, for her part, with an estate valued at seventy-three pounds, was poor by colony standards, but she still reserved the majority of her wealth for her daughters while only offering her son five shillings. Perhaps mother-son hostilities led Ann Peschaire to take a similar

worked as mariners and operated the "new great boat or wherry" that she had "built" in her widowhood. Sixty percent of female will makers were mothers. Census records do not provide enough detail about the free population to show whether widows made up the majority of the single women on the island, but they conclusively comprised the majority of female will makers. Forty-six of the mothers with children of both sexes distributed estates equally between sons and daughters. See Jamaica Wills, I–XXXII.

44. Will of Mary Tuckey, 1705, Jamaica Wills, XI, Will of Ann Hansis, 1720, XVI, Will of Elizabeth Price, VII, 1692. Burnard also determines that inter vivos gifts were unpopular in colonial Maryland, where testators showed a disinclination to transfer property, even to adult male heirs, during their lifetimes, which would effectively make them dependent on their children. See Burnard, "Inheritance and Independence," *WMQ*, 3d Ser., XLVIII (1991), 96. According to Charles Leslie, when Peter Beckford died in 1710, he was the wealthiest landholder in Jamaica, and perhaps the entire empire. See Leslie, *A New History of Jamaica*, 267.

action: she also allotted her son five shillings while her daughter stood to inherit two enslaved women together with the rest of her possessions. Likewise, Mary George only left a mourning ring for her son; her daughter received all of her property. In command of family estates, Scott, Pestana, and Peschaire had the legal power to omit sons from their wills if they chose, yet parents rarely went to such extreme lengths to exclude daughters from their wills.[45]

Sons, it seems, created more intense conflicts within colonial families headed by widowed mothers. Girls might disobey parents when it came to choosing marriage partners. Boys, on the other hand, could test the veracity of female authority in more potent ways. Conscious of inheritance traditions that benefited male heirs, they might have begrudged sharing legacies with sisters and resented the control exercised by their mothers over family resources. Knowledge of these gendered dynamics within families might have led Dorothy Williams, a free woman of African descent who lived in Saint Catherine, to be concerned about her son's behavior after her death. Worried that he would defy her intention to offer a more substantial legacy to her daughter, Williams attempted to thwart her son's actions in her 1731 will by offering him seventy-four pounds in gold and silver, a bequest that would be voided "if he ever" attempted to "disturb or molest" her daughter "in her goods chattels or estate." By tendering cash to her son, Williams strove to shield her daughter from his future meddling. As Williams's will suggests, she was conscious of the masculine prerogative claimed by all male colonists, which could be used to challenge the claims of female property holders.[46]

If rancor motivated a few women to limit the legacies they offered sons, pragmatism likely inspired the majority of Jamaica's property-holding mothers to choose daughters. One-quarter of the women who had sons and daughters still elected daughters to be their primary heirs. For instance, the widow Rebecca Sutton of Kingston devised four slaves, ten mules, and £560 to her son, but she transferred the "rest and residue" of her holdings to her daughter. Mary Elding left only £36 to her son "in full barr of any claim" to her £492 estate; her granddaughters inherited the remainder. By supporting younger, female, and single children, these women adhered to British standards. Giving more generously to daughters and granddaughters balanced out the legacies that male heirs received from fathers and other rela-

45. Will of Elizabeth Scott, 1726, Jamaica Wills, XIV, Will of Judith Pestana, 1726, XVII; Inventory of Judith Pestana, 1727, Jamaica Inventories; Will of Ann Peschaire, 1747, Jamaica Wills, XXVI, Will of Mary George, 1749, XXVII.

46. Will of Dorothy Williams, 1731, Jamaica Wills, XVIII.

tives. Free and freed women carefully transferred resources along homosocial lines, using their property to support several generations of female heirs.[47]

Elderly widows also made gendered inheritance choices that benefitted female heirs: 69 percent transferred the bulk of their estates to nieces and granddaughters, in particular. In 1721, Joan Enoome, a widow in Spanish Town, favored her granddaughter over her grandson, offering her £3,077. He would receive nothing unless his sister died. Mary Fox left her entire fortune to her granddaughter. Women who did not have any children or grandchildren to support explicitly preferred female heirs, offering them financial protection and patronage. Mary Bradshaw transferred her assets to her mother in 1700 and ordered that it be passed on to another "female kinswoman" when she died. A few decades later, Alice Anderson and Susannah Tilton allotted their property to sisters. Mary Crawford, identified as a "spinster," also singled out female relatives, giving all of her "household furniture, apparel, rings" to her niece. Her sister would receive half of the estate for life and then it, too, would pass on to her niece. These extranatal relationships forged between female colonists counteracted the havoc wreaked by the island's high mortality rates.[48]

47. Will of Rebeca Sutton, 1730, Jamaica Wills, XVIII, Will of Mary Elding, 1748, XXVI; Inventory of Mary Elding, 1749, Jamaica Inventories. Forty-six of the mothers with children of both sexes distributed estates equally between sons and daughters; twenty-nine gave the majority to sons; twenty-six gave the majority to daughters. See Jamaica Wills, I–XXXII. One of the purposes of women's wills was to "lessen the unequal effects of primogeniture" on a family's other children. See Froide, *Never Married,* 119.

48. Will of Joan Enoome, Apr. 12, 1721, Abstracts of Jamaica Wills, 1625–1792, Add MS 34181; Will of Mary Fox, 1748, Jamaica Wills, XVI, Will of Mary Bradshaw, 1700, IX, Will of Alice Anderson, 1739, XXII, Will of Susannah Tilton, 1739, XXII, Will of Mary Hutchinson, 1739, XXII, Will of Mary Crawford, 1749, XXVII. One-third of Jamaica's female will makers made no mention of children. Of course, some of the women who fell into this category never started families, either within or outside of wedlock. They were the exception, though. The majority of women identified themselves as widows. Of the 706 female will makers, 241 did not refer to children in their wills. I include women who only referred to grandchildren in the group of childless women because I have no evidence that their children were still alive. One hundred three women who fell into the childless category made bequests to close relatives (grandchildren, nieces, nephews, siblings, parents, spouses). Sixty-seven gave the majority of their estates to female kin, and 36 gave the majority to male kin. Most were widows. Of the 103 women who made bequests to relatives but not children, 25 identified themselves as spinsters by occupation or as a "free negro woman" or "free mulatto woman." See Jamaica Wills, I–XXXII.

Women favored female heirs whom they shared closer bonds with. Boys were raised to be independent. They spent more time away from home than girls. Lower and middling sons were apprenticed to artisans or professionals (merchants, attorneys, physicians). When they came of age, they could provide for themselves. Wealthier families sent their sons across the Atlantic to be educated in Britain. The life options of free and freed women, in contrast, were far more restricted, and most remained on the island. However, growing up in the colony also afforded new opportunities to daughters. They developed local knowledge, contacts, and experience with family businesses, ranging from shopkeeping and tavernkeeping to planting and trading. Colonial expertise enhanced the prestige of female members within free families. Just as husbands considered their wives to be the most suitable managers and, often, owners, of family estates, parents identified island-based daughters as the most capable kin to oversee island-based enterprises.

Thousands of inheritance decisions made by spouses and parents were designed to protect colonial estates and increase the fortunes and legal independence of female heirs. Though free and freed women never amassed the resources held by men, high mortality rates, the vast riches produced by slave labor on the island, and the value of enslaved people themselves resulted in material gains for female colonists. Regularly widowed at young ages, women then assumed legal authority over substantial fortunes. In command of both financial and legal power, widows and women who never married then transferred property, which often included slaves, along female lines.

"FOUR BEST NEGRO GIRLS . . . FROM MY WHOLE PARCEL"

Free islanders treated enslaved people as malleable possessions and multifaceted laborers, especially when it pertained to enhancing the property of female heirs. An enslaved person's usefulness changed depending on the life phase and marital status of the woman who commanded them. Captives acted as companions and servants for free girls, but, once those young women came of age, the enslaved people in their possession became a means of attracting suitors as a costly form of property. Some families also placed slaves in separate estates to provide material assets for daughters who married. The bequests made by the first three generations of colonists turned enslaved people into a key currency—one that became the primary means of supporting free and freed women. Building on precedents established in the late seventeenth century, locals defined slaves as gendered, moveable goods.

TABLE 3: *Bequests Specifically Designating Enslaved People to Heirs, 1661–1771*

BEQUESTS	NUMBER	PERCENTAGE N	PERCENTAGE %
Husbands to wives	96	330	29
Fathers to daughters	120	217	55
Fathers to sons	24	170	14
Mothers to daughters	167	240	69
Mothers to sons	68	185	37

Source: Jamaica Wills, 1661–1771, I–XXXVIII, Island Record Office, Spanish Town, Jamaica.
Note: The flow of enslaved men, women, and children into female hands via inheritance was considerable. It is difficult to quantify nondescript bequests of "all estate," "all real and personal estate," or "half" of an estate, but the majority probably included enslaved people. Hence, the numbers of people inheriting slaves from spouses and parents was in all likelihood significantly higher.

Equated with furniture, livestock, and plate, captives were deemed to be particularly suitable for women, who traditionally received these types of movable items via inheritance.[49]

The flow of enslaved people into female hands through men's inheritance bequests was considerable. One-third of the 330 husbands studied here specifically reserved captives for wives (Table 3). Some men, like carpenter Henry Lamb, who gave his "whole estate, chattels, slaves" to his wife to share with their daughter "in lieu of her dower," explicitly referred to "slaves" in the one-sentence descriptions of their estates. It is also reasonable to conclude that the majority of the nondescript bequests of "all real and personal estate" made by husbands included slaves. Altogether, an estimated three-quarters of married men transferred enslaved people to spouses.[50]

49. Michael Jarvis observes a pattern of families bequeathing enslaved people to daughters in Bermuda. His findings, together with my own, hint at a broader Anglo-Atlantic inheritance trend wherein slaves were a favored means of supporting female heirs. Jarvis also observes that the relationships between white mistresses and their captives often outlasted their marriages, suggesting that enslaved people were considered to be women's property during and after marriage. See Jarvis, *In the Eye of All Trade*, 265–266.

50. Will of Henry Lamb, 1700, Jamaica Wills, IX. In making this claim, I disagree with Lucille Mathurin Mair, who concluded that in comparison with women in North America the property rights of free women in the Caribbean were "narrowed" and the "marriage noose tight-

In 1700, planter Richard Turpin offered "all negroes and other slaves and personal estate" to his wife, explicitly identifying them as a form of "personal" property. Turpin's view of slaves as "personal estate" was widely shared among inhabitants from diverse backgrounds. When mariner John Bevis wrote his will in 1722, he also conveyed "all personal estate, house, lands, negro slaves male and female, and plate" to his wife. Decades later, Joseph Bennet bequeathed "all land slaves outstanding debts furniture and all real and personal [property]" to his wife, while carpenter George Bishop left his wife "all real and personal, plate, negroes forever."[51]

Husbands like Turpin, Bevis, Bennet, and Bishop used African captives as a source of income that would protect wives from future dependency or destitution. When bricklayer John Frazier left slaves to his spouse in 1748, he instructed her to hire them out to maintain the couple's children. Frazier not only expected his wife to become a slaveholder, he also assumed that she would participate in the slave trade, instructing her to sell land to buy more captives from Africa. Enslaved people, of course, commanded a higher monetary worth in the marketplace than other forms of moveable goods customarily bequeathed to women while also providing female legatees with labor and enhancing their social status and legal authority.[52]

In the early eighteenth century, captive Africans comprised a significant portion of the resources devised to all female heirs, not just wives. More than half (120) of the fathers whose families included daughters also provided them with slaves. This estimate does not account for the enslaved people who were included in less descriptive bequests of "real and personal estates." Realistically, three-quarters of all the legacies fathers conferred to daughters included captives. Prudence Gale's father was one of these men. When her father, who worked as a carpenter in Port Royal, made his will in 1699, he left Prudence eight hundred pounds, a house, and four enslaved people. That same year, when a surgeon named Edward Smith bequeathed his holdings to

ened." See Mathurin Mair, *Historical Study of Women in Jamaica,* ed. Beckles and Shepherd, 155–156. Chancery Court, in her estimation, was inefficient, but this chapter details the numerous other ways that colonists modified common law customs. Of the 330 husbands, 101 referred specifically to slaves as part of the property they bequeathed to wives; 235 either referred specifically to slaves as part of their bequests to their wives or gave their wives their entire estates. See Jamaica Wills, I–XXXVIII.

51. Will of Richard Turpin, 1700, Jamaica Wills, IX, Will of John Bevis, 1722, XVI, Will of Joseph Bennet, 1740, XXII, Will of George Bishop, 1750, XXVII.

52. Will of John Frazier, 1748, Jamaica Wills, XXVII.

his wife, he forbade her from selling the family's captives, whom he reserved for the couple's daughters. In contrast, only twenty-four fathers specified slaves in bequests to male heirs.[53]

By 1730, Kingston tavernkeeper Samuel Hinton held nine men, two women, and seven children in bondage. His daughter would inherit them all. Ten years later, Hugh Williams, a merchant in Kingston, bequeathed eighteen hundred pounds to his daughter and instructed his wife to select "four best negro girls . . . from my whole parcel" for her. Planter Job Williams left the majority of his assets to his son, but he offered his daughter two three-hundred-acre plots of land and made provisions for her to capitalize on the slave trade by purchasing eight "new negroes" from slave ships.[54]

Mothers, who had likely received enslaved people from their parents and husbands, displayed an even stronger preference for bequeathing captives to daughters. Nearly 70 percent of the women who gave property to daughters specifically referred to enslaved people. Including mothers who only described "real and personal estate" increases this number to 85 percent. Female slaveholders identified captives as an especially gendered movable asset. Only 21 percent of the 321 women who made bequests to children and grandchildren reserved enslaved people for male heirs. Female enslavers exhibited a strong partiality for providing captives to girls irrespective of their wealth, legal status, or race. Even the poorest free and freed women conveyed slaves to daughters and granddaughters. When Esther Tacey made her will in 1742, her meager holdings were comprised of fourteen sheep and two enslaved people. Her daughter received the sheep, and the slaves went to her granddaughter. Ten years later, Sarah Gregory of Kingston divided five enslaved people among her daughter and her "spinster" granddaughters, who also each inherited one mare. She passed the remainder of her modest estate to her daughter. Just like men, poorer women like Tacey and Gregory identified captives as movable chattels, which they grouped with livestock and designated for female heirs.[55]

53. Will of John Gale, 1699, Jamaica Wills, IX, Will of Edward Smith, 1699, VI. Of the 217 men who left legacies for their daughters, 120 men specifically identified slaves as part of such legacies. Out of the 266 men who made bequests to children, 24 men mentioned slaves for sons. Men's bequests were generally less descriptive than women's though, and the number of male heirs who inherited slaves was likely larger, including boys who received "the rest" of estates or entire estates. See Jamaica Wills, I–XXXVIII.

54. Will of Samuel Hinton, 1730, Jamaica Wills, XVIII, Will of Hugh Williams, 1740, XXII, Will of Job Williams, 1748, XXVII.

55. Will of Esther Tacey, 1742, Jamaica Wills, XXIII, Will of Sarah Gregory, 1752, XXVIII.

TABLE 4: *Female Slave Ownership by Decade, 1675–1769*

DATE RANGE	NUMBER OF ESTATES PROBATED	TOTAL ESTATE VALUE (TEV)	NUMBER OF SLAVES	TOTAL VALUE OF SLAVES	PERCENTAGE OF TEV HELD IN SLAVES	AVERAGE NUMBER OF SLAVES PER ESTATE
1675–1689	15	7,659	208	2,954	39	14
1690–1699	17	14,892	309	4,741	32	18
1700–1709	22	13,313	393	6,554	49	18
1710–1719	52	39,474	970	18,718	47	19
1720–1729	85	83,839	1,344	32,244	38	16
1730–1739	83	67,076	939	24,118	36	11
1740–1749	165	186,856	2,387	78,738	42	14
1750–1759	110	131,014	1,658	61,107	47	15
1760–1769	236	377,582	4,007	186,574	49	17
Total	785	921,705	12,215	415,748		

Source: Jamaica Inventories, Jamaica Archives, 1674–1784, Spanish Town, Jamaica.

Note: Although the majority of the book focuses on the period 1665 to 1765, I have expanded the date range for my study of probated inventories to show the dramatic increase between 1760 and 1769 in both the number of free women and the number of enslaved people whom they owned.

Women property holders transferred resources, including enslaved people, along female lines, while also capitalizing on their wealth to acquire more captives. Second- and third-generation women benefited from these developments. Between 1665 and 1765, an estimated three-quarters of all the women who made wills controlled slaves. The probated inventories of women's estates that were made between 1675 and 1769 suggest that the total was closer to 80 percent. As the number of estates held by women increased, their investment in slavery deepened. Between 1690 and 1699, a total of seventeen female-owned estates were inventoried. Altogether, the women commanded 309 captives (Table 4). Seventy years later, the number

---

Of the 241 women who made bequests to daughters, 167 specifically referred to slaves. Of the 321 women who mentioned children in their wills, only 68 made provisions for sons to receive slaves. It is possible that more mothers explicitly referred to specific captives in bequests to sons than fathers because enslaved people comprised a higher portion of women's estates. See Jamaica Wills, I–XXXII.

of female-owned estates had increased more than tenfold—so, too, had the number of enslaved people whom they posessed.[56]

The bequests made by spouses and parents created a new form of female dependency on unfree labor. As the flow of enslaved people into free families increased in the early eighteenth century, colonial women gained unprecedented access to a new and substantial form of property to offer female heirs. Women might have favored daughters to balance out the bequests made by fathers to sons. African-descended captives provided them with a novel means of accomplishing this. By 1720, Mercy Bars could offer five slaves to her son while transferring several families of enslaved people to her daughter. Eight years later, when Catherine Byndloss received her husband's consent to write her own will, she conveyed enslaved people, whom she held in a separate estate in her "own right," to her children. Like Bars, Byndloss offered fewer slaves to her son, who received one man. In contrast, she devised a woman named Betty, Betty's three daughters, and another woman named Quasheba to one daughter. Her other daughter received an enslaved mother and child.[57]

The inheritance choices made by free and freed women normalized female slaveholding, ensuring that future generations of female colonists would be deeply invested in Jamaica's unfree labor regime. Mary Penlerick's 1716 will exposes this familial process. Penlerick's ancestor James Pennelerick, among the first group of English settlers in Jamaica, bequeathed slaves as well as money for purchasing more African captives to his wife. When Mary Penlerick offered seventeen pounds for a "negro young woman" "to be bought" for her granddaughter "after marriage," she was following a well-established family precedent, one that ensured the investment of her granddaughter's generation in slavery.[58]

In Jamaica, parents and grandparents recognized emotional connections to heirs by giving them specific slaves. Colonists carefully distinguished the captives whom they intended for female recipients. James Leller gave the bulk of his property to his sons in 1700, but he spilled far more ink detail-

56. Nearly 80 percent of the estates owned by women that were probated between 1674 and 1765 contained slaves. Of the 825 female-held estates that were probated between 1674 and 1765, 648 also included slaves. See Jamaica Inventories. These figures support my estimates of men giving three-quarters of all wives and daughters slaves as legacies and suggest that inheritance transactions undergirded women's investments in slavery.

57. Will of Mercy Bars, 1720, Jamaica Wills, XV, Will of Catherine Byndloss, 1728, XVII.

58. Will of James Pennelerick, 1668, Jamaica Wills, I, Will of Mary Penlerick, 1716, XIV.

ing the movable items his daughter would receive, including £560, a silver tankard and sugar box, her mother's wedding ring, and "one negroe girl Savannah by name." Leller handled Savannah like a talisman—viewed as a sentimental object, she served a similar purpose to his deceased wife's wedding ring. Both the ring and Savannah signified his bond with his daughter. Similarly, when Mary Walker disbursed her £223 estate, she grouped Hannah and her daughters, Flora, Bella, and Gibba, together with a silver tankard, "porringers" (the small bowls that were used to feed infants), and silverware for her daughter. Leller and Walker equated enslaved people with feminized moveable goods that they imbued with personal meanings.[59]

Naming enslaved people and recognizing their family connections exposed the limitations of defining human beings as property. Mariner James Neal, for example, carefully listed "Dover, Tower Hill Kent Tour Deal Celia Mimbo Venus" as legacies for his wife and daughter in 1722. James Haughton "esquire" offered moveable goods, including "all plate, chariot and horses," to his wife. She also received eleven slaves, including "Imoundao and son, Nanny and children Elsy and Flora, Hercules, mulatto Quaco, Marlborough, Dorinda, and her child Betty and Mary a washerwoman." Perhaps Haughton recognized these parental ties in an effort to keep enslaved families intact. That same year "gentleman" John Gourlaw singled out a "negro woman Dafne" from the cattle, horses, household goods, money, and outstanding debts he awarded to his wife. Likewise, William Hunt lumped together a "negro woman Jane" with a "bald face horse" that he intended for his wife.[60]

When thousands of colonists defined and bequeathed people as assets, they did more to protect and further chattel slavery than Jamaica's slave codes or imperial policies could accomplish. On one hand, owners individualized slaves by naming them "Dafne" and "Jane" and distinguished them from other forms of personal property. On the other hand, colonists also participated in quotidian yet insidious acts of cultural and social destruction by equating "Dafne" and "Jane" with animals and giving them English names. If the women were African, the naming practices captured in colonial wills erased their African identities while enforcing their commodification. Inheri-

59. Will of James Leller, 1700, Jamaica Wills, I, Will of Mary Walker, 1718, XV.

60. Will of James Neal, 1722, Jamaica Wills, XVI, Will of James Haughton, 1722, XXII, Will of John Gourlaw, 1710, XIII, Will of William Hunt, 1710, XIII. For more on the implicit violence of the creolization process, which included giving captives English names, see Jennifer L. Morgan, *Laboring Women: Reproduction and Gender in New World Slavery* (Philadelphia, 2004), chap. 4.

tance transactions like the ones made by Neal, Gourlaw, Haughton, and Hunt continually reiterated and reinscribed object status onto enslaved people. In a colony where inheritance was the most instrumental means of allocating material possessions, these processes mattered. Collectively, bequests turned abstract legal definitions into lived realities for tens of thousands of captives.

HE TOOK HER SLAVES

Though wills strove to transform enslaved people into objects, these efforts were never fully successful. Legal conflicts over the possession of slaves highlight the manifest challenges involved in holding a large number of people in bondage. Owners, and captives themselves, readily contested each other's rights to claim people as slaves. People who engaged in legal disagreements over claims to a few enslaved people appeared in Grand Court in Spanish Town. Here, islanders sued each other for the act of detaining or "taking" slaves. Suits involving detainment were civil, not criminal, cases; litigants did not accuse defendants of harboring runaways, stealing enslaved people, or transporting them off the island, which were all serious and even felonious offenses. Instead, court scribes used words like "took" or "detained" to describe colonists' actions as the cases discussed here show. When locals invoked the English legal concepts of detainment and distraint, they displayed a sophisticated knowledge of property law.[61]

61. Anyone who kept someone else's slave for more than ten days faced a stiff fine of twenty pounds. Transporting a stolen slave off the island was a felony and carried the death penalty without the benefit of clergy. See "An Act for the Better Ordering of Slaves," in *The Laws of Jamaica, Passed by the Assembly and Confirmed by His Majesty in Council, April 17, 1684* . . . (London, 1684), 142–143. Detainment referred to the esoteric English legal actions of "trover" and "conversion." According to Sir William Blackstone, the eighteenth-century's preeminent legal scholar, a person who "*found* another's goods, and refused to deliver them on demand, but *converted* them to his own use" committed trover and conversion. Blackstone describes the actions of trover and conversion and the issues surrounding these actions as follows: "The injury lies in the conversion: for any man may take the goods of another into possession, if he finds them; but no finder is allowed to acquire a property therein, unless the owner be for ever unknown: and therefore he must not convert them to his own use, which the law presumes him to do, if he refuses to restore them to the owner; for which reason such refusal alone is, *prima facie,* sufficient evidence of a conversion. The fact of the finding, or *trover,* is therefore now totally immaterial: for the plaintiff needs only to suggest (as words of form) that he lost such goods, and that the defendant found them; and, if he proves that the goods are *his* property, and that the defendant had them in his possession, it is sufficient. But a conversion must be fully proved: and then in this action the

Conducting a comprehensive survey of the island's early court records is not feasible. Most of the materials are deemed too fragile for handling. The only cases available for viewing are from the 1680s, 1743, and 1761. These previously unstudied instances of slave detainment bring a varied group of free and enslaved people into the foreground. Jamaica's high mortality rates aggravated conflicts over slaveholding. Deeds, schedules of slaves, bills of sale, or mortgages could all be lost or forged. People died or moved away, leaving their captives behind. Detainment created opportunities for subterfuge. The bar was low for initiating detainment suits—anyone who paid a nominal court fee could accuse another person of unlawfully withholding his or her slaves. The looseness of the law meant that colonists could take a gamble that might have a large payoff. Accordingly, most of the plaintiffs and defendants who appeared in these suits were professionals or artisans—not elites. They often knew each other and quarreled over a few captives—not hundreds. Familiarity, and sometimes kinship ties, added a personal edge to disputes while also hinting at the ambiguously intimate relationships between enslavers and slaves, who had their own motives for influencing and even instigating conflicts between owners.[62]

The claims of female slaveholders whose property rights varied depending on their marital status, were especially unstable. Elizabeth Prothers, the wife of a bricklayer, pursued another married couple for "holding" eight captives whom she believed she was entitled to from a previous marriage. Perhaps the couple took advantage of Prothers's limited authority once she remarried and fell under coverture again. The result of Prothers's suit is unknown. At the time the case's verdict was recorded, free and freed women were as likely as men to win their suits. Though men dominated the upper echelons of colonial society—and ran the island's legal institutions—they preferred to uphold the property rights of slaveholders over enforcing the prerogatives of white men. Mary Phillips, a widow living in Kingston, sued her neighbor, the carpenter John Turner, in 1743 because he allegedly "took her slaves" from her at the courthouse. Phillips asserted that she was the rightful owner

plaintiff shall recover damages, equal to the value of the thing converted, but not the thing itself; which nothing will recover but an action of *detinue* or *replevin*." See "Of Injuries to Personal Property," in Blackstone, *Commentaries on the Laws of England,* Book III, Chapter 9, Lonang Institute, https://lonang.com/library/reference/blackstone-commentaries-law-england/bla-309/.

62. Of Injuries to Personal Property," in Blackstone, *Commentaries on the Laws of England,* Book III, Chapter 9, Lonang Institute, https://lonang.com/library/reference/blackstone-commentaries-law-england/bla-309/.

of a woman named Clara, Clara's child, and a girl, Jenny, whom she valued at £140. The court found Turner guilty and ordered him to return the captives to Phillips.[63]

As minors who lacked legal rights and parental protection, orphans were also vulnerable to challenges to their claims. An orphan named Christian Fea and her guardian, a butcher from Kingston, for instance, brought a suit against the town's deputy marshal in 1743, arguing that he "took a negro woman slave of her" named Venus and "detains her." The deputy marshal probably held Venus, who was valued at sixty pounds, as a means of collecting on debts owed by the orphan's estate. When he failed to appear in court, Fea's suit remained outstanding. As Fea's case shows, free women began defending their claims to enslaved people early in life. The same year that Fea sued the deputy marshal, another orphaned minor, Anna Mary Booth, was indicted by three of her male kin—Peter, Thomas, and Henry Booth—who were also parentless youths, for taking an adult enslaved man named Abraham from them. Booth probably held Abraham as a form of debt collection for cattle the Booths' father had purchased from her on credit. He died before paying his debt to the young woman, and she took Abraham to recoup the loss. By protecting her claim to Abraham, Anna Mary Booth engaged in an act of distraint.[64]

In England, distraint was typically considered to be a feminine practice through which women asserted their responsibility to protect their households. The majority of distraint suits there involved women who resisted or

63. James and Susanna Wellin v. Thomas and Elizabeth Prothers, Jamaica Grand Court Records, 1743, XLI, JA, John Turner v. Mary Phillips, Jamaica Grand Court Records, 1743, XLI. My assessment is based on a handful of court records that are accessible to the public. Limited access to the sources makes it difficult to conduct a more comprehensive study comparing male and female appearances in court.

64. Christina Fea and Daniel Stinger (guardian) v. William Lamb, Jamaica Grand Court Records, 1743, XLI, JA, Anna Mary Booth v. Peter Graves Booth, Thomas Henry Booth, and Henry Booth, Jamaica Grand Court Records, 1743, XLI. It is possible that the deputy marshal had mistreated Venus while she was in his custody and wanted to avoid the forty pound penalty he might be liable for if he appeared in court. The *Laws of Jamaica* required the provost marshal to pay forty pounds to the owner of any slaves that he employed or failed to provide adequate food and water to while under his custody. The penalty was probably high because it aimed to deter colonial officials from abusing their offices. See "An Act for the Better Ordering of Slaves," in *Laws of Jamaica* . . . (1684), 141. Christian could be a female name in Jamaica, and the usage of "her" in Christian Fea's case indicates that Fea was a female. Women named Christian made wills and had their estates probated.

illegally repossessed movable goods or livestock that had been seized to settle debts. In Jamaica, Booth won her case. The court supported her behavior, lending institutional power to colonial practices that expanded the category of movable goods to include captives like Abraham. Booth's suit also yields clues about enslaved people's experiences. The deceased man who owed money to the orphaned woman was a millwright. He probably trained Abraham in the profession, which significantly enhanced the captive's monetary value. If he was hired out to work as a millwright, Abraham would have enjoyed a degree of independence and possibly earned a modest income. Though Booth, as a free woman, wielded more authority than Abraham on paper, he might have used his de facto influence as an older man to instigate the dispute. Perhaps he conspired with, or even directed Booth, to challenge the claim of her young relatives to his person. Maybe he negotiated higher wages, more time off, or even manumission from Booth in exchange for remaining with her.[65]

Although these are, of course, conjectures, the appearance of other female colonists in similar suits hint at equally complicated social dynamics that were influenced by competing axes of power, including legal status, marital status, age, gender, and race. In 1743, five family members, including a widow, a "spinster," a baker, and a blacksmith, accused Jane Sedgewick, another Kingston widow, of taking two captives, Cato and Rachel, from them at the Wherry Bridge in town. Sedgewick did not appear in court to defend herself, and the case remained against her. In another suit that same year, Dr. John Brook charged two sisters, Mary and Ruth Grey, with taking an enslaved man named Cubah from him when Cubah was walking in Kingston's town square.[66]

Similar to the Booth case, both suits involved women who stood accused of detaining other adults. Additionally, Sedgewick and the Grey sisters supposedly abducted these men and women in public and highly visible locations, indicating that other residents did not perceive foul play. Perhaps they even viewed Cato, Rachel, and Cubah as belonging to the enslavers who stood accused of taking them. The public nature of these acts both complicates and elucidates the relationships forged between enslaved people and

65. The act of distraint was called "forcible rescue." See Garthine Walker, *Crime, Gender, and Social Order in Early Modern England* (New York, 2003), 89–90.

66. Jane Sedgewick v. John Standish, Martha Standish, Caleb Standish, Jane Miller, Robert Standish, 1743, Jamaica Grand Court Records, XLI, JA, Mary and Ruth Grey v. John Brook, 1743, Jamaica Grand Court Records, XLI. The sisters in the latter case were found guilty.

their purported captors. The Grey sisters who were faulted for taking the enslaved man Cubah on the town square, for instance, must have known him. The widow Sedgewick, who supposedly held Cato and Rachel from the Standish family, was likewise on familiar terms with the enslaved people in question. Detainment and distraint were not furtive acts of abduction. On the contrary, participants claimed possession of captives at courthouses, bridges, and town squares. The widow Elizabeth Sharpe charged two men with illegally withholding her slaves, one of whom was taken in a churchyard. The court found both men guilty. Two adolescent sisters, Mary and Elizabeth Jarum, also accused a man with taking three captives from them at a church.[67]

Enslaved people were not necessarily passive victims in such transactions. Adults who were allegedly seized, particularly those who were acquired by younger women, likely agreed to the exchanges. Otherwise, it would have been difficult for defendants in these scenarios to physically coerce adults, especially men, without attracting attention. Though the Grey sisters might have threatened Cubah, Cato, and Rachel with punishments if they did not comply, it is equally plausible that the captives also shaped these encounters. The small-scale slaveowners who normally appear in distraint suits shared close quarters with enslaved people, who would have been privy to personal information about the financial and legal positions of their owners. Cubah, Cato, and Rachel might have used the legal ambiguities surrounding slave ownership to their advantage. If one can imagine Sedgewick or the Grey sisters whispering threats into the ears of the people they wanted to claim, one should also envision Cubah, Cato, and Rachel strategically sharing family secrets and persuading colonists to capitalize on the deaths or debts of neighbors and friends. Free and enslaved people probably conspired to enact seizures in public locations where they could easily slip away together.

Such actions are not equivalent to earning legal freedom, but they are still suggestive of the varied tactics used by enslaved people to exercise a small degree of influence and shape the contours of their captivity. Moving to different owners might have afforded some people with better treatment, protection from abuse, and proximity to loved ones. Distraint suits might even reveal acts of maroonage. The laws called for harsh punishments of runaways, specifically repeat offenders. Yet slaves and servants were not considered to be runaways until they had been absent for several months or

67. John Hammon v. Elizabeth Sharpe, 1743, Jamaica Grand Court Records, XLI, JA, John Wilson v. Mary and Elizabeth Jarum, 1743, Grand Court Records, XLI.

if their owners identified them as "rebellious" or thieves. Cases of distraint suggest that slaveholders accepted captives' temporary hiatuses on occasion or preferred to identify certain actions as property transgressions rather than criminal activities.[68]

On a more basic level, distraint suits show that free and enslaved people considered women enslavers to be ordinary figures in colonial society. If bequests of slaves enriched the coffers of female islanders, inheritance practices also made slaveholding a commonplace activity for them, so much so that nobody deemed it unusual for an adult woman of European or Euro-African descent to appear alongside two enslaved adult men on the street. If bequests contributed to the construction of the slave as a specific form of legal estate, thereby supporting colonial laws, then distraint cases disclose the latitude between law and practice. As their wills show, colonists were certainly invested in exploiting the material value of enslaved people. The Jamaica Assembly devised some of the most brutal slave codes in the Anglo-Atlantic world, but islanders did not necessarily choose to enforce them. They were intently concerned with property, not necessarily with the type of policing that the laws aimed to encourage. Occasionally, free and unfree people colluded with each other, using this maneuverability to their advantage.

Despite the catastrophic conditions endured by islanders, Jamaica was not a failed settler society. By the 1740s and 1750s, free people had constructed the most important colony in the British Empire. They accomplished this by adapting to Jamaican circumstances. In the face of demographic volatility, colonists modified aspects of British inheritance customs that upheld masculine privilege, preferring to support local kin irrespective of gender rather than distant male heirs. Displaying an impressive legal savvy and a keen awareness of the gendered disabilities experienced by wives, free people used equity to shield married women's property. Equity enabled wives to maintain ownership of assets, making them less dependent on husbands. Acting in their capacities as executors, household heads, and enslavers, legally independent widows and unmarried women wielded forms of authority traditionally correlated with masculine privilege.

During the first half of the eighteenth century, colonists turned captive Africans into an essential resource for female heirs. By treating enslaved

68. Later in the eighteenth century, deserters were defined as "incorrigible runaways" after a six-month period and tried in slave courts. See Diana Paton, "Punishment, Crime, and the Bodies of Slaves in Eighteenth-Century Jamaica," *Journal of Social History*, XXXIV (2001), 930.

people as fungible assets, they created a form of wealth that was flexible, easily saleable, and suitable for any free person on the island. Islanders used these measures to more fully commodify and exploit slaves, providing additional material support to all of the members in their kin group. Free and freed women were often the beneficiaries of this trend. The influx of captives into colonial families augmented the size and value of the portions female heirs received. Once women assumed control of estates, which normally included enslaved people, they showed a marked interest in transferring their holdings to other women. By the early eighteenth century, these practices were so pervasive that even women like Sarah Harrison, who likely spent part of her own life in bondage, also inherited and sold enslaved people.

Colonial circumstances made free and freed women instrumental to the accumulation and transmission of material wealth on the island. Though familial needs might have driven islanders to develop their own inheritance customs, their actions had much broader consequences for the British Empire. Wives, daughters, and granddaughters sustained fragile kinship networks that were ravaged by disease and death and kept family resources intact across multiple generations. In doing so, they ensured the stability and continuity of British control over an increasingly valuable Caribbean territory. As free and freed women became more reliant on enslaved people to serve as a vital form of property, they furthered the demand for more African captives to be exiled to Jamaica and deepened the empire's commitment to Atlantic slavery.

5. Nonmarital Intimacies

In 1752, Mary Barrow, a "mulatto woman," and her "white" partner, Lawrence Reid, brought their eight-month-old daughter, Anne Reid, to be baptized at the main church in Kingston, Jamaica. Through this action, the couple publicly recognized their child—and their relationship, though they were not married—before the largest congregation in Britain's wealthiest colony. Anne Reid's baptism served spiritual, social, and legal purposes. By giving his surname to the infant, Lawrence Reid asserted his paternity, bringing Anne into the fold of the Reid kin group and establishing her membership in the island's free Christian community. At the same time, he muted his daughter's African ancestry, distanced her from a past marked by enslavement, and weakened her connection to her mother. Mary Barrow's own baptism twenty-seven years earlier had served similarly complicated objectives. She was the daughter of an enslaved woman named Sarah and a free man, Thomas Barrow.[1]

Colonial inhabitants like Barrow and Reid, and her parents before them, laid the groundwork for the development of a sexual culture and modes of family formation that diverged sharply from the legal and social trends reshaping reproduction and marriage in other parts of the Anglo-Atlantic world. With the passage of the Hardwick Marriage Act in 1753, Britain sought to uphold a more rigid, restricted, and legalistic definition of marriage, one that marginalized illegitimate children and their unwed mothers.

1. Baptism of Anne Reid, June 1752, Kingston Parish Register, Baptisms, I, 1722–1792, Jamaica Copy Registers, 1669–1761, Island Record Office (IRO), Spanish Town, Jamaica, Baptism of Mary Barrow, 1725, Kingston Parish Register, I.

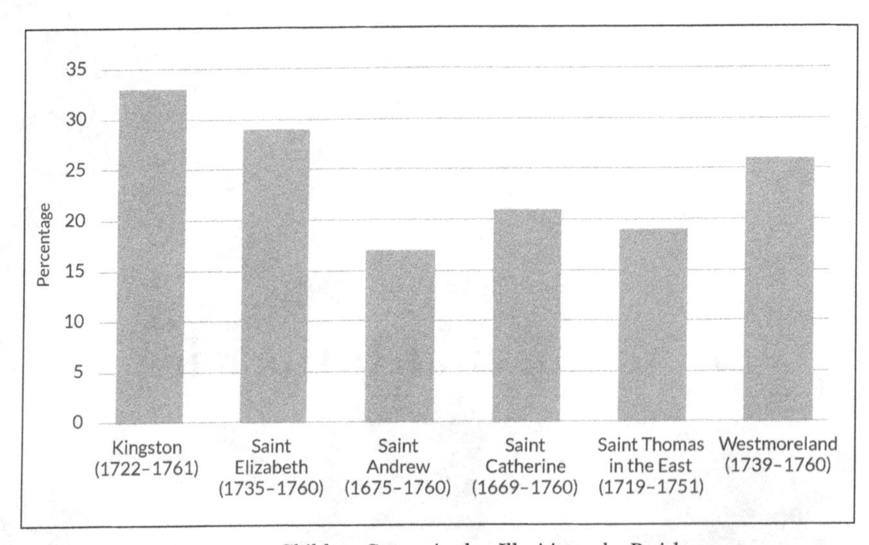

FIGURE 3. Children Categorized as Illegitimate by Parish.
Source: Jamaica Copy Registers, 1669–1761, Island Record Office, Spanish Town, Jamaica.

A study of two thousand parish register entries made in Jamaica between 1675 and 1767, however, shows Jamaican colonists adopting a very different approach toward gender, sex, and marriage (Figure 3). A survey of the six parishes with surviving records—Kingston, Saint Andrew, Saint Catherine, Saint Elizabeth, Saint Thomas in the East, and Westmoreland—reveals that Jamaica had the highest illegitimacy rate in the empire: 25 percent of the children who received baptisms in the colony were born to unmarried parents. If it was possible to include infants who died before their christenings, whose parents had different faiths, or who were born into slavery, the number of illegitimate children would be higher. Illegitimacy rates in Britain, by comparison, ranged from 0.5 to 5.5 percent, and, even in Philadelphia, which has been characterized as a sexually permissive space, only 2.6 percent of the children who received christenings were born out of wedlock.[2]

2. Instead of focusing on literary representation and policy, this chapter explores the intimate relationships of individuals. It responds to the call for scholarship on sexuality in early America to study people's interactions, rather than attend solely to regulations. I use baptism records as a means of studying the sexual and personal connections between people whose relationships are otherwise obscured in the archives. See Kirsten Fischer and Jennifer L. Morgan, "Sex, Race, and the Colonial Project," *WMQ*, 3d Ser., LX (2003), 197–198. For the Hardwick Marriage Act, see Daniel Livesay, *Children of Uncertain Fortune: Mixed-Race Jamaicans in Britain and the Atlantic Family, 1733–1833* (Williamsburg, Va., and Chapel Hill, N.C., 2018), 52–61. Parish registers

As Jamaica's parish registers demonstrate, a significant number of free and freed people who possessed the means to marry and had access to licensed ministers chose not to do so. Variations in the racial makeup of unwed couples can be partially explained by the demographic disparities between free and enslaved people in the various parishes. For instance, in Saint Thomas in the East, where legally free "masters and mistresses" together with indentured servants and a handful of free people of African descent made up 14 percent of the population and enslaved persons constituted the remaining 86 percent, captive women accounted for more than half of the mothers of the illegitimate children who received baptisms in the parish. Yet illegitimacy rates in other rural parishes indicate that demographics alone cannot explain

---

were considered important documents in the colony. They were often the sole source of demographic information, and falsifying them was a crime. See "An Act for the Maintenance of Ministers, and the Poor, and Erecting and Repairing of Churches," in *The Laws of Jamaica, Passed by the Assembly and Confirmed by His Majesty in Council, April 17, 1684* . . . (London, 1684), 57–58; and [Charles Leslie], *A New History of Jamaica: From the Earliest Accounts, to the Taking of Porto Bello by Vice-Admiral Vernon* . . . (London, 1740), 190. My calculations are based on a survey of the baptism registers kept in the parishes of Kingston, Saint Andrew, Saint Catherine, Saint Elizabeth, Saint Thomas in the East, and Westmoreland between 1675–1761. See Jamaica Copy Registers. Among the children who were baptized, 634 were born to mothers who had a different surname than their child's father, who appeared alone when presenting their baby for baptism and did not name their child's father, or who were enslaved. Furthermore, the legal status of "mulattos" was often not recorded in Saint Catherine. Overall, the children born to enslaved women are, for the most part, not represented in baptismal records. A study of the baptism records made in Kingston between 1722–1753 by Clare A. Lyons supports my findings. She, like me, determines that more than one-third of the children baptized by white women in the city were illegitimate. Likewise, she describes the "magnitude of disregard for marriage" in Jamaica as unprecedented in the Anglophone world. See Lyons, "Cities at Sea: Gender and Sexuality in the Eighteenth-Century British Colonial City, Philadelphia, Kingston, Madras, and Calcutta," in Deborah Simonton, ed., *Routledge History Handbook of Gender and the Urban Experience* (New York, 2017), 433. Jamaica had the highest illegitimacy rates in the Anglo-Atlantic world. See Richard Adair, *Courtship, Illegitimacy, and Marriage in Early Modern England* (Manchester, U.K., 1996), 53, cited in Trevor Burnard, "'Gay and Agreeable Ladies': White Women in Mid-Eighteenth-Century Kingston, Jamaica," *Wadabagei: A Journal of the Caribbean and Its Diaspora,* IX, no. 3 (Fall 2006), 44. For illegitimacy rates in Philadelphia, see Clare A. Lyons, *Sex among the Rabble: An Intimate History of Gender and Power in the Age of Revolution, Philadelphia, 1730–1830* (Williamsburg, Va., and Chapel Hill, N.C., 2006), 64. Kathleen M. Brown also notes that bastardy rates in seventeenth-century Virginia were much higher than they were in England in *Good Wives, Nasty Wenches, and Anxious Patriarchs: Gender, Race, and Power in Colonial Virginia* (Williamsburg, Va., and Chapel Hill, N.C., 1996), 75.

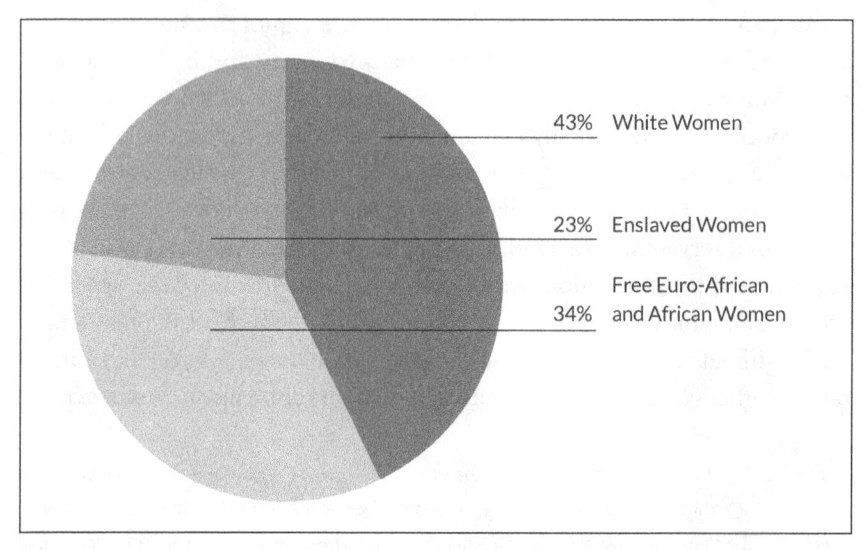

FIGURE 4. Race and Legal Status of Mothers of Illegitimate Children.
Source: Jamaica Copy Registers, 1669–1761, Island Record Office, Spanish Town, Jamaica.

the broader interest in seeking public recognition for nonmarital relationships. White people comprised 78 percent of the unmarried couples in the plantation parish of Saint Andrew, where they also formed a small minority. Similarly, in the agricultural region of Saint Elizabeth, white couples represented 59 percent of unmarried parents (Figure 4). Perhaps the actions of individual ministers shaped these trends, encouraging parishioners of European descent to christen their children. Or, white colonists might have been more likely to use churches.[3]

3. A census, which included "mistresses" and "female servants," was taken of Jamaica's population by parish in 1730. The parish of Saint Thomas in the East was inhabited by 437 free people, including 85 "masters and mistresses," 204 "white men servants," 56 "white women servants," 65 "white children," and 27 "free negro, indian, and mulatto" men, women, and children. See "Jamaica to His Majesty, Relating to the Unhappy Situation of Affairs of That Island," Correspondence to the Lords of Trade and Plantations, CO 137/19, II, The National Archives (TNA), Kew, U.K. Similar patterns appeared in other agricultural parishes. Twenty percent of all the illegitimate children baptized in Saint Elizabeth had an enslaved mother while 27 percent of the natural children christened in Westmoreland were born to unfree women. The 1730 record of Westmoreland's population is spotty: the census taker recorded 61 masters and mistresses, 289 white male servants, and 7,137 slaves. No record of white children, white female servants, or free people of color was created, though these groups certainly existed in the parish. The record for Saint Elizabeth is even sparser: it only identifies 398 white male servants and 6,529 slaves. The

Parish registers are, of course, incomplete archival sources. The high turnover of clergymen who either died soon after arriving in Jamaica or left after a few years there resulted in uneven and erratic record keeping in most of the churches on the island. Those who survived did not adhere to a uniform terminology for children who were born to unmarried parents. The minister in Saint Catherine used the terms "illegitimate" and "bastard" interchangeably while his counterpart in Saint Elizabeth described them as "base" born. Nevertheless, the parish registers still provide the most voluminous, and often the only, evidence of the complex, yet otherwise invisible, intimate connections people forged across racial and legal divides. Cumulatively, these records deepen our understanding of how second- and third-generation islanders adapted British practices related to sex, marriage, and reproduction to suit colonial circumstances.[4]

During the first half of the eighteenth century, free and freed people treated legal and religiously sanctioned marriage as one of a variety of possible intimate relationships. Couples living in both rural and urban areas, including those who had access to licensed ministers, displayed a preference for starting families outside of wedlock. The parents of more than one-third of all the children baptized in Kingston—where the island's largest church was located—were unwed, and 50 percent of these people were white. Ministers who worked in sparsely populated hinterland parishes, such as Westmoreland and Saint Elizabeth, baptized nearly the same numbers of illegitimate infants as their urban peers.[5]

Jamaica's single mothers comprised a diverse group. Surprisingly, more than half the women who baptized illegitimate children were identified as "white" in the parish registers. Although the relative scarcity of women of European descent made them desirable marriage prospects, especially if they

racial categorizations of unwed parents are derived from baptism records. See Saint Elizabeth Parish Register, I, Jamaica Copy Registers, Saint Thomas in the East Copy Register, Baptisms, and Westmoreland Parish Register.

4. The baptismal records logged by ministers serving in the agricultural parishes of Saint Elizabeth, Saint Thomas in the East, and Westmoreland, for example, are far sparser than the scrupulously kept Kingston register. The legal status of men identified as "negro" or "mulatto" in the parish of Saint Catherine was not recorded, making it difficult to precisely count the number of enslaved mothers who baptized children there. Between 1690–1754, ministers of Saint Catherine Parish used the term "bastard" nine times and "illegitimate" six times. The ministers in Saint Elizabeth Parish used the label "base" seventy-three times between 1753–1761. See Saint Catherine Parish Register, I, Jamaica Copy Registers, and Saint Elizabeth Parish Register, I.

5. Kingston Parish Register, Baptisms, I, Jamaica Copy Registers.

were young and wealthy, a large portion of white female colonists declined from marrying their sexual partners. Free African and Euro-African women like Mary Barrow accounted for another 30 percent of the unwed mothers who baptized children (Figure 5). Their prominence among the group of single parents is more predictable. Despite that interracial marriage was legal in Jamaica and European men occasionally wed women of African descent, the growing hostility toward free and freed people of color probably triggered social censure of interracial marriage. Captives like Mary Barrow's mother, Sarah, occupied the most vulnerable and marginalized positions on the island. These women, who made up an estimated one-quarter of the mothers who baptized illegitimate children, rarely married free men. Doing so would have unsettled the legal basis of slavery that defined them as property. Still, the small number of enslaved mothers like Sarah whose children became free as a result of their baptisms were the fortunate ones. The vast majority of infants born to enslaved women would never be christened, acknowledged by free fathers, or released from bondage.[6]

It is, of course, impossible to know whether all single mothers in Jamaica remained unmarried by choice, and attributing agency to their actions is a fraught endeavor. Jamaica's sexually permissive environment created a culture that sanctioned the widespread exploitation of enslaved women by free men. But, when the fragments of evidence from parish registers and wills are pieced together and situated within the island's tolerant attitudes toward sexuality, it becomes clear that a large number of women, many of whom were of middling status, preferred long-term relationships outside of wedlock. Hardly desperate or abandoned, this group of female colonists possessed social respectability and, often, considerable material resources.[7]

6. Wills and baptism records from the colony disclose very few examples of interracial marriages—almost none of the couples made up of white men and free or enslaved women of African descent who baptized children were married. Free and freed husbands and wives of African descent were slightly more common. My study of the parish registers, however, focuses on baptisms, not marriages. A comprehensive study of all the marriage records in the parish registers has yet to be done.

7. Scholars have observed that the sexual exploitation of enslaved women by male colonists in the British Caribbean, and Jamaica in particular, was especially pernicious. See Trevor Burnard, "'Rioting in Goatish Embraces': Marriage and Improvement in Early British Jamaica," *History of the Family*, XI (2006), 185–197; and Burnard, *Mastery, Tyranny, and Desire: Thomas Thistlewood and His Slaves in the Anglo-Jamaican World* (Chapel Hill, N.C., 2004). Richard Godbeer describes all sexual relationships between white men and enslaved women as "implicitly coercive" (Godbeer, *Sexual Revolution in Early America* [Baltimore, 2002], 199). See also Sharon Block,

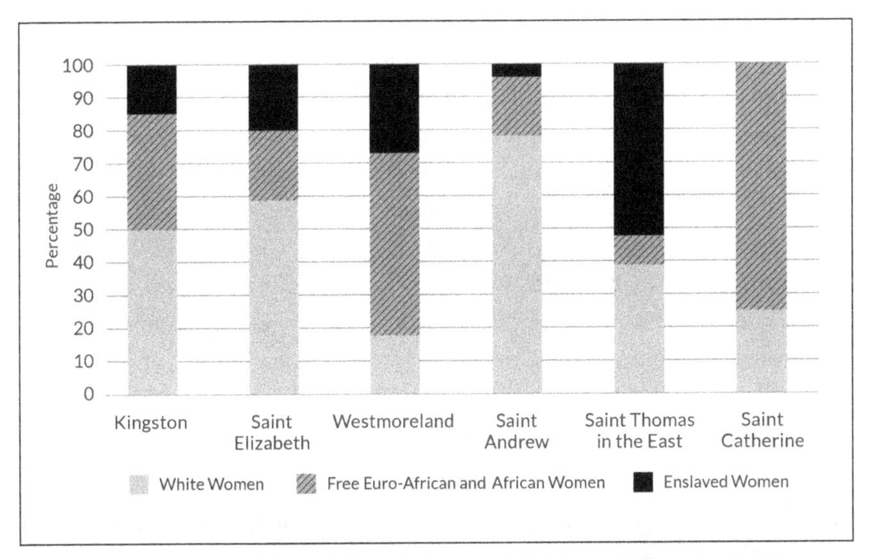

FIGURE 5. Race and Legal Status of Mothers of Illegitimate Children by Parish. Source: Jamaica Copy Registers, 1669–1761, Island Record Office, Spanish Town, Jamaica. *As the graph shows, illegitimacy was not associated with one racial category or legal status. White women represented more than half of the unwed mothers in Saint Elizabeth and Kingston, for instance, whereas women of African descent christened three-quarters of the illegitimate children in Saint Catherine Parish, where Spanish Town was located.*

On the whole, islanders disavowed English legal precedents that defined all children who were born out of wedlock to be fatherless and thus children "of no one," preferring instead to use baptism as a means of recognizing and legitimizing nonmarital families. In England, illegitimate children could not make legal claims to the estates of their parents based on patrimony. Although Jamaica passed no acts related to illegitimacy that would modify common law principles, colonists regularly acknowledged paternity and maternity of infants who were born out of wedlock and bequeathed property to them. In a society saturated by slavery, baptism also took on new legal and quasi-legal meanings. Couples made up of free and enslaved individuals used the Christian ritual as the first step toward establishing the free status of their children.[8]

Rape and Sexual Power in Early America (Williamsburg, Va., and Chapel Hill, N.C., 2006); and Wendy Anne Warren, "'The Cause of Her Grief': The Rape of a Slave in Early New England," *Journal of American History*, XCIII (2007), 1031–1049.

8. English law diverged from the Roman laws adopted by France and Spain, which allowed

The proliferation and tolerance of a multiplicity of nonmarital relationships in Jamaica was especially significant for free women of European, Euro-African, and African descent. In Jamaica, unwed mothers did not face legal or social repercussions for sexual impropriety, as they did elsewhere in the empire. Women throughout much of the Anglo-Atlantic world were increasingly subjected to an uncompromising sexual double standard that equated feminine respectability with sexual virtue, which could only be established within marriage. In England, women who committed the acts of fornication, adultery, prostitution, or bastard bearing faced social ostracism, expulsion from their communities, or imprisonment. The majority of inmates in English houses of correction were women who had engaged in petty crimes, including prostitution and bastard bearing.[9]

---

for children to be recognized as legitimate if their parents entered into wedlock later in their lives. Sir William Blackstone describes the rights and incapacities of a bastard according to eighteenth-century English law: "The rights are very few, being only such as he can acquire; for he can inherit nothing, being looked upon as the son of nobody, and sometimes called *filius nullius* [son of no one], sometimes *filius populi* [son of the people]. Yet he may gain a surname by reputation, though he has none by inheritance." See "Of Parent and Child," in Blackstone, *Commentaries on the Laws of England* (London, 1765–1769), Book 1, Chapter 16, Lonang Institute, https://lonang.com/library/reference/blackstone-commentaries-law-england/bla-116/. The laws passed in Barbados, Jamaica, and South Carolina, in particular, focused intensively on "the consolidation and elaboration of a slaveholding interest." Edward B. Rugemer raises this point in a footnote in which he identifies the need for "a more nuanced understanding of racial formation that is attuned to geography and political economy *as well as gender* [emphasis my own]." See Rugemer, "The Development of Mastery and Race in the Comprehensive Slave Codes of the Greater Caribbean during the Seventeenth Century," *WMQ*, 3d Ser., LXX (2013), 432n. See also Barbara Bush, "White 'Ladies,' Coloured 'Favourites,' and Black 'Wenches': Some Considerations on Sex, Race, and Class Factors in Social Relations in White Creole Society in the British Caribbean," *Slavery and Abolition*, II, no. 3 (December 1981), 248; Zacek, *Settler Society in the English Leeward Islands*, 178–179; and Heather Miyano Kopelson, "Sinning Property and the Legal Transformation of Abominable Sex in Early Bermuda," *WMQ*, 3d Ser., LXX (2013), 495.

9. Trevor Burnard, "European Migration to Jamaica, 1655–1780," *WMQ*, 3d Ser., LIII (1996), 769–796; Burnard, "A Failed Settler Society: Marriage and Demographic Failure in Early Jamaica," *Journal of Social History*, XXVIII (1994), 63–82; Cornelia Hughes Dayton, *Women before the Bar: Gender, Law, and Society in Connecticut, 1639–1789* (Williamsburg, Va., and Chapel Hill, N.C., 1995), esp. chaps. 4 and 5; Godbeer, *Sexual Revolution in Early America;* Kristen Fischer, *Suspect Relations: Sex, Race, and Resistance in Colonial North Carolina* (Ithaca, N.Y., 2002), 161; Kenneth A. Lockridge, *On the Sources of Patriarchal Rage: The Commonplace Books of William Byrd and Thomas Jefferson and the Gendering of Power in the Eighteenth Century* (New

The criminalization of women's sexual misconduct intensified across the Atlantic, where a large portion of the suits in many colonies involved sexual transgressions related to extramarital sex and took on a racial cast. As colonial officials struggled to maintain control of a growing slave population in British North America, they, too, began passing laws that penalized free inhabitants for interracial sex and targeted white women specifically. Virginia established legal codes in 1662 fining "any Christian" who committed the crime of "fornication" with a "negro man or woman" and then banned interracial marriage altogether in 1691, as did Maryland. North Carolina outlawed marriage between white people and people of African or Indian descent in 1715. Yet, as Kirsten Fischer shows, only white women were punished "explicitly" for interracial sex. In 1717, South Carolina added seven years to the indentures of white female servants who bore children with black men while free interracial couples were forced into seven years of servitude. Less than a decade later, Pennsylvania passed stringent laws that sought to ban interracial sex. White men and women who cohabited with "any negro" under the "pretense of being married" were punished with a hefty fine of thirty pounds or seven years of servitude. Any child born to an interracial couple was indentured until she or he turned thirty-one, and partners of African descent faced re-enslavement. Although acts passed by several colonies referred to

---

York, 1992); Mary Beth Norton, *Founding Mothers and Fathers: Gendered Power and the Forming of American Society* (New York, 1996); Stephanie Wood, "Sexual Violation in the Conquest of America," in Merril D. Smith, ed., *Sex and Sexuality in Early America* (New York, 1998), 9–34. Communities subjected women's intimate lives to harsh scrutiny, while the sexual escapades of men were often tolerated and even celebrated. See Natalie A. Zacek, *Settler Society in the English Leeward Islands, 1670–1776* (New York, 2010), 208–209; and Clare A. Lyons, "Mapping an Atlantic Sexual Culture: Homoeroticism in Eighteenth-Century Philadelphia," *WMQ*, 3d Ser., LX (2003), 123–124. Tim Hitchcock argues that as sex in England was more narrowly equated with activities that led to pregnancy, more women bore the responsibility for bastard bearing. See Hitchcock, *English Sexualities, 1700–1800* (New York, 1997), 40–41. According to Karin Wulf, single women were a "nexus for cultural tensions and thus provide a prism through which vital connections among politics, economics, and gender were refracted" (Wulf, *Not All Wives: Women of Colonial Philadelphia* [Ithaca, N.Y., 2000], 5, 9). Houses of correction were designed to discipline crimes associated with single women: prostitution, petty larceny, living out of service, and bastard bearing. See Amy M. Froide, *Never Married: Singlewomen in Early Modern England* (New York, 2005), 38, 40–41. As Kirsten Fischer notes, one in ten court cases in North Carolina involved immoral behavior related to sexuality. Likewise, a large number of criminal prosecutions in New England and Virginia were also related to sexual behavior (Fischer, *Suspect Relations*, 112–113).

white men and women, the courts rarely punished men who engaged in interracial intimacies.[10]

By comparison, free and freed women in Jamaica exercised a remarkable degree of sexual liberty. Though enslaved people comprised the large majority of the population, the colony's lawmakers adopted a different approach toward female sexuality from their counterparts in North America and Britain. The Jamaica Assembly neither punished women who bore illegitimate children nor forbid interracial sex and marriage. Indeed, the only references to illicit sex in all of Jamaica's legal codes related to indentured servants. Acts passed in 1683, for example, charged "Free-m[e]n" who fathered children with female servants twenty pounds, which they were required to pay to the woman's "Master or Mistress." The money would be used to either support their offspring or pay for a replacement servant if the father planned to marry his paramour. If the fathers of their children failed to comply, indentured women risked having their time in servitude doubled. Male servants were also denied the right to start families during their indentures. Marrying without a master's or mistress's consent or bearing a child with another servant would result in an extension of service. These types of statutes, which sought to control and extract labor rather than enforce moral or religious values, were not unique to Jamaica. With the exception of Antigua and Bermuda, most British colonies in the Caribbean ignored issues related to gender and interracial sex. Instead, officials invested institutional resources in controlling large enslaved populations. As the British territory with the largest number of slaves in the Anglo-Atlantic world, the colony's legal and correctional institutions focused on surveilling and disciplining enslaved people, not free islanders.[11]

10. William Waller Hening, ed., *The Statues at Large; Being a Collection of All the Laws of Virginia, from the First Session of the Legislature in the Year 1619*, II (New York, 1823), 170, quoted in Godbeer, *Sexual Revolution in Early America*, 202–203; Fischer, *Suspect Relations*, 123–124; "An Act for the Better Regulation of Negroes in This Province," in James T. Mitchell et al., comps., *The Statutes at Large of Pennsylvania* (Harrisburg, Pa., 1896–1915), IV, 59–64, quoted in Lyons, *Sex among the Rabble*, 91. See also John Ruston Pagan, *Anne Orthwood's Bastard: Sex and Law in Early Virginia* (New York, 2003).

11. Grand Court Records, 1A/5/1, JA; [Leslie], *New History of Jamaica*, 173, 302; "An Act for Regulating Servants," in *The Laws of Jamaica, Passed by the Assembly and Confirmed by His Majesty in Council, Feb. 23, 1683 . . .* (London, 1683), 11–12; "Of Parent and Child," in Blackstone, *Commentaries on the Laws of England*, Book 1, Chapter 16, Lonang Institute, https://lonang.com/library/reference/blackstone-commentaries-law-england/bla-116/. An act was passed in 1683 for the establishment of a Supreme Court of Judicature in Spanish Town. Charles Leslie

The Church of England's anemic authority in Jamaica further contributed to a secularized society that enhanced the legal rights and social authority of the individual and largely ignored sexual behaviors considered spiritual crimes elsewhere. Few of the English clergymen who traveled to Jamaica survived or remained there for long. In 1720, William May, the Anglican minister in Kingston, reported that five parishes were vacant. Those who stayed decried their inability to regulate colonists' spiritual and moral affairs. The island's legal codes expressly forbid "Ecclesiastical Law or Jurisdiction" and granted royal governors, not English bishops, the right to issue marriage licenses, weakening the legal power of religious officials and disavowing the spiritual element of marriage. One clergyman wrote, "If we have not Somewhat of the Ecclessast. Law on our Side to help us to suppress Immorality and vice, we cannot expect to come much more speed [in] our way than Soldiers goeing to War without weapons."[12]

called it both the Supreme Court and the Grand Court, and it sat four times a year. Cases involving illicit sex are also absent from early eighteenth-century court records, further emphasizing institutional disinterest in controlling colonists' sexual behaviors. The suits that I have examined suggest that this court was mainly used for litigating smaller financial disputes. It is plausible that the records related to illicit sex have not survived the passage of time or that local justices of the peace handled cases relating to sexual indiscretions. Access to the Grand Court records is limited. Only one volume from the eighteenth century has survived, and it is considered too fragile to be handled by researchers. However, the dearth of laws to regulate sex would have made it difficult for colonists to pursue each other legally for sexual matters.

12. "An Act for the Maintenance of Ministers, and the Poor, and Erecting and Repairing of Churches," in *Laws of Jamaica . . .* (1684), 59; John Kelly, "Queries to Be Answer'd by Every Minister," Apr. 15, 1724, Fulham Papers, Colonial, General Correspondence, West Indies, XVII, fols. 219r–220v, Lambeth Palace Library (LPL), London. For the vacant parishes, see William May to [Bishop John Robinson], Mar. 6, 1720, Fulham Papers, Colonial, General Correspondence, West Indies, XVII, fol. 147r; and Anon., *The Importance of Jamaica to Great-Britain Consider'd . . .* (London, [1740]), 14. British clergymen who traveled to Jamaica contended with high mortality rates and ministered to a spiritually diverse community. They received little support from the local government, and the Church of England's infrastructure on the island was weak. The situation did not improve with time; in the later eighteenth century, there was one clergyman per fifteen hundred white inhabitants, and five parishes still lacked churches. See Edward Brathwaite, *The Development of Creole Society in Jamaica, 1770–1820* (Oxford, 1971), 21, 25. By stripping the institution of its customary authority over spiritual, sexual, and domestic life, colonial leaders participated in a "quiet lay revolution against church discipline" occurring in plantation colonies throughout British America. For a description of this broader trend, see Nicholas M. Beasley, *Christian Ritual and the Creation of British Slave Societies, 1650–1780* (Athens, Ga., 2009), 56. For an account of the de-emphasis of church authority and formal reli-

Licensed clergymen were alarmed by the island's policy of religious tolerance which went hand in hand with its laissez-faire approach toward sexuality. Anyone could settle in Jamaica irrespective of confessional faith. By the 1720s, people who were exiled or experienced severe discrimination elsewhere in the British Empire—Jews, Quakers, and Catholics—had moved to the colony. One minister stated that "any Jew, Turk, Mahometan, Papist may teach publick school, provided he does not openly profess his Religion." His colleagues asserted that half of the three hundred families in Port Royal, fifty families in Kingston, and another thirty-eight families in Spanish Town were Jewish. Enslaved Africans, who made up the vast majority of the island's population, brought their own diverse spiritual beliefs and practices to Jamaica, strongly influencing its religious eclecticism.[13]

Their criticisms of Jamaica's spiritually diverse and sexually permissive environment notwithstanding, representatives of the official church certainly did not act as the moral exemplars of their parishes. One clergyman in Port Royal had allegedly fled from Virginia following the discovery of his polygamous marriages to three different women. After learning of the "Notorious profligate and Vitious" conduct of another minister, Governor Archibald Hamilton incited the Jamaica Assembly to pass an act in 1713 empowering

---

gion on the island, see James Robertson, "Late Seventeenth-Century Spanish Town, Jamaica: Building an English City on Spanish Foundations," *Early American Studies*, VI (2008), 361–362. The assembly divested the church of the "Power to inforce or establish any penal Mulcts or Punishment, in any Case whatsoever." See law quoted from Charles Leslie's publication of the laws in force in Jamaica during his visit in the 1730s; [Leslie], *A New History of Jamaica*, 191. The law was originally passed in 1684 (*Laws of Jamaica* . . . [1684], 59). Couples who desired to marry were supposed to announce their banns in a parish church three times or obtain a license from the governor. The minister who entered marriages into the parish of Saint Catherine's register in the late seventeenth century, for example, noted whether couples had procured a license from the governor to marry or "duly published their bans." See "An Act for the Maintenance of Ministers, and the Poor, and Erecting and Repairing of Churches," in *Laws of Jamaica* . . . (1684), 59. One clergyman complained of the governor for appointing ministers without obtaining a license from the bishop of London. See "The State of the Church in Jamaica," undated and unsigned, (refers to events of 1722), Fulham Papers, Colonial, 1626–1822, General Correspondence, West Indies, XVIII, fols. 228–233, LPL.

13. James White to [Bishop Gibson], Mar. 5, 1723/4, Fulham Papers, Colonial, General Correspondence, West Indies, XVII, fols. 173r–174v, Calvin Galpine, "Queries to Be Answer'd by Every Minister," Apr. 20, 1724, XVII, fols. 215r–216v, William May, "Queries to Be Answer'd by Every Minister," [1724], XVII, fols. 224r–225v, John Scott, "Queries to Be Answered by Every Minister," XVII, fols. 230r–231v.

him to remove clergy who lived "scandalous" lives. The sexual behavior of the island's religious officials only served to undermine the church's credibility on the island.[14]

In the absence of a strong church presence—the cornerstone of parish life in Britain—islanders established their own syncretic spiritual rituals. They read Bibles at home and buried the dead on family land rather than church graveyards. Parents turned baptisms into lively events, offering local delicacies of barbequed pork, yam pudding, turtle soup, tropical fruit, and generous helpings of rum punch to their guests. Just as they reshaped and personalized religious practices, colonists asserted authority to individualize and customize the sexual, marital, and reproductive dimensions of their lives. Free people constructed complex families comprised of overlapping kinship groups that regularly included illegitimate and legitimate children as well as free, freed, and sometimes enslaved members of African descent.[15]

Free and freed women played essential roles in the creation of this distinctively Caribbean sexual culture and the complicated kinship groups that it fostered, helping to shore up Jamaica under British rule. English clergymen might have derided the alleged promiscuity and debauchery of colonists, but the empire benefited from the adaptations made by islanders to gender roles, intimate relationships, and family arrangements. Although single mothers could not make legal claims on the estates of men with whom they started families, preserving their legal status as single enabled these women to better safeguard their kin from endemically high mortality rates, the rapid expansion of the slave population, chronic warfare, privateering, and piracy. Indeed, some couples took advantage of the colony's sexually permissive environment and avoided wedlock for strategic reasons. Nonmarital alliances became an alternative means of accruing family resources and shielding them from men's debts. Affording female colonists more latitude in their sexual lives and accepting children born out of wedlock as legitimate members replenished free communities that were continually decimated by disease

14. [Governor] Archibald Hamilton to the Bishop of London [John Robinson], Mar. 22, 1713/4, Fulham Papers, Colonial, General Correspondence, West Indies, XVII, fol. 107r–110v, "An Act for Regulating the Ministers of This Island," Feb. 17, 1713, XVII, fol. 105r–106v, "The State of the Church in Jamaica," undated and unsigned, (refers to events of 1722), XVIII, fols. 228–233. Leslie writes, "The Clergy here are of a Character so vile . . . they are generally the most finished of our Debauchees." See [Leslie], *A New History of Jamaica,* 303.

15. For baptisms at home in Jamaica and Barbados, see Beasley, *Christian Ritual and the Creation of British Slave Societies,* 67–68.

and protected Jamaica holdings, which sometimes amounted to significant fortunes.

"BELOVED FRIENDS"

"Spinster" Sarah Barnwell lived in the agricultural parish of Westmoreland and never married. Her "beloved brother" William Singleton, "a free mulatto" and the "reputed son of a man named William Singleton," a planter in her parish, was one of the only two people with whom Barnwell formed a close relationship. Barnwell and Singleton might have been siblings or half-siblings who shared the same mother of African descent but had different fathers. Barnwell emphasized her brother's importance to her by offering him three enslaved women and an acre of land. Though Barnwell did not marry, she also forged a connection with a merchant named Richard Hungerford, whom she nominated as her primary heir. Barnwell described her largess toward Hungerford as a means of compensation for his "many favors." Barnwell, like the majority of the free women who established partnerships outside of marriage, treated Hungerford like a surrogate husband. He would receive the majority of her land and thirteen slaves and serve as the sole executor of her estate, a role that spouses and children typically performed.[16]

By the 1750s, when Barnwell made her will, the nonmarital attachment she formed to Hungerford—one she recognized and formalized by making him her sole executor and primary heir—was common among Jamaica's free female population. Although Barnwell's reference to her "free mulatto" brother suggests that she also had African ancestry, her legal status as a free person had a stronger influence on the character of her intimate relationship than her race. Barnwell joined a varied group of free and freed women who pursued sexual relationships outside of marriage. Many then baptized the children who were born of these intimacies. A combination of local and imperial developments shaped this pattern. The accelerated growth of the British Empire in the eighteenth century destabilized marriage and gave rise to illegitimacy throughout the Anglo-Atlantic world. In Britain, the army, the navy, and private mercantile ventures drew large numbers of able-bodied men away from their homes. Similar conditions existed in Jamaica, which served as both a major port and a military base. In addition to sailors and merchants, the colony received thousands of soldiers who were garrisoned in Fort Augusta, located between Kingston and Spanish Town. The large popu-

16. Will of Sarah Barnwell, 1754, Jamaica Wills, 1661–1771, XXIX, IRO.

lation of transient seafaring and military men who caroused in Kingston's numerous rum shops undoubtedly left single mothers in their wake. Mothers Mary Nowell, Mary Willis, and Johanna Smith all appeared alone when they baptized their children and did not name the fathers, who might have been soldiers or sailors.[17]

Though Nowell, Willis, and Smith fit the profile of the typical unwed mother from the early modern era, they were the minority in Jamaica. White children comprised nearly half of the 634 illegitimate infants who were baptized in Jamaica between 1675 and 1767. Most of the mothers who baptized these infants forged long-term partnerships outside of marriage. Living on an island that invested its resources in policing enslaved people and privileged free status made it possible for white women to pursue intimate relationships outside of wedlock. Far from destitute, the women in this group typically commanded either middling or sizable fortunes. Many of them abstained from marriage as a legal strategy for protecting the wealth they accumulated via the larger inheritance bequests, slaveholding, and enhanced professional opportunities afforded by colonial circumstances.[18]

17. Baptism of Jane, 1722, Kingston Parish Register, Baptisms, I, Jamaica Copy Registers, Baptism of William, 1723, Baptism of Johana, 1725. Lawrence Stone observes that wars between England and France in the seventeenth and eighteenth centuries physically separated hundreds of thousands of spouses while also stationing single officers and soldiers in local communities. Warfare thus led to marital breakdown, adultery, and divorce. See Stone, *Broken Lives: Separation and Divorce in England, 1660–1857* (New York, 1993), 15. In Britain, these disruptions led to higher illegitimacy rates in port towns, as many women turned to prostitution as a means of supporting their families on their own. Felicity A. Nussbaum refers to M. Dorothy George's labeling of 1720–1750 as an era of "waste of life" in London "because of the high burial rate, high infant mortality rate, the inebriated lower class, and the pauperization of women" (Nussbuam, *Torrid Zones: Maternity, Sexuality, and Empire in Eighteenth-Century English Narratives* [Baltimore, 1995], 26, 29). After 1773, three thousand troops were permanently stationed on the island. By 1787, there were 270 rum shops in Kingston alone. Owners hired out female slaves as prostitutes to the soldiers stationed at Fort Augusta. Runaways also worked as prostitutes at the fort. See Brathwaite, *Development of Creole Society in Jamaica,* 135, 137, 160.

18. Only 10 percent of the parents (mother or father) who brought illegitimate children to be baptized appeared alone in the samples taken from the Kingston parish registers between 1722–1761. See Kingston Parish Register, Baptisms, I, Jamaica Copy Registers. Trevor Burnard estimates that, by eighteenth-century standards, 80 percent of the white population were adults in the prime marrying ages. He finds the percentage of adults who did marry to be "distinctly unimpressive." See Burnard, "'Rioting in Goatish Embraces,'" *History of the Family,* XI (2006), 188. My calculations are based on a survey of the baptism registers kept in the parishes of Kings-

Second- and third-generation colonists created a range of nonmarital family arrangements. They used baptisms, rather than weddings, as a means of conferring legal and social legitimacy on their children. John Dawkins and Mary Wilson, Mary Blackbourne and Andrew Stewart, and Susanna Howard and David Grant all baptized natural children during the 1720s. They were reasonably well-off and firmly settled in Kingston—which was becoming a major slave-trading hub. In 1730, 1,468 white people, 269 free people of color, and 2,724 slaves made up the town's population. Kingston's free residents were neighbors who engaged in credit transactions, attended church together, and socialized at local rum shops and taverns. When these three couples went to Kingston's church to baptize their children, they sought public recognition from the local community for their nonmarital relationships and "illegitimate" families.[19]

Kingston resident Sarah Robinson was among the group of legally single white women who forged families outside of wedlock during the early eighteenth century. She and her partner, John Drinkwater, baptized their first son in 1722, another son two years later, and a third son the following year. Given the spacing of the baptisms, Robinson would have been continually pregnant during a four- to five-year period, indicating that she had an ongoing sexual relationship with him. The couple probably lived together, but Robinson never assumed Drinkwater's surname. He still appeared as the father of her children at their christenings and further established his paternity by giving all of them his surname and one son his forename. Perhaps the couple did not marry because Robinson was a woman of lower status. Neither a will nor a probated inventory of Robinson's estate exists. Drinkwater, on the other hand, died a wealthy man with a fortune of nine thousand pounds and adopted the title of "gentleman" in his 1745 will. Aside from a possible difference in wealth, the Robinson-Drinkwater couple had every reason to marry. They were both categorized as white, and Drinkwater had ample resources to support his family. The partners easily accessed the Kingston church to bap-

---

ton, Saint Elizabeth, Saint Andrew, Saint Catherine, Saint Thomas in the East, and Westmoreland between 1675–1761. See Jamaica Copy Registers.

19. Baptism of George, 1726, Kingston Parish Register, Baptisms, I, Jamaica Copy Registers, Baptism of Whilemina Charlotte, 1727, Baptism of Charles, 1728. The mothers of these children did not assume their children's father's surnames, indicating that they were unmarried at the time of the christening. Census data from: "Jamaica to His Majesty, Relating to the Unhappy Situation of Affairs of That Island, by the Increase and Success of Their Rebellious Negroes," Feb. 11, 1731, CO 137/19, II, The National Archives (TNA), Kew.

tize their children. Yet Robinson and Drinkwater chose not to legally consecrate their own relationship through wedlock.[20]

The Robinson-Drinkwater couple's decision was not unique. One out of every six white infants born in Kingstown was illegitimate. The proliferation of alliances outside of marriage in Jamaica suggests that marriage for a large portion of Jamaica's free female population was either unattainable, impractical, or unappealing. Their disinclination to marry mirrored a trend away from wedlock in Britain, where an estimated 27 percent of the population never married. However, British women who openly pursued the kind of intimate sexual partnership Sarah Robinson engaged in faced severe social censure and possible disciplinary actions. In other parts of the Anglo-Atlantic world, Robinson, too, might have been punished, or at least ostracized from her community, for committing the crimes of fornication and bastardy. The absence of similar gendered laws and social stigmas in Jamaica made marriage only one of a range of possible intimate relationships available to free and freed women. Some women married and then acquired legal independence during their widowhoods while others established partnerships and started families outside of wedlock. Such nonmarital families were considered to be unremarkable and socially acceptable on the island.[21]

The women in the Hall family pursued all of these kinds of relationships. Though Grace Hall identified herself as a "spinster" in her will, implying that she never married, she appeared together with Charles Cooper to baptize their illegitimate daughter, Elizabeth, in Kingston in 1729. At some point, Grace had a second daughter, Agnes Hall, who adopted the Hall family surname. Like many of the free women who started families outside of wedlock, Hall maintained control of her assets and bequeathed her entire estate to her daughter, Agnes. Esther Hall, Grace Hall's kinswoman, forged relationships within and outside of wedlock with several men. Esther married John Hall, and the couple christened a son, Edward, in Saint Catherine in 1725. Though Esther described herself as a widow in her will, she did not remain single

20. Baptism of William, 1722, Kingston Parish Register, Baptisms, I, Jamaica Copy Registers, Baptism of John, 1724, Baptism of William, 1725; Inventory of John Drinkwater, 1745, Jamaica Inventories, 1674–1784, Jamaica Archives (JA), Spanish Town, Jamaica. It is possible that their first son, William, died, and they named their third son after him.

21. Margaret R. Hunt describes several factors that made marriage unattractive to women in Britain. See Hunt, "The Sapphic Strain: English Lesbians in the Long Eighteenth Century," in Judith M. Bennett and Amy M. Froide, eds., *Singlewomen in the European Past, 1250–1800* (Philadelphia, 1999), 277–280.

after her husband's death. Instead, she established a marriage-like relationship with a man from Vere Parish. The couple probably met in Spanish Town, where planters lived for months at a time to attend social and political events. Their attachment produced a "natural" daughter, Johanna White, and a son, George White, both of whom assumed their father's surname. As a widow, Esther achieved social respectability; as a slaveowner, she commanded authority and wealth. She was not driven by poverty or desperation to pursue a nonmarital alliance. Nor did she need to remarry. Remaining legally single enabled Esther to devise her estate to her children as she desired.[22]

The Halls might have eluded public disapproval, but more extreme cases of female sexual transgressions also failed to elicit strong reactions from the authorities or the local community. Two women who were accused of marital infidelity, interracial sex, and even incest in high-profile court cases escaped with their wealth, and possibly their reputations, intact. Sarah Pearsall describes the suit brought against Ann Tharp by her husband for committing adultery with her own son-in-law and then bearing his illegitimate daughter. Though the couple separated, Tharp upheld her social standing and received a generous annuity from her spouse. Similarly, in 1739, Edward Manning brought the first colonial divorce case to occur before the Jamaica Assembly against his wife, Elizabeth, on grounds of adultery and then sought to obtain his divorce through a private act of Parliament. Manning accused Elizabeth of "cohabiting" with Ballard Beckford, a member of one of Jamaica's richest and most politically powerful families, "in his own house," a charge other witnesses corroborated. The Mannings' housekeeper claimed that Elizabeth engaged in sexual relationships with men of African descent. In spite of these allegations of carnal impropriety, Elizabeth would have been entitled to the £2,143 portion she brought to the marriage if the divorce had been granted—a considerable sum of money. But nobody offered evidence of the couple "being seen in bed together," and the crown refused to dissolve the marriage

22. Baptism of Elizabeth, Kingston Parish Register, Baptisms, I, Jamaica Copy Registers, Baptism of Edward Hall, 1725, Saint Catherine Parish Register; Will of Grace Hall, 1735, Jamaica Wills, XIX, Will of Esther Hall, 1740, XXII. I have been unable to find a baptism record for Agnes Hall, though she is the only child whom Grace Hall refers to in her will. Perhaps Grace called her daughter Elizabeth "Agnes" or perhaps Elizabeth had married or died before Hall wrote her will. It is possible that John White was related to the minister James White, who also settled in Vere Parish in the 1720s. The planter would receive Hall's slaves if their children died before him. Esther Hall's son from her marriage to John Hall either died or received an estate from his father.

on the grounds that the adultery was not "positively proven." Manning's effort to malign his wife failed, and he was not granted a divorce.[23]

Although it is possible that their reputations were besmirched, neither Ann nor Elizabeth experienced financial hardship as a result of their suspected sexual transgressions. But the Manning divorce case does hint at a social taboo against interracial sex between white women and free or enslaved men of African descent. Despite the absence of laws prohibiting these kinds of behaviors and white men's public engagement in an array of relationships with free and enslaved women of African descent, the Manning suit intimates that islanders considered allegations of intimacy between white women and black men to be a form of sexual slander. Anxiety about the legal implications of relationships between enslaved men and white women likely motivated this social restriction. A child born to an enslaved man and a free woman held an especially ambiguous legal position in a society where free children were supposed to assume the status of their fathers and enslaved children that of their mothers. Furthermore, captive fathers, who were themselves considered to be property, could not assert their paternal rights to their offspring. These dynamics strained the legal principles that undergirded a slaveholding colony while also challenging patriarchal laws and customs that privileged the authority of fathers.[24]

Women's reticence to acknowledge intimacies with enslaved or free men of African descent in their wills suggests the operation of strong community disapproval, even if the law did not criminalize miscegenation. Yet female silence in legal documents should not necessarily be interpreted as a reflection of lived practice. A few records have survived that offer clues about

23. Sarah M. S. Pearsall, "'The Late Flagrant Instance of Depravity in My Family': The Story of an Anglo-Jamaican Cuckold," *WMQ*, 3d Ser., LX (2003), 549–582. In Britain, divorce by act of Parliament was costly and rare. Parliament granted only 325 divorces between 1670 and 1857. See Amanda Vickery, *The Gentleman's Daughter: Women's Lives in Georgian England* (New Haven, Conn., 1998), 73. Edward and Elizabeth Manning sent a request for divorce to the Lords of Trade and Plantations in 1739. See "Mr. Fane's Report to the Lords of Trade and Plantations, on an Act Passed in Jamaica . . . to Dissolve the Marriage of Edward Manning Esq. with Elizabeth Moore," May 12, 1739, CO 137/23, fol. 60, TNA. The king in council observed of the Manning case that this was the "first instance of an act of divorce" that had ever passed in the American colonies. They did not believe that adultery was positively proven though, and the act was repealed and disallowed (741, CO 137/23, fol. 130, TNA). See also Evelyn O'Callaghan, *Women Writing the West Indies, 1804–1939: "A Hot Place, Belonging to Us"* (London, 2004), 24.

24. For more on the gendered ramifications of white women bearing the children of enslaved men, see Fischer, *Suspect Relations*, 122–125; and Pagan, *Anne Orthwood's Bastard*, 108.

white women's relationships with black men. Barbara Davis bore three children with two enslaved men. Though she appeared as white in the baptism records, she also assumed the surname of one of her partners, Thomas Davis, who "belonged to Mr. McFarlane." The Davis couple formed a long-term relationship. In 1740, Barbara Davis baptized all of her children: a thirteen-year-old son who assumed the name Davis; a daughter, Elizabeth Beckford, whom she bore to a different man, "a negro man belonging to Rob. Hamilton named John Beckford"; and a seven-year-old girl, who was the second daughter of Thomas Davis, suggesting that Barbara resumed her connection with Davis after her dalliance with Beckford. That same year, Sarah Tirmmons christened her twenty-two-year-old "Indian daughter," whom she named Sarah. Islanders might have frowned on these interracial families, but mothers of Euro-African children were not disciplined. Instead, women like Davis and Tirmmons went to Kingston's popular church, where the minister William May baptized their interracial children before the local community.[25]

A court case involving an adolescent white woman in Kingston also indicates that colonial attitudes toward interracial sex between white women and men of African descent were less rigid than one might assume. In 1730, a fourteen-year-old named Sarah Jennings brought a suit against her stepfather for viciously beating her. During the trial, the neighbors reported that they heard him saying: "Dam her he would whip her for she had got a foul distemper by laying with a negro." Jennings's stepfather was enraged with Jennings for catching a venereal disease from the man, claiming that "it had cost him a great deal of money for the curing of her." His statement suggests that he punished his stepdaughter as much for the expense elicited by her sexual activities as for the race of her partner. Moreover, rather than castigating Jennings for illicit interracial sex, her neighbors sided with the young

25. Baptism of Joseph Davis, 1740, Kingston Copy Registers, Baptism of Elizabeth Beckford, 1740, Baptism of Barbara Davis, 1740, Baptism of Sarah Tirmmons, 1740. Scholars have studied interracial couples in other parts of colonial America as well as in the antebellum South. See Terri L. Snyder, "Marriage on the Margins: Free Wives, Enslaved Husbands, and the Law in Early Virginia," *Law and History Review*, XXX (2012), 141–171; and Fischer, *Suspect Relations*, chap. 4. For a comparative work on this topic, see Martha Hodes, *White Women, Black Men: Illicit Sex in the Nineteenth-Century South* (New Haven, Conn., 1997). Using a 1715 census, Hilary McD. Beckles has found evidence of working class white women who started families with free and enslaved men of African descent in Barbados. Similar dynamics likely existed in Jamaica. See Beckles, *Centering Woman: Gender Discourses in Caribbean Slave Society* (Kingston, 1999), 68–69.

woman, testifying against her stepfather. Although it is possible that Sarah and her neighbors considered her stepfather's racialized sexual slur to be damaging enough to her reputation to warrant legal action, the case indicates that the community took issue with his abusive actions, not her sexual behavior. Jennings lived in a busy maritime town where poorer white women likely interacted with men of all sorts on the bustling wharves and in the crowded taverns. Local residents probably considered the sexual and social connections that developed between such female colonists and men of African descent to be ordinary and unremarkable. Women like Davis, Tirmmons, and Jennings, who acknowledged intimate interracial relationships are archival outliers. The majority of Jamaica's white female colonists who forged connections to free or enslaved men of African descent did not use legal practices and documents to recognize their partners or baptize their children. In contrast, white women readily acknowledged the illegitimate infants whom they bore to white men, even if those men were of lower social standing.[26]

Legally single women typically veiled their nonmarital relationships in the language of friendship. The kinds of bequests these women made to their male, and sometimes female, friends nonetheless betray the existence of long-term marriage-like connections. Some middling and wealthy women left considerable legacies for male "friends" of artisan status—the men who poured their drinks, shoed their horses, and built their homes. "Singlewoman" Elizabeth Smith and widow Eleanor Walters, who lived in the fading maritime town of Port Royal, chose to preserve their legal independence while also forming connections to men whom they described as "beloved friends." Smith's companion was a barber, and Walters's "beloved friend" was a surgeon. When they made their wills in 1712 and 1719, each gave her entire estate to her male companion and nominated him to act as her sole executor. These women treated their partners like spouses, rather than friends, who were typically recognized in bequests by the receipt of small tokens, not the command of estates.[27]

26. "Commission, from King to John Wyllys Esq, (to Take Depositions) . . . Relating to Maltreatment and Other Unkind or Cruel Usage of Sarah Jennings a Minor about the Age of Fourteen Years Daughter of Henry Jennings Late of the Parish of Kingston Mariner Dead by William Rogers and Sarah His Wife . . . ," June 29, 1730, Jamaica Wills, XVIII, IRO. This investigation was randomly recorded in the volume of wills.

27. Will of Elizabeth Smith, 1712, Jamaica Wills, XIV, Will of Eleanor Walters, 1719, XV. The relationships between legally single women and their male "friends" are ambiguous and difficult to define using early modern understandings of intimacy. *Intimacy* referred to a person's

Legal and financial concerns might have motivated white women—who tended to marry at a young age, outlive their husbands, and inherit sizable estates from spouses—to start families outside of wedlock during their widowhoods. If a woman remarried, the laws of coverture would have subjected her property to her new husband's possession and his debts. Furthermore, some widows inherited property saddled with restrictions that would be enforced if they chose to marry again. A small number of mothers also stood to lose the guardianship of their children. Obtaining a divorce in the eighteenth century was difficult, and partners who separated could not legally remarry. All of these factors made marriage an unattractive option, especially in a colony that afforded women a wider degree of sexual latitude. When faced with the prospect of the strictures coverture imposed on wives, free women like Smith and Walters might have reasoned that nonmarital attachments were more preferable and practical. These women were not alone. One out of every ten free women who made a will between 1665 and 1757 also offered her entire estate to a single man who was not related to her through blood or marriage.[28]

---

innermost thoughts. The word did not take on a sexual connotation until the late nineteenth century. In this chapter, I will use *intimacy* in its early modern sense while also recognizing that people's intimate relationships veered into erotic and sexual realms. When couples had children together, they obviously forged bonds that involved sex. See *Oxford English Dictionary,* s.v. "intimate" and "intimacy," http:www.oed.com. Port Royal was inhabited by 718 white people, 76 free people of color, and 1,562 enslaved Africans in 1730, more than a decade after the women made their wills. The term "friendship" itself was evolving in the eighteenth century, as the practices of sociability and the availability of new leisure activities, from tea drinking to theater going, encouraged people to socialize in mixed-gender company. Friendships between married men and women became socially acceptable in colonial North America. Women's wills indicate an even more capacious definition of the term in colonial Jamaica. See Cassandra A. Good, "Friendly Relations: Situating Friendships between Men and Women in the Early American Republic, 1780–1830," *Gender and History,* XXIV (2012), 18–34. See also Richard Godbeer, *The Overflowing of Friendship: Love between Men and the Creation of the American Republic* (Baltimore, 2009). Husbands commonly transferred their entire estates to wives. Married women did not have the legal right to bequeath property unless they established separate estates, and widows typically transferred estates to their children or other female heirs. For further information on the gendered transference of property, see Chapter 4, above.

28. As Lawrence Stone has observed, "England thus had the worst of all worlds: marriage was all too easy legally to enter into, but all but impossible to legally get out of." Stone explains that Protestant England was unique in Europe because it preserved the medieval canon laws related to marriage that were considerably revised in Catholic countries by the Council of Trent.

The expansion of slavery on the island further enhanced the life possibilities of female colonists. By providing them with alternative sources of income and labor, slaveholding made free women less reliant on husbands for support. Women even used enslaved people as symbolic tokens to mark their affection for "beloved friends." Walters carefully set aside a horse and saddle together with an enslaved boy named Fortune for her companion. Fortune probably acted as Walters's domestic servant. In making the gift, she might have envisioned him acting in a similarly personal capacity for her "loving friend" after her death. Another of Port Royal's single women, widow Mary Bazill, commemorated her connection to a tavernkeeper by offering a captive girl, Abbah, to his daughter—who might have also been Bazill's illegitimate child. Perhaps Bazill's gift of Abbah signified her maternal connection to the girl.[29]

Though Kingston widow Mary Adams was wealthier than either Walters or Bazill, she, too, established an intimate relationship with a single man, Samuel Adams, a cooper by trade, whom she described as her "very good friend." Although they shared the same surname, Adams did not identify Samuel as her husband, son, or cousin. She might have adopted his surname as a means of signifying their bond, which she further established in her 1737 will. Adams offered her "very good friend" a generous legacy that included the use of her house on Beeston Street in Kingston, which he was *"personally"* to "enjoy possession" of. Adams also gave him furniture from "one chamber," two enslaved women, and a three-hundred-acre plantation near "Ginger River" on the outskirts of town. Her offerings were imbued with material and sentimental value. Adams wanted Samuel to live amid her possessions when she died. They comprised an important part of Adams's financial and emotive support of her partner.[30]

In making her bequest, Mary assumed a husband-like position in relation to Samuel, whom she treated like her dependent. Mary was able to perform this inversion of gender roles precisely because she remained single and thereby retained command of her sizable holdings, including urban property,

---

See Stone, *Broken Lives,* 10. I surveyed all of the female-authored wills made between 1665 and 1757 to determine the number of women who made bequests to single men. See Jamaica Wills, I-XXXII.

29. Will of Eleanor Walters, 1719, Jamaica Wills, XV, Will of Mary Bazill, 1727, XVII. The size of Bazill's estate is unclear. She identified "real and personal" in a single line, and the enslaved girl, Abbah, was the only part of her estate that she specified.

30. Will of Mary Adams, 1737, Jamaica Wills, XXI (emphasis is my own).

a plantation, and slaves. Though Samuel worked in a respectable profession as a cooper, he did not possess the kind of wealth, property, or rank that she did. The widow also had a daughter from a previous marriage, which might have further dissuaded her from remarrying. As a widow, she could offer the remainder of her estate to her child without restrictions. Conscious of the limitations coverture imposed on wives, widows like Mary Adams were able to enjoy affectionate and lasting relationships while avoiding the legal strictures of wedlock.[31]

Another Kingston resident "single woman" Elizabeth Sanderson pursued a similar path, starting a family outside of marriage with Patrick Montgomery. The couple had four children, all of whom they baptized in Kingston's Anglican church. Patrick died in 1736, leaving Elizabeth a modest £180 estate. Over the next eighteen years, the entrepreneurial mother enlarged her family estate, purchasing plots of land in the growing port town from "Messrs. Spencer and Paplay merchants" and amassing cash and enslaved people. When she made her own will nearly twenty years later, thirty years after the birth of her first child, Sanderson still described herself as a "single woman." Elizabeth gave the majority of her property to her unwed thirty-year-old daughter, who was also named Elizabeth, displaying a preference for her female heir that many of Jamaica's property-holding women exhibited. Elizabeth ensured that her daughter had the resources to follow a similar path and defer from marrying if she chose.[32]

According to English law, Elizabeth and Patrick's children were bastards, which made Elizabeth a sexually transgressive and debauched woman, but locals in Jamaica perceived of her family differently. Instead of marrying, the

31. Ibid.; Inventory of Mary Adams, 1738, Jamaica Inventories. Adams commanded eight slaves and owned property valued at three hundred pounds when she died. Brathwaite lists the numerous occupations for white islanders who lived in towns. See Brathwaite, *Development of Creole Society in Jamaica*, 136.

32. Baptism of Elizabeth, 1724, Kingston Parish Register, Baptisms, I, Jamaica Copy Registers, Baptism of Denis, 1725, Baptism of Patrick, 1726; Inventory of Patrick Montgomery, 1736, Jamaica Inventories; Will of Elizabeth Sanderson, 1754, Jamaica Wills, XXVIII. All of the children were listed in the baptism records as being the "son" or "daughter" of Elizabeth Sanderson "by Patrick Montgomery." Sanderson referred to two sons in her will, John and Denis, and two daughters, Margaret and Elizabeth. It is possible that Patrick had died by the time that she made her will. There is no baptism record for Margaret. Though he was hardly wealthy by local standards, Patrick was listed as an "esquire," signaling his aspiration to elite status. Chapter 4, above, explores the gendered dimensions of local inheritances customs in greater depth. John and Margaret do not appear in the baptism register. The son Patrick, named after his father, likely died.

couple used baptisms to affirm Patrick's paternity of their children, whom he recognized by giving them his surname. Kingston's free community accepted the Sanderson-Montgomery family, and their children grew up to join the town's artisan and middling classes. The eldest son became a bookkeeper, the other worked as a cooper, and one daughter wed a mariner. Couples like Elizabeth and Patrick joined a free minority outnumbered by an enslaved population that continually contested the conditions of bondage. The cohesion and stability of free society relied on the participation of every colonist, male and female alike. These circumstances turned freedom into the primary qualifier for social status, which, in turn, reduced the significance of a woman's sexual virtue. By accepting a wider range of relationships among free inhabitants and empowering female colonists, locals were better able to sustain their grip on Jamaican wealth and slavery.

FEMALE FRIENDS AND GODPARENTS

The intimate bonds female colonists established with each other further reinforced and expanded the social networks that undergirded free society. Women's homosocial friendships often traversed emergent racial categories. Sarah Harrison and Hannah Richardson, two free women of African descent, forged close relationships with women who might have been European, African, or Euro-African, giving them prized personal items like clothing and jewelry. Harrison offered tokens of affection to female friends, including Elizabeth Moore, a carpenter's wife, whom she presented "a gold ring with a stone set in it." Richardson, who lived in Port Royal, was far wealthier than Harrison. When she died in 1743, Richardson had amassed a fortune of nearly one thousand pounds and held four people in bondage. Although she gave the bulk of her estate to her son, who worked as a mariner, Richardson left meticulous instructions for divvying up personal jewelry among her female friends. Lucey Stretch received two gold finger rings, a necklace of gold beads went to Lucey Harris, and gold lockets went to Hannah Jacobs and Elizabeth Penniston. Another close acquaintance, Dorothy Christian, would inherit her set of china, while several other women would inherit her wearing apparel.[33]

Free and freed women like Harrison and Richardson participated in an early modern culture of female gift-giving that spanned the Atlantic world.

33. Will of Sarah Harrison, 1737, Jamaica Wills, XXI, Will of Hannah Richardson, 1743, XXIII.

As Amanda Herbert shows, personal offerings and handmade items served as mementos that strengthened female alliances in England. Colonial woman shared these practices, describing cherished household objects, jewelry, and apparel that they gave to other women in painstaking detail. Captive Africans also became precious possessions female islanders used to signify their close ties to one another. The widow Catherin Custis gave the majority of her estate to relatives in Ireland, but she devoted most of the text in her will to designating the items that her close friend, a "free negro woman" named Elizabeth Thomas, and her son would receive. Custis offered Thomas the intimate gift of a pair of "gold sleeve buttons I now wear," together with a house in Port Royal, her "small canoe," most of her furniture, and twenty-eight pounds. Custis also gave an enslaved person named Cudjoe to her friend. Additionally, the widow lavished attention on Thomas's son, leaving him her "best milk goats," a set of china and six silver teaspoons, and money for his "care." After offering seven pounds to Elizabeth Thomas's brother, she made provisions to manumit a "blind negro man named Cesar," whom she held in bondage.[34]

The bequests made by Custis to Thomas might signal their kinship connection. Or, perhaps it discloses the existence of a marriage-like relationship between the women. The outlines of their ambiguously intimate dynamic defies contemporary notions of sexualized, gendered, and racialized identity. Ultimately, defining the precise nature of their bond also misses the point. The two women formed their own version of a family, one that challenges simple categories and requires acceptance of its opacity. A handful of female testators, most of whom were childless, offered even larger bequests to their female companions whom they explicitly described as "beloved friends," hinting at the existence of homoerotic ties. Elizabeth Hagon, a widow who lived in Saint Catherine, described Mary Burdges as her "beloved friend." Mirroring the bequests husbands typically made to their wives, Hagon gave her entire estate to Burdges in 1708 and asked her friend to act as her sole executor. Nearly a decade later, the Kingston widow Dorothy Sapporton offered a similar legacy to her "good friend," another widow who lived in town. In 1742, Sarah Shewell (Showell) made her "loving friend" Margaret Grant the sole heir and executor of her modest estate in return "for the many

34. Will of Catherin Custis, 1739, Jamaica Wills, XXII. For more on women's homosocial alliances and gift-giving practices in early modern England, see Amanda E. Herbert, *Female Alliances: Gender, Identity, and Friendship in Early Modern Britain* (New Haven, Conn., 2014), 54–78.

favors she has done me and her love and kindness towards me." Hagon, Sapporton, and Shewell treated female friends like family members or surrogate spouses.[35]

"Singlewoman" Elizabeth Tonge went a step further. Tonge created an exclusively homosocial community, and she paid homage to her female world in her 1764 will. She appointed one woman to act as her executor and gave another the majority of her estate. Tonge was wealthy, and she offered a generous £857 in South Sea annuities to her goddaughter; four other "spinsters" received £71 in gifts. Tonge also provided a legacy to a married friend in a trust, emphasizing that the money was for her "sole use" to ensure that her friend's husband could not access the bequest. Tonge might have enjoyed a marriage-like relationship with one of her friends. Such an arrangement would not have been viewed as unusual in the Caribbean or in Britain, where widows often lived together with their sisters or mothers-in-law. Same-sex female couples attracted little attention in places like Philadelphia. Such partnerships were even less likely to generate interest in Jamaica, a more diverse, transient, and sexually permissive space. Perhaps women like Tonge preferred homosocial and homoerotic relationships to marriage for similar reasons as those that prompted other female colonists to live outside of wedlock with their "beloved" male friends. Marriage offered few material or legal advantages to well-off single women, especially those who were past their childbearing years. Same-sex friendships, in contrast, could provide female colonists with practical and emotional support and possibly sexual intimacy without triggering the financial and legal restrictions of marriage. Indeed, women who forged partnerships with each other might have developed an alternative to the social and cultural subjugation of masculine authority.[36]

35. Will of Elizabeth Hagon, 1708, Jamaica Wills, XII, Will of Dorothy Sapporton, 1717, XV, Will of Sarah Shewell, 1742, XXIII; Inventory of Sarah Showell [Shewell], 1743, Jamaica Inventories. Shewell survived off the labor of one slave. When she died a year after making her will, her estate was only valued at £108. One hundred thirty-eight of the 241 childless women who made wills did not refer to relatives by blood or marriage; 69 gave the majority of their estates to women, and 69 gave them to men. See Jamaica Wills, I–XXXII.

36. Will of Elizabeth Tonge, Aug. 13, 1764, Abstracts of Jamaica Wills, 1625–1792, Add MS 34181, British Library (BL), London; Amy Louise Erickson, *Women and Property in Early Modern England* (New York, 1993), 189. I follow Clare Lyons's lead in using the terms *homoerotic* and *heteroerotic*. Doing so avoids anachronistically imposing the heterosexual-homosexual binary onto more complex eighteenth-century notions of gender and desire. Little evidence exists to suggest that colonists had any interest in defining or policing sexual deviance in Jamaica. They exhibited a similarly liberal attitude toward sexuality as their northern counterparts in Philadel-

As women's bequests show, islanders fostered a range of intimate relationships that included close friendships, expanding and strengthening fragile kinship networks that were otherwise susceptible to extinction from rampant death and disease. Colonists further enlarged their kinship networks by acting as godparents for the children of their close friends and, sometimes, even for the people whom they held in bondage. During the early modern era, godparents were important figures who served as patrons and assumed familial responsibilities for their godchildren. In Jamaica, godparenting took on additional social and quasilegal purposes that were especially important for free and enslaved people of African descent. Elizabeth Sanderson was a slaveholder who lived within walking distance of Kingston's slave market, where she probably acquired a "negro man," Ned, whom she then gave to one of her sons. Though Elizabeth offered captives as a form of material support to her own illegitimate children, she also became the godmother of Sarah Sparks, the daughter of a free "negro woman." Sanderson's creation of a kinship tie with Sparks indicates that female networks were not racially segregated. As a godmother, Sanderson became Sparks's patron and assumed important social and financial obligations toward her. Having a connection to a presumably white godmother, in turn, strengthened Sparks's membership in Kingston's free community.[37]

Certain slaveholders also elected to serve as the godparents of children who were born to their own captives. Kingston slaveowner, Cornelia Robillyer, along with two other white people, volunteered to act as godparents for Elizabeth Christopher, the five-year-old daughter of Robillyer's captive, Luce, in 1729. When Robillyer made her will five years after Elizabeth's christening, she left instructions to free the girl, who would then become a "bound apprentice" to another free woman and learn "to read to write work at her needle and other husery"—the essentials of an eighteenth-century woman's education. Ten years later, Sarah Jackson held a baptism at her home in the agricultural parish of Saint Thomas in the East for Rebecca, the daughter of her slave, Nancy, and a (white) man, Philip Tosh. She also became Rebecca's

---

phia. See Lyons, "Mapping an Atlantic Sexual Culture," *WMQ*, 3d Ser., LX (2003), 126, 149. Writing about eighteenth-century England, Margaret Hunt describes women whom she identifies as lesbians as an "unproblematic, unobtrusive feature of mainstream society, not an alienated minority" (Hunt, "Sapphic Strain," in Bennett and Froide, eds., *Singlewomen in the European Past*, 271).

37. Will of Elizabeth Sanderson, 1754, Jamaica Wills, XXIX; Baptism of Sarah Sparks, 1729, Kingston Parish Register, Baptisms, I, Jamaica Copy Registers.

godmother. The reasons that led Robillyer and Jackson to establish kinship ties with children whom they owned are not readily transparent. Some godparents treated their roles seriously, offering material support, professional training, and occasionally even manumitting their enslaved godchildren while others might have used these intimate ties to manipulate and strengthen their authority over families whom they held in bondage.[38]

By acting as godmothers, Robillyer and Jackson simultaneously recognized and undermined the parent-child bonds forged between Luce and Mary and their daughters. Both of the enslaved children had free fathers who attended their baptisms. Elizabeth's father gave her his surname, Christopher. Robillyer and Jackson might have baptized Elizabeth and Rebecca and nominated themselves as godmothers without the consent of the girls' mothers. Perhaps these baptisms were charged events where female slaveholders and free fathers contested each other's claims to young people. It is also possible that Robillyer and Jackson were inspired by their religious beliefs to convert Africans to Christianity. From this perspective, then, baptism, which involved the naming and renaming of captive infants, was an act of cultural erasure that intensified the daily violence of the creolization process. If mothers were coerced into baptizing their sons and daughters, then this Christian ritual would have been a distressing event that emphasized their disempowerment and alienated their children from African spiritual beliefs. Elizabeth and Rebecca also might have been conceived through acts of sexual violence. If baptisms granted public recognition to perpetrators of rape, then they would have been even more disturbing to mothers.[39]

Yet there are other ways to interpret this nebulous and multifaceted ceremony that take into account the interests and influence wielded by enslaved

38. Baptism of Elizabeth Christopher, 1729, Kingston Parish Register, Baptisms, I, Jamaica Copy Registers; Baptism of Rebecca, 1738, Saint Thomas in the East Copy Register, Baptisms, Jamaica Copy Registers; Will of Cornelia Robillyer, 1734, Jamaica Wills, XIX.

39. Jennifer L. Morgan describes this tension in slaveowners' minds between acknowledging parent-child bonds while also destroying them. "Obliterated and mispronounced African names," she writes, "did violence to a crucial part of African culture and symbolized the willingness of Europeans to engage in many other kinds of violence toward the Africans they enslaved." See Morgan, *Laboring Women: Reproduction and Gender in New World Slavery* (Philadelphia, 2004), 119, 121. The journals created by Thomas Thistlewood, a small Westmoreland planter in the 1750s and 1760s, document only too well the degree to which white men exploited their power. For a detailed account of Thomas Thistlewood's life, see Burnard, *Mastery, Tyranny, and Desire.* For an investigation of the racial dimensions of sexual violence in the mainland colonies, see Block, *Rape and Sexual Power in Early America,* 185.

mothers. Perhaps Luce and Nancy urged Robillyer and Jackson to call the fathers of their children to account and extract symbolic restitution for their sexual exploitation. It is possible that the christening offered a venue for publicly shaming their abusers. Rather than treating baptism as an act of cultural domination, then, it is also necessary to consider whether Luce and Mary were already familiar with the ritual. They were members of a sizable and diverse African community in Jamaica that included peoples from the Bight of Biafra, the Gold Coast, West Central Africa, Sierra Leone, the Bight of Benin, and Senegambia. If Luce and Mary came from west Central Africa, they might have been converted to Catholicism before they were enslaved and shipped to the Caribbean. Certain West African religions also used water in sacred rites, which made the Christian ceremony more familiar to some slaves. They continued to employ observances involving water to signify rebirth or transformation and to establish kinship ties in the Americas. In the early eighteenth century—the very time when Luce and Mary christened their daughters in Jamaica—Moravian missionaries who lived in the Danish sugar colony of Saint Thomas witnessed Congolese captives performing a baptism-like ritual where they poured water over the heads of recent arrivals, put salt in their mouths, and prayed over them. This custom provided "foster parents" for alienated and terrified newcomers who in turn called their mentors "baptismal fathers and mothers." Luce and Mary might have participated in similar ceremonies on their arrival in Jamaica, where a much larger flow of captives from many ethnic groups in West Africa ensured the persistence of African customs on the island.[40]

From an African outlook, baptism was not necessarily a foreign act. Its very familiarity might have been a source of comfort, rather than grief, for enslaved mothers. Additionally, women and children who mediated between African and European cultures did not necessarily view the belief systems of

40. Christian Georg Andreas Oldendorp, *History of the Mission of the Evangelical Brethern on the Caribbean Islands of St. Thomas, St. Croix, and St. John*, ed. Johann Jakob Bossart, English trans. and ed. Arnold R. Highfield and Vladimir Barac (Barby, 1777; republished, Ann Arbor, 1987), 220, 263, quoted in Jon Sensbach, *Rebecca's Revival: Creating Black Christianity in the Atlantic World* (Cambridge, Mass., 2005), 92. Vincent Brown provides a map detailing the origins of enslaved immigrants to Jamaica. His book begins in 1741 when people from the Bight of Biafra and the Gold Coast comprised the majority of the captives who were transported to Jamaica. However, the island's slave population was diverse before 1741. See Brown, *The Reaper's Garden: Death and Power in the World of Atlantic Slavery* (Cambridge, Mass., 2008). Sensbach considers the varied meanings of baptism for Africans in *Rebecca's Revival,* 87–93.

their ancestors, parents, or even captors as being mutually exclusive. In slave societies like Jamaica, African religions and Christianity "coexisted side by side, overlapped, and merged in complex ways." Baptism also took on significant legal meanings for enslaved people, which Mary and Luce were likely aware of. Membership in the Church of England was a key criteria for manumission and an official requirement for free people of Euro-African descent who wished to petition the crown for the same rights and privileges held by white people. Asserting a child's Christianity, identity as the son or daughter of a free, and increasingly, white father, and kinship ties to white godparents all worked to move him or her toward free status. Perhaps Mary's and Luce's children's baptisms represented the culmination of years of effort on their part navigating the rocky terrain of the mistress-slave relationship and carefully cultivating ties with their enslavers to secure patronage and, possibly, manumission, for their daughters. Enslaved women could also leverage their intimate ties with slaveholders as a means of exerting some influence over the fates of their children.[41]

THE "SCANDALOUS DETESTABLE VICE"

Baptism records reveal a range of complicated alliances between free, freed, and enslaved people, showing how their intimate ties directly influenced the ethnic and cultural diversity of free society through the births of free Euro-African children and the manumissions of enslaved children who had a free parent. As baptisms show, colonists expanded their kinship groups to include African and Euro-African members who were free and enslaved, thereby turning the free family into a complex hierarchy where each member's position in relation to the others was determined by her or his age, gender, wealth, legal status, race, religion, education, and local connections. Colonial lawmakers recognized that the proliferation of interracial relationships and the intricate kinship networks they spawned helped to stabilize a free society that was otherwise wracked by disease and, until 1739, seriously threatened by the Maroons. English outsiders developed a less favorable impression of the island's lenient approach toward sex, reproduction, and family formation, which seemed to diverge sharply from metropolitan norms

41. Sensbach, *Rebecca's Revival*, 88. Daniel Livesay discerns that "Christian piety and political loyalty, evidence of economic advancement, and a genealogical map highlighting white kinship" were all necessary markers for petitioning for "white" status. See Livesay, *Children of Uncertain Fortune*, 45.

related to gender and sexuality. The English minister William May sent a withering critique of the colony's sexual culture to the bishop of London in 1733. In it, he denounced colonial officials for sanctioning miscegenation, asserting that the speaker of the Jamaica Assembly had stated that "people ought to be Encourag'd, or Rewarded, for begetting Mulattos and that That was the best way to People the Islands." May equated sexual depravity with interracial sex, which he described as the "scandalous detestable vice" of "keeping negro concubines." His letter highlights two conflicting worldviews in relation to sex, gender, and race. Whereas the minister portrayed interracial intimacies as an immoral contagion and evidence of the evils of empire, islanders, including colonial elites, believed that such relationships would add loyal members to the free population who would aid in securing the island for British rule.[42]

As it turns out, May's disapproval of interracial sex was more of a discursive performance than a reflection of his lived reality. Rather than despising Jamaica, he thrived there. After surviving a horrific hurricane that killed his wife, May went on to become the island's longest practicing minister, running Kingston's church for thirty years. May succeeded precisely because he adapted to local circumstances and customs. By 1730, just a few years after he penned his letter to the bishop of London, 2,724 slaves lived in Kingston. Invoking increasingly familiar tropes enabled the clergyman to veil his ac-

42. William May to Bishop Gibson, Apr. 11, 1733, Fulham Papers, Colonial, General Correspondence, West Indies, XVII and XVIII, LPL. As Daniel Livesay points out, by the 1730s "three generations of interracial relationships had produced a diverse society" (Livesay, *Children of Uncertain Fortune,* 39). In the 1730s, members of the Jamaica Assembly believed that interracial relationships were the key to establishing a strong settler society on the island. My study of baptism records complements Livesay's work and shows how colonists developed a variety of intimate and patronage-based relationships that secured free society. However, I also emphasize the gendered implications of these local developments, which altered free and freed women's sexual behavior and their approaches toward marriage. Livesay refers to this quote as well and explains that May was reacting to the passage of an act by the Jamaica Assembly that recognized people who were four generations removed from an Africa ancestor as being white. Describing sexually debauched bachelors who preferred the company of "negro concubines" to white wives, May was an early contributor to a discursive tradition of portraying West Indians as sexual deviants; this discourse would culminate in Edward Long's oft-repeated descriptions of white men "rioting in goatish embraces" with African women. See May to Gibson, Apr. 11, 1733, Fulham Papers, Colonial, General Correspondence, West Indies, XVII and XVIII; Livesay, *Children of Uncertain Fortune,* 38–39; and Trevor Burnard, "'Rioting in Goatish Embraces': Marriage and Improvement in Early British Jamaica," *History of the Family,* XI (2006), 185–197.

tions in the colony even as he baptized many of the children who were born to interracial couples comprised of free and freed and enslaved partners in Kingston. May's meticulous records afford the most detailed and consistent evidence from Jamaican parish registers of the long-term partnerships established between free men and enslaved women. These couples made up 15 percent of the unwed parents who baptized their children in Kingston. Only 30 percent of the men in this group owned the mothers of their offspring. Although the dynamics between enslaved women and (white) men were always mediated by power, these numbers hint at the limited influence wielded by female captives in their connections with free partners.[43]

The relationships that some free men established with enslaved women in rural parishes are equally nebulous and open to multiple interpretations. For example, Denis O'Brien and a slave, Venus, baptized their son Henry in 1732 in the plantation parish of Saint Thomas in the East; another man held Venus in captivity. Eight years later, George Leith and a slave named Diana, who was also owned by another man, christened a daughter, Frances, in the same parish. If Venus and Diana labored as field hands, they would have been under the continual surveillance of men like O'Brien and Leith, who were probably among the large numbers of Irish and Scottish migrants who traveled to Jamaica to work as servants, overseers, or bookkeepers on plantations. If the women acted as domestic servants, cooking meals, washing clothes, and cleaning rooms would have further increased their daily interactions with free men. Venus and Diana lived in a society that was suffused with sexual violence, and their children might have been the fruits of coercive encounters.[44]

43. *Great-Britain Consider'd* (London, 1740), 13; "Jamaica to His Majesty, Relating to the Unhappy Situation of Affairs of That Island," CO 137/19, II, TNA; Kingston Parish Register, Baptisms, I, Jamaica Copy Registers. Just months after William May and his wife had moved to the colony from England in 1722, a terrible hurricane whipped across Kingston Harbor. It sank twenty-six ships, drowning the men caught onboard. The storm flattened buildings and crushed the town's occupants. More than four hundred people were killed, and it was reported that May was one of the casualties. May suffered a broken leg, but he survived. His wife was not so lucky: when the hurricane blew down their house, she was crushed under the rubble and died. He became the longest-serving minister on the island. See David Longshore, *Encyclopedia of Hurricanes, Typhoons, and Cyclones,* new ed. (New York, 2008), 268. Charles Leslie described hurricanes in Jamaica in *A New History of Jamaica,* 41. See also Anon., *Importance of Jamaica to Great Britain Consider'd,* 13.

44. Baptism of Henry, 1732, Saint Thomas in the East Copy Register, Baptisms, Jamaica Copy Registers, Baptism of Frances, 1740. O'Brien is an Irish surname; Leith is Scottish. For

Still, it is worth considering the roles played by Venus and Diana in determining their intimate connections. The baptism records reveal the presence of Venus and Diana, who would otherwise remain invisible in the archives, at these ceremonies. As one scholar has observed, the types of partnerships they formed are not evidence of sexual agency, but these intimacies show how enslaved women who were otherwise disempowered or marginalized could use sex as a means of negotiating their position. Perhaps Venus and Diana kept both African husbands and European lovers, as other enslaved women on the island did. Their life options were severely circumscribed, making sexual relationships with free men who could offer them protection, lighten their workloads, and give them occasional gifts one of the only avenues they could pursue to improve their conditions. Most critically, the children whom enslaved women bore to free men were more likely to derive the social and material benefits of having white fathers. Henry's and Frances's fathers both publicly recognized their sons and established their membership in Jamaica's Christian community. Twelve years after baptizing his son Henry with Venus, O'Brien went on to marry a white woman. No records exist that offer clues about what happened to the family that O'Brien created with Venus. The enslaved mother probably remained in bondage. Henry's publicly recognized kinship connection to his free father, however, might have yielded more positive results. Fathers preferred to manumit their biological children.[45]

The local community might have even believed Henry to be legally free as a result of his baptism. A more descriptive register from another agricultural parish, Westmoreland, lends credence to this assertion. One-quarter of the illegitimate children born in the parish were labeled as "free mulatto," even if they had enslaved mothers. This was even true in cases where the free father

---

Scottish migrants to Jamaica, see Alan L. Karras, *Sojourners in the Sun: Scottish Migrants in Jamaica and the Chesapeake, 1740–1800* (Ithaca, N.Y., 1992).

45. Baptism of Mary Diana, Dennis, and Margaret O'Brien, 1744, Saint Thomas in the East Copy Register, Baptisms, Jamaica Copy Registers. Scholarship on other locations in the Atlantic world has added more nuance to our understanding of enslaved women's sexuality. Writing about witchcraft cases involving women of African descent, including enslaved women in colonial Cartagena, Nicole von Germeten suggests that the women used sex to "achieve certain practical goals and to create a specific persona for themselves." See Von Germeten, *Violent Delights, Violent Ends: Sex, Race, and Honor in Colonial Cartagena* (Albuquerque, N.Mex., 2013), 129–130. Danielle C. Skeehan describes an enslaved woman sewing the initials of her friend's husband and her free white lovers onto her smock in "Caribbean Women, Creole Fashioning, and the Fabric of Black Atlantic Writing," *The Eighteenth Century*, LXVI (2015), 105.

did not own the woman who bore his children. One woman Elizabeth was recorded as the "free mulatto daughter" of Sarah, who "belonged" to the estate of John Lewis. Another woman named Leah bore two "mulatto" sons who were categorized as free to a man who did not own her. John Hawkins fathered a free girl, Rachel Hawkins, with an enslaved woman, Amba, who had a different owner. Jacob Johnson owned Kate and Leanor when he engaged in polygamous relations with them. Their children were categorized as "free mulattos" at their christenings. Although the fathers might have paid to manumit their children prior to christenings, it is also possible that their community, or the local minister, considered baptism itself to be an act of manumission. Colonists and religious officials invested baptism with their own legal and spiritual meanings, and these interpretations sometimes challenged official slave codes that sought to deny the connection between Christianity and freedom.[46]

Parish registers indicate that some islanders treated baptism as a deliberate strategy to ensure the liberty of children who were born to enslaved women. The enslaved Sarah, "belonging to Mrs. Beech," and her free partner, Thomas Barrow, who appear at the start of this chapter, purposefully brought their daughter, Mary Barrow, to be baptized by May in 1725. Sarah and Thomas hardly expected the event to be anonymous when they went to Kingston's "handsome" and busy church, where May preached from a pulpit adorned with a red velvet cloth with gold fringe and a "good Organ" supplied the music that attracted a sizable congregation. One observer reported seeing fourteen to twenty coaches and chariots parked outside every Sunday.[47]

The sparse entries in parish registers provide shadowy evidence of the motives that led enslaved women like Sarah and free men like Barrow to baptize their children. The nature of these relationships is equally obscure. In the absence of more detailed sources, it is only possible to speculate. Perhaps Barrow and the men who appeared alongside their enslaved partners in colonial churches did so to fulfill spiritual obligations or assuage their guilt for coercive sex. If this was the case, then Barrow's actions were not unusual. Free white men living throughout British America used their gen-

46. Baptism of Elizabeth, 1750, Westmoreland Copy Register, Baptisms, Jamaica Copy Registers, Baptism of James and Robert, 1750, Baptism of Elizabeth, 1760, Baptism of Bonella and William, 1760. Of the thirty-three illegitimate children born in Westmoreland, nine were labled as being "free mulatto." See Westmoreland Copy Register, Baptisms, Jamaica Copy Registers.

47. Baptism of Mary Barrow, 1725, Kingston Parish Register, Baptisms, I, Jamaica Copy Registers; Anon., *Importance of Jamaica to Great-Britain Consider'd*, 6, 14.

dered and racialized authority to exploit marginalized, impoverished, and vulnerable enslaved women while emasculating enslaved men, who faced severe and even capital punishments if they sought to protect female kin. Jamaica's draconian slave codes, its lenient handling of sexuality, and the island's large slave majority made sexual violence an endemic part of colonial society. Additionally, free men who fathered children with enslaved women were under no legal obligation to provide for them or their mothers. As many scholars have argued, these conditions negate the possibility for sex between enslaved women and white men to have ever been consensual.[48]

That Sarah only shows up in the historical record because of her carnal connection to a free (white) man emphasizes the profoundly unequal position each person occupied in relation to the other. Such evidence makes her sexual subjectivity a fraught subject. Barrow's actions as a father and Sarah's potential involvement in the decision to baptize her daughter deserve a more nuanced interpretation—one that takes into account Sarah's interior life, desires, and needs. Some scholars have posited that the power differentials that defined the master-slave relationship did not deny the possibility for captive women like Sarah to experience intimacy and pleasure. Perhaps Sarah sought Thomas out and engaged him in conversation on one of Kingston's busy streets or shared a drink with him at one of the town's numerous rum houses. Or, maybe Sarah's connection to a free man afforded her moments of release from the relentless objectification and dehumanization of slavery.[49]

48. Jane E. Mangan proposes that similar motives led Spanish men to make bequests to indigenous women they fathered children with in colonial Peru. See Mangan, "Indigenous Women as Mothers in Conquest-Era Peru," in Sarah E. Owens and Mangan, eds., *Women of the Iberian Atlantic* (Baton Rouge, La., 2012), 87. Sharon Block investigates the racial dimensions of sexual violence in Block, *Rape and Sexual Power in Early America,* 185. Sarah Pearsall raises this point in "'The Late Flagrant Instance of Depravity in My Family,'" *WMQ,* 3d Ser., LX, no. 3 (2003), 581. Scholars have long asserted that violence or the threat of violence permeated all sexual encounters between enslaved women and free men. Marisa J. Fuentes cautions against conflating enslaved women's sexuality with agency. See Fuentes, "Power and Historical Figuring: Rachel Pringle Polgreen's Troubled Archive," *Gender and History,* XXII (2010), 566–568. See also Block, *Rape and Sexual Power in Early America;* Warren, "'The Cause of Her Grief,'" *Journal of American History,* XCIII (2010), 1035–1049; and Godbeer, *Sexual Revolution in Early America,* 202–201.

49. It was possible for erotic intimacy to exist between free and enslaved people. Other scholars have rejected the binaries of consent or nonconsent in studies of intimate violence and slavery. Treva B. Lindsey and Jessica Marie Johnson provide a list of scholars who study the "terrain of intimate violence that crosses gender, race, and status" in "Searching for Climax: Black

If Sarah's sexual relationship with a free man fulfilled her desires and offered her an escape from bondage, it also had important and potentially life-changing legal ramifications for their child. The baptism of Mary Barrow was a performance that both Sarah and Thomas participated in and might have orchestrated together. It is possible that the ritual represented the fruition of Sarah's emotional, sexual, and reproductive efforts as much as it did Barrow's authority as a free white man. Though she did not possess any legal rights, Sarah could wield personal influence over her lover. Perhaps she urged Barrow to publicly acknowledge his daughter in an effort to establish a family that was partitioned from her life in captivity.

Although the infants born to enslaved mothers and free fathers who were baptized represent a small fraction of the children who remained in bondage for the rest of their lives, the symbolic significance of these young people far exceeds their numerical import. The christenings of daughters like Mary Barrow brought two competing visions of social order—a secularized hierarchy based on increasingly rigid categories of racial difference that enshrined the property rights of a white slaveholding class and an older model rooted in patriarchal privileges and Christian identity—into conflict. The Jamaica Assembly passed an act in 1684 that explicitly denied the connection between baptism and freedom, stating that "no Slave shall be free by becoming a *Christian*." They aimed to replace older associations between Christianity and freedom with a newer racialized model of slavery. As the baptism records show, their efforts were not entirely successful. The legal, ideological, and

---

Erotic Lives in Slavery and Freedom," *Meridians: Feminism, Race, Transnationalism*, XII, no. 2 (2014), 180–181. Barbara Bush argues that relationships between white men and black women were not "purely repressive" and defined by "rape, seduction and 'heinous forms of sexual torture'" in Caribbean slave societies. See Bush, "White 'Ladies,' Coloured 'Favourites,' and Black 'Wenches,'" *Slavery and Abolition*, II, no. 3 (December 1981), 246, 253. Similarly, writing about colonial Latin America, Karen Vieira Powers describes a spectrum of modalities for interpreting relationships between European men and indigenous women ranging from "rape and betrayal" to "mutual consent, economic opportunism, physical attraction, political alliances, social mobility, genuine love." See Powers, *Women in the Crucible of Conquest: The Gendered Genesis of Spanish American Society, 1500–1600* (Albuquerque, N.Mex., 2005), 71. Lindsey and Johnson argue for new approaches to the study of enslaved women's experiences of intimacy and desire that allow "the interior lives and erotic subjectivities of enslaved blacks to matter." The authors imagine what sex might have meant for enslaved women: "On a more quotidian level, finding moments of sexual pleasure with oneself, a partner, or partners meant rejecting the dehumanizing status designation of property." See Lindsey and Johnson, "Searching for Climax," *Meridians: Feminism, Race, Transnationalism*, XII, no. 2 (2014), 187.

spiritual meaning of baptism was fraught throughout the Anglo-Atlantic world. Imperial authorities in Britain failed to clarify the matter, and metropolitan judges issued contradictory decisions about whether slaves who converted to Christianity obtained freedom. The crown also failed to present a uniform imperial policy deciding the issue.[50]

Despite passing a law to the contrary, parish registers indicate that some colonists remained uncomfortable with enslaving Christians. The confusion and contradiction surrounding baptism led some islanders to fiercely oppose the efforts of English ministers to convert slaves, precisely because they believed in the leveling potential of Christianity. May stated that clergymen did not "dare" to convert slaves "without the consent of masters which they do not give." Writing from the agricultural parish of Westmoreland, another minister described "a swarm of unbaptized negro's mulatto's Indians etc." who were "so strictly kept to labor they cannot be converted." Seeking to maximize the labor of their captives, enslavers also resisted attempts to convert slaves for practical reasons: they were loath to give captives time off to attend church. Although certain colonists fought against slave baptisms, others who desired to convert captives found their efforts thwarted by clergymen themselves. The minister James White cynically claimed that "multitudes" of colonists "bring Negroes to us both children and adult to be baptiz'd" and disparagingly attributed the demand for christening enslaved people to the illicit sexual behaviors of islanders, writing that his parishioners used

50. "An Act for the Better Ordering of Slaves," in *Laws of Jamaica* . . . (1684), 140–141. Generally, far less of an effort was made in English colonies to baptize slaves than in French, Spanish, and Portuguese colonies. Nicholas Beasley observes that few slaves in Jamaica, for example, were offered or sought out baptism during most of the eighteenth century (Beasley, *Christian Ritual and the Creation of British Slave Societies,* 75–76). In contrast, the Portuguese crown and the Catholic Church viewed slaves' conversion to Catholicism as important. See Kathleen J. Higgins, *"Licentious Liberty" in a Brazilian Gold-Mining Region: Slavery, Gender, and Social Control in Eighteenth-Century Sabará, Minas Gerais* (College Park, Penn., 1999), 122–123. James H. Sweet, however, argues that, although slaves were baptized en masse in Africa before being transported to Brazil, the majority had no knowledge of basic Christian precepts. The Christianization of Africans occurred slowly there. See Sweet, *Recreating Africa: Culture, Kinship, and Religion in the African-Portuguese World, 1441–1770* (Chapel Hill, N.C., 2003), 197–210. Issued in 1685, the Code Noir required all enslaved people who were transported to French colonies to be baptized. See Louis XIV, Code Noir, 1685, Article II, "The Code Noir (The Black Code)," Liberté, Egalité, Fraternité: Exploring the French Revolution, http://chnm.gmu.edu/revolution/d/335/. See also Travis Glasson, *Mastering Christianity: Missionary Anglicanism and Slavery in the Atlantic World* (New York, 2012), 78–79.

"All meanes" to "induce us [to baptize them]" such as "recommendation of the persons good qualities if Adult [adultery], flattering addresses to our selves, good presents." White rejected their requests on racist grounds that "Negroes" could never come to "the sacraments of salvation."[51]

Although the majority of Jamaica's enslaved population would never be baptized, recognized by free parents, or join the colony's Christian community, free parents who started families with enslaved people, as White's comments show, continued to view baptism as an important act that had the potential to move their children on the continuum from bondage to liberty. Their actions covertly, and sometimes overtly, challenged the logic of *partus sequitur ventrem* (offspring follows the womb), which islanders generally followed. But, the Jamaica Assembly chose not to enshrine the principle in colonial law as their counterparts in Virginia did, which contributed to the ambiguity surrounding the legal status of children who were born to enslaved mothers and free fathers. Thomas and Sarah's decision to baptize Mary enabled them to assert a counterclaim to Sarah's owner Mrs. Beech's right to Mary. Beech could have assumed legal command of Mary according to partus sequitur ventrem. By baptizing their daughter, Thomas and Sarah ensured that Mary received her free father's surname and contested Mary's illegitimate status as *fillias nullius* (daughter of no one). Although it is unclear if the act of baptism itself marked Mary as free, if Thomas purchased her freedom, or if Mrs. Beech manumitted her, she appeared as a free woman by 1752. Like Thomas Barrow and Sarah, a number of second- and third-generation colonists used baptism as a foil to civil law and custom, suggesting that Jamaica's inhabitants considered the religious ritual to be a legal act that established a child's freedom.[52]

51. William May to Edmund [Gibson], April 1724, Fulham Papers, Colonial, General Correspondence, West Indies, XVII, fol. 185–188, John Dickson to Gibson, Apr. 23, 1724, XVII, fol. 185–188, James White to Gibson, Apr. 23, 1724, XVII, fols. 185r–188v. Neither Jamaica's colonists, nor the British clergymen who were sent over to minister to them, exhibited a uniform attitude toward baptizing enslaved people. Some defied efforts to christen captives while others sought out baptisms for those in bondage. Colonists continued to view Christianity as a crucial marker of status, one which was distinctive from and had the potential to override differences in skin complexion. See Roxann Wheeler, *The Complexion of Race: Categories of Difference in Eighteenth-Century British Culture* (Philadelphia, 2000), 146–147.

52. For more on the influence of the principle of partus sequitur ventrem in the Anglo-Atlantic world, see Morgan, *Laboring Women;* Jennifer L. Morgan, "*Partus sequitur ventrem:* Law, Race, and Reproduction in Colonial Slavery," *Small Axe,* XXII, no. 1 (March 2018), 1–17; Fischer, *Suspect Relations;* Brown, *Good Wives;* Snyder, "Marriage on the Margins," *Law and*

That baptisms were performed by licensed ministers in public spaces discloses the acceptance of and even support offered by local communities to couples composed of free and enslaved persons who adopted this strategy. Their actions took on de facto meanings that could both reinforce and undermine newer legal codes that sought to define and strengthen bondage. Euro-African children whose liberty was confirmed during baptisms joined a small but growing population of free African and Euro-African colonists. By 1730, "negro, indian," and "mulatto" people accounted for 17 percent of the free populations in Kingston, Spanish Town, and Port Royal. Women and children made up 87 percent of the people in this group. During the 1730s, Jamaica's local militia and the British army were losing the war against the Maroons, which generated increasing hostility toward free people of African and Euro-African descent. Colonial officials identified people whom the government categorized as "negro" or "mulatto" as a serious threat to Jamaica and the empire. Allegedly, colonists who fell into this group established close connections to friends and family who were still enslaved and possibly aided the Maroons. In 1730, a "Mr. Popple" sent an alarmist letter to the Lords of Trade in which he argued that people of African descent were "not likely to make war against their own color," whom "they are most certainly attached to." Popple viewed the Maroon War as a racial conflict of attrition and accused individuals with African ancestry of giving arms to the "rebels" (Maroons) and avoiding military service, writing "Free negroes skulk and abscond to prevent their being sent out against the rebells."[53]

In this tense climate, interracial intimacies enlarged the population of free and freed people of color on the island who were then targeted for imperiling colonial security. As Popple wrote, "free mulattoes and negroes increases daily," bolstering the ranks of furtive enemies to the crown. Governor Robert Hunter supported Popple's view, describing the homes of free Afro-Europeans as "receptacles of rebellions and runaway slaves," whom they

History Review, XXX (2012), 141–171; and "Of Parent and Child," in Blackstone, *Commentaries on the Laws of England,* Book 1, Chapter 16, Lonang Institute, https://lonang.com/library/reference/blackstone-commentaries-law-england/bla-116/.

53. "Jamaica to His Majesty, Relating to the Unhappy Situation of Affairs of That Island," Correspondence to the Lords of Trade and Plantations, CO 137/19, II, TNA, Mr. Popple to the Lords of Trade and Plantations, "A Short State of Jamaica with Respect to the Rebellious and Runaway Negroes," July 25, 1730, fol. 104, CO 137/18. As we will see in Chapter 6, below, male and female slaveholders preferred to manumit women and children. Of the 587 free people of color living in Kingston, Spanish Town, and Port Royal, 242 were women, and 271 were children. For more background information on the Maroon War, see Chapter 3, above.

provided with "powder, arms, and ammunition." The governor even proposed an act to restrict manumissions, ordering that "no mulatto, indian or negro, should hereafter be made free, unless the owner allotted them a sufficient maintenance during life." Although Hunter's proposal to limit enslaved people's access to manumission failed to pass, the colony restricted the rights of people who were freed from slavery. They were not allowed to vote, sit in the legislature, serve on a jury, or give evidence against whites or freeborn people of African descent. Elite Euro-Africans had to petition the crown to obtain the same "rights and privileges" as white people. In addition to substantial land ownership and education abroad, christening in the Anglican Church became a critical requirement for these privileges.[54]

Jamaica's increasingly antagonistic and divisive racial climate intensified the significance of baptism for free and freed people of African descent. The ritual emphasized the free legal status of their children while also strengthening their spiritual and cultural allegiance to white Christian society. After securing freedom for himself and his wife, John Williams petitioned the crown in 1717 to obtain the "rights and privileges" accorded to white people for his family. William stressed their Protestant identity, emphasizing that his family members had all "been baptized in the christian faith and do all profess the protestant religion." A free (white) woman, Frances Oldfield, signed an affidavit attesting to their baptisms. In his petition, Williams argued that "negroes and other infidels" should not be allowed to give evidence against them in court, conflating religion, race, and legal status. Through his petition, he established his legitimacy as the husband and father of a Protestant patriarchal household. The rights the crown granted to Williams were gendered—they primarily benefited men, not women, who were barred from voting, sitting on juries, and holding political offices irrespective of race.[55]

For the majority of Jamaica's free women of African and Euro-African descent, colonial baptisms, not imperial petitions, served as the primary

54. Mr. Popple to the Lords of Trade and Plantations, "A Short State of Jamaica with Respect to the Rebellious and Runaway Negroes," July 25, 1730, fol. 104, CO 137/18, TNA, Governor Robert Hunter to the Lords of Trade and Plantations, May 10, 1730, CO 137/18; Brook N. Newman, "Gender, Sexuality, and the Formation of Racial Identities in the Eighteenth-Century Anglo-Caribbean World," in Kevin P. Murphy and Jennifer M. Spear, eds., *Historicising Gender and Sexuality* (West Sussex, U.K., 2011), 59–76; Livesay, *Children of Uncertain Fortune*, 40–41; Brathwaite, *Development of Creole Society in Jamaica*, 170–171.

55. "Attorney General's Report upon an Act Pass'd in Jamaica in November 1716 to Prevent Negroes Being Evidence against Dorothy the Wife and John Thomas, and Francis, Sons of John Williams a Free Negro," April 1717, fol. 130, CO 137/12, TNA.

means of establishing the free legal status of their children and also buttressing their own liberty. Many forged relationships with white men who could offer precious patronage ties and additional economic and social security to their families. Sarah Hart, a "free mulatto" woman living in Kingston, went with a man named "Cathurst," the father of her child, to church to baptize her daughter, Mary, in 1729. Hart further emphasized her ties to free society by having two white women and one man, Taylor Hart, serve as her daughter's godparents. Sarah shared the surname Hart, suggesting that Taylor Hart was related to her. As Mary's baptism shows, free and freed people of African descent used the ceremony for varied purposes. It signified and legitimized their legal status, it was a means of publicly recognizing their social and sexual connections to free partners, friends, and patrons, and it confirmed their families' affiliation with free society.[56]

As a spiritual, social, and legal practice, baptism also exposed the tenuousness, fluidity, and ambiguity of racial categories based on skin color. Sarah Hart was identified as a "free mulatto" in 1729. When she made her will twenty years later, her race was not referenced, implying that she was categorized as a white woman. It is impossible to know whether the person who recorded Hart's will at the secretary's office assumed that she was white, viewed her race as unimportant, or if Hart herself deliberately obscured her African ancestry—and her connection to a past marked by slavery. Whatever the case, Hart's African heritage was expunged from the legal record by 1749. Though she was looked on as white, Hart sustained close connections to other free and freed people of African descent. Her daughter married John Darby, a "free negro," and Hart nominated her son-in-law, not a white man, to be her executor while also bequeathing her estate to her grandsons.[57]

If only Hart's will survived in the archive, and the record of her daughter's baptism did not exist, then it would make sense to assume that she was a white woman. Piecing together these shreds of evidence from her will and her baptism brings into view a more complicated story about the interplay between gender, race, sex, and power. Though colonial lawmakers increasingly treated race as a legible and indelible feature of a person's identity, Hart's shifting status in colonial documents, and baptism records more generally, suggest that race-making was an uneven and sometimes contested process. Race did not necessarily dictate the lived practices, or the social positions, occupied by women like Sarah Hart, whose own racial status was ambigu-

56. Baptism of Mary, 1729, Kingston Parish Register, Baptisms, I, Jamaica Copy Registers.

57. Will of Sarah Hart, 1749, Jamaica Wills, XXVII.

ous at best. Instead, Hart and other women like her forged important friendship and kinship ties with colonists of European, Euro-African, and African descent. These intimate connections radiated outward, strengthening free people's bonds with each other while also confirming their commitment to slaveholding as a source of material wealth and symbolic status. Intimate ties that traversed legal and racial categories could complicate, undermine, and even collapse the boundaries between enslavement and liberty.

Jamaica's lax handling of sexual behavior gave free men and, significantly, free women license to establish varied family arrangements outside of legal marriage, and islanders developed sexual, marital, and familial strategies that responded to local conditions. The baptism records show this process at work. Both free couples and couples where one party was free and the other enslaved repurposed baptism, using it to legitimize marriage-like arrangements. Locals simultaneously upheld slavery while also ignoring the racial barriers that colonial slave codes sought to erect. They recalibrated and stretched the meaning of family and determined who was included or excluded from kinship groups. During the early decades of the eighteenth century, legal, spiritual, and emotional ties wove free, freed, and enslaved people together in uneasy alliances and sometimes loving partnerships.

The colony's laissez-faire approach toward sex, combined with its draconian slave codes, also left female captives particularly vulnerable to sexual coercion. Yet some enslaved women and free men established what appeared to be stable relationships. When they baptized their children, free fathers and enslaved mothers disrupted the racial divide between "white" and "negro" that local laws aimed to establish and undermined the principle at the heart of colonial slavery: that children followed the legal condition of their mother.

By treating illegitimate children of European, African, and Euro-African descent as legitimate family members, colonists bolstered their meager numbers, ensuring the survival of a free minority that was continually ravaged by disease. Islanders of all races regularly raised these children to be slaveholders, thereby strengthening Jamaica's commitment to chattel slavery. In a place where captive Africans formed the majority of the population, the meaning of legitimacy itself changed. The marital status of a person's parents mattered less in this context. Race, of course, was mapped onto legal status. The children born to white parents could never be enslaved. In contrast, even children with African ancestry who were born free still experienced disenfranchisements of all sorts and could face the prospect of reenslavement. The valuation of skin color created new barriers to social legitimacy and advancement, just as the legal status of being free or enslaved came to matter more than whether one's parents were married.

The baptism records also highlight the mutability of whiteness as a category of identity. Race remained an unstable and changeable signifier of status in colonial Jamaica, and, for a select few, enslavement could also be a temporary condition, rather than a permanent, heritable state. Closeness with free people could yield financial security, legal protection, and even liberty, especially for children born to interracial couples. For other women of African descent, intimate relationships also created opportunities to alter their own legal conditions and racial labels. Their children and grandchildren embodied the contradictions of a slave society. Some, like Anne Reid, the daughter of Mary Barrow and Thomas Reid, were enfolded into free families over the course of a few generations, while others remained in captivity for the rest of their lives.

6. Manumissions

When Mary Cussans, a widowed sugar planter living in Clarendon Parish, made her will in 1745, she gave a "free negro woman" named Elizabeth Dunning thirty pounds to purchase the freedom of her husband, James Dunning, whom Cussans held in her "possession" as a slave. She also manumitted her coachman, Whan, and a "mulatto child," offering them "free liberty to reside" on her estate "or wherever they shall like best." Cussans then furnished them with financial support. Concerned about their vulnerability as formerly enslaved people after her death, she emphasized their right to live on her property "without any molestation or hindrance" and asserted that the man and the child "should not at any time hereafter be called upon or employed in or about any labor or servitude whatsoever." Cussans's reasons for leaving money to Dunning to free her spouse are unclear. Perhaps she and Dunning were close companions. Interracial friendships were not unusual in Jamaica. Or, maybe the two women were related. The widow's relationships with her coachman, Whan, and the unnamed "mulatto child" are equally inscrutable. Whan occupied a privileged position in Cussans's household. As her coachman, he likely spent hours alone with the widow traveling Jamaica's notoriously poor dirt roads. Perhaps these lengthy trips fostered an intimate bond that motivated Cussans to free him. Maybe the unnamed "mulatto child" was the son of Cussans's deceased husband. Or possibly Cussans herself was the youth's mother, and freeing him signaled a covert acknowledgement of her maternal bond. Although Cussans's brief instructions provide few answers to these questions, her closeness to free and enslaved people of African descent, her decision to liberate people based on these personal ties, her offer of financial support and property to former slaves, and her anxiety about their possible exploitation in her absence, are all characteristic of women's approaches toward freeing slaves.[1]

Very little is known about women's manumission bequests in Jamaica. Typically, manumission has been configured as a reward proffered by white men to enslaved women in exchange for sexual companionship (and sometimes domestic labor). As the first major survey of manumission provisos in wills that were recorded in eighteenth-century Jamaica, this chapter interrogates these gendered, racialized, and sexualized assumptions. Concentrating on 126 female slaveholders who left directives to free people between 1683 and 1771, with reference to a sample of men's wills, it illuminates the centrality of women like Mary Cussans in both constructing and undoing the boundary between freedom and slavery.[2] During much of the eighteenth century, colonial lawmakers handled manumission, like baptism and inheritance bequests, as a personalized practice. The right to free someone was considered customary and hence required no legal definition. This treatment enhanced the power wielded by individual slaveholders in relation to local

1. Will of Mary Cussans, 1745, Jamaica Wills, 1661–1771, XXV, Island Record Office (IRO), Spanish Town, Jamaica.

2. Because my archival research focused on testamentary evidence, I was unable to review the manumission books that contain the certificates of freedom issued between 1747 and 1838. These records are held at the Jamaica Archives (JA) in Spanish Town and have been recently digitized. A comprehensive survey of them would provide a useful point of comparison to my analysis of colonial wills. Unfortunately, the first four volumes of the certificates are missing. See Manumission of Slaves, 1747–1838, JA. The British Library has digitized the volumes as part of its Endangered Archives Programme. See https://eap.bl.uk/collection/EAP148-3-1. I study a compilation of all 741 wills made by women between 1683 and 1771 and use a sample of 503 men's wills to derive the number of male-offered manumissions. My survey of women's wills does not include the years between 1762 and 1770. I primarily recorded the wills made by married men, and my sampling process was as follows. Starting in 1679, I sampled men's wills in roughly ten-year intervals based on the condition of the records, including 1699–1700, 1710, 1722, 1730, 1740, 1748–1750, 1759–1760, and 1770 (the wills from the 1660s and 1670s are incomplete). I also sampled the wills of men who either were or had been married. This factor might have led them to liberate fewer enslaved women in particular. My book is primarily focused on free and freed women — not men. To conduct a more accurate comparison of men's and women's manumission practices, one would need to do a comprehensive survey of all of the men's wills created between 1762 and 1770. For more on inheritance and baptism practices on the island, see Chapters 4 and 5, respectively, above. As Chapter 4 explains, married women did not have the right to dispose of their property unless they created separate estates; their husbands claimed their property under coverture.

and imperial institutions. In the absence of official restrictions and rules, male and female testators alike expanded the customary privilege to disburse estates into the authority to transform enslaved "property" into free persons.[3]

The Jamaica Assembly's laissez-faire approach toward manumission was specific to the British Empire. Unlike their counterparts among their Catholic rivals, British officials in London and the colonies displayed little interest in codifying and regulating paths to freedom. In contrast, Louis XIV issued a Code Noir that dictated the treatment of enslaved people for all French territories in the Americas in 1685. The Code Noir required single men who fathered children with female captives to marry the women, an action that released the mothers and their children from bondage and made them "free and legitimate." No such laws were passed in Jamaica, where colonial administrators deferred from establishing a system for registering free people

3. David Beck Ryden has conducted the first substantial analysis of manumission deeds in eighteenth-century Jamaica. However, his work focuses on the records from a two-year period between 1772 and 1774. See Ryden, "Manumission in Late Eighteenth-Century Jamaica," *New West Indian Guide/Nieuwe West-Indische Gids,* XCII (2018), 211–244. My study, in contrast, investigates all of the manumission provisos made by female testators between 1683 and 1771 as well as a sample of men's manumission provisos during the same era. A few studies have also been done of manumissions in nineteenth-century Jamaica. See, for instance, B. W. Higman, *Slave Population and Economy in Jamaica, 1807–1834* (Kingston, Jamaica, 1995); and D. A. Dunkley, *Agency of the Enslaved: Jamaica and the Culture of Freedom in the Atlantic World* (Lanham, Md., 2013). Higman claims that women "more often obtained manumission through sexual relationships with whites or freedmen," but he does not provide data to support this claim. See Higman, *Slave Populations of the British Caribbean, 1807–1834* (Kingston, Jamaica, 1995), 383. See also John F. Campbell, "How Free is Free? The Limits of Manumission for Enslaved Africans in Eighteenth-Century British West Indian Sugar Society," in Rosemary Brana-Shute and Randy J. Sparks, eds., *Paths to Freedom: Manumission in the Atlantic World* (Columbia, S.C., 2009), 143–145. Campbell draws on Hilary McD. Beckles, "Property Rights in Pleasure: The Marketing of Slave Women's Sexuality in the West Indies," in Roderick A. McDonald, ed., *West Indies Accounts: Essays on the History of the British Caribbean and the Atlantic Economy in Honour of Richard Sheridan* (Kingston, Jamaica, 1996), 169–187. Referring to Edward Long's observation in 1754 that "Domesticks" were the primary group of slaves to receive manumissions, Campbell argues that a "domestick" was invariably the sexual companion of a white man and contends that white men used the promise of manumission to control enslaved women's sexuality. He does not consider the manumission of "domesticks" by female slaveholders nor does he refer to children who were freed by their fathers. See also Christer Petley, "'Legitimacy' and Social Boundaries: Free People of Colour and the Social Order in Jamaican Slave Society," *Social History,* XXX (2005), 481–498; and Richard Godbeer, *Sexual Revolution in Early America* (Baltimore, 2002), 218–222.

or for adjudicating manumissions. The absence of bureaucratic procedures and institutions made formerly enslaved inhabitants reliant on a miscellany of wills, baptism records, testimonies, and manumissions—paper records easily lost or destroyed in the tropical weather—to establish their legal independence.[4]

Owing to the unstructured and individualized nature of Jamaica's manumission system, sources on manumission practices are also limited. The majority of directives in colonial wills do not specify whether testators were presenting freedom unconditionally or if they had received payments in exchange for manumissions. Though a few owners added monetary or labor contingencies to their bequests, most of them simply stated that a person was to be liberated immediately on their death. Likewise, figuring out how many people were actually released from bondage as a result of the directives in wills is also challenging. Most colonists made wills at the end of their lives and died soon thereafter (as evidenced by their estates being probated). Although it is reasonable to assume that they intended for specific captives to be freed after their deaths, the evidence is not definitive. In spite of these shortcomings, the provisos in eighteenth-century wills comprise one of the most detailed, substantive, and well-preserved resources of information about Jamaican manumission patterns.[5]

4. Louis XIV, Code Noir, 1685, Article IX, "The Code Noir (The Black Code)," Liberté, Egalité, Fraternité: Exploring the French Revolution, http://chnm.gmu.edu/revolution/d/335/. The process of freeing enslaved people was not systematized in the British Caribbean as it was in Francophone colonies. Scholars have described the manumission records in Barbados and Jamaica as disorganized, a reflection of the haphazard approach to manumissions in both locations. See Ryden, "Manumission in Late Eighteenth-Century Jamaica," *New West Indian Guide/Nieuwe West-Indische Gids,* XCII (2018), 213–214, 234, 220; and Kit Candlin and Cassandra Pybus, *Enterprising Women: Gender, Race, and Power in the Revolutionary Atlantic* (Athens, Ga., 2015), 81.

5. Though entrepreneurial enslaved people did save money, Ryden's study of the manumission deeds recorded between 1772–1774 leads him to conclude that very few captives purchased their own freedom. The lack of references to self-purchasing in the manumission provisos made earlier in the eighteenth century suggests likewise. See Ryden, "Manumission in Late Eighteenth-Century Jamaica," *New West Indian Guide/Nieuwe West-Indische Gids,* XCII (2018), 237–238. The archives do not enable me to distinguish between "granting freedom" and transferring "ownership" in manumission transactions as James Sweet does, for example, with manumissions in Brazil in *Domingos Álvares: African Healing, and the Intellectual History of the Atlantic World* (Chapel Hill, N.C., 2011), 91–92.

Though men and women claimed the same legal right to manumit enslaved people, gendered variances in both the scale of slaveholding and the nature of the work performed by the captives on the island influenced manumission trends. The average male colonist was twice as rich and owned twice as many slaves (26) as his female counterpart (16). Nevertheless, a strikingly high number of female slaveholders determined to free captives, even though they controlled a smaller portion of the colony's wealth. More than a quarter (126) of all 452 women who specifically referred to slaves in descriptions of their estates made provisions to liberate at least one person, indicating that enslaved people who had female owners stood a greater chance of being freed. Comparatively, only 15 percent (76) of the 503 men in the sample of male-authored wills manumitted someone.[6]

The average woman in the group of female manumitters was of middling status. She held an estate worth a mean value of £1,096 and a median value of £508 and commanded between 8 (median) and 20 (mean) enslaved people. Unsurprisingly, nearly 90 percent of the women who left manumission directives were identified by their marital status as widows; most of the others appeared as "spinsters," and a few were listed as "shopkeeper," "planter," "free black woman," or "free mulatto woman." By contrast, men were categorized by their professions and more than half of them claimed elite status in colonial society. One-third (28) of the 76 men were listed as "planter." Another

6. My calculations of the average number of slaves owned by women and by men are based on data from all of the inventories of estates probated in the colony between 1674 and 1765. See Jamaica Inventories, 1674–1784, Jamaica Archives (JA), Spanish Town, Jamaica. For a detailed chart of the average number of slaves owned by women, see Chapter 4, above. Of the 741 women who made wills between 1683 and 1771, I identify 452 women who were definitely slaveholders. As I explain in Chapter 4, many women who only referred to "real and personal estate" in their wills probably owned slaves. I do not include them in this figure though because I cannot state with certainty that they were slaveholders. See Jamaica Wills. In reality, the portion of male manumitters was probably larger. My sample of men's wills includes all of the men who made wills during that period, not just those who specifically referred to slaves. But the average male colonist owned more slaves, which diminished the impact of a manumission on his estate. Ryden's study of the deeds of manumission recorded during a two-year period between 1772 and 1774 supports my conclusion about the significance of women among the manumitters in colonial Jamaica. Ryden determines that women of European, Euro-African, and African descent appeared in one-fifth of the deeds made during this time. See Ryden, "Manumission in Late Eighteenth-Century Jamaica," *New West Indian Guide/Nieuwe West-Indische Gids*, XCII (2018), 230–231.

17 appeared to be "gentlemen" or "esquires." Only 15 percent (12) of the men worked as lower-ranking artisans or mariners.[7]

Comparatively, the women who released people from bondage made up a more economically, socially, and racially diverse lot. Ann Russell, a widowed inhabitant of Port Royal, lived on the margins of colonial society. Though African captives comprised the majority of her wealth, Russell left instructions to "discharge from slavery" a "negro woman Phibba" and provide her with £7—a significant sum for a woman whose total estate was valued at £63. Russell divided up her remaining slaves, a woman and her two children, between a local carpenter, a mariner, and her sister-in-law. Rebecca Pereira Mendes, a member of Kingston's Jewish mercantile community, commanded an estate valued at £9,100 and controlled forty-six captives. When Mendes died in 1771, her estate was valued at £9,100, and she controlled forty-six captives. The rich widow entrusted the majority of her fortune to her "friend" Moses Brandon, a bookkeeper who was perhaps her intimate partner. Mendes also determined to "manumize" several enslaved women, including Rosanah, Silvia, Agar, Beneba, Grace, Perla, Judith, and Ruthy, together with one man, Ned, and furnished each of them £7. She further instructed her executors to pay Judith, who had acted as her nurse, "6 shillings 3 pence" every week for the rest of Judith's life. Though Mendes freed nine people, the effect on the total value of her estate was negligible in comparison with Russell's action in releasing one person from bondage and giving her £7 from more meagre resources.[8]

Though their holdings were radically disparate, as urban dwellers Russell and Mendes both fit the profile of the typical female manumitter. One-third of the women in this group lived in Kingston, which was home to the largest number of free and freed women on the island (Table 5). Female colonists

7. I have determined the average wealth and marital status of these female slaveholders using the forty-three probated inventories made between 1675–1769 of the estates held by women who also left instructions to manumit slaves in their wills. Manumission information for male slaveholders was derived from a sample of men's wills made between 1679–1770. See Jamaica Inventories; and Jamaica Wills.

8. Will of Ann Russell, 1750, Jamaica Wills, XXVII; Inventory of Ann Russell, 1750, Jamaica Inventories; Will of Rebecca Pereira Mendes, 1770, Jamaica Wills, XXXVIII; Inventory of Rebecca Pereira Mendes, 1771, Jamaica Inventories. As I explain in Chapter 5, above, women typically made large bequests to single male friends who were their sexual companions. For more on manumissions made by Jewish slaveholders, see Ryden, "Manumission in Late Eighteenth-Century Jamaica," *New West Indian Guide/Nieuwe West-Indische Gids,* XCII (2018), 229–230.

TABLE 5: *Geographic Distribution of Women Who Made Manumission Provisos, 1683–1771*

PARISH	NUMBER	PERCENTAGE
Clarendon	4	3
Hanover	2	2
Kingston	41	33
London (Britain)	2	2
Port Royal	10	8
Saint Andrew	13	10
Saint Ann	3	2
Saint Catherine	26	21
Saint David	2	2
Saint Dorothy	3	2
Saint Elizabeth	6	5
Saint James	2	2
Saint Thomas in the East	2	2
Vere	6	5
Westmoreland	3	2
Total	125	101

Source: Jamaica Wills, 1661–1771, III, IV, V–XXXVIII, Island Record Office, Spanish Town, Jamaica.

Note: Rounding produces small discrepencies, hence, the percentages total 101.

who resided in the parishes in neighboring urban areas also represented significant portions of the women who made manumission provisos. Of those women who freed slaves in their wills, 21 percent resided in Saint Catherine, where Spanish Town was located, 10 percent resided in Saint Andrew Parish, on the outskirts of Kingston, and 8 percent in Port Royal. The remainder lived in agriculture parishes. As these figures suggest, captives who were held by urban-dwelling women on the south coast of the island were more likely to be freed than their rural counterparts who labored on large plantations.[9]

The divergence in urban and rural manumissions partially explains why men, who controlled the majority of Jamaica's large plantations and the people who labored on them, also released fewer captives from bondage. Female slaveholding was typically more small-scale in nature, and their slaves performed work that either required the owner's direct supervision

9. Jamaica Wills, 1661–1771, I–XXXVIII.

or allowed for greater independence. The enslaved people who labored for women owners in urban areas worked as servants, washerwomen, seamstresses, cooks, footmen, coach drivers, wharf hands, sailors, and artisans. Those toiling in the countryside aided female planters who operated more diversified agricultural ventures than their male planters did. Their captives were employed in the cultivation of sugar, but they also grew ginger, pimento, and provision crops and reared livestock. Altogether, women commanded an enslaved labor force that was more skilled and often employed in more independent occupations than the people who were under men's control. Consequently, female enslavers needed to personally manage, cooperate with, and trust their captives, whom they were more likely to labor alongside. Although the intimate quality of these work relationships could intensify their intrusive and coercive nature, closeness with enslavers also increased the likelihood of preferential treatment, improved living conditions, and, for a select few, a release from bondage.[10]

Manumissions served multiple and contradictory purposes in Jamaica. Some slaveholders deployed the reward of freedom as a subtle form of coercion, dangling the promise of future manumission before captives in return for a lifetime of compliant and loyal service. From this angle, manumission was a mercenary and exploitative practice colonists used to control slaves during the prime of their lives before callously discarding them when they were too old to work. Perhaps such a strategy inspired the planter Francis Flowaires to have his son "ratify and confirm" the freedom of a woman named Moll, "provided that she behave herself in the meantime as an orderly slave ought to do," in 1710. Similarly, a female slaveholder manumitted a woman named Grace and her three children in return for Grace's obedience and "severall years of faithful service" in 1734. Likewise, a woman named Joan obtained her liberty and an annuity of four pounds "in consideration of several years faithful service," and a doctor in Saint Catherine used comparable language when he manumitted Chloe for the "good deeds and services she has done and performed for me during my life." Chloe's "liberty and freedom," however, was conditional; the slaveholder empowered his wife with the "discretion" to manumit the woman at her "pleasure."[11]

10. Chapter 2, above, studies the economic activities of female colonists who lived in urban areas of the island. Chapter 3, above, focuses on free and freed women who oversaw plantations and livestock pens.

11. Will of Francis Flowaires, 1710, Jamaica Wills, XIII, Will of Elizabeth Woodland, 1734, XIX, Will of Elizabeth Totterdell, 1735, XIX, Will of William Stanverton, 1748, XXVII.

As the vocabulary in these manumission provisos suggests, freeing a handful of people who exhibited qualities that appealed to enslavers—faithfulness, deference, and obedience—served as an important security measure. By turning certain captives into valuable allies who could inform owners of malcontents and runaways and even uncover brewing uprisings, slaveholders sought to strengthen their control over a large and restive enslaved population. Freed people possibly acted as exemplars, conferring false hope to a captive majority who would never be released from bondage.[12]

To an extent, manumitting certain slaves was a symbolic act that aided in mollifying and controlling those who remained enslaved. Scholars have determined that the manumission rate in the late eighteenth and early nineteenth centuries was approximately 1.5 per thousand slaves. Although the actual number of people who received freedom was miniscule, manumission served critical colonial and imperial objectives. Manumission acts had the potential to quell unrest among the enslaved and boost the free minority population without compromising the integrity of the slave system. Assigning freedom to a select group of inhabitants, therefore, aided in the preservation of British Jamaica.[13]

Colonial manumission provisos are, on the whole, more inscrutable and nuanced than such interpretations initially suggest. Islanders' directives evince a localized view of slavery as a conditional legal status rather than an intrinsic biological and heritable racialized identity. Moreover, manumission bequests manifest African understandings of kinship, familial belonging, and slavery as much as they display emerging European notions of individuality, self-hood, and autonomy. As Suzanne Miers and Igor Kopytoff point out, individual autonomy was considered to be "meaningless and dangerous" in most African societies. Africans defined liberty in familial terms as a form of belonging to a patron or kin group. If they signal slaveholder aspirations, these directives also allude to the roles played by enslaved people, and espe-

12. As in Barbados, the majority of Jamaica's slave population stood little chance of ever being freed. For manumissions in Barbados, see Jerome S. Handler and John T. Pohlmann, "Slave Manumissions and Freedmen in Seventeenth-Century Barbados," *WMQ*, 3d Ser., XLI (1984), 400.

13. Ryden calculates the rate of manumission for the late eighteenth and early nineteenth centuries in "Manumission in Late Eighteenth-Century Jamaica," *New West Indian Guide/Nieuwe West-Indische Gids*, XCII (2018), 239, which he supports using data from the following works: Higman, *Slave Population and Economy in Jamaica;* and Dunkley, *Agency of the Enslaved.*

cially enslaved women, in procuring freedom for themselves and their children. The sway of African women might account for the strong interest displayed by colonists in manumitting young people. Women who had grown up in patrilineal African communities where enslaved concubines were considered to be outsiders possibly interpreted their own degraded positions in Jamaica as a new form of outsider status. From this perspective, it made sense to forge close connections with slaveholders, thereby increasing their belonging to the host community. Acts of manumission, like baptism, transitioned people from positions of marginality to greater belonging and incorporation into the "host society" and conferred "second generation" status on children.[14]

Though slaveholders undoubtedly defined captives as property, they also strove to integrate former slaves into free families and, more broadly, into the free "host society" in Jamaica. Colonists lived in an environment plagued by demographic catastrophe, and they adapted manumission, like inheritance bequests and baptism, to suit local needs. Although enslaved people were commodified, they were also valued according to African principles as "producers of more people." By treating certain slaves as blood relatives and "quasi blood members," islanders defined kinship and enslavement as mobile relationships, rather than fixed genealogical or racial statuses, and constructed intricate and multilayered families. Young people, who were more malleable than adults, received special attention in slaveholder bequests. Starting in infancy, they were taught the cultural literacy, especially the language and social skills, that would mark them as free people. Formerly enslaved children who joined free families, in turn, stabilized the island's free minority population, thereby representing wealth in the form of people. Manumission was one way for colonists to strengthen and expand their kinship groups and weather the vagaries of a volatile place. In doing so, slaveholders also undermined rigid definitions of racial difference and legal status.[15]

14. Suzanne Miers and Igor Kopytoff, eds., *Slavery in Africa: Historical and Anthropological Perspectives* (Madison, Wis., 1977), 17, 19, 31–34, 37. Concubines were often women who lacked the requisite bridewealth to attract husbands in Africa.

15. Ibid., 37, 55–56; Sweet, *Domingos Álvares,* 91. Colonists' manumission practices indicate that "naked capitalism" did not depersonalize relationships between enslaved and free people to the extent that scholars have claimed. Michael Craton, for example, argues that the commodification of slaves and the "immense cultural differences between white European masters and black African slaves made the creation of a social . . . matrix" between the two "virtually impossible." See Craton, "Reluctant Creoles: The Planters' World in the British West Indies,"

"MY LITTLE SLAVE"

In 1740, a modest planter named Francis Israel made bequests to his free, freed, and enslaved children. Israel used legacies to support and also distinguish between legitimate, illegitimate, and enslaved heirs. Three legitimate daughters received slaves. He granted his free illegitimate "mulatto" daughter three horses. He also left money and instructions for his executors, including his legitimate son and heir, to "buy" his other son, Thomas, who was still enslaved. Israel's son would then support his half-brother, Thomas, until the boy was old enough to enter an apprenticeship. That same year Isaac Pereira Brandon, a merchant and member of Kingston's Jewish community, selectively freed an enslaved woman, Percer, and her daughter Judith, a "mulatto girl of 13 years" who was probably Brandon's child. Brandon also bequeathed Judith an annuity of eighteen pounds. Brandon's decision to free the "mulatto girl" Judith renders his intimate connection to Percer visible. His severe treatment of Percer's other three "negro" children, "none of whome their freedom is given or intended in my will," emphasizes the personalized nature of manumission, which was only bestowed on people who established close emotional, and possibly sexual, ties to enslavers.[16]

On average, men owned similar numbers of male (54 percent) and female captives (46 percent). Yet, like Israel and Brandon, most male manumitters freed their biological children and, sometimes, the women they forged relationships with: 48 percent of the captives whom men released from bondage were children, 37 percent were adult women, and 15 percent were adult men. Similarly, female slaveholders, who also controlled nearly equal numbers of male (47 percent) and female slaves (52 percent), also preferred to manumit women and children. Altogether, female slaveholders made provisions to free 270 people (Table 6). Adult females comprised 45 percent of people whom female testators referred to in manumission provisos; 37 percent were children, and 18 percent were adult males. Manumissions, then, cannot just be

---

in Bernard Bailyn and Philip D. Morgan, eds., *Strangers Within the Realm: Cultural Margins of the First British Empire* (Williamsburg, Va., and Chapel Hill, N.C., 1991), 337. I draw on Rachel Sarah O'Toole's reference to anthropological scholarship that defines kinship as a set of "mobile" relations created through daily practices in her study of manumissions in colonial Peru. See O'Toole, "The Bonds of Kinship, the Ties of Freedom in Colonial Peru," *Journal of Family History*, XLII (2017), 4.

16. Will of Francis Israel, 1740, Jamaica Wills, XXII, Will of Isaac Pereira Brandon, 1740, XXII.

TABLE 6: *Distribution of People Freed by Female Owners by Age and Sex, 1683–1771*

	NUMBER	PERCENTAGE
Adults	171	63
Men	49	18
Women	122	45
Children	99	37
Girls	62	23
Boys	37	14
Total	270	

Source: Jamaica Wills, 1661–1771, III, IV, V–XXXVIII, Island Record Office, Spanish Town, Jamaica.

correlated to the gender ratios of the captives held by owners. It is also necessary to consider how the gendered dimensions of slaveholding influenced colonists' actions.[17]

Overall, men chose to manumit their own children, and women manumitted other women, despite that both owned equivalent numbers of adult men. Interestingly, the majority (70 percent) of the fifty-five adult women who were freed by male slaveholders appear to be childless, suggesting that they either did not start families with the men who freed them or that the men determined to keep their children in bondage. Fathers tended to manumit children separately. Sparse manumission instructions, however, shroud certain relationships between male slaveholders and female captives in ambiguity. In 1722, John Marshall left instructions to "enfranchize and set free a negro woman slave that belongs to me in Jamaica called Betty formerly house servant of my former wife Margarett." Furthermore, Marshall bequeathed a substantial estate to his legitimate wife and daughters. Perhaps Marshall freed the woman in recompense for her years of service to his wife. Or he could have manumitted her as a means of acknowledging a past intimacy. In any case, even though he had relocated to London, Marshall still remembered Betty. Wharfinger James Ker's instructions to "enfranchize and make free my negro woman slaved called Nancy, and bequeath unto her full freedom and liberty from all slavery" are less ambiguous, though certainly not

17. Calculations of the gender ratios of slaves owned by male and female slaveholders are based on data from estates probated between 1675–1769 in Jamaica Inventories. Figures are derived from colonial wills, Jamaica Wills, 1661–1771, I–XXXVIII.

definitive. Ker left his small estate to his "poor relatives" in Ireland; Nancy was possibly his intimate partner in Jamaica. Although these brief provisos allude to close connections, the absence of children makes the sexual dimension less certain.[18]

When men recognized and manumitted their biological children, their intimate connections with enslaved women come into view more clearly. For the fathers of enslaved infants, manumission served a similar purpose as baptism. It became part of a multistep process to establish a child's free status. During the first half of the eighteenth century, some men who started families with captive women had their children christened, freed, and educated. Collectively, their actions released a handful of young people from bondage. However, fathers did not treat their legitimate and illegitimate offspring equally. Whereas legitimate heirs often received large portions of family estates, formerly enslaved sons were typically placed in apprenticeships to learn skilled crafts. Although this differentiated treatment ensured the second-class status of freed children within families, apprenticeships were still a valuable form of training that promised a stable income and possible membership in the colony's middling class. For formerly enslaved boys, such instruction served multiple purposes: it authenticated their legal status as free people, brought them into the fold of the colony's skilled artisan community, and confirmed their gendered status as independent adult males.

Greater toleration of illegitimate and formerly enslaved children, combined with the demand for tradesmen, made it easier for fathers to establish freed sons in respectable professions on the island. With so few European artisans surviving, there was a high demand for carpenters, coopers, blacksmiths, millwrights, and shipwrights. Claudius Archbould's plans for his son, Samuel Blake, in 1740 took advantage of these conditions. Archbould wanted Samuel to be enfranchised, sent to school to achieve literacy and "to be educated in the Christian faith," and then bound as an apprentice to a trade. At the completion of his apprenticeship, he was to receive ten pounds to purchase tools. By making provisions for Samuel's professional education, Archbould performed his paternal duty toward the boy while also acting as his patron. He and other men who freed enslaved children subscribed to powerful early modern ideals of masculinity that linked patriarchal authority to fatherhood. Like Samuel, the majority would not, however, be treated as legitimate heirs.[19]

18. Will of John Marshall, 1722, Jamaica Wills, XVI, Will of James Ker, 1722, XVI.

19. Will of Claudius Archbould, 1740, Jamaica Wills, XII.

Men's wills also show how gendered expectations influenced life options for sons and daughters born to enslaved women who were then freed by their fathers. Sons were typically placed in apprenticeships that promised future financial independence; daughters' prospects, in comparison, were more limited. In 1748, Robert Cole, for example, assigned two slaves to his Euro-African son Samuel before he entered an apprenticeship. Cole also had a daughter, Mary, with another free woman of African descent. He granted Mary an enslaved girl and made provisions for his executors to purchase another captive for her when she turned fourteen. Her father offered her some support, but when she came of age, Mary would need to attract a husband, survive as a small-scale slaveholder, or rely on assistance from her brother.[20]

Two years later, Mathias Philip furnished even larger legacies for his illegitimate Euro-African children. He wanted both his sons and daughters to be educated, but Philip did not envision the same level of instruction for all of his children. He awarded his son, Samuel, a large sum of eight hundred pounds when he turned twenty-one and a supplementary annuity of forty pounds for an apprenticeship as a carpenter, bricklayer, or "some other profitable employ." Philip's executors were also instructed to purchase "four likely boys to be bound to same trade" with Samuel who could then serve as his enslaved laborers. Philip's two daughters, Nancy and Kitty, would each inherit substantial portions of five hundred pounds when they turned sixteen and receive thirty pounds a year for their maintenance and education. Though still generous, their legacies were smaller than their brother's, and their futures were far less certain. Like Mary Cole, the girls faced the prospect of attracting spouses, relying on their brother for extra financial support, or joining the group of free and freed women in Jamaica who engaged in a range of lower-skilled occupations to support themselves.[21]

The planter Henry Lord made similar provisions for his two Euro-African sons, John and Nathaniel, who, in addition to learning to read, write, and do arithmetic, would be joined by four captive African children when they began their apprenticeships. Lord charged his executors to purchase "new" captives, two boys and two girls, from a slaving ship for his sons on their manumission. The enslaved boys would be bound to the same millwright or persons of "other good trades" as John and Nathaniel while the "new" African girls would serve as their washerwomen, cooks, and seamstresses. By

20. Will of Robert Cole, 1748, Jamaica Wills, XVII.

21. Will of Mathias Philip, 1750, Jamaica Wills, XVII.

simultaneously freeing John and Nathaniel and making them slaveholders, Lord engaged in an act that became a common feature of Jamaica's manumission process. Acts of manumission melded familial and professional interests and made freedom inextricable from slaveholding. As Lord understood, slaveholding was a crucial signifier of independence in Jamaica. The logic of a slave society dictated arrangements that turned recently freed children into the masters of other young people who had been captured and transported to the island for their benefit.[22]

Men's provisos reveal both the advantages and the limitations of the relationships forged between fathers and their enslaved children, whom they provided for but also kept at arm's length from legitimate kin groups. By fulfilling their paternal duties, men like Lord confirmed their manhood. Fathers treated sons and daughters who were born to enslaved women as illegitimate offspring, expecting them to act as lower-ranking members in free legitimate families while achieving respectable artisan or middling—not elite—status in colonial society. In a transaction that highlights the overlapping and competing interests of kinship and slaveholding within free families, Lord also set aside seventy pounds to purchase the freedom of Dorothy, the mother of John and Nathaniel, whom his legitimate daughter held in bondage. Not trusting his daughter to follow his directions, Lord instructed his executors to grant Dorothy the interest on the manumission money if his daughter refused to free her.[23]

Lord's relationship with Dorothy and the children who were born of their bond created a multilayered family and bred a high potential for conflict. The proviso in his will suggests that Lord's legitimate daughter had a financial stake in holding Dorothy in captivity. It is also plausible that she resented John and Nathaniel, the half-brothers of her father's paramour. Nevertheless, Lord's family was hardly atypical. The absence of laws prohibiting interracial sex together with the local acceptance of children who were born out of wedlock made these kinds of complicated kinship groups commonplace, if not socially acceptable.

Though women's reasons for freeing children are less obvious, they also used manumission as a means of recognizing and adopting enslaved children into their families. References to the mothers of the young people they freed indicate that the children were not their biological offspring. Yet that

22. Will of Henry Lord, 1740, Jamaica Wills, XII.

23. Ibid.

both men and women engaged in this practice points toward the emergence of a localized and flexible notion of family that accommodated members who were not just blood relations or sexual companions. Even as free and freed women rarely acknowledged intimate connections to men of African descent in their wills, manumission bequests show that female islanders still established complicated and significant relationships with enslaved people that defy straightforward interpretations. One might assume that widows who freed captive women were resentfully honoring legal obligations to fulfill husbands' bequests, but their actions were rarely so transparent.[24]

The widow Elizabeth Turnbridge, for example, wielded the legal authority to make a will, distribute property, and free slaves according to her own preference. Turnbridge chose to release her deceased husband's enslaved daughter, Jenny, whom she described as "begot by my late husband . . . on his negro woman named Lucretia" in her 1727 will. Rather than viewing Jenny as a bitter reminder of her husband's infidelity, Turnbridge expressed anxiety about the child's future, using a combination of rewards, threats, and alternative inheritance strategies to shelter Jenny from her husband's brother and sister, who were also her sole heirs. The widow reserved the "best part" of her estate for them if they complied with her instructions. Turnbridge directed her executors to fund the girl's release directly from her estate if "they [her heirs] refuse" to free her. Jenny would then be placed "under the care" of a close friend and receive ten pounds to buy clothes. Turnbridge took an enslaved girl who was akin to a stepdaughter under her wing, claimed a kinship connection to her, and strove to alter her legal status.[25]

By the early decades of the eighteenth century, women like Turnbridge exhibited a distinctively colonial understanding of familial affiliation—one that bore the imprint of European and African beliefs and responded to local conditions. Like most other female slaveholders who manumitted children, Turnbridge herself was childless. Her reference to a son-in-law in New York

24. Well into the nineteenth century, female Creole domestics were still the most probable group of enslaved people to be freed in the British Caribbean. However, as my research shows, they were more likely to be manumitted by female owners. Male owners, in contrast, preferred to free their biological children. These findings suggest that manumission was not just a reward for sexual companionship that was extended by white men to captive women. Instead, as I argue in this chapter, other dynamics were at play. See Higman, *Slave Populations of the British Caribbean,* 383–386.

25. Will of Elizabeth Turnbridge, 1727, Jamaica Wills, XVII.

suggests that her own daughter had died. Turnbridge possibly considered the enslaved girl, Jenny, to be a fictive child of sorts. Though the widow did not make Jenny her primary heir, she expressed considerable concern for the girl's future and devised intricate inheritance plans to protect her. By drawing Jenny into her kinship group, Turnbridge might have even evinced an African-influenced view of slavery as wealth building in people.

Turnbridge's will reveals the complex relationships forged between female slaveholders, enslaved mothers, and enslaved children. These dynamics turned the colonial household into an emotionally charged space. Turnbridge made no mention of Jenny's mother, Lucretia. It is not known if Lucretia supported the widow's plan to free her daughter, whether she was coerced into agreeing to it, or if she was still alive. Turnbridge's harsh treatment of her three other captives, whom she transferred to her niece and nephew, as well as her gift of twenty pounds to an acquaintance, John Sheen, "to buy him a negro," indicates a generalized lack of empathy for enslaved people. Rather, the widow, like most of Jamaica's slaveholders, extended privileges, which sometimes included freedom, to select people for whom she developed affection. When Turnbridge made provisions to manumit another captive, Moll Green, "after serving faithfully and honestly" for twelve months following the widow's death, she expressed no qualms about separating Green from her children, whom she wanted to be "immediately sold" after she died. Her direction to put an enslaved man, Simon, "in irons till the first opportunity serves to send him off to be sold," further emphasized her coercive power while underscoring the idiosyncratic and individualistic nature of colonial manumissions.[26]

The dynamic between Anna Maria Langley, a widow and a contemporary of Turnbridge's, and her "mulatto wench Betty" is equally opaque. Langley seemingly manumitted Betty "according to the request of my husbands will" when she made her own will in 1728. The widow left detailed instructions for Betty's release, giving her an estimated annual annuity of three pounds. Moreover, Langley's manumission package invested Betty with command of Beatrice, whom Langley instructed to "attend and waite upon her [Betty] and work for her during her life." Through this action, Langley expanded Betty's slaveholdings. Betty already owned a woman, Margarett, "which was bought with Betty's money," and the widow formally recognized Betty's claim to her. Her proviso indicates that Langley fostered her own close tie

26. Ibid.

to Betty, one that overrode any resentment she bore toward a woman who was possibly her husband's former mistress. With an estate valued at roughly thirteen hundred pounds, Langley was wealthy. The widow made her fortune acting as a moneylender and held the majority of her assets in outstanding debts—not captives. She possessed eight enslaved people: one, Betty, whom she freed, and two more whom she recognized as belonging to Betty. Langley, not her husband, crafted intricate instructions for Betty's release. Men's provisos rarely included such descriptive particularities.[27]

In drawing attention to Betty's actions, Langley's will disrupts a binary construction of the relationship between slavery and freedom. Though Betty was enslaved, she seemed to live in a state of de facto liberty that Langley supported. Perhaps the widow hired Betty out, enabling her to earn enough income to purchase her own slaves, very expensive forms of property on the island. Or Betty's "slaves" Beatrice and Margarett could have been Betty's relatives whom Langley "gave" to her as a means of allowing her to defend her kin. It is equally likely that Betty used slaveholding to establish the credibility of her own status as a free person. Holding someone else in bondage was a crucial means of signifying and performing one's legal status in a colony that revolved around slaveholding.

The wills made by Turnbridge and Langley unravel ostensibly straightforward manumission bequests initiated by an obvious motive: a white man's sexual relationship with an enslaved woman. Female slaveholders did not simply transcribe their husbands' orders. They instigated, reshaped, and amended manumissions to reflect their own interests and ties to enslaved people. Besides freeing Betty, Langley also released her coachman from bondage while giving two "mulatto" children to her niece and nephew. The widow's instructions outline the hierarchy that existed among the captives within her household. Betty, a slaveowner herself, was at the top, the coachman occupied a rung below her, and Beatrice and Margarett, who would become the slaves of a former slave, clung to the lowest rung. Perhaps the "mulatto" children she referred to were the offspring of Betty and Langley's late husband. If that was the case, then it appears as though the widow vindictively separated the mother from her children. Yet other interpretations are possible. Female slaveholders, including women of African descent, also transferred children to free relatives. Such acts allowed young people to re-

27. Will of Anna Maria Langley, 1728, Jamaica Wills, XVII; Inventory of Anna Maria Langley, 1728, Jamaica Inventories.

main close to their parents and protected them from being sold when owners died. Perhaps Langley's arrangements were motivated by a similar reason.[28]

It is also worth considering a third scenario: that the "mulatto" children were Langley's own offspring. Because free women rarely referred to relationships with men of African descent, especially enslaved men, it is impossible to support this conjecture with evidence. Yet reticence in the sources should not be equated with actual behavior in Jamaica's racially and sexually entangled communities. A handful of manumission provisos made by other women hint at this possibility. Twenty years earlier, Mary Chidloy, a widow from Vere Parish, freed an enslaved man named Dick and his daughter, Taroconte. Chidloy called the child "my little negro girl Taroconte." Female slaveholders often used the possessive "my" when referring to enslaved children, verbally emphasizing their legal ownership and negating the claims of the actual parents. But Chidloy took the less common step of providing Dick with an annuity of three pounds and leaving Taroconte a considerable legacy of eighty-six pounds to be put out at interest and used as her marriage dowry. Chidloy further asked her executors to oversee the girl's education.[29]

The attention the widow lavished on Taroconte, combined with her decision to enfranchise the girl's father, suggests that Taroconte was Chidloy's and Dick's child. Chidloy also maintained close ties to a man named Thomas Cargill, whom she nominated to act as her executor and primary beneficiary. It is also conceivable that he was an intimate partner, for unmarried women commonly forged nonmarital connections to men on the island. In any case, Chidloy's manumission provisos are suffused with shadowy clues about the dynamics between a free widow, an enslaved girl, an enslaved man, and a free man. These rare archival traces lead to conjectures without yielding satisfactory and comprehensive answers.[30]

Thirty years after Chidloy freed Dick and Taroconte, Kingston widow Hannah Dennis manumitted a "negro boy christened William Dennis." He bore her surname, which indicates that the two were likely related, though Dennis did not specify whether William was her son, grandson, or a child whom she adopted into her family. Whatever their connection, Dennis considered William to be kin and wanted the boy to join her free family. His christening was the first critical step toward securing his freedom. Dennis de-

28. Will of Anna Maria Langley, 1728, Jamaica Wills, XVII.

29. Will of Mary Chidloy, 1708, Jamaica Wills, XII.

30. Ibid.

sired her namesake to adopt further attributes of a free colonist. After being granted his "absolute freedom," Dennis planned for William to be "Christianly trained up and liberally educated." If the boy had the "capacity for learning any trade or livelihood," he was "to be taught the same"; if not, he was still to be "maintained and provided for in a handsome manner as a Christian." Rather than perceiving Dennis as a slave, the widow envisioned him becoming an accomplished craftsman and a godly member of the Kingston community.[31]

As the above manumission provisos show, slaveholders maintained porous boundaries between their families and the people whom they held in bondage. The interests of free and freed women like Chidloy and Dennis were intertwined with those of their captives. Though the motives of female slaveholders are rarely legible, their manumission provisos emphasize the personalized nature of slavery. Women's plans for children, bestowing financial support and placing boys, in particular, in apprenticeships, paralleled the actions of fathers who liberated their offspring.

Manumission practices were more than performances of patrimony made by men. By the 1740s, slaveholders had developed a widely shared set of strategies for integrating young people into free society. The wealthy planter Ann Elphinston had already freed the daughter of her slave Sue when she made her will in 1749. She also manumitted Sue and her son Barkshire (Berkshire), whom Elphinston diminutively called "my little slave." The family was to receive a house with nine acres of property "near old harbor bay" in which to reside. Elphinston granted the boy fifty pounds to "bind him apprentice to a trade" that was both "agreeable to him" and "shall seem most convenient" to her executors, two Kingston merchants who would act as his guardians. Elphinston's manumission tactics resemble the instructions left by fathers who placed freed sons into apprenticeships. Her financial support and her affectionate description of Barkshire as her "little slave" might even provide a glimpse of a kinship tie between the planter and the enslaved family whom she planned to release from bondage.[32]

Like their male counterparts, female slaveholders also enforced gender norms when they freed people. Whereas they established boys in skilled trades like carpentry, brickmaking, coopering, masonry, and blacksmithing,

31. Will of Hannah Dennis, 1739, Jamaica Wills, XXII.

32. Will of Ann Elphinston, 1749, Jamaica Wills, XVII; Inventory of Ann Elphinston, 1750, Jamaica Inventories. Elphinston commanded an estate valued at an estimated £780, including nine slaves, when she died.

women typically instructed that girls acquire literacy and domestic skills, especially the ability to sew. Mary Hadwen, a wealthy woman living in Saint Catherine, released two girls, Amelia and Monemmia, from bondage in 1749. Hadwen bequeathed them the small sum of approximately three pounds to finance four years of "education and improvement in needlework." A year later, at the same time that Kingston widow Mary Welsh left her urban property, which included several stores, to her nieces, she also made provisions for Olive, a "mulatto girl," to be "manumized and enfranchised" when she turned sixteen. Her nieces would acquire Olive's mother as a captive while Olive, in contrast, would live with them as a free person and be "educated in reading and working at the needle." The plans made by Hadwen and Welsh reflect the gendered occupational limitations faced by most early modern women. Sewing was a feminized and often unpaid skill, and nearly every woman was expected to be capable of "working at the needle." Yet sewing, as slaveholders were undoubtedly aware, had the potential to become a lucrative occupation. Women dominated the needle trades, working as seamstresses, mantuamakers, and milliners throughout the Atlantic world, and perhaps Hadwen and Welsh envisioned similar paths for Amelia, Monemmia, and Olive.[33]

Colonists like Hadwen and Welsh carefully groomed young protégés, hoping that baptism, education, and guidance in a skilled occupation would prepare formerly enslaved youths to succeed in free society. Manumission afforded a release from enslavement but not from the grip of former enslavers. Rather than creating distance, freedom further bound girls such as Amelia, Monemmia, and Olive to their patron families. For children, manumission was typically accompanied by the expectation of cultural and spiritual assimilation into free society. When Elizabeth Wilds made plans to manumit a girl named Martha Parlour in 1747, she insisted that Martha had been "bap-

33. Will of Mary Hadwen, 1749, Jamaica Wills, XXVII; Inventory of Mary Hadwen, 1749, Jamaica Inventories; Will of Mary Welsh, 1750, Jamaica Wills, XXVII. Hadwen owned nineteen slaves and held an estate valued at approximately £739 when she died in 1749. A large number of free women of color identified their occupations as seamstresses in a 1754 census of Spanish Town, and the girls might have joined their ranks later in life. See "Census of St Jago de la Vega [Spanish Town] undertaken by Charles White, gent, in July and August 1754," Feb. 19, 1754, SAS/RF 20/7, Jamaica Papers of Rose Fuller (1729–1763), Removal Acts, Deeds and Documents Relating to Lands Formerly Belonging to the Family of Fuller of Brightling, East Sussex Record Office (ESRO), Lewes, U.K. Chapter 3, above, explains the role played by seamstresses in greater detail. For a more comprehensive explanation of women's involvement in the textile trades, see Chapter 2, above.

tized in the Christian faith and learned to read in order to know her duty as a Christian." Martha's Christianity, and her possession of an English surname, either indicating that she had a free father or free godparents, burnished her legal independence by eradicating her African heritage.[34]

Yet female slaveholders did not necessarily act in isolation when they manumitted children. Their directives disclose the shadowy efforts of enslaved mothers as much as they do enslavers. Parlour's liberty came at a cost. Wilds observed that the girl's enslaved mother, Venus, would be "obliged to work" for the "maintenance and education" of her daughter until she turned twenty-one. Wilds also planned for the child to be placed under the "care" and "tuition" of a free woman — not her birth mother. If Venus managed to save twenty-one pounds, then she had the financial means to purchase her freedom and that of her daughter's. Perhaps the enslaver forced mother and child apart and then created an unrealistic goal for a desperate parent. Or maybe Wilds hoped to protect the girl from being abused or sold by placing Parlour in the care of another free woman when she died. In other English Caribbean colonies, owners presented captives with the money to purchase their own liberty as a means of establishing the legality of the transaction. Perhaps Wilds and Venus devised a similar strategy for the enslaved woman to buy her family's freedom when her daughter came of age, using Wilds's money to create the illusion of a financial exchange. Jamaica's laissez-faire policy toward manumissions made any of these options plausible. In the absence of strong institutional guidelines or governance, women like Wilds customized manumission plans that catered to their own and, sometimes their captives', interests.[35]

Women's manumission provisos were personalized, but they were not idiosyncratic. Female slaveholders who liberated young people manifested a desire to ensure their respectability and prosperity. They also acknowledged the vulnerabilities freed children stood to encounter in the absence of benefactors. Elizabeth Sharpe expressed a high degree of concern for the future of an enslaved girl, Ann Good, whom she intended to manumit. The widow lived in Kingston where she probably ran a mercantile enterprise, a boarding house, or a tavern with the help of nineteen slaves. Sharpe manumitted

34. Will of Elizabeth Wilds, 1747, Jamaica Wills, XXVI.

35. Ibid. Kit Candlin and Cassandra Pybus describe self-purchase, or claim that the purchase of a slave was made with the slave's own money, as a common manumission strategy in Barbados. Given the similarities between the two colonies, it is reasonable to assume that a similar practice existed in Jamaica. See Candlin and Pybus, *Enterprising Women*, 80–81.

Good immediately on her death "so that she may not come into the hands custody or possession of my executor or any other person whatsoever or be made subject to the payment of any legacies . . . funeral expenses or debts." The widow wanted Good to join the free community as a slaveholder, giving the girl an enslaved woman named Violet.[36]

Though Sharpe freed two other girls and allotted an annual annuity of seven pounds along with part of her apparel to each of them, she claimed a special connection to Good, reserving four of her "best gowns" and a quilt for the child—the kinds of gifts that women normally bequeathed to daughters or close female friends. Sharpe treated the girl like a surrogate family member. Nevertheless, as with Parlour and her mother, Venus, Good's manumission came at the expense of her own mother, whom Sharpe sold. Even as Sharpe's varied treatment of Good and her enslaved mother illustrate the callous cruelties enslavers inflicted on their captives, it is also plausible that Good's enslaved mother urged Sharpe to agree to a harrowing transaction that would secure a better future for her daughter. Perhaps the mother even negotiated her own sale in exchange for Ann's freedom, which she further supported by making her child a slaveholder. Although Venus's status as an enslaved woman deprived her of the right to raise her daughter, she could have still influenced her owner's decisions about Martha's future, even if it meant spending her life apart from her child.[37]

Another contemporary of Wilds and Sharpe, "spinster" Mary Carpenter, also planned to manumit enslaved sisters at the sacrifice of their mother. Carpenter owned ten slaves and freed two of them—girls named Betsy and Molly—in her 1740 will. Like Wilds, Carpenter carefully cultivated a genteel English Christian identity for the siblings, baptizing them and renaming them Elizabeth Brodgin and Mary Carpenter. Perhaps Elizabeth Brodgin née Betsy assumed the name of her free father at her christening. In giving Molly her own name, Carpenter established a familial connection to the girl. Carpenter also planned for the children to be educated. Molly's mother, an Indian woman named Diana, would remain enslaved until they completed their schooling. Carpenter directed Diana and another enslaved woman to work to pay for the girls' "maintenance and education." Carpenter placed a premium on their successful transition to the middling echelon of the free community. If the two enslaved women were unable to earn enough money to

36. Will of Elizabeth Sharpe, 1747, Jamaica Wills, XXVI; Inventory of Elizabeth Sharpe, 1747, Jamaica Inventories.

37. Will of Elizabeth Sharpe, 1747, Jamaica Wills, XXVI.

finance her plan, then Carpenter's estate would "keep them at school" until they turned fifteen, at which point Elizabeth and Mary would be "left at their own discretion and management" and, as their owner advised, "may therefore want friendly care instruction and admonition." She ordered the sisters to seek out her attorney for guidance "in what manner they had best dispose of themselves," and she urged them to be "obedient" in following the man's recommendations.[38]

Carpenter's manumission plans were not benign, nor were they entirely malevolent. On one hand, she possibly coerced the children into changing their names, thereby symbolically erasing a connection to their mother, Diana. She directly linked Diana's obedience with the promise of freedom, lauding the girls' mother for her "many good and faithful services," which "justly entitled her to some share of my esteem." This made Diana's future manumission conditional. It would only occur if the enslaved woman were to "behave herself with all due obedience and as a good and faithful slave ought to do." When Carpenter died, Diana's freedom would depend on whether the estate's executor discerned that she had displayed the characteristics of "a good and faithful slave."[39]

On the other hand, perhaps Diana, like the enslaved mother Venus, shaped her owner's designs for her daughters. It is plausible that Diana encouraged and fostered a connection between the girls and the woman who held them in captivity, understanding that such an alliance had the potential to result in better opportunities for them. By informally adopting one of Diana's daughters and educating and financially supporting both girls, Carpenter established a life trajectory for them that would have been impossible if they remained in bondage. If Diana nurtured these ties, the mother ensured a strong bond between her girls and a patroness who, though far from wealthy, still claimed the authority to direct their futures. When they came of age in the 1750s, Mary and Elizabeth would be free, educated, and capable of either attracting suitable husbands or living independently as members of the island's growing population of free and freed people of color.

In their preference for manumitting children, the actions of women like Wilds and Sharpe mirror those of male slaveholders, who favored young

38. Will of Mary Carpenter, 1740, Jamaica Wills, XXII; Inventory of Mary Carpenter, 1744, Jamaica Inventories.

39. Will of Mary Carpenter, 1740, Jamaica Wills, XXII. Carpenter gave her estate to Samuel Dicker, Mary Elbridge's son-in-law, revealing the close ties among free and freed people on the island.

people. Like men, women treated the manumission of a young person as a multistep process that often involved confirmation of the child's Christian identity through baptism, some formal schooling, and career experience in gender-specific skills. Men typically freed their biological children, though, whereas women like Wilds and Sharpe manumitted youths whom they were not related to by blood or marriage. Free and freed women rarely recognized children whom they bore with enslaved men in legal records. However, colonial society accepted the integration of freed children into women's extended families via manumissions. A slaveholder's gender, then, had a greater influence on manumission practices than emergent beliefs about racial difference. Locals deemed it appropriate for childless women to free certain young people and act as their patrons, guardians, godparents, or surrogate parents. Manumission provisos disclose a view of race and legal status as malleable dimensions of identity, especially for children, that could be recrafted through financial support, religious conversion, education, and socialization with members of the island's the free community.

Although familial interests and emotional attachments seemed to inspire slaveholders to free certain people, their actions had broader imperial consequences. By developing a more plastic definition of kinship through manumission provisos—one not restricted to blood and marriage nor limited to rigid racial categories—women slaveholders, in particular, helped to replenish a free minority that was decimated by disease and death. Though the community of free and freed people of African descent was minute in comparison with the slave population, they still acted as an essential stabilizing force that aided in securing Jamaica under British control.

TO "ENJOY PRIVILEGES THAT FREE NEGROS ENJOY"

Although manumission provisos in colonial wills were legally binding contracts, they provide evidence of intent, not action. A few sentences in a will did not necessarily guarantee freedom. Jamaica lacked a system for recording, enacting, and enforcing manumission bequests, which resulted in an erratic and poorly documented process. In the absence of regulations and institutional involvement, enslaved people were reliant on the mercurial goodwill of executors and surviving kin to comply with the instructions of deceased testators. Free relatives were loath to relinquish slaves, who comprised a valuable currency and source of labor, and beneficiaries often created roadblocks to thwart manumissions from being enacted. Furthermore, legal freedom in itself did not afford protection from poverty, degradation, and possible re-

TABLE 7: *Material Gifts in Women's Manumission Provisos, 1683–1771*

GIFTS	NUMBER	PERCENTAGE
Money	34	26
Land	11	8
Clothing / Moveables	7	5
Slaves	2	2
Education / Apprenticeship Fees	9	7
Tenancy / Maintenance	10	8

Source: Jamaica Wills, 1661–1771, III, IV, V–XXXVIII, Island Record Office, Spanish Town, Jamaica.

Note: In my survey of wills, 126 women left some form of material gifts as part of a manumission proviso. Hence, the percentages in this table are based on N=126.

enslavement. Former captives who lacked the necessary social connections to free people and the job skills to earn a living faced new depredations, including homelessness and starvation.

In the absence of a bureaucratic administration and established procedures, freedom was precarious. Recently manumitted people would need to perform their independence on multiple fronts and in various contexts, often for the remainder of their lives. This might explain why some islanders preferred to manumit children. Baptized, literate, professionally competent slaveholding youths possessed the constellation of material and immaterial markers that safeguarded their liberty. Rather than using freedom to casually discard elderly or injured laborers, many of the islanders who manumitted adults recognized their vulnerability and sought to ameliorate their conditions and fortify their claims to liberty, awarding them manumission packages that included land, money, and moveable goods as well as invaluable patronage ties with free society. Nearly half (61) of the 126 women who manumitted captives also bestowed on them gifts of wearing apparel, annual annuities, land, and education (Table 7). Slightly more than half (44) of the 76 men who freed slaves also supplied them with legacies. These manumission provisos aimed to transform former captives into credible and self-sufficient colonists.[40]

As well as furnishing financial support, some slaveholders expressed an interest in protecting the mobility as well as formal and informal property claims of freed people. In 1730, John Cossley wanted an enslaved man, Joe,

40. See Jamaica Wills, 1661–1771, I–XXXVIII.

together with three women whom he bequeathed to his son to have the liberty to "work for themselves in any place in this island where they please," warning his executors not to disturb their pursuits. The three people would "keep profits from their labors to themselves, for their support and maintenance" until his son reached the age of twenty-one, at which point they would be manumitted. In the event of his son's early death, Joe and the two women would immediately be "set free," and his estate would "never after" be allowed to claim them.[41]

When John Campbell drafted his will a decade later, he asked his wife to "set free" a woman, Marina, and her "mulatto child" and gave the woman an estimated three-pound annuity. It would be easy to assume that Campbell was the father of Marina's child, but his reference to her partner, Cuffee, who was either a free or enslaved man of African descent, suggests otherwise. After arranging to manumit Marina and her child, John further instructed his wife to free her "mulatto" maid, Nelly, "on condition she behave well and faithful to her Mrs." The planter also acted as a surrogate father for a "poor boy," described as "living in my family," whom he planned to send to Boston to be educated and "bound to a trade." When he made his will, Campbell carefully considered the needs of the enslaved and orphaned dependents in his household and sought to support them. Though the "poor boy," who was presumably white, would be sent to Boston, he would be bound as an apprentice, just like the children born to enslaved women. Marina and her child might scrape by on the parsimonious annuity he allotted to her, and his wife's servant also stood to be released from bondage. Although Campbell's actions were not necessarily generous, he presented these members of his household forms of support that were fine-tuned to their varying legal, social, and economic positions in colonial society. His patronage and financial provisions, in turn, would help all of them establish tenuous footholds in Jamaica's free community.[42]

Like Cossley and Campbell, female slaveholders exhibited a sharp awareness of the relationship between property ownership, legal status, and authority on the island. When they included bequests with manumission provisos, women turned people who were defined as assets into property holders. Their bequests emphasize the fragility of the positions occupied by former captives. Dolorosa Knight, who owned 132 slaves and managed a sizeable plantation, manumitted one person in her 1722 will, a woman named "Black

41. Will of John Cossley, 1730, Jamaica Wills, XVIII.

42. Will of John Campbell, 1740, Jamaica Wills, XXII.

Molly." She bequeathed her a five-pound stipend and a hog, along with the "liberty" to continue living on her plantation. Knight's insistence that "Black Molly" be allowed to reside on the estate "without molestation or abuse from any overseer or other person" exposes the freed woman's vulnerability. Priscilla Guy, a contemporary of Knight's, owned 20 slaves. She made similar arrangements for an "old negro man" named Peter to receive a house, one acre of land, and the "fruit trees growing thereon," together with the "liberty of running or grazing two mares in my pasture" and six pounds per annum. Peter would also assume legal ownership of an enslaved boy who might have been a son, a grandson, or just a young person whom Guy wanted to assist Peter in his old age.[43]

Molly and Peter were probably elderly when their enslavers made their wills. Freedom, a hog or a horse, a house, and a few pounds per year were hardly just recompense for a lifetime of hard labor. But such bequests contributed enough material support for freed people to subsist on the island. Annual annuities of four to six pounds, like the ones assigned to Molly and Peter were not insignificant. During the same time period, domestic servants in Britain earned between two and fifteen pounds per annum. The legacies bestowed by some owners to people whom they manumitted represented considerable portions of their own estates. For example, though Rachell Shergill (Shergot), a Port Royal widow, possessed an estate valued at a mere twenty pounds and survived with the help of one captive, she still presented her "former slave," a woman named Daphne "who I have set free by manumission," a piece of land in town, carefully detailing the dimensions of the thirty-eight-foot by thirty-nine-foot plot, "bounding on the house in the alley that did formerly belong to my husband." Aside from the slave, this piece of property was the most valuable asset the widow held. She passed it on to Daphne and her husband, Cudjoe, to live on for the remainder of their lives.[44]

43. Will of Dolorosa Knight, 1722, Jamaica Wills, XVI, fol. 2; Inventory of Dolorosa Knight, 1723, Jamaica Inventories; Will of Priscilla Guy, 1748, Jamaica Wills, XXVI; Inventory of Priscilla Guy, 1749, Jamaica Inventories. It was also common in Barbados for owners to make bequests of money and sometimes land or an education to slaves at the time of manumission. See Handler and Pohlmann, "Slave Manumissions and Freedmen in Seventeenth-Century Barbados," *WMQ*, 3d Ser., XLI (1984), 402–403.

44. Will of Rachell Shergill, 1751, Jamaica Wills, XXVIII; Inventory of Rachell Shergot [Shergrill], 1752, Jamaica Inventories (I assume that this is the same woman because she lived in Port Royal and died within one year of writing her will). As I explain in the Introduction, above, all Jamaican currency has been converted to British pounds sterling, including this comparison. See Clive Emsley, Tim Hitchcock and Robert Shoemaker, "London History—Currency, Coin-

Shergill's penury enhances the significance of her bequest to Daphne and Cudjoe. The bequest made by Kingston resident Mary Hallwood of a "piece of garden land with buildings on it . . . to hold for their common use" to five enslaved people whom she intended to manumit was, relative to Shergill's legacy, less substantial. Hallwood commanded an estate worth nearly three thousand pounds and owned thirty-five slaves; five people represented 14 percent of her total slaveholdings. The land that she transferred to them possibly formalized their informal claim to property they had already occupied for years. Though enslavement created extreme power differentials, it was still a negotiated relationship. These kinds of bequests disclose the pressures that captives placed on owners to recognize their customary rights to homes and provisioning grounds. This is likely why the widow Amy Pallmer left Scipio and his wife Diana three pounds per annum "in lieu of their plantation and pimento walk" when she manumitted them in 1751. Pallmer held the couple in bondage, but she still recognized a parcel of land on her estate as "their" property.[45]

A contemporary of Pallmer's, Mary Williams, made far more generous provisions for eight people whom she freed. Williams lived in a rural area and ran a medium-sized plantation with the labor of forty-one slaves. She did not accrue her fortune from planting. Rather, the woman's moneylending activities produced her considerable £6,000 fortune. Numerous people had outstanding debts with Williams when she died. The savvy financier set aside nearly 10 percent of her wealth to support select captives whom she deemed worthy of freedom, cash, and land to live on. Williams instructed her executors to buy the group of people "a piece of good land worth two hundred pounds and build thereon two houses for their immediate settlement." Additionally, Williams bequeathed each of them an annuity of £7 "towards their support and maintenance," which was to be paid from the interest earned on the substantial sum of £714 that she set aside for their use. Perhaps Williams hoped to establish and protect the independence of her former captives by providing them with land and money.[46]

As other manumission provisos show, freed people were never really dis-

---

age, and the Cost of Living," Historical Background, London and Its Hinterland, *Old Bailey Proceedings Online* (www.oldbaileyonline.org, version 7.0, Mar. 20, 2014).

45. Will of Mary Hallwood, 1761, Jamaica Wills, XXXII; Inventory of Mary Hallwood, 1761, Jamaica Inventories; Will of Amy Pallmer, 1751, Jamaica Wills, XXVIII.

46. Will of Mary Williams, 1753, Jamaica Wills, XIX; Inventory of Mary Williams, 1753, Jamaica Inventories.

tanced from slavery in Jamaica. Their liberty often sparked the purchase of other captives who had been recently transported from Africa, thereby increasing the colony's involvement in the slave trade. When James Crawford manumitted an enslaved woman Grace and their daughter, Janetta, he emphasized his desire for them to "enjoy privileges that free negros enjoy." Slave ownership was an essential "privilege" in Jamaica. That is why, along with giving Grace money to "bring up" Janetta, her father also conferred on his daughter a "negro girl Mary." Janetta and Mary would live together in captivity until Crawford died. Then, Janetta would take possession of the other child as a marker of her own "privilege" as a "free negro." Crawford, Grace, and Janette understood that slave ownership was one of the "primary mechanisms" for upward social mobility.[47]

By the early decades of the eighteenth century, colonists like Crawford defined freedom and slavery as mutually constitutive. From this point of view, slaveholding reinforced one's free status. Former captives who became enslavers gained material wealth while also validating their own liberty in contrast with a rapidly expanding enslaved population. Planter Henry Boon manumitted Pheba and Suky, giving them "their absolute freedom forever," in 1750. He also left money for them to support Suky's infant daughter, Sarah Ware, who was most likely his child, with four slaves and 120 acres of land at "Ginger's River" in Saint Andrew Parish. Although she did not assume the surname of the man who might have been her father, Sarah was likely baptized. By giving her land and enslaved laborers, Boon made Sarah a property owner who had the ability to support herself or attract a marital partner when she came of age.[48]

Some colonists transferred captives to people who were still being held in captivity themselves. John Sibbald, a carpenter in Kingston, allotted an enslaved woman, Venice, to a "negro woman slave named Joan," who was owned by another man. Perhaps lacking the funds to purchase Joan's freedom, Sibbald sought instead to support her by making her a slaveholder. On top of transferring Venice to Joan, he also gave her his household goods and twenty pounds and directed his friend to act as her protector. Sibbald issued a warning in his will to anyone, including her master, who "disturbed

47. Will of James Crawford, 1748, Jamaica Wills, XXVII. In Rio De Janeiro, Brazil—a place where thousands of Africans who were transshipped from Kingston ended up—free and freed people used slaves to emphasize their own independent status. See Sweet, *Domingos Álvares*, 89–91.

48. Will of Henry Boon, 1750, Jamaica Wills, XXVII.

or molested" her "enjoyment" of the money, goods, and the labor of the enslaved woman Venice. If this occurred, then Sibbald instructed his friend to take the property and protect it for Joan. Colonists like Crawford, Boon, and Sibbald invested in the Atlantic slave trade to support themselves, but they also formed a variety of relationships with enslaved Africans who, in turn, received material support, occasionally in the form of other captives, from their benefactors.[49]

Some owners even funded manumissions by selling other enslaved people in their households. In 1737, Magdalen Gason of Kingston made provisions to free a woman named Sarah and Sarah's six children. She willed Sarah a gift of six silver spoons—the kind of personal items that free grandmothers normally reserved for their grandchildren, revealing a strong emotional connection if not kinship tie. More significantly, Gason made provisions for the rest of her moveable goods and captives to be sold to discharge her debts; anything that remained would go to Sarah. By making Sarah her primary heir, Gason treated the enslaved woman like a close relative. Colonists normally bequeathed their estates to spouses and children, not slaves. In what was a familiar transaction by the 1730s, Sarah and her family benefited from the sale of other enslaved people. The proceeds would then fund their own dramatic conversion from bondage to liberty and property ownership.[50]

African ancestry and the experience of enslavement did not necessarily turn freed people into antislavery advocates. On the contrary, former captives who were either born in Africa or had African parents imbued slaveholding with their own meanings, whereas island-born freed people viewed slavery as a fundamental facet of colonial life. Indeed, slave ownership was an even more critical marker for those who experienced deprivations as a result of their African ancestry. Freed people lived in a colony where legal status was increasingly conflated with racial complexion. With only the most fragile of legal protections—one line in a will or a baptism record—to assert their own liberty, former captives used slaveholding as one of the chief means of signifying their own legal independence to Jamaica's free community.[51]

49. Will of John Sibbald, 1740, Jamaica Wills, XXII.

50. Will of Magdalen Gason, 1737, Jamaica Wills, XXI. Chapter 4, above, provides an in-depth study of the kinds of personal items women normally offered to female heirs, who were typically kin or intimate friends.

51. Using the petitions made by free people of color living in early nineteenth-century Barbados, Candlin and Pybus describe slaveholding as a "preoccupation for many people of color" that was more important to them than the right to vote. Former slaves living in eighteenth-

The dual-step process of manumitting certain captives and then transferring specific slaves to them also presented a strategy for keeping families intact. As the legal owners of kin, relatives protected them from separation and sale. For example, Goody Jacobson, a butcher and "free negro" from Port Royal, set aside thirty-five pounds in "pursuance of my bill of sale" to purchase the freedom of his daughter Judy in 1724 and left her a ten-pound legacy. Jacobson was also the legal owner of his sons-in-law. He commanded them to be freed immediately after his decease and consigned a steer and a cow to each heir. Participating in the slave system afforded families like the Jacobsons with a smokescreen. As the legal owner of his sons-in-law, Jacobson had the power to support and safeguard them while he was alive and then assert his right to manumit them on his death.[52]

Cecelia Mayo, a "free black woman" who also lived in Kingston, devised a similar plan in 1745 when she manumitted her slave Sarah and "gave" Sarah's sons to her as slaves to "serve" their mother during her lifetime. When Sarah died, her sons would be released from bondage. Mayo was not a wealthy woman. The enslaved woman Sarah comprised her most valuable asset. On manumitting her, Mayo entrusted Sarah's family a piece of land. Like Jacobson, Mayo was only one step removed from slavery herself, and some of her family members were still enslaved. Mayo set aside the other half of her estate for the man who owned her sister, Phoeba, whom she described as a "negro woman." Mayo instructed the owner to allow Phoeba's use of the property during her lifetime. It would then pass on to Sarah and her sons. Mayo also furnished her enslaved sister with wearing apparel and jewelry. Once freed, Sarah's family stood to inherit the "rest and residue" of her estate. These kinds of bequests indicate that Sarah was either a close friend or a relative of Mayo's. It is possible that Mayo, like Jacobson, held Sarah in bondage to protect her. The two women, appearing as mistress and slave, then reproduced the strategy by turning Sarah into the legal owner of her own sons.[53]

Jacobson and Mayo were among the island's first few generations of free and freed people of African descent to establish families after the English conquest. They used manumissions to carefully construct and extend their networks of free kin, friends, and patrons who, in turn, furnished their families with social and material support. Sarah Sparks, a free woman of African

---

century Jamaica had just as much, if not more, reason to use slaveholding as means of protecting their freedom. See Candlin and Pybus, *Enterprising Women*, 40.

52. Will of Goody Jacobson, 1724, Jamaica Wills, XVI.

53. Will of Cecelia Mayo, 1745, Jamaica Wills, XXV.

descent, took all of these steps when she made her will in 1743. She had a son, Robert Sparks, who was still held in bondage by a "Captain Barnett." Sparks was also a slaveowner. She left instructions to purchase her son's "liberty and freedom" and reserved seven pounds for "his commencement of a livelihood," seeking to bolster Robert's independence with an apprenticeship. Sparks also had another son and two daughters who were already free. Aside from her wearing apparel and twenty shillings each, she barred her daughters from making any other demands on her estate, which she left to her sons.[54]

Sparks was not a wealthy woman. The majority of her estate's value was composed of five slaves—one man and four women—whom she owned. When she died, her sons would assume possession of these people. The Sparks family, with its overlapping connections to free, freed, and enslaved kin, was increasingly typical of the kinds of kinship groups that comprised Jamaica's free population. Oblique references like the one made by Sparks to her enslaved son reveal families who were in the process of slowly pulling themselves out of slavery, one member at a time. Yet, as Sparks's will and inventory indicate, the foundations of freedom for families like hers was built on slaveholding. Sparks supported herself with the labor of the five people whom she held in bondage. She also used her status as a slaveholder to distance her family from a past marked by slavery.[55]

Sparks's complex status as a slaveholding woman of African descent whose own children were still enslaved was produced by Jamaica's culture of slavery. She lived in an era when racial categories were still in formation. Though her complexion possibly belied her connection to past enslavement, it did not solely determine her position on the island. Manumission provisos expose the amorphous character of liberty in Jamaica. The legal document in itself was not enough to establish the credibility of a person's independence. Sparks, other freed people, and the slaveholders who manumitted captives all defined freedom as a performative and sometimes mercurial state of being that demanded continual signification. To adequately distance herself from captivity, a person like Sparks needed to acquire a host of characteristics that legitimated her free status. In a colony that depended on slavery, slaveholding became one of the chief attributes denoting a person's liberty.

Jamaica's free population used manumission as a powerful tool for maintaining stability on the island. Locals coped with the ravages that disease, the

54. Will of Sarah Sparks, 1743, Jamaica Wills, XXIV.

55. Inventory of Sarah Sparks, 1744, Jamaica Inventories.

prolonged absences of relatives from the colony, slave insurgencies, and imperial warfare wrought on their families by enlarging their kinship groups. Selectively manumitting enslaved people bolstered the meager numbers of depleted communities, enabling free families to better maintain continuity across generations. Colonial manumission committed formerly enslaved people to slaveholding, further strengthening control over Jamaica's captive population. Manumissions, however, were more than just simple strategies for extending slaveholder power. The practice implicitly undermined the legal system that was designed to enforce the status of enslaved people as property. Manumission provisos indicate that free people did not perceive of captives as fundamentally distinctive beings from themselves, either because of their legal status or their race. Slaveholders' actions disclose an understanding of enslavement as a mutable status—one that they, as individuals, not colonial or imperial authorities—claimed the power to alter.

Just as colonists recognized children who were born out of wedlock as legitimate kin, they used manumission provisos for similar purposes, to confirm and consecrate their intimate connections with enslaved people. Through practices like baptism and manumission, islanders constructed increasingly complicated families that included free and freed members and sometimes people who were still enslaved. Cumulatively, the actions of individual colonists to manumit, baptize, financially support, and educate the formerly enslaved created a growing community of free and freed African-descended people on the island. Between the 1730s and the 1770s, the population of free people of color nearly quadrupled, rising from 1,010 to 4,093, and people of African descent came to comprise more than one-third of the free population.

Female slaveholders played crucial roles in shaping these colonial developments. The absence of laws or institutions governing manumission turned it into another gender-neutral legal act that amplified the power of the individual slaveholder irrespective of sex. Though they were on average less wealthy than men, women exhibited an equal interest in freeing people and incorporating certain individuals into their extended kinship groups. However, unlike men, who typically manumitted biological offspring, women preferred to release other adult women and children, whom they treated as relatives. In doing so, female slaveholders made more radical alterations to the colonial family than their male counterparts, adding members who were not related to them by blood.[56]

56. Trevor Burnard, *Planters, Merchants, and Slaves: Plantation Societies in British America, 1650–1820* (Chicago, 2015), 172–173.

The largely unregulated nature of manumission in Jamaica made it a customizable, multivalent, and sometimes contradictory practice that had the potential to stabilize the free population by adding a vital stream of new members while also disrupting slave codes that sought to commodify and racialize people. On one level, manumission provisos, like baptisms, enacted slaveholder command. On another level, the instructions manifest a mediation of power and disclose the actions of enslaved people themselves. Though colonial laws placed all authority in the hands of slaveholders, the realities of daily life, especially in families headed by poor and middling women, also influenced the dynamics between owners and captives, who were as pragmatic and self-interested as their enslavers. Nurturing close ties with slaveholders was a judicious survival strategy. Tactical relationships were a less dangerous and often more effective path to independence; running away or openly challenging a free person triggered brutal physical punishments, transportation, and even death. People who established trust with their captors stood to earn material rewards, greater independence, and lighter workloads. The most fortunate among this group were liberated and awarded money, land, and captives of their own. Freed people then benefited from the ties that they formed with former owners or other members of free society, who served as valuable patrons and protectors. Manumission directives disclose the formation of a slave system that was upheld and, on occasion, undermined, by thousands of daily interactions, negotiations, and concessions. These quotidian acts—more so than Jamaica's slave codes, the spectacular displays of violence and brutality on the island, or imperial directives—entrenched slavery in the Anglo-Atlantic world while also creating loopholes for a select few to escape bondage.

Conclusion

During the first half of the eighteenth century, free and freed women helped to place Jamaica at the center of Britain's commercial empire. Female islanders displayed pragmatism, entrepreneurialism, and creativity in their business dealings, their legal tactics, and their family arrangements. The different strands of their lives were complicated, their motives diverse, and their morals ambiguous. Driven by the need to survive and to provide for future generations, women invested deeply in Atlantic slavery—and some profited substantially from their participation. In an era when women's life possibilities were typically restricted, slaveholding enabled those living in the Caribbean to achieve greater prosperity and more independence than was possible elsewhere in the Anglo-Atlantic world.

Mary Rose, a free woman of Euro-African descent who lived in Spanish Town, best embodies the economic and social trends charted in this book. On the one hand, she exemplifies the gendered, racialized, and sexualized inequities that suffused slave societies like Jamaica. On the other hand, to focus solely on the disempowering and oppressive dimensions of her life would not do justice to her accomplishments as a successful and politically connected entrepreneur who exhibited literary panache and cosmopolitan taste. Her letters offer a glimpse into the bustling world of the interconnected cities that sprang up throughout the Atlantic world, offering new economic opportunities for free and freed women. She is representative of this group of middling and elite European, Euro-African, and African-descended women who became prominent members of their communities throughout the circum-Caribbean basin.[1]

1. Chapter 5, above, offers a more detailed study of intimate relationships between people of African and European descent. It also provides an exhaustive study of illegitimacy rates in

In colonies that revolved around money, property, slaveholding, and social networking, it was possible for free and freed women with African ancestry like Mary Rose to distance themselves from slavery, grow wealthy, and become slaveowners themselves. A savvy businesswoman, Mary Rose rented out a large house in Spanish Town to island luminaries and also operated a profitable livestock business on the outskirts of town with the support of enslaved ranch hands. She earned more than eight hundred pounds a year (worth approximately one hundred ten thousand pounds in today's economy). Her business ventures, which melded urban and agrarian pursuits, connect Mary Rose to the women whose varied economic activities are detailed in the first half of this book. But she is singular in one respect—she is only one of a handful of people of African descent whose own words have survived in the archive in the form of eloquently sharp missives to her long-term partner, Rose Fuller, a rich and politically powerful white man who would become a member of Parliament.[2]

Baptized in 1700, Mary Rose was the child of Elizabeth Johnston, derisively labeled as a "negro wench" in the Spanish Town parish register, and an unknown white man. Though Mary's father's presence at her baptism was not recorded, he was probably one of the few white men with the surname Johnston who lived in Spanish Town at the time of Mary's birth. Elizabeth Johnston's origins are uncertain. She might have been born in Africa and forcibly transported to Jamaica, living for years in captivity before she achieved legal freedom with the help of her child's white father. Or maybe her

---

Jamaica. Mary Rose's letters, which display a mastery of eighteenth-century epistolary conventions, were preserved as part of the Jamaica Correspondence of Rose Fuller and Stephen Fuller, 1747–1775, SAS/RF 21, Deeds and Documents Relating to Lands Formerly Belonging to the Family of Fuller of Brightling, East Sussex Record Office (ESRO), Lewes, U.K.

2. George Alpress to Rose Fuller, May 26, 1759, Jamaica Correspondence of Rose Fuller and Stephen Fuller, SAS/RF 21/240; Measuring Worth, www.measuringworth.com. According to Alpress, Fuller's estate manager, Mary Rose grossed £134 from renting out Fuller's "great house" in town, and her revenue from livestock totaled roughly £714. Dominique Rogers and Stewart King make a similar point about free and freed women of Euro-African and African descent gaining entrée to the marketplace in Jamaica's counterpart, Saint Domingue. They argue that money rather than gender facilitated their participation. Their research, together with my findings about urban Jamaica, suggests that gender and race did not necessarily constrain women's commercial activities in the colonies. See Rogers and King, "'Housekeepers, Merchants, Rentièrs': Free Women of Color in the Port Cities of Colonial Saint-Domingue, 1750–1790," in Douglas Catterall and Jodi Campbell, eds., *Women in Port: Gendering Communities, Economies, and Social Networks in Atlantic Port Cities, 1500–1800* (Leiden, 2012), 372.

parents were local descendants of African slaves who had been manumitted by Spanish colonists years earlier. Perhaps she received the name Elizabeth Johnston at her christening as a means of signaling her independent status and connection to the island's white Christian community. After all, colonists used baptism to achieve all of these objectives. Whatever her background, Johnston's decision to baptize her daughter distanced the family from slavery and strengthened its ties to the island's free community, which formed a minority on the island.[3]

Following in her mother's footsteps, Mary Rose took measures to further disassociate herself from her African heritage, forming attachments to white men. Two of these relationships produced sons, Thomas Wynter and William Fuller. In the colonial context, there was nothing unusual about her establishing a family outside of wedlock. As we have seen, during the first decades of the eighteenth century, unmarried couples and their illegitimate children had come to form a considerable portion of free society. Mary Rose's effort to "whiten" her family, however, exposes the gendered and racialized restrictions she labored under. When Mary Rose was growing up, the Maroon War exacerbated racial tensions in the colony, turning race into a shorthand for a person's loyalty to the colony and, more broadly, the British Empire. For women of color who operated under growing constraints, partnerships with white men generated invaluable kinship and patronage ties for themselves and their children. Although the vast majority of the island's inhabitants joined an ever-growing enslaved population, a small but rising number of free African and Euro-African colonists who were either born to free parents, baptized and considered to be free, or manumitted entered the lower, middling, and even elite ranks of colonial society. Women of African descent who forged intimate ties with free partners were primarily responsible for this development.[4]

3. Baptism of Mary Elizabeth Johnston, July 5, 1700, Saint Catherine Parish Register, fol. 43, I, Jamaica Copy Registers, 1669–1761, Island Record Office (IRO), Spanish Town, Jamaica. Five men with the surname Johnston or Johnstone made wills between 1717 and 1740 and could have been Mary's father. See Madeleine E. Mitchell, *Alphabetical Index to Early Will of Jamaica, West Indies, 1655–1815* (self-published, 2000).

4. Linda L. Sturtz observes that Mary Rose served as her mother's administrator when she died in 1753, indicating that the two remained close. See Sturtz, "Mary Rose: 'White' African Jamaican Woman? Race and Gender in Eighteenth-Century Jamaica," in Judith A. Byfield, LaRay Denzer, and Anthea Morrison, eds., *Gendering the African Diaspora: Women, Culture, and Historical Change in the Caribbean and Nigerian Hinterland* (Bloomington, Ind., 2010), 81n. Edward Winter Nedham might have been the father of Mary Rose's son Thomas Wynter.

In an environment of intensifying enmity, Mary Rose sought to improve her family's position and protect their legal status, which also meant assuming a veneer of whiteness. Both of her children received their father's surname. Mary Rose also joined a handful of Euro-African people who petitioned the colonial and imperial governments to secure the rights held by white colonists in eighteenth-century Jamaica. Her petition was successful, and, in 1746, the crown granted her family "the same rights and privileges with English subjects born of white parents."[5] Mary Rose further emphasized her elite "white" status by adopting her long-term partner Rose Fuller's

He died in Saint Catherine, the parish where she lived, in 1722. His brother William Nedham is another candidate. Several "mulatto" children with the surname Wynter also appear alone without parents in the Saint Catherine parish register, indicating that the Wynter men were fathering multiple children with enslaved or freed women of African descent. Edward Winter Nedham freed an enslaved woman named Lucretia Greenwhich in his will, and these children might have been hers. See Will of Edward Winter Nedham, 1722, Jamaica Wills, 1661–1771, XVI, IRO; Inventory of William Needham, 1772, Jamaica Inventories, 1674–1784, Jamaica Archives (JA), Spanish Town, Jamaica; and Saint Catherine Parish Register, Jamaica Copy Registers.

5. Francis Fane to Lords of Trade and Plantations, "An Act to Entitle Mary Johnstone Rose of the Parish of St. Catherine in the Said Island a Free Mulatto Woman and Her Two Sons Thomas Wynter and William Fuller Begotten of White Fathers to the Same Rights and Privileges with English Subjects Born of White Parents," [1744 and 1745], CO 137/24, fol. 165, The National Archives (TNA), Kew, King in Council approves act, 1746, CO 137/24, fol. 187. During the early decades of the eighteenth century, freed men of African descent were barred from serving in the legislature, testifying in court against white people, and voting. They also could not work as supervisors on plantations. These restrictions, which targeted men, did not necessarily affect women, who were barred from public office based on their gender. However, the legislation contributed to a culture of discrimination against free and freed people with African ancestry. Nevertheless, the Jamaican Assembly did allow free people of color to apply for the privileged rights of "white subjects" (not including political rights). See Daniel Livesay, *Children of Uncertain Fortune: Mixed-Race Jamaicans in Britain and the Atlantic Family, 1733–1833* (Williamsburg, Va., and Chapel Hill, N.C., 2018), 36–43; and Gad Heuman, "The Free Coloreds in Jamaican Society," in Heuman and James Walvin, eds., *The Slavery Reader* (New York, 2003), 655–656. As we saw in Chapter 5, above, it was common practice for unmarried couples to give their children their father's surname. In addition to bearing Fuller's surname, Mary Rose also mentioned his emotional and financial support of her son, informing him, "my Son, through your friendship and interest goes on in life very well." Unlike other fathers of illegitimate children on the island, Fuller did not acknowledge Thomas Fuller as his son in his will. Thus, Thomas could make no claims as his heir. It seems as though Fuller supported Thomas in a more informal capacity, as he did Mary. See Mary Rose to Rose Fuller, Mar. 21, 1759, Jamaica Correspondence of Rose Fuller and Stephen Fuller, SAS/RF 21/232.

first name as her surname. As Mary Rose née Johnston undoubtedly knew, Rose was also the maiden name of Fuller's mother, Elizabeth Rose. Assuming the name connected her to one of the island's original planter and slave trading families, and it is even possible that the Rose family profited from a slave ship that transported Mary Rose's ancestors to Jamaica in the late seventeenth century. Mary Rose née Johnston therefore tied herself to a colonial family that had transformed its investments in the Atlantic slave trade and the sugar industry into imperial power.[6]

Colonists accommodated and recognized a broad range of intimate relationships, including the one between Mary Rose and Rose Fuller, as legitimate, thereby furthering the life possibilities for a varied group of women, including those whose parents were unwed or even enslaved. Mary Rose adeptly and shrewdly used the tools offered by Jamaica's slave society to better her standing. She established a stable, lifelong, sometimes marriage-

6. Rose Fuller's mother, Elizabeth Rose, and her sister Ann both inherited property on Jamaica from their father. Elizabeth received Knollis Plantation in Saint Thomas in the Vale, along with property in Spanish Town and agricultural land in Saint Catherine. On marrying, however, the two sisters diverged in the way they handled their ownership of their respective property. Whereas Anne conveyed her land to her husband, Elizabeth maintained control over her portion. Like many women with a Jamaican heritage, she placed these estates in a trust for "her own disposal" and "benefit" during her marriage to John Fuller. Though Elizabeth relocated to England with her husband, she emphasized her Caribbean genealogy by naming her son Rose. When he came of age, Rose Fuller would travel to the tropics to manage his mother's, not his father's, property there. His relationship with Mary Rose would enmesh her family and her livelihood in the Fuller business ventures. See Indenture between Thomas Isted and His Wife Anne, and John Robinson and John Ekins, no. 1423, National Library of Jamaica (NLJ), Kingston, Indenture between Elizabeth Rose, John Fuller, and John Southcott, no. 1133. Fuller's mother had been one of the daughters of Fulke Rose, a physician whose involvement in the slave trade and sugar planting produced the family fortune. Fuller's family was also associated with Sir Hans Sloane, a member of the Royal Society who authored the first exhaustive study of Jamaica. When Sloane visited the island, he befriended Rose Fuller's grandfather, Fulke Rose, a fellow physician, and quickly married his widow when Rose died, assuming control of the fortune Fulke had amassed from the slave trade and sugar planting. Fulke Rose left his wife, Elizabeth, one-third of the family estate for life and two thousand pounds in addition to plate, jewels, and furniture. See Will of Fulke Rose, June 17, 1691, Abstracts of Jamaica Wills, 1625–1792, Add MS 34181, British Library, London; and Indenture between Philipa Rose, and Hans Sloane, Doctor in Physick and Elizabeth His Wife, Late Wife of Fulke Rose, Mother of Philippa, and Executors of Will and Testament of John Heathcote, London, no. 1233, NLJ. See also James Delbourgo, "Slavery in the Cabinet of Curiosities: Hans Sloane's Atlantic World," *British Museum,* 2007, https://www.britishmuseum.org/PDF/Delbourgo%20essay.pdf.

like partnership with Fuller that was mutually beneficial. The two met when Fuller moved to Spanish Town in 1735 to oversee his mother's Jamaica estate. As this book has shown, women of Euro-African and African descent wielded their own forms of social and financial influence, and Mary Rose's local connections undoubtedly helped Fuller launch his political career in Jamaica. Fuller quickly scaled the ranks of the local political echelon, serving in the Jamaica Assembly, on the Council, and as a judge of the Supreme Court. His contentious dealings with Governor Edward Trelawny drove him back to England permanently in 1755. Fuller parlayed his political experiences in the colony into metropolitan power. A year after returning to England, he was a member of Parliament.[7]

After Fuller's departure, he and Mary Rose exchanged letters and gifts that maintained their connection across the Atlantic. Fuller regularly sent her an assortment of European luxuries at her request, including tea, silken shoes in a rainbow of colors, and a "woman's white beaver hat." These items attested to her taste and awareness of metropolitan fashions. Like any person of higher social status on the island, Mary Rose did not walk. She owned a horse and drove through town in a kittereen, or a small two-wheeled coach, lived in comfortable home, dressed in European clothing, and hobnobbed with elite houseguests. She reciprocated Fuller's affection, shipping him tropical delicacies like tamarinds and "six pots of sweetmeats," which she affectionately wrote in an accompanying letter "will serve to remind you that you have left here a person who always thinks of you."[8]

When Fuller moved to England, he placed Mary Rose in charge of renting out his "great house" in Spanish Town to illustrious guests. There she hosted the most prominent local politicians, including members of the Jamaica Assembly and court officials. Even the governor stayed at one of Fuller's properties, which Mary Rose prepared for him. The personalized nature of the early modern economy created opportunities for women like Mary Rose to play important roles in family-run commercial endeavors, and her letters manifest this intersection of personal and financial concerns—a theme that has surfaced throughout the book. Mary Rose framed her connection to Fuller

7. John Brooke, "Fuller, Rose (?1708–77), of Rose Hill, Suss.," History of Parliament, http://www.historyofparliamentonline.org/volume/1754-1790/member/fuller-rose-1708-77.

8. Mary Rose to [Rose Fuller], May 4, 1756, Jamaica Correspondence of Rose Fuller and Stephen Fuller, SAS/RF 21/44. For a description of Mary Rose's public presentation, see also Sturtz, "Mary Rose," in Byfield, Denzer, and Morrison, eds., *Gendering the African Diaspora*, 79.

in terms of intimacy, believing their close relationship "entitled" her to his ongoing "friendship." When she reminded him of "the service I did for you while you were here besides the intimacy between us," she was not just alluding to sexual companionship. Both the terms "intimacy" and "service" operated on multiple registers. From her perspective, "service" included her professional work for Fuller as his estate manager, and she described her "intimacy" with him as one of close friendship, writing, "You told me all your friends would be mine and yet I find the first frown comes from yourself of consequence I must shortly expect the frowns of the whole World."[9]

Fuller's actions paralleled Mary Rose's perception of their rapport. By entrusting her to administer his colonial property, Fuller ensured her a comfortable income and recognized their bond. His payment of an annual stipend in return for her managerial work mirrored the kinds of arrangements husbands commonly made with wives to oversee estates after they died. Fuller also gave her a dwelling house in Spanish Town and several enslaved people, underscoring the colonial practice of using real and movable property, and slaves in particular, to strengthen close ties. Additionally, Fuller provided her with livestock for a ranching business that she operated on his pen land called the Grange. This gift would become the center of a bitter contest between Mary Rose and one of Fuller's estate managers, George Alpress, that revealed the limits of her influence. Although it is unclear if Alpress resented Mary Rose's wealth, local connections, and relationship with a rich patron or whether he simply cared about maximizing the profits of the Fuller estate, his complaints to Fuller about her monopolization of the Grange for her own advantage were direct: "You have not made a shilling from yor pens, two-thirds of the stock on the Grange Pen claime by Mary Rose and you slaves." Alpress both recognized and contested the authority Mary Rose claimed, writing in one letter that "she had a power for what she did." This seemingly mundane disagreement about access to pastureland captures the gendered, racialized, and sexualized tensions that suffused slave societies like Jamaica. Though free and freed women commanded social stature, the conflict between Alpress and Mary Rose offers a final example of the ways masculine prerogatives were at odds with newer modes of ordering society based on individual property rights and localized customs such as baptisms and manumissions.[10]

9. Mary Rose to Rose Fuller, Aug. 27, 1759, Jamaica Correspondence of Rose Fuller and Stephen Fuller, SAS/RF 21/265, Mary Rose to Rose Fuller, May 27, 1759, SAS/RF 21/241.

10. George Alpress to Rose Fuller, Mar. 14, 1757, Jamaica Correspondence of Rose Fuller and Stephen Fuller, SAS/RF 21/97, Alpress to Fuller, May 26, 1759, SAS/RF 21/240. The line in

Though Alpress made no mention of Mary Rose's race in his letters, his concern about the behavior of enslaved people who seemed, from his perspective, to assert an unwarranted degree of independence, might have also influenced his struggle with her and the captive ranch hands whom she commanded. When he wrote to Fuller in 1758, Alpress depicted a chaotic and unruly slave society where "no less than 18 negroes riding mares, in spanish town every night of their lives" boldly challenged colonial rule. The slaves who raced through town astride horses overturned a social order wherein the privilege of horseback riding was typically associated with middling or elite status—enslaved people were supposed to walk barefoot. Though he did not make the connection explicit, the enslaved people whom Alpress portrayed were exactly the kind of captives Mary Rose employed at her ranch: expert horseman who enjoyed a high degree of independence. Alpress's letters therefore implicitly implicated Rose and women like her in the construction of a tumultuous society, one wherein female slaveholders and their captives covertly and overtly defied white male power.[11]

Of course, this is not how Mary Rose perceived the situation. Hoping to stave off action from across the Atlantic, she deployed her superior literary skill to flatter, cajole, and convince Fuller to take her side in the dispute over her ranching activities. In a tone reminiscent of correspondence composed by other women such as Sarah Shanks and Mary Elbridge, Rose modulated between feminine submissiveness and business-like assertions, pertly reminding Fuller that the new "instructions" instigated by Alpress "entirely disagree with those you left behind" while also playing on her womanly weakness, referring to "the promises you have made and the assurances you have constantly given me that you would always take care of me and render the remainder of my days easy and happy to me." When delicacy failed, her letters grew more forceful. She was "greatly chagrined," she wrote, to learn that Fuller had followed Alpress's advice to block her access to the Grange and candidly asked him to "recant" his orders.[12]

Like most of the women studied in this book, Mary Rose relied on the labor of enslaved captives to run her business ventures, yet she did not legally

---

Alpress's letter about Mary Roses's "power" suggests that Fuller had given Mary Rose power of attorney over the property.

11. George Alpress to Rose Fuller, June 19, 1758, Jamaica Correspondence of Rose Fuller and Stephen Fuller, SAS/RF 21/189.

12. Mary Rose to Rose Fuller, Aug. 27, 1759, Jamaica Correspondence of Rose Fuller and Stephen Fuller, SAS/RF 21/265.

own these people—Fuller did. Thwarting access to the Grange also threatened her position as a slaveholder—a key signifier of her free and elite status. Mary Rose adamantly insisted that Fuller's actions "contradicted the positive instructions given under your own hand as to the allowance of the negroes you left me, and the pasturage of my cattle." As she knew, her ability to support her enslaved ranch hands depended on Fuller's permission and his funding. Given the centrality of slaveholding to free society, she must have experienced a minor crisis when one of Fuller's employees reported that he had "removed the negroes stock from the grange as per RFs [Rose Fuller's] orders." In an effort to maintain her control of the captives, she diminished their value, describing seven of them as "children of no use to any body as yet and the mothers but of very little"—not the sort of emboldened adults whom Alpress described riding through town every night. Her effort to keep her livestock and her enslaved employees on the Grange ultimately failed. By 1760, Fuller's attorneys reported that they had "ord'd off all the goats from this and Roses pen and all strange stock of every kind" that belonged to her.[13]

Mary Rose might have lost the battle, but she did not necessarily lose the war. Fuller had spent roughly twenty years during the prime of his life with her. Although he never acknowledged Mary Rose as his wife or their son as his heir, Fuller remained a bachelor for the rest of his days. Fuller's ongoing correspondence with her, and his decision not to marry, suggest that she was a significant woman to him. An island intimacy, perhaps, ultimately prevailed. When he died, Fuller bequeathed her his great house in Spanish Town, which she had desired for a long time. He also left arrangements for her to obtain the manumissions of two enslaved girls, Fanny and Molly, from his family.[14]

Though slaveholding bolstered Mary Rose's wealth and status, she treated slavery as a flexible status that could be modified through individual acts such as baptisms and manumissions. In 1756, she used her influence with Fuller to release Fanny and Molly, legally owned by Fuller's aunt Anne Isted, from bondage. Gently reminding him of his "promise" to obtain the "freedoms of Fanny and Molly the two children you desir'd me to take care of," Mary Rose

13. John Lee to Rose Fuller, Dec. 11, 1757, Jamaica Correspondence of Rose Fuller and Stephen Fuller, SAS/RF 21/165, Zachary Bayly and Peter Kay to Rose Fuller, Mar. 17, 1760 SAS/RF 21/286.

14. Mary Rose to Rose Fuller, Mar. 21, 1759, Jamaica Correspondence of Rose Fuller and Stephen Fuller, SAS/RF 21/232.

implored Fuller to ask his aunt to sign the manumission deeds. On another occasion, she further importuned him, "I must beg of you not to forget mentioning it to her." In this case, Mary Rose's sway with Fuller succeeded. Isted wrote to Fuller promising to sign the deeds liberating Fanny and Molly from slavery as a "small token" of her "gratitude" toward her nephew.[15]

Mary Rose might have assumed the appearance of a white woman in colonial records, but her interest in the fates of Fanny and Molly also discloses her intimate ties to people in Spanish Town who were still enslaved as well as her desire to free a few of them from captivity. Her overlapping allegiances to the free and enslaved communities and her own shifting racial categorization mark Mary Rose as one of the liminal figures who made up free societies throughout the Atlantic world. By the middle of the eighteenth century, African and African-descended women fluidly navigated between enslaved and free communities and creatively combined African and European knowledge and skills. Their ambiguous racial identity and nebulous relationships with enslaved people undermined institutional efforts to demarcate racial boundaries and control African captives. Indeed, in Jamaica, the inconsistent usage of unclear racial categories, the local policies of religious and sexual tolerance, and the considerable presence of African peoples made it difficult to track and pigeonhole locals.[16]

Through their personal and financial dealings, islanders forged dense social networks that incorporated free, freed, and enslaved people. Yet there were also limitations to the authority women derived from sexual and emotional ties with men and financial gain, limitations Mary Rose painfully experienced in the loss of her livestock venture. Her words convey both the command and the weakness of female islanders who possessed money, social connections, and slaves but lived in a world that excluded them from male-dominated networks of power. In one letter, she directly attacked Fuller's wealth and privilege, writing, "Your circumstances are full as good as when

15. Mary Rose to [Rose Fuller], May 4, 1756, Jamaica Correspondence of Rose Fuller and Stephen Fuller, SAS/RF 21/44, Ann Isted to Rose Fuller, Oct. 3, 1756, SAS/RF 21/60.

16. Wendy Wilson-Fall describes the *signares* of Senegal and *zany malatta* of Madagascar as powerful slave traders who forged alliances between local communities and Europeans. See Wilson-Fall, "Women Merchants and Slave Depots: Saint-Louis, Senegal, and St. Mary's, Madagascar," in Ana Lucia Araujo, ed., *Paths of the Atlantic Slave Trade: Interactions, Identities, and Images* (Amherst, N.Y., 2011) 278–279. Similarly, Rogers and King demonstrate that women of color owned substantial property, worked in a range of occupations, and amassed considerable fortunes in Saint Domingue. See Rogers and King, "Housekeepers, Merchants, Rentières," in Catterall and Campbell, eds., *Women in Port*, 357–397.

you left me, and the little indulgences which cost you but a very triffle was of infinite service to me." Female slaveholders like Mary Rose might have surpassed their counterparts who lived in societies without slaves, but their material and social advances did not translate into political and institutional power. Quite simply, Fuller could use his colonial gains—both material and political—to become a member of Parliament and hold the reigns of empire in his hands; Mary Rose could never aspire to reach such dizzying heights.

By the middle of the eighteenth century, the colonial world Mary Rose inhabited was fully developed. The end of the Seven Years' War in 1763 marked Britain's dominance of the global stage and a shift in its imperial ambitions. Yet the 1760s were also a period of turmoil in Jamaica. In 1760—the very year Fuller ordered the removal of Mary Rose's livestock and the enslaved ranch hands whose independence so troubled men like George Alpress—Tacky's Revolt stunned the island. The event represented a spectacular reaction to the everyday violence of colonial life. During the uprising, more than one thousand enslaved people struck at the heart of colonial power and colonial slavery, attacking several of the most prominent plantations in Jamaica. Led by two enslaved African men, Tacky and Jamaica, the number of rebels quickly swelled as fleeing slaves joined their ranks. Even though the two leaders were captured during a battle and beheaded, the gruesome display of their heads on pikes outside of Spanish Town did little to quell the insurrection. Captives in other parts of the island rose up, massacring the people who enslaved them and destroying the property they labored on.[17]

Tacky's Revolt was the most well-organized, destructive, and threatening slave insurgency to occur in the Anglo-Atlantic world before the Haitian Revolution. It took a combination of British troops, local militia, and free Maroons six months to stop the insurrection and another year to capture all of the participants. At least sixty people of European descent and sixty free people of African descent were killed during the revolt. More than four hundred slaves died in battle, and another one hundred rebels endured brutal executions. Some were slowly burned to death, while others were gibbeted alive and left to die of starvation. Local officials shipped off another five hundred slaves to Honduras in an effort to weed out any potentially unruly people.[18]

17. Vincent Brown, *The Reaper's Garden: Death and Power in the World of Atlantic Slavery* (Cambridge, Mass., 2008), 148.

18. Trevor Burnard and John Garrigus, *The Plantation Machine: Atlantic Capitalism in French Saint-Domingue and British Jamaica* (Philadelphia, 2016), 122–127, 131.

The revolt's participants caught free society completely off guard, exposing the fragility of Britain's control of the island. In the end, however, Jamaican society was shaken but not fundamentally altered by the event. Tacky's Revolt did little to dismantle Jamaica's draconian labor system, its considerable role in the Atlantic slave trade, or the island's pride of place in the British Empire. The lure of wealth and affordable land overrode metropolitan fears of another slave revolt. Rather than decreasing, the flow of free and enslaved migrants to the island increased during the latter half of the eighteenth century. The majority of the British indentured servants who were bound for America also went to Jamaica. Just fourteen years after the insurgency, the number of white inhabitants had nearly doubled in size, reaching eighteen thousand by 1774. Likewise, the number of captives who were transported to the island between 1750 and 1807 increased significantly, further enlarging the slave population.[19]

Colonists also ignored the revolt's dire warning. No efforts were made to ameliorate the conditions of the enslaved—that project would wait decades for the antislavery movement to gain steam in Britain. Instead, the revolt inspired the Jamaica Assembly to target wealthy free people of Euro-African and African descent. In an effort to curb the riches of this group, who allegedly controlled two to three hundred thousand pounds in estates, the assembly passed a measure prohibiting colonists who were identified as nonwhite from inheriting more than twelve hundred pounds sterling from white testators. Other laws were also enacted to police free people of African descent, who were required to register with local authorities and to wear badges. Yet these piecemeal measures did not alter the local customs, which had been established over the course of three generations. Practices related to property and family legitimacy that had taken root in the 1720s and 1730s intensified, rather than diminished, during the latter part of the eighteenth century.[20]

19. Jack P. Greene, *Pursuits of Happiness: The Social Development of Early Modern British Colonies and the Formation of American Culture* (Chapel Hill, N.C., 1988), 161; Simon P. Newman et al., "The West African Ethnicity of the Enslaved in Jamaica," *Slavery and Abolition,* XXXIV (2013), 379–380. Newman et al. estimate that 255,683 enslaved Africans arrived from the Bight of Biafra, 196,241 from the Gold Coast, and 56,977 from the Bight of Benin between 1750–1807. The slave population was still far from being self-reproducing during this period.

20. In 1774, there were twenty-three thousand people designated as "mulattoes" on the island, and only four thousand of them were free. See Brown, *Reaper's Garden,* 111. See also Livesay, *Children of Uncertain Fortune,* 69–75; Gad J. Heuman, *Between Black and White: Race, Politics, and the Free Coloreds in Jamaica, 1792–1865* (Westport, Conn., 1981), 5–6; Christer

Free islanders skirted the new race-based inheritance restrictions and continued to offer large legacies to women and children of Euro-African and African descent and treat them as legitimate heirs. In 1770, for instance, Judith Alcraft, a "free mulatto woman" received her planter partner James Hugh's entire estate and also became his executor, a bequest and role that, as seen in Chapter 4, husbands commonly assigned to wives. That same year, Doctor John James Gorse bequeathed his partner Fanny Duncan, a free "mulatto" woman, one acre of land and one captive. This meagre legacy was symbolic: Gorse transferred the majority of his estate to the couple's children, whom he claimed were "by me begotten on the body of Fanny Duncan" and gave them his surname. They would inherit a one-hundred-acre property called "Shutter's Hill," along with thirty-two slaves, which would be leased out to safeguard the profits in a trust, and join Jamaica's middling planter class. Islanders like Hugh and Gorse were the beneficiaries of customs that had been in formation for a century. That the number of free and freed people with African ancestry continued to grow after Tacky's Revolt attests to the persistent popularity of colonial practices despite the alleged threat posed by freed people to Jamaica's security.[21]

Colonists who had been constructing their own signifiers of status and legitimacy continued to recognize kin who fell outside the purview of social and legal legitimacy elsewhere in the empire. Planter Joseph Martiny fathered a child with his enslaved woman, Flavia, and then manumitted her in 1770. As was commonplace, Flavia simultaneously gained her freedom and became a slaveholder—Martiny gave her two slaves of her own to command. Martiny also displayed a remarkably tolerant attitude toward his legitimate daughter, who bore a "natural" son out of wedlock. Rather than holding her to a sexual double-standard while he engaged in illicit interracial sex, as one might expect of an eighteenth-century patriarch, Martiny made his illegitimate grandson, John Shickle, his legitimate heir. Martiny further signified his desire to remain close to his family, which included his formerly enslaved partner, their child, his legitimate daughter, and her illegitimate son, by asking for his "corpse" to "be buried in a garden" on the estate that his grandson would inherit. At the end of the eighteenth century, colonial men like Martiny main-

---

Petley, "'Legitimacy' and Social Boundaries: Free People of Colour and the Social Order in Jamaican Slave Society," *Social History*, XXX (2005), 486; and Brooke N. Newman, "Gender, Sexuality, and the Formation of Racial Identities in the Eighteenth-Century Anglo-Caribbean World," *Gender and History*, XXII (2010), 589–590.

21. Will of James Hugh, 1770, Jamaica Wills, XXXVIII, Will of James Gorse, 1770, XXXVIII.

tained a permissive approach toward female relations that conflicted with paternalist prerogatives and established families made up of overlapping kinship ties that linked free, freed, and enslaved people.[22]

Yet some aspects of Jamaica's social world did change after Tacky's Revolt. By the 1760s and 1770s, colonists expressed a greater awareness of race and the ways that it shaped their lives than earlier generations. In their wills, islanders began invoking racial labels to describe kin, friends, and slaves, thereby revealing the seepage of racial discourse into local practice and personal records. The will made by Diana Cole, who identified herself as a "free negro," hints at this shift. In many respects, her life resembled the lives of the three generations of free and freed women who preceded her. Cole attained material wealth and social status. She was a slaveholder who forged close friendships with female kin and other women in her community and established an intimate relationship with a man whom she did not marry. In keeping with local tradition, she, like most female property holders, bequeathed the majority of her estate to other women. Cole gave one of her nieces a "padded bridal" for riding, a pair of earrings "set with porcelain stones," a coral necklace, mahogany furniture, and an expensive bed furnished with a bolster, counterpane, and mosquito net. Another niece received a necklace, while Cole's mother got clothing and furniture. These objects represented the material trimmings and trappings of a feminine world, where gifts of furniture, clothing, and jewelry—all forms of personal property—connected women throughout the Atlantic world.[23]

Following another colonial ritual, Cole transferred enslaved people to mark her intimate relationships, giving her mother an adult woman and a girl and recognizing her "loving friend"—a man named William Allen who was likely her paramour—by offering him an enslaved man and woman along with a one-hundred-pound legacy. Certain lines in Cole's will, however, signal the transition to a different era in Jamaican history. Unlike her predecessors, Cole placed race-based restrictions on the captives whom she bequeathed to her relatives. She transferred one slave to a woman named Caterine Ancelloy, who might have been her natural daughter, but included a condition that only allowed Ancelloy to bequeath the captive to her own children "begotten by an unnamed "L—" and whom Cole specified was a "white man." If Ancelloy died, Cole instructed that the enslaved girl would be passed on to the heirs of Cole's niece "of her body to be begotten by a white man." By the

22. Will of Joseph Martiny, 1770, Jamaica Wills, XXXVIII.

23. Will of Diana Cole, 1771, Jamaica Wills, XXXVIII.

end of the eighteenth century, racial categories were entrenched in the Cole family and in colonial society more broadly. Cole viewed her female kinship network through the prism of race. She was overtly conscious of the privileges associated with whiteness, so much so that she used the gift of an enslaved girl to influence the intimate relationships of the next generation of women in her family.[24]

Jamaica's slave system functioned, not by the force of colonial institutions, but, rather, through laissez-faire administrative policies that emphasized individual privileges and required slaveholders to do their dirty work themselves. Instead of restricting the behavior of the free populace in the wake of Tacky's Revolt, the Jamaica Assembly continued to maintain an uneasy control over the slave majority by upholding the rights of individual slaveholders. Colonists were accustomed to making their own choices about inheritance, religion, sexuality, marriage, and manumissions without government interference. In return for the expanded liberties they enjoyed, free men and women were expected to police slaves, who outnumbered them nearly ten to one. Consequently, when the cruelty and excesses of slavery that produced a particular type of empire came under increasing attack, Jamaica, once the epitome of Britain's imperial commercial success, became the hallmark of its wrongdoing.[25]

Ideas about race and gender had also categorically changed. The antislavery movement put Caribbean colonists on the defensive. Forced to justify their lifestyles and their livelihoods in the face of growing condemnation, Jamaican-born slaveholding intellectuals like Edward Long turned to arguments about the "natural" suitability of Africans as slaves. At the end of the eighteenth century, race was becoming an immutable, inherited, biological facet of identity. During this time, ideas about gender also altered. Just as black and white were conceived of as binary categories of difference, so, too, were men and women defined as distinctive biological types, with women increasingly confined to a moralizing role of domesticity. The assertive colonists who appear throughout this book, women like Sarah Shanks, Mary Elbridge, and Mary Rose, who openly negotiated their positions in relation to men, no longer fit in this newly gendered and racialized landscape.

By the end of the eighteenth century, ardent critics of the slave trade were gaining traction throughout the Anglo-Atlantic world. A few decades later, Atlantic slavery, the cornerstone of Britain's imperial success—which found

24. Ibid.

25. See Brown, *Reaper's Garden*, chap. 5.

its fullest expression in Jamaica—was slowly unraveling. Instead of uncritically accepting slavery as a key component of commerce, antislavery activists attacked the slave trade and characterized slaveholders as vicious, evil, and aberrant members of an empire in need of reform. In 1772, the *Somerset* case confirmed the illegality of slavery in England. Britain then lost thirteen of its American colonies but clung onto its most valuable territory in the Caribbean and shifted its focus to India and Southeast Asia. Britain formally ended the slave trade in 1804 and abolished slavery throughout the empire in 1832.[26]

After more than a century of intensive participation in colonial slavery, it should come as no surprise that British women with ties to the Caribbean made up nearly half of the people who petitioned the Slavery Compensation Commission for remuneration after the abolition of slavery. Yet that visitors to Westminster Abby still overlook Anna Hassall, the wealthy but historically obscure merchant, privateer, and slaveholder whose life is detailed in Chapter 2, testifies to the ongoing erasure of female slaveholders from the history of the British Empire. Hassall was buried in Islip Chapel in Westminster Abby in the middle of the eighteenth century. Her legacy is curiously conjoined with a far more famous person, William Wilberforce. The family of the renowned antislavery activist placed a memorial for Wilberforce in Islip Chapel, which they also helped to restore. Commemorated together in death in the most hallowed ground of empire, Hassall, the entrepreneurial enslaver, and Wilberforce, the avowed enemy of the slave trade, both juxtapose and inform one another. One is remembered with reverence; the other is consigned to the ash heap of history. Yet Hassall and Wilberforce each represent a crucially distinctive but equally important epoch in the joined histories of colonialism and slavery. Hassall died when the British slave trade was reaching its zenith. Wilberforce died the year that slavery was abolished throughout the empire.[27]

It is impossible to understand the era that produced Wilberforce without recognizing Hassall and the female-dominated dimension of imperial history she embodies. If Wilberforce participated in altering the character of the empire, then women like Hassall aided in its creation, building the contours of

26. Trevor Burnard, *Planters, Merchants, and Slaves: Plantation Societies in British America, 1650–1820* (Chicago, 2015), 228–234.

27. Hannah Young, "Women, Slavery Compensation, and Gender Relations in the 1830s" (Undergraduate thesis, University College of London, 2010), http://www.ucl.ac.uk/lbs/media-new/pdfs/hyoung.pdf; "William Wilberforce and Family," Westminster Abbey, http://westminster-abbey.org/our-history/people/william-wilberforce.

a remarkably profitable, durable, and exploitative node in the heart of the Caribbean. Jamaica's dismal mortality rate, its favoring of the privileges of free individuals, and, most importantly, its investment in slavery, all fostered an environment that was especially conducive to free and freed women. The first three generations of female islanders derived considerable social and material benefits from slavery that afforded them novel forms of wealth accumulation, labor, and social authority. Their ill-gotten gains were considerable. By the 1760s and 1770s, a handful of female islanders commanded massive fortunes, including "spinster" Sarah Haughton, who oversaw 283 enslaved people and controlled a £17,537 estate, and Mary Wait, a Port Royal widow who held 336 people in captivity and commanded £11,428. Slaveholders like Haughton and Wait made essential contributions to a new form of society precariously held together by a web of kinship ties that connected the free and freed minority. Even women like Mary Rose, whose ancestors had been enslaved, still relied on slaveholding. Whether they were driven by the need to survive, the desire to protect their families, or, like Mary Rose, to secure their own fragile independence, free and freed women laid the foundation for a brave new world, one that hinged on relentless profit-seeking, coercive colonialism, and profound exploitation.[28]

28. Inventory of Sarah Haughton, 1767, Jamaica Inventories, Inventory of Mary Wait, 1761.

Index

Page numbers in italics refer to illustrations.

CPSIA information can be obtained
at www.ICGtesting.com
Printed in the USA
LVHW110753031220
673231LV00005B/444

9 781469 658797